PHOTOGRAPHIC GUIDE TO THE BIRDS OF BRITAIN AND EUROPE

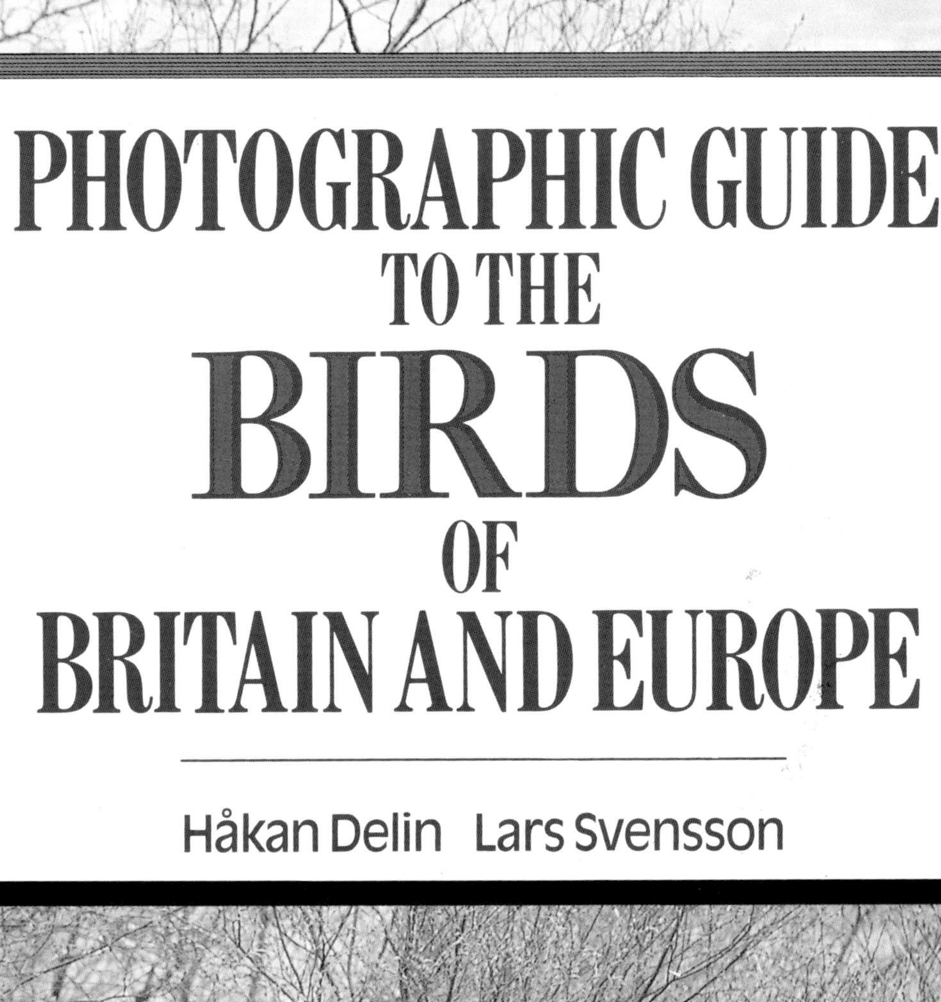

PHOTOGRAPHIC GUIDE TO THE BIRDS OF BRITAIN AND EUROPE

Håkan Delin Lars Svensson

TED SMART

First published 1988

Revised edition published 1990 by The Hamlyn Publishing Group Limited
part of Reed International Books
Michelin House, 81 Fulham Road, London SW3 6RB

Some of the text and map material used in this book previously published in the Country Life Guides: Birds of Britain and Europe

This edition published in 1991
for The Book People

ISBN 0 600 55808 8

Produced by Mandarin Offset
Printed in Hong Kong

Page 1 Skylark

Page 2-3 Golden Eagle with young at the nest

We would like to thank a number of people for their assistance in the preparation of this book. David Christie did much valuable work in selecting pictures and writing drafts for the captions. Peter J. Grant helped with some groups of birds and checked some of the identifications. The many agencies and individuals who supplied photographs and Nature Photographers, in particular, who provided us with many hours of help and allowed us the full run of their excellent library. Karel Feuerstein designed the book including the attractive picture layout. The Publisher, Andrew Branson, initiated the whole undertaking and maintained his equanimity in the face of the many problems which arose. But most of all our gratitude goes out to all the photographers from all over Europe who made the book possible.

Håkan Delin, Lars Svensson

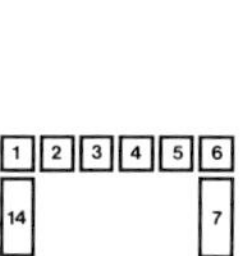

1 White-billed Diver 1st-summer **2 White Pelican** adult in flight **3 Bewick's Swans** adults and juvenile (at front) **4 Mallard** female with chicks **5 Long-legged Buzzard** adult in flight **6 Sparrowhawk** adult female at nest **7 Barn Owl** adult **8 Water Rail** adult **9 Upland Sandpiper** juvenile **10 Lapwing** adult male summer **11 Rock Thrush** adult male with lizard **12 Blackbird** first winter male **13 Scarlet Rosefinch** adult male summer **14 Grey Wagtail** adult male summer

Contents

Left-hand page
Green Woodpecker adult male
Kingfisher adult male
Arctic Tern adult

Right-hand page
Shag adult early summer
Stock Dove adult
Red-throated Diver adult summer

Introduction

This book provides a comprehensive identification guide to the birds of Britain and Europe illustrated throughout in colour. It contains over 1,300 photographs, selected to show as far as possible every variety of plumage of the nearly 600 species of birds treated here. At the same time it is also a fine collection of pictures to browse through, vividly conveying the beauty and rich variety of the European bird fauna.

The bringing together of such a large number of photographs in a single volume has not been an easy task and, although there are still a handful of species for which we have not been able to find a single useful picture, we are nevertheless confident that the book represents a landmark of its kind.

Ten years ago it would have been much more difficult, even impossible, to produce such a book. However, during the last decade interest in bird photography has been growing rapidly all over Europe. More and more skilled amateurs are carrying cameras equipped with advanced telephoto lenses. Moreover, the emphasis has shifted from traditional nest photography taken from a hide to freehand shots of birds in all seasons and in a variety of situations. The advantages of this are twofold: less disturbance for the birds during their vulnerable breeding season and more abundant and less stereotyped bird pictures. Less than 10 per cent of the photographs in this book have been taken at the nest, considerably less than in previous comparable books. In fact, a special feature of the *Photographic Guide* is the striking pictures of birds in flight.

Bird photography has never been a true profession except for a devoted few. 'Amateurs' have always contributed significantly to the photographic portrayal of birds in books and magazines. However, for this project we have made a real effort to complement the work of the professionals and established amateurs with a considerable number of photographs taken by young enthusiasts which have not previously been published.

Many of the photographs in this book, with not only the bird but also its natural habitat in focus, give us the delightful feeling of viewing the results of pioneering achievements. We invite you to enjoy these pictures, taken with patience and sheer hard work in areas as remote as the Varanger Peninsula and the Negev Desert. What would we have done without the efforts of the 'young boys of Finland', the increasingly professional British birders/photographers and all the other expert birders who have crawled with their cameras through mud, waded in water up to their armpits and climbed steep mountains in order to capture on film a rarely photographed bird or plumage? This book is a tribute to them all.

Anyone who has ever been a bird-watcher or who has an interest in bird books will surely ask the question: should a book on identification have photographs or colour artwork? We believe that the two complement each other. A small standard field guide will normally do best with colour artwork. Since space is limited the artist can place illustrations of several plumages close together. But, with a larger format, as here, the advantages of photographs as a *complement* to artwork can be profitably employed. However talented the artist is, he or she is unlikely to be familiar with *all* the European species. There will always be some less successful portraits, in which small but important details are wrongly depicted. With photographs, on the other hand, we can trust what we see: this is how at least one bird really looked on one particular occasion. The subtle differences in jizz and facial expression between even closely related species can generally best be learnt from photographs. And we are confident that our readers have the imagination required to enable them to compensate for differences in light and in posture, the main drawback of using photographs for identification purposes.

So, instead of taking one course, we should like to recommend both. Most bird-watchers already own more than one guide. Here we offer a new picture reference source for all those who want to check the artwork of their favourite field guide against photographs and increase their knowledge about birds.

If you think that you possess pictures of superior quality, the publisher would be most grateful if you could send them in for consideration and possible inclusion in future editions.

We are pleased that our text from the Country Life Guides *Birds of Britain and Europe*, published in 1986, has been selected to accompany the photographs. Only minor additions and amendments have been made to the text. The maps and line drawings are unchanged.

This photographic guide covers the continent of Europe bordered by the Atlantic, the Mediterranean, the Bosphorus, the Black Sea, the Caucasus Mountains, the Caspian Sea, the Ural River and Mountains and the Arctic Ocean. This is a land mass of 3,900,000 square miles (10,000,000 square km). The geographic and climatic environment varies from the Arctic areas in the far north to the Mediterranean in the south with its subtropical climate. In the east the zones merge into those of the Asian continent. Europe, most of Asia, and northernmost Africa form the *Palaearctic* region.

The book covers the breeding birds, the regular visitors, and the casual visitors which have been recorded at least five times in this century. Among the breeding birds are counted introduced species which are well established in a feral state.

The English names in this guide are those in common use. Local or foreign names are not as a rule included, though a number of common alternative names have been included in the index. The scientific name follows the English name. The scientific name consists of two parts: the genus, followed by the specific name.

Closely related birds are grouped together in genera, closely related genera into subfamilies, subfamilies into families and families into orders. Within a species several subspecies may be recognized. Only where subspecies are easily identifiable are they included in this book. Colour phases or morphs may occur; unlike subspecies these are not usually geographically separated, though their proportion in the population may vary in different regions. Where distinctive phases or morphs occur these have been mentioned.

The sequence is that of an evolutionary order, progressing from the least to the most advanced families of birds. Exceptions are made where they are deemed practical for identification. For instance, the white herons are grouped together, and the Hemipode put next to the closely similar but unrelated Quail.

Text, map and illustration of each bird are placed together.

The text gives the English name, the scientifc name, the total length (and in some cases the wing span) in centimetres (unless otherwise stated), the abundance, habitat, characteristic features of plumage and silhouette, behavioural characteristics, and songs and calls of each bird.

There are introductions to each order and family. In some cases smaller groups are also furnished with introductory notes where this is of value. Furthermore the status of each species in the British Isles and Ireland is given in abbreviated form.

R: resident S: summer visitor W: winter visitor P: passage visitor V: vagrant

A species may belong to several of these categories.

The distribution maps have been carefully compiled from the most recent references and in order that as much detail as possible can be represented four colours have been used. The purple areas represent the residential range of the species. The red areas

Introduction

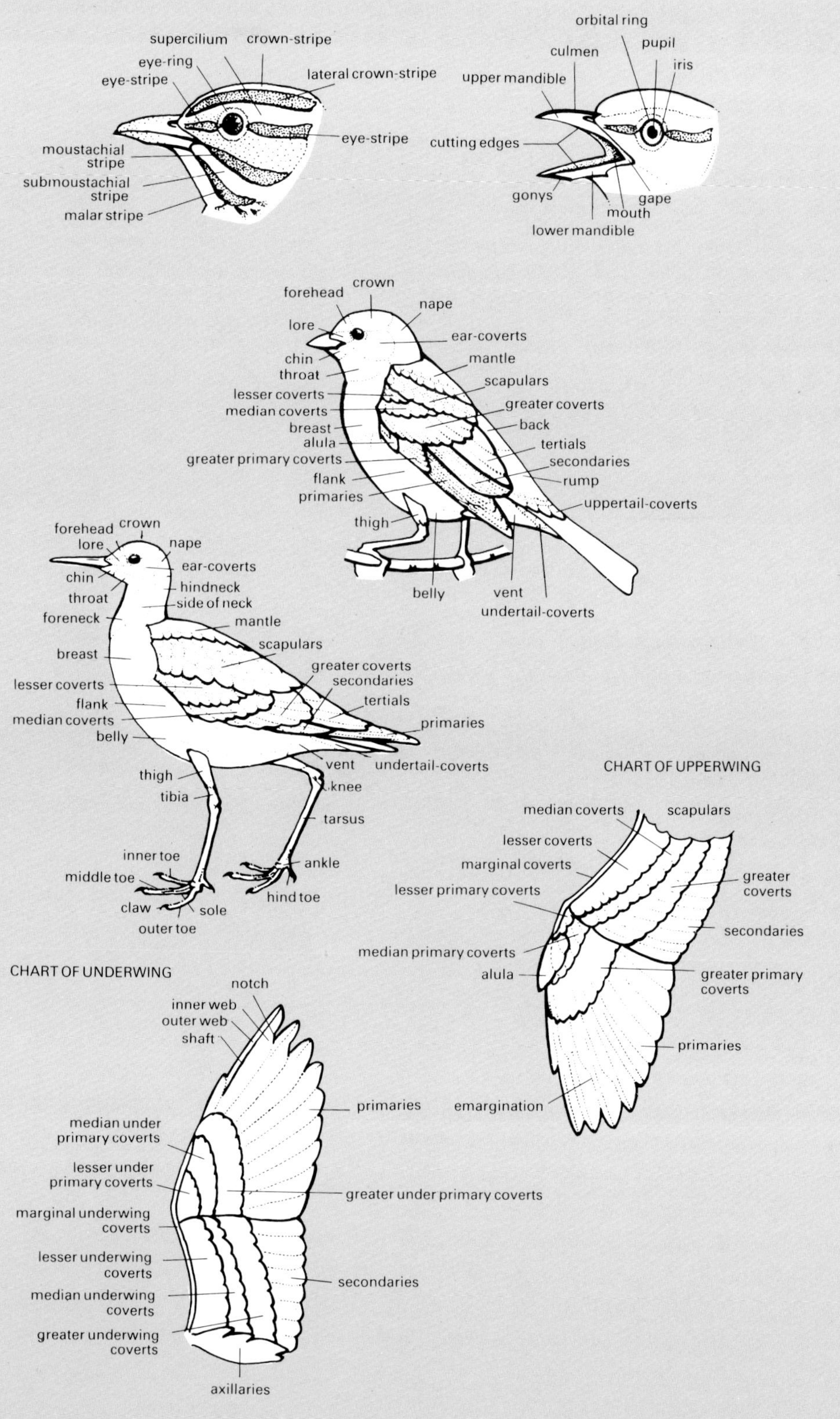

supercilium
crown-stripe
eye-ring
eye-stripe
lateral crown-stripe
eye-stripe
moustachial stripe
submoustachial stripe
malar stripe

orbital ring
pupil
culmen
iris
upper mandible
cutting edges
gonys
gape
mouth
lower mandible

crown
forehead
nape
lore
ear-coverts
chin
mantle
throat
scapulars
lesser coverts
greater coverts
median coverts
back
breast
alula
tertials
greater primary coverts
secondaries
flank
rump
primaries
uppertail-coverts
thigh
belly
vent
undertail-coverts

forehead
crown
lore
nape
ear-coverts
chin
hindneck
throat
side of neck
foreneck
mantle
scapulars
breast
greater coverts
lesser coverts
secondaries
flank
tertials
median coverts
primaries
belly
vent
undertail-coverts
thigh
knee
tibia
tarsus
inner toe
ankle
middle toe
hind toe
claw
sole
outer toe

CHART OF UPPERWING

median coverts
scapulars
lesser coverts
marginal coverts
greater coverts
lesser primary coverts
secondaries
median primary coverts
alula
greater primary coverts
primaries
emargination

CHART OF UNDERWING

notch
inner web
outer web
shaft
primaries
median under primary coverts
lesser under primary coverts
greater under primary coverts
marginal underwing coverts
lesser underwing coverts
secondaries
median underwing coverts
greater underwing coverts
axillaries

Illustration by permission of *British Birds*

Diagram showing topography of typical European birds.

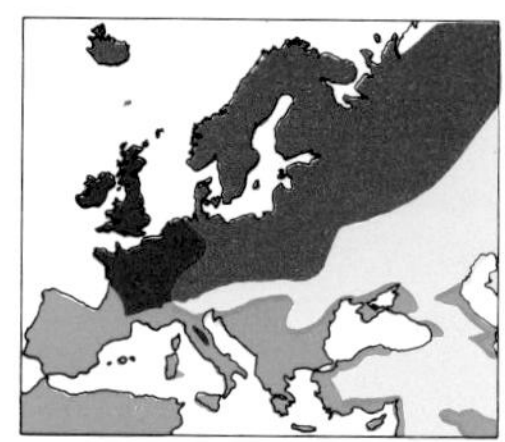

The distribution maps give wintering areas in blue, breeding areas in red and where the bird occurs all year round in purple. Migration areas are shown in yellow. The irregular winter and summer limits are shown as broken blue or red lines. The irregular migration limits are shown as a solid yellow line.

Introduction

represent the summer breeding range only. Blue areas are the winter ranges and the yellow represents those areas where the species occurs on migration. Broken lines in the appropriate colour represent the irregular limits in the range of the species; for example, a broken blue line indicates the irregular winter limits. A solid yellow line represents the irregular migration limits of the species.

Neighbouring areas outside Europe are included although this book does not comprehensively cover the birds of these areas. The small size of the maps clearly limits the amount of detail which can be incorporated and readers are referred to more local guides and lists for such details.

The arrangement of the photographs generally follows (with minor exceptions) the order in which the description of the species is given on the opposite page. Location symbols placed alongside the caption will help the reader quickly to find each picture. Although much care has been taken to ensure accuracy about age and sex, some photographs are not sufficiently clear, or else the plumages are not unambiguous enough, to enable a positive identification to be made.

Scientific terms are kept to a minimum. *Adult* means mature (a bird in its definitive plumage), *juvenile* (juv.) young (and wearing its first plumage necessary for flight) and *immature* intermediate between these two without a firmer specification. The expression *subadult* is sometimes used to indicate that the bird is very nearly adult but still shows traces of immaturity. A *first-winter* bird is one that has moulted some or all of its juvenile plumage and can be seen any time between, say, the August of the year in which it was born and April of the following spring. A *first-summer* bird is roughly one year old and has moulted some or all of its first winter plumage. *First-year* can be used to describe a bird which is up to one year old, from hatching to the summer of the following year. *Race* (or *subspecies*) is the classification level below species which expresses a geographically discernible variation in plumage colour or size within a certain species. *Phase* (or *morph*) denotes a colour variant within a species which is not strictly linked with range.

BIBLIOGRAPHY

A great many bird books are published every year. Each country has its own wealth of bird literature, and a complete list of books dealing with European birds would alone simply fill this volume. Some books are, however, of special interest and the following list gives the most important literature on identification and the best regional works.

Bannerman, D. A. & W. M. 1971. *Handbook of the Birds of Cyprus and Migrants of the Middle East*. Edinburgh.

Bannerman, D. A. & Lodge, G.E. 1953-63. *The Birds of the British Isles*. 12 vols. London.

Bergmann, H.-H. & Helb, H.-W. 1982. *Stimmen der Vögel Europas*. Munich.

Bernis, F. 1954. *Prontuario de la Avifauna Española (incluyendo Aves de Portugal, Baleares y Canarias)*. Madrid.

British Ornithologists' Union. 1971. *The Status of Birds in Britain and Ireland*. Oxford.

Bruun, B., Delin, H. & Svensson, L. 1986. *Birds of Britain & Europe*. London.

Campbell, B. & Lack, E. 1985. *A Dictionary of Birds*. Calton.

Cramp, S. (chief ed.), *et al.* 1977-. *Handbook of the Birds of Europe, the Middle East and North Africa: The Birds of the Western Palearctic*. vols 1, 2, 3, 4 & 5. London. (Further vols in course of publication.)

Delacour, J. & Scott, P. 1954-64. *The Waterfowl of the World*. 4 vols. London.

Dementiev, G. P. & Gladkov, N. A., *et al.* 1951-54. *Birds of the Soviet Union*. 6 vols. (Israel Program for Scientific Translation, Jerusalem, 1966-70).

Dunn, J. L., Blom, E. A. T. (eds), *et al.* 1983. *Field Guide to the Birds of North America*. Nat. Geographic Society, Washington.

Etchécopar, R. D. & Hüe, F. 1967. *The Birds of North Africa*. Edinburgh.

Farrand, Jr, J. (ed.), *et al.* 1983. *The Audubon Society Master Guide to the Birds of North America*. 3 vols. New York.

Ferguson-Lees, J., Willis, I. & Sharrock, J. T. R. 1983. *The Shell Guide to the Birds of Britain and Ireland*. London.

Fjeldså, J. 1977. *Guide to the Young of European Precocial Birds*. Tisvilde.

Flint, V. E., *et al.* 1984. *A Field Guide to Birds of the USSR*. Princeton.

Forsman, D. 1984. *Rovfågelsguiden*. Helsinki.

Génsbøl, B. 1986. *Birds of Prey of Europe, North Africa and the Middle East*. London.

Géroudet, P. 1947-57. *La Vie des Oiseaux*. 6 vols. Neuchâtel & Paris.

Glutz von Blotzheim, H.U.N. (chief ed.), Bauer, K. & Bezzel, E. 1966-. *Handbuch der Vögel Mitteleuropas*. Wiesbaden. (11 vols appeared up to 1989; further vols in course of production.)

Grant, P. J. 1986. *Gulls: a guide to identification*. 2nd edn. Calton.

Hancock, J. & Kushlan, J. 1984. *The Herons Handbook*. London & New York.

Harrison, C. 1982. *An Atlas of the Birds of the Western Palaearctic*. London.

Harrison, P. 1986. *Seabirds: an identification guide*. 2nd edition. Beckenham.

Harrison, P. 1987. *Seabirds of the World*. A Photographic Guide. London.

Hayman, P., Marchant, J. & Prater, T. 1986. *Shorebirds*. An identification guide to the waders of the world. London.

Heinzel, H., Fitter, R. & Parslow, J. 1972. *The Birds of Europe with North Africa and the Middle East*. London.

Hollom, P. A. D. 1962. *The Popular Handbook of British Birds*. London.

Hollom, P. A. D. 1980. *The Popular Handbook of Rarer British Birds*. London. (2nd edition.)

Hollom, P. A. D., Porter, R. F., Christensen, S., & Willis, Ian. 1988. *Birds of the Middle East and North Africa*. Calton.

Hüe, F. & Etchécopar, R. D. 1971. *Les Oiseaux du Proche et du Moyen Orient de la Mediterranée aux Contreforts de l'Himalaya*. Paris.

Jonsson, L. 1978-82. *Birds of Lake, River, Marsh and Field; Birds of Sea and Coast; Birds of Wood, Park and Garden; Birds of Mountain Regions; Birds of the Mediterranean and Alps*. 5 vols. London.

Madge, S., & Burn, H. 1988. *Wildfowl. An identification guide to the ducks, geese and swans of the world*. London.

Peterson, R. T., *et al.* 1984. *A Field Guide to the Birds of Britain and Europe*. London.

Pforr, M. & Limbrunner, A. 1981-82. *The Breeding Birds of Europe*. 2 vols. London.

Porter, R. F., *et al.* 1981. *Flight identification of European Raptors*. 3rd edition. Berkhamsted.

Prater, A. J., Marchant, J. & Vuorinen, J. 1977. *Guide to the Identification and Ageing of Holarctic Waders*. BTO Guide 17. Tring.

Scott, P. 1968. *A Coloured Key to the Wildfowl of the World*. London.

Stresemann, E., Portenko, L. A., *et al.* 1960-. *Atlas der Verbreitung Palaearktischer Vogel*. Berlin. (In course of production.)

Svensson, L. 1984. *Identification Guide to European Passerines*. 3rd edition. Stockholm.

Vaurie, C. 1959, 1965. *The Birds of the Palearctic Fauna*. 2 vols. London.

Voous, K. H. 1977. *List of Recent Holarctic Bird Species*. *Ibis* suppl. London.

Williamson, K. 1967, 1968. *Identification for Ringers*. 3 vols. Tring.

Witherby, H. F., *et al.* 1938-41. *The Handbook of British Birds*. 5 vols. London.

ACKNOWLEDGEMENTS

Note: the numbers of the pages on which the photographs occur are followed by letters indicating the position of the photographs on the particular page, moving horizontally across from left to right.

Per Alström 215E, 219F; Aquila/Kevin Carlson 215H, 221G/G. D. and Y. S. Dean 183G, 217D, 219E, 239L, 267I, 283J/Paul Doherty 121C, 127J, 131I, 143G, 153B, 153D, 153H, 155A, 179G, 193I, 195D, 225C, 235I, 239E, 243I, 263D, 263E, 271H/R. Glover 105C, 241C, 269B, 269F, 275A/Conrad Greaves 63E, 65I, 103E, 143J, 173E, 173G, 185J, 185K, 191G, 199J, 225B, 237F/James Hancock 49I, 65A/Wayne Lankinen 47C, 171F, 271K, 273G, 273H, 285F/Robert Maier 89E/Ed Mackrill 137C, 139D/Richard T. Mills 6C, 41E, 47K, 111L, 117A, 131L, 139C, half title and 187A, 193C, 233D, 255H, 267J, 271J/A. T. Moffett 6A, 71A, 159A, 175B, 175F, 265B, 265G, 279E/J. L. Roberts 27H, 31G, 205E, 209F, 221H/Colin Smith 207H/B. Speake 5:6, 71D, 99F/M. C. Wilkes 4:12, 25A, 151I, 205C, 209G, 255E, 263G/S. Young 135E, 197F; Ardea/J. A. Bailey 267B/J. B. Bottomley 277D/G. K. Brown 55K, 267C/John Daniels 115E/M. D. England 245A, 267D, 285I/Peter Steyn 23G, 23H/David and Katie Urry 207B/Wolfgang Wagner 65J; Peter H. Barthel 41F; Per-Göran Bentz 5:10, 31B, 49E, 51F, 51H, 59D, 61I, 75L, 81C, 81F, 81K, 87A, 101I, 117E, 117I, 125I, 137A, 157C, 165D, 167D, 169C, 169F, 185E, 199C, 199L, 207G, 235D, 235H, 263A, 263C, 277F; Arnoud B. van den Berg 17E, 17H; Ola Bondesson 25C, 29E, 31C, 39F, 43B, 53G, 67K, 69B, 69E, 69I, 69J, 71C, 71F, 77H, 95H, 97H, 101D, 139E, 139I, 147C, 147D, 169G, 187C, 187H, 195H, 197D, 203C, 243F, 249D; Bertil Breife 75K, 233B; J. J. Brooks 17D, 19G, 63C; Tony Broome 15I, 39L, 55I, 127G, 183A, 183B, 209K; Graham Catley 37F, 191C, 201K, 227C, 233A; R. A. Cawthorne 215C, 231G; Bruce Coleman Ltd/Jack Dermid 285J/J. Fennell 21D/Carmel Galea 263F/M. P. Price 201B/Hans Reinhard 89F, 179E, 261A/Gunter Ziesler 87B; David M. Cottridge 5:9, 17F, 23F, 101F, 103K, 111A, 113J, 119G, 119J, 123L, 135C, 135L, 139J, 139K, 141D, 143B, 143I, 159G, 159H, 173F, 185G, 189C, 191D, 199E, 203E, 219B, 219D, 221C, 223E, 225E, 225G, 225K, 229K, 237E, 247A, 247C, 249H, 269E, 271A, 273F, 275E, 281G, 285B, 285C, 285D; Dennis Coutts 53I, 57E, 57H, 75B, 81B, 141I, 143E, 153A, 183F, 201C, 213F, 213G, 271E, 271F, 271G, 285G; Jeff Delve 111E; Paul Doherty 47H, 199F; Göran Ekström 27E, 49B, 55F, 55G, 59A, 61G, 67B, 67H, 73F, 73G, 73I, 75C, 77F, 81H, 119H, 119K, 123I, 129E, 139G, 143K, 157A, 169D, 169E, 195A, 199K, 211D, 211E, 219G, 231B, 245D; Dick Forsman 7A, 89D, 99I, 105H, 107B, 109A, 157G, 163C, 173H, 239D, 283F; Hannu Friman 63G, 185C; Peter Gerdehag 63B, 63F; Waldemar Gleinich 63H; Axel Halley 69D; Peter Harrison 19C, 21E, 21F, 21I, 25F, 129F; Stellan Hedgren 171D; Pekka Helo 7C, 37B, 43D, 53C, 57F, 57I, 63A, 63D, 73J, 75D, 75F, 75G, 75I, 83A, 83C, 85F, 109H, 117J, 121G, 121I, 121J, 123D, 129G, 129J, 133F, 155C, 155F, 161D, 161F, 163A, 163F, 163G, 163H, 163I, 163J, 165A, 165B, 165C, 165I, 165K, 180-1, 203A, 249B, 251D, 255A, 265F, 267F, 271B, 271D, 271L, 273D, 275C, 275D, 275F, 281D, 283G; Teemu Helo 57G; Teppo Helo 117K; David Hosking 155E, 233F, 235C; Eric and David Hosking 55H, 219A; Jon Østeng Hov 77A, 115B; M. Huhta-Koivisto 157F; Svante Joelsson 85E; Lars Jonsson 101B, 111B, 123G, 133D, 227E, 229E, 245G; A. Knystautas 247F; Heikki Kokkonen 47J, 199A, 241A; Pekka Komi 31E, 69H, 219I; M. Komulainen 79D; Volkes Konrad 93D, 147I; Lasse J. Laine 43A, 43G, 45C, 67C, 69G, 79C, 183E, 191J, 205H, 211F, 215G, 217E, 221A, 231E, 235L, 239A, 239H, 239I, 271I, 279A, 279B, 279G, 279I, 281E, 281F/O. Belialov 153G; Frank Lane Picture Agency/Leo Batten 205G/B. Borrell 261D/Hans Dieter Brandl 177F, 257G/A. Christiansen 17C, 55E, 69C/Eichorn/Zingel 73A, 173J, 201A/G. Håkansson 235E/A. R. Hamblin 45F/Hannu Hautala 175E, 179A/G. Moon 145G/Silvestris 167B, 205A/H. Schremp 77I/B. S. Turner 257F/Roger Wilmshurst 55B, 59C, 189E, 189G, 253E; O. Zingel 177G; Tim Loseby 275G, 285E; Tomas Lundquist 69L; John Marchant 107F, 113B, 113I, 121L, 145F, 167G, 259C, 267A; A. V. Moon 15G, 145H, 149E, 149H; Karel Mauer 35E; Natural Image/Bob Gibbons 41D; Nature Photographers Ltd/T. Andrewartha title page, 77C, 85A, 97I, 107A, 109L, 143A, 151C, 179C, 265K/Frank V. Blackburn 79A, 79B, 117F, 167A, 175C, 177H, 187E, 203H, 209E, 217C, 223B, 227B, 229C, 229D, 233C, 241B, 243A, 243B, 253C, 257C, 273A, 275B, 279F, 281H/S. C. Bisserot 91D/Mark Bolton 21G, 23A, 61C, 107H, 125H, 161A, 189D, 203D, 277A/Derick Bonsall 191A/L. H. Brown 35I, 83J, 97K, 97L/N. A. Callow 45G, 49C, 49H/Kevin Carlson 4:11, 29D, 31A, 33B, 33K, 35D, 37I, 51L, 59J, 59K, 61D, 61E, 61J, 67D, 67E, 67F, 73H, 75A, 75E, 75H, 81D, 81I, 89A, 91A, 93A, 93B, 93C, 93E, 101E, 105J, 121A, 127A, 159F, 163B, 173B, 177I, 183H, 189F, 189H, 193F, 199D, 201I, 203F, 211B, 213D, 217A, 219C, 221B, 223H, 223I, 225F, 227A, 227D, 229B, 229G, 231A, 239F, 241I, 241K, 243C, 243G, 249E, 263H, 267E, 277B, 277C, 281B, 281I, 283E/Colin Carver 69A, 83G, 107G, 151G, 169A, 195B, 205B, 215B, 223F, 235J, 241D, 245C, 251A/R. J. Chandler 101C, 109F, 119B, 125E, 133I, 133L, 195G, 197H, 255G, 265D/Bob Chapman 135D/Hugh Clark 39A, 49D, 83E, 161H, 165G, 171B, 171C, 175A, 177D, 189A, 189B, 189J, 197C, 205D, 209D, 233E, 255I/Andrew Cleave 19F, 27D, 49A, 51D, 59G, 95I, 133K/R. S. Daniell 25G, 31F, 159E/A. K. Davies 147A/Thomas Ennis 17G, 45L, 51K, 133C, 135G, 205F, 261C/R. J. Fairbank 243E/ R. H. Fisher 161C/Stephen Gantlett 185I/C. H. Gomersall 15D, 61F, 81A, 177E/Michael Gore 25D, 27A, 31D, 35B, 35C, 35J, 37H, 39K, 65D, 87C, 87G, 93F, 99H, 103H, 107D, 109J, 117H, 123H, 127B, 143H, 145I, 149D, 161B, 165F, 171E, 173D, 173I, 223A, 235A, 241J, 253B, 283A, 283B/James Hancock 33L, 95C, 125C, 167F, 245H, 249J, 285K/M. P. Harris 19A, 141B, 149J/Dr M. R. Hill 17J, 27F, 33D, 33E, 35F, 39B, 39C, 39I, 41B, 47I, 55A, 63I, 91E, 97F, 99E, 101L, 103B, 103J, 105K, 113H, 115A, 117D, 119C, 119D, 119E, 121B, 121F, 123B, 129C, 131G, 159C, 185D, 193D, 193J, 195F, 199B, 199H, 237C, 237G, 239B, 263B/Michael Hollings 73E/Jeff Hunt 195E/David Hutton 97B, 209B/E. A. James 6B, 7B, 45K, 109G, 113C, 113F, 165J, 203G, 207D, 221F, 221I, 235B, 243D, 243K, 249F, 251E, 265E, 265H, 265I, 265J/John Karmali 33J, 97A/Paul Knight 51C, 97J, 115D/Chris Knights 39H, 85B/Chris and Jo Knights , 4:3, 45H, 51I, 125G/Michael Leach 5:7, 41C, 45D, 81G, 155B, 163D, 165H, 223C, 267H, 279H/E. C. G. Lemon 23B/C. K. Mylne 17A, 57A, 83B, 147G/P. J. Newman 95A, 123A, 129H, 147F, 209C, 213A, 221E, 221J, 237B, 261E/Charles Palmar 43E, 49G, 135I/W. S. Paton 5:4, 25B, 83F, 149I, 169B/Mark Pidgeon 31I/B. Mearns 105A/R. Mearns 107J, 117L/Hugh Miles 12-13, 39G, 83K/M. Müller/H. Wohlmuth 33F, 33I, 61L, 65B, 65F, 69K, 71G, 71H, 73K, 95E, 95F, 99L, 103G, 107K, 143F, 183D, 195C, 223G, 225D, 277E, 281J/J. F. Reynolds 61A, 77G, 81E, 99B, 103I, 121H, 123F, 125A/P. J. Roberts 19B/J. Russell 87E, 87F, 157B, 269D/David Sewell 45B, 197A/Don Smith 15E, 21B, 21C, 53B, 53D, 61H, 73C, 77D, 77E, 85C, 119I, 125F, 127E, 129A, 131H, 135A, 155G, 161G, 187F, 193E, 193K, 201F, 201H, 207K, 253D, 269G, 285H/Robert T. Smith 53F, 85D/Paul Sterry 4:14, 5:8, 19E, 23E, 27G, 35A, 49F, 51A, 51G, 51J, 53A, 53H, 55D, 55J, 57B, 57C, 57D, 57J, 59F, 59I, 79G, 95G, 99A, 99C, 101G, 113K, 117B, 119F, 123C, 127C, 127L, 129B, 129D, 131E, 133A, 133E, 135J, 135K, 137H, 137I, 137J, 139H, 147L, 149F, 151D, 151H, 159B, 165E, 171A, 173A, 191B, 197B, 197E, 207J, 237A, 251B, 269A, 269H, 281A, 281C, 283C, 283H, 283K/Derick Summers 279D/J. M. Sutherland 33C/Roger Tidman 17L, 19D, 27C, 29B, 29C, 31J, 33G, 33H, 37A, 37C, 37E, 39D, 39E, 39J, 43C, 45A, 45E, 45J, 47D, 51B, 59B, 81J, 87D, 89B, 89C, 95B, 97C, 97D, 97E, 97G, 101A, 101K, 105B, 105D, 105E, 105L, 107C, 107E, 107I, 109B, 109C, 109E, 109I, 111I, 111J, 111K, 115C, 115G, 117C, 117G, 123E, 123J, 123K, 125B, 127I, 131K, 137D, 137G, 141A, 145A, 145B, 145C, 147J, 149A, 149G, 151B, 151E, 157D, 157E, 179F, 187B, 187D, 189K, 191E, 193A, 193B, 193L, 201D, 201E, 201J, 203B, 207A, 209A, 211A, 235K, 241E, 255B, 255C, 257E, 265A, 265C, 267G, 273B, 273C, 273E, 285A/Maurice Walker 99D, 177A, 177B, 207C, 209H, 215A, 229A, 243J, 251G, 253A, 255D, 257A, 259A, 269C/Dereck Washington 249C/Anthony Wharton 207E/Keri Williams 105G/Jonathan Wilson 29A, 33A, 109D; Pekka J. Nikander 35G, 35H, 65K, 67A, 67G, 67J, 83H, 93H, 99J, 127D, 137B, 137E, 271C; Blair Nikula 147H; Göran Nyrén 71B, 91B, 229H; Dieter Oelkers 135B; Bengt O. Olsson 79F; Urban Olsson 4:2, 5:5, 17K, 21J, 25E, 27B, 29F, 31H, 31K, 37D, 37G, 43H, 45I, 47A, 47B, 47E, 47F, 47G, 51E, 53E, 61B, 61K, 65C, 65E, 65G, 65H, 67I, 73B, 79H, 91F, 93G, 95D, 99G, 99K, 101J, 103A, 103C, 103D, 103F, 105I, 107L, 111D, 111F, 111G, 111H, 113A, 113D, 113E, 115F, 119A, 121D, 121E, 121K, 125D, 127F, 127K, 129I, 129K, 129L, 131A, 131B, 131C, 131D, 131J, 133B, 133G, 133J, 135F, 135H, 137K, 137L, 139A, 139B, 139F, 139L, 141C, 141E, 145D, 147B, 147E, 147K, 149B, 149C, 151A, 151F, 153E, 153F, 159D, 161E, 169H, 171G, 183C, 189I, 191F, 191H, 191I, 193H, 195I, 195J, 195K, 197G, 201G, 207I, 209J, 211G, 213B, 215D, 215F, 217B, 219H, 221D, 223D, 225I, 225J, 229J, 231H, 237D, 239C, 239J, 241G, 241H, 243H, 245I, 247E, 249I, 251C, 251F, 255F, 257D, 261B, 279C, 283D, 283I; Orion Press/NHPA 254B; William S. Paton 41A; R. Pop 4:1, 15B, 15C, 15H, 15J, 15K, 15L, 17I, 21A, 83I; R. F. Porter 21H, 25H, 71I, 91C, 145E, 153C, 173C, 185A, 185B, 185F, 185H, 199G, 229I, 235F, 253F, 263I, 277G;, Viggo Ree 229F; Rune O. Roalkvam 69F, 207F; Alan Roberts 23D, 55C, 59H, 113L, 213C, 213E, 225A, 245F; Staffan Rodebrand 155H, 225H; D. I. Sales 167E, 245E, 249G; Olli Sassi 247B; Reinhard Siegel 175D; Olle Staaf 75J; Bruno Sundin 15A, 41G, 59E, 71E, 101H, 105F, 109K, 127H, 131F, 155D, 163E, 179B, 179D, 187G, 193G, 231F, 235G, 249A, 257B, 259B; Pavel Tomkovitch 141F; G. Tucker 199I, 211C; Dr Pete Wheeler 15F, 77B, 111C, 113G, 141G, 141H, 231C, 231D, 239K, 247D; J. S. Wightman 281K; Steve Young 17B, 23C, 43F, 137F, 143C, 143D, 241F; Dan Zetterström 133H, 167C, 209I, 239G

Introduction to non-passerines

This group includes all the orders of birds except the Passeriformes, in Europe a total of 20 orders. These range from the divers, through waterfowl, birds of prey and shorebirds to the pigeons, the owls and the woodpeckers. Within this essentially artificial grouping there is a great diversity, both in appearance and in habits, though each order and each family has its own particular characteristics.

The non-passerines include birds as small as storm-petrels, the stints and the vagrant Little Swift (12 cm), as well as the long-winged albatrosses, the huge pelicans and vultures and the enormously heavy (up to 16 kg) bustards. The world's largest bird, the Ostrich *Struthio camelus*, is a non-passerine, but so too is the smallest, the 6-cm Bee Hummingbird *Mellisuga helenae* (weighing only 2 g).

Among Europe's non-passerines there are conspicuously brightly coloured birds such as the bee-eaters, the male pheasants and some male ducks, and comparatively drab species, such as some of the shearwaters and petrels, many female ducks and winter-plumaged shorebirds, or the swifts.

Not unexpectedly, the non-passerines, encompassing as they do so many different orders, display an extraordinary variety of life styles among their members. Some are almost entirely oceanic, coming ashore only to breed (tubenoses), others are totally aquatic (divers and grebes); the swifts spend almost all of their time in the air, whereas the gallinaceous birds spend most of theirs on the ground. The non-passerines include grouse that breed well above the tree line in mountains, open-country and steppe-dwelling sandgrouse and bustards, woodland-inhabiting woodpeckers, and marsh-loving herons and crakes. Specialists include the nest-parasitic cuckoos and the nocturnal nightjars and owls.

Within this diverse group are birds that perform amazing feats. The terns and the shorebirds number among them some of the longest-travelling of all birds; some migrate from the far north to the Antarctic and back every year. Young auks jump from the cliff ledges where they were born 50 m and more to the water below and, still incapable of flight, proceed to swim out to the open sea with their parents. The birds of prey include species capable of lifting and carrying prey even heavier than themselves and species which can reach speeds in excess of 180 km per hour in a dive.

The sequence in which orders and their respective families should be placed has been much debated over many decades, and various treatments have been proposed by taxonomists over the years. It has been claimed that a logical sequence should start with the most primitive orders/families and lead through to the most specialised ones; in practice, however, this is not so easy to devise, even within the relatively small confines of Europe, since insufficient is known about many families and orders and their true relationships with other orders. For convenience, the systematic arrangement adopted here is more or less the 'traditional' one; it does at least group together some of the seemingly closely related orders and families, and has the advantage that it is widely recognised and accepted.

Long-tailed Skua adult summer in flight

Divers

Divers (order Gaviiformes, family Gaviidae) are completely adapted to a life on and in the water. Powerful legs, placed far back, with webbed feet. In flight the head is often held slightly lower than the body. The wingbeats are relatively fast, and the birds never use gliding flight. Over longer distances they fly high (often at heights of 20–70 m), in contrast to grebes, which almost touch the tops of the waves. When diving, the divers disappear with a smooth, neat dip. They nest at the water's edge, usually 2 eggs.

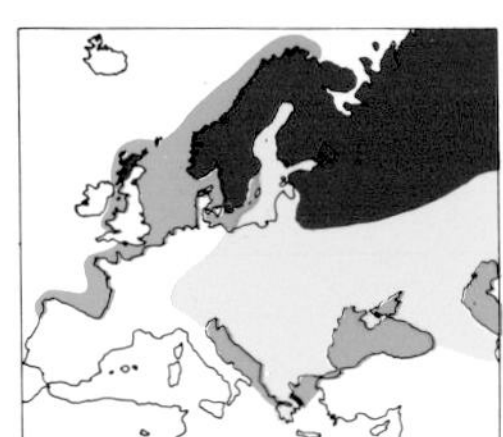

Black-throated Diver *Gavia arctica* L 65. Breeds in N Europe and Scotland on lakes and lochs with deep, clear water and fish; rarely at coast. Migratory, winters along sea coasts. Character in summer are *black throat and chin* and pale grey crown. In winter plumage, back is dark grey; *on swimming birds a white patch is often visible on rear of body at the water line. Bill held almost horizontal* when swimming, is dagger-shaped, medium-heavy and straight, proportionately slimmer than in Great Northern Diver. Call on the breeding grounds (most often at night) is a desolate, mournful, far-carrying 'kloowee-kow-kloowee-kow-kloowee-kow-klowi'. Other calls: a resounding 'aah-aw' like calling gull, and hard 'knarr-knorr'. Silent in flight. RWP

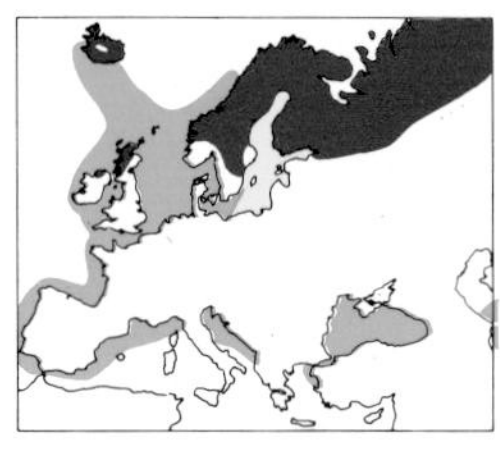

Red-throated Diver *Gavia stellata* L 57. Breeds in N Europe and Scotland on pools or open water, bogs and tundra. Often flies long distances to larger lakes or the sea to fish. Winters mainly along coasts. When swimming often holds its *head and bill* (slender and upturned) *pointing markedly upwards*. In summer easily recognised by *reddish-brown throat*. In flight very like Black-throated but can often be told by *feet projecting less*, greater tendency towards *hunched back* and *sagging neck*, quicker wingbeats, higher upstroke and more backwards-angled wings. Winter plumage paler than in Black-throated and with *more restricted grey on hindneck*, and *eye usually clearly white-framed*; back is sprinkled with small white spots; *side of body completely dark above water line*. Male has continuously repeated, loud display call, 'oo rrOO-U, oo rrOO-U, oo rrOO-U, . . .', accompanied by female's louder and shriller 'AArroo-AArroo-AArroo- . . .'. Also has drawn-out wailing 'eeaaooh'. Most often heard call is rapid goose-like cackle in flight, 'gak-gak-gak-gak- . . .'. RWP

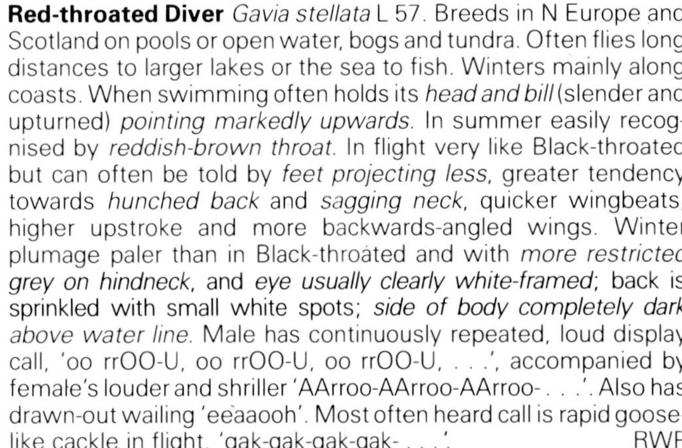

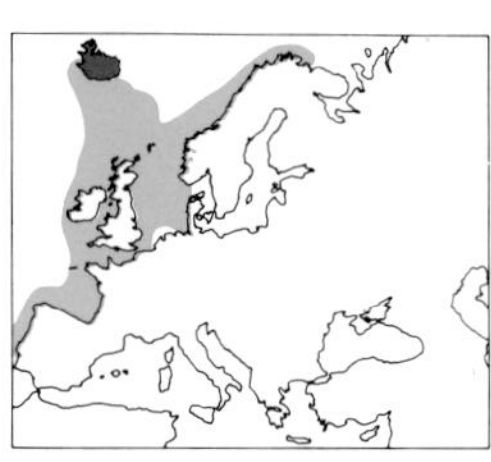

Great Northern Diver *Gavia immer* L 75. Mainly a New World species. In Europe breeds on inland lakes in Iceland. Winters mainly along coasts of N and W Europe. Size rather variable, usually considerably larger than Black-throated Diver (note that occasional giant examples of Black-throated can exceed small Great Northern). Has proportionately much more powerful neck and bill. Immatures and winter plumage adults as a rule have quite pale, greyish-white bill (but *culmen and tip* always dark; mostly pale in White-billed). Note that adult in summer plumage can have whitish outer part of bill (can appear pale in flight). Winter plumage like Black-throated's but has *white eye-ring*, has crown and hindneck darker than back (converse in Black-throated) and often *broad dark half-collar* on lower neck. Flight heavy. Feet protrude far behind. Call during breeding season consists of loud screams and yodels ('maniacal laughter'). W

White-billed Diver *Gavia adamsii* L 80. Breeds in N Russia and Alaska. Winters chiefly in Norwegian waters. The largest diver, near enough identical to Great Northern but with *bill greyish-yellow-white, slightly upturned* and on average a shade longer. The culmen is completely straight in adults, in immatures (and in Great Northern Diver at all ages) usually convex. When swimming, holds the *bill pointing upwards* like Red-throated Diver. In summer plumage the white spots on back and neck are a shade larger and fewer than in Great Northern. In winter and immature plumages *the neck and the side of the head are paler* than in Great Northern and the *culmen is pale*, at least on the outer part (rarely only the outer third pale). Like Great Northern, has a *dark half-collar* on lower neck. The flight is heavy. V

■□□ **Black-throated Diver** adult summer pair

□■□ **Black-throated Diver** adult winter

□□■ **Black-throated Diver** juv.

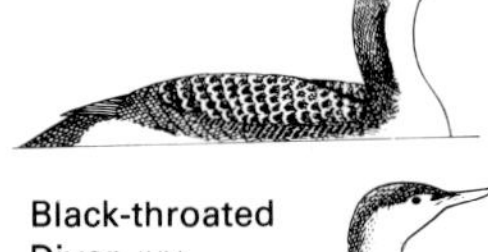

Black-throated Diver, juv.

Red-throated Diver, winter

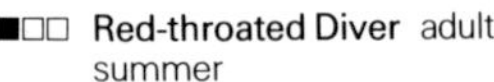

■□□ **Red-throated Diver** adult summer

□■□ **Red-throated Diver** adult summer taking off from water

□□■ **Red-throated Diver** adult winter

Great Northern Diver

White-billed Diver

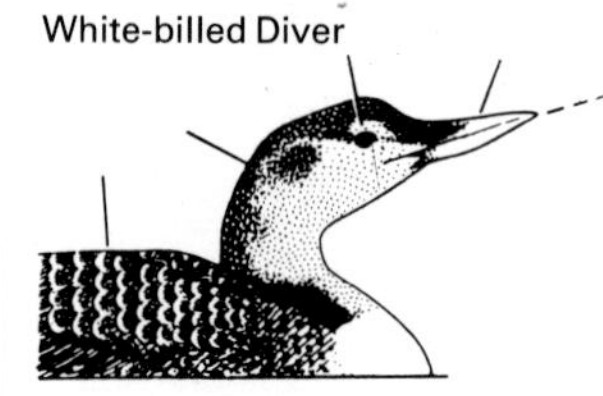

■□□ **Great Northern Diver** adult summer

□■□ **Great Northern Diver** adult winter (showing traces of summer plumage)

□□■ **Great Northern Diver** juv.

Great Northern Diver, adult summer

White-billed Diver, adult summer

■□□ **White-billed Diver** 1st-winter in flight

□■□ **White-billed Diver** adult winter moulting into summer

□□■ **White-billed Diver** juv.

Grebes

Grebes (order Podicipediformes, family Podicipedidae) are accomplished diving birds, but are smaller than the divers and have lobed toes. They have short legs placed far back; tail very short. The flight is swift, with the head held low. They live on fish and aquatic insects, and build a floating nest of plant material. Clutch 2–7 eggs.

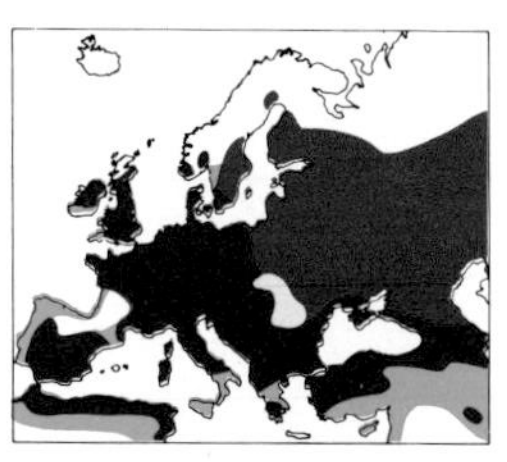

Great Crested Grebe *Podiceps cristatus* L 50. Locally common on inland lakes and rivers with reed cover. During migration and winter, along the coasts and on large lakes and reservoirs, usually in small flocks. In winter plumage the ear tufts and tippets are absent, confusion can then occur with Red-necked Grebe. Distinguished from latter by *white above the eye, longer, paler neck and longer, pink bill* with dark culmen. The courtship display is remarkable and is frequently performed. Characteristic is the breast-to-breast 'flirting' with vigorous head-shaking. Its seldom-seen climax is the so-called 'penguin-dance'. Calls include a far-carrying, rumbling 'koorrr' (often at night) and a harsh cackling 'vrek-vrek-vrek-'. The young beg with a loud 'ping-ping-ping-'. RW

Red-necked Grebe *Podiceps grisegena* L 45. Fairly common but local on lowland lakes and shallower marshy ponds, usually with tall surrounding cover. Winters mostly on coasts, occasionally on inland lakes, reservoirs. In summer plumage unmistakablo, in winter plumage easily confused with Great Crested Grebe. Dis-In flight, compared with Great Crested, appears stunted at front, and the front white wing patch (quite big) does not reach inner part of rear one. Noisy in spring. The call most resembles the Water Rail's squealing call but is considerably more intense. It starts with a Pheasant-like stutter, is then drawn out in a roaring howl. W

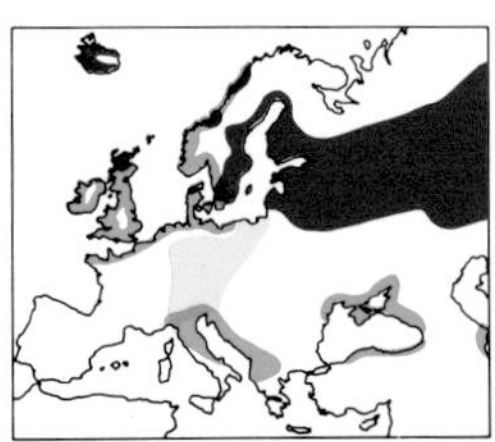

Slavonian Grebe *Podiceps auritus* L 35. Rare breeder in Scotland, locally fairly common elsewhere in N Europe, on sheltered reedy lakes. On migration and in winter on sheltered coasts and estuaries, occasionally on inland waters. Reddish-brown neck of summer can look black at distance, but the 'shaving brushes' are always well visible. In winter plumage told from Black-necked Grebe by whiter sides of head and neck, straight bill together with *flat crown* and *angular nape*. Most common call, heard in spring, summer and autumn, is feeble but far-carrying, plaintive, rattling 'hij-aarrr', repeated in short series. Display call trilling, but *pulsating*, each wave of whinnying sounds begins with a rapid giggling but drops and dies away nasally. RWP

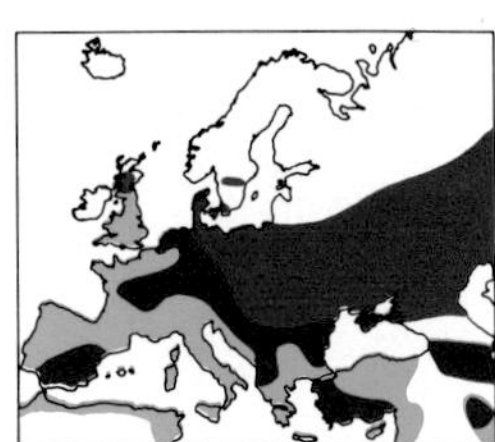

Black-necked Grebe *Podiceps nigricollis* L 31. Breeds locally in N Britain (rare) on shallow, well-reeded lakes in colonies, often among Black-headed Gulls. More common on Continent. During migration and in winter on open waters, along shallow coasts and in estuaries. In summer, plumage *narrow* black *neck, high forehead* and flattened, *fan-like, slightly drooping cheek tufts* characteristic. Like Slavonian Grebe in winter plumage but neck and sides of head greyer, bill slender and slightly upturned, and *the forehead is steep* and *the crown pointed.* Commonest call a plaintive whistle, 'ooo-eet'. RWP

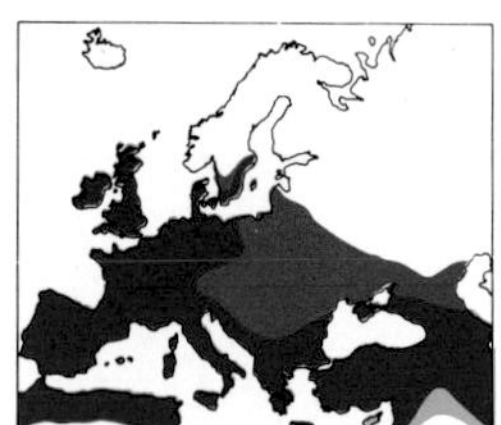

Little Grebe *Tachybaptus ruficollis* L 25. Widespread and generally common on densely vegetated lakes and small rivers. A master at keeping out of sight during breeding period. Rather uniformly coloured plumage and *small size* characteristic at all times of the year. *Cheeks, chin and foreneck brownish-red* in summer plumage. *Bright whitish-yellow gape patches.* More greyish-brown in winter plumage, and pale gape not so conspicuous. *Lacks white on wing* (but trailing edge paler). On breeding grounds utters loud, drawn-out, shrill cackling trills, like female Cuckoo. Contact call 'beeheeb'. RW

Pied-billed Grebe *Podilymbus podiceps* L 35. Rare vagrant from North America. *Thick, stubby bill* is typical; the dark transverse band is present only in summer plumage. In flight wings all-dark. Spring call a rapid string of powerful, rattling, hollow barks. V

■□□ **Great Crested Grebe** adult summer pair in head-shaking courtship display

□■□ **Great Crested Grebe** adult winter starting to assume summer plumage

□□■ **Great Crested Grebe** adult summer in flight

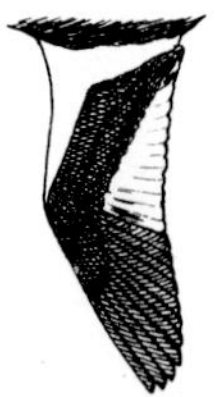

Great Crested Red-necked
upperwings

■□□ **Black-necked Grebe** adult summer at nest

□■□ **Black-necked Grebe** adult winter

□□■ **Red-necked Grebe** adult summer

Slavonian Grebe

■□□ **Slavonian Grebe** adult summer

□■□ **Slavonian Grebe** adult winter

□□■ **Red-necked Grebe** adult winter

Black-necked Grebe

■□□ **Little Grebe** adult summer on nest

□■□ **Little Grebe** adult winter

□□■ **Pied-billed Grebe** adult summer

Tubenoses

Tubenoses (order Procellariiformes) have external, tube-shaped nostrils from which excess salt is secreted. They are birds of the oceans and come ashore on remote islands and shores only to nest. Colonial nesters. Live on fish, plankton etc. All have hook-tipped bills. Sexes alike. Utter calls only on the breeding grounds.
The tubenoses that visit European waters and coasts belong to the following families:

ALBATROSSES (family Diomedeidae), very large birds with long narrow wings and very powerful bills.
FULMARS, SHEARWATERS AND PETRELS (family Procellariidae), nearest in size to gulls. Bill equipped with tube-shaped nasal openings.
STORM PETRELS (family Hydrobatidae), small birds, barely larger than swallows. Bills short and legs fairly long.

Albatrosses belong mainly to the southern hemisphere and visit Europe only as accidentals. Wingspan strikingly large. Although they may beat their wings in flight, for the most part they are seen gliding along following the contours of the waves on rigidly extended wings. Lay only one egg and do not breed every year. The Black-browed Albatross is the species most frequently seen in Europe.

Black-browed Albatross *Diomedea melanophris* L 80–95, W 213-246. Very rare, but the albatross one can most expect to see in Europe. Single individuals have on several occasions overflown to Scotland and the Faeroe Islands and lived there for many years on bird cliffs among Gannets ('Solan Goose' in folk dialect). Very large. Appearance similar to the even rarer Yellow-nosed and Grey-headed Albatrosses but *entirely yellow bill, dark eyebrow streak* and fairly broad dark borders on underside of wing, *widest in front*, are characteristic features of the Black-browed. The immature has a grey crown, grey neck and dark bill. Most observations in Europe have been made during the summer months. V

Wandering Albatross *Diomedea exulans* L 110-135, W 275-345. Extremely rare visitor to SW European waters. *Enormously big*, long-winged and with *wholly pale, powerful bill*. The immature is dark brown with white head, neck and belly as well as white underwings. The development to full adult plumage – with all-white upperwing-coverts – takes many years. A fully grown bird weighs between 8 kg and 10 kg – almost as much as a Mute Swan – but nevertheless has complete mastery of the air: can follow ships for days (and nights) over stormy seas.

True fulmars resemble the larger gulls in appearance and feeding methods. Usually live farther out at sea. Often nest on coastal cliffs, lay one egg.

Fulmar *Fulmarus glacialis* L 45, W 105. Nests in colonies on N Atlantic bird cliffs, has increased during the 1900s. Nesting-cliff ledges are surrounded by greenery. Vomits stinking secretion over intruders at the nest. Between large and small gulls in size, but behaviour and proportions immediately distinguish it from these: flies like a miniature albatross, sails along in *long glides on stiff, straight wings*, exploiting the air currents close above the wave crests or alongside the nesting cliff faces. Wingbeats stiff. When swimming, floats high on the water. Leaps into flight when it takes off from the water. Has characteristically *robust head and neck area*, short tail and *short, thick bill*. Upperparts grey with *pale patches on 'wrists'*, underparts white (light phase) or pale grey ('blue' phase; of northern origin). Lacks white trailing edge to wing shown by gulls. Silent, but cackling calls can be heard at the nest and from flocks searching for food (sometimes 1000s of birds). Follows ships. RS

■□□ **Black-browed Albatross** adult in flight from below
□■□ **Black-browed Albatross** adult in flight from above
□□■ **Wandering Albatross** adult in flight from below

Wandering Albatross, subadult

■□ **Fulmar** in flight from above
□■ **Fulmar** in flight from below

■□ **Fulmar** party scavenging around dead whale
□■ **Fulmar** adult on nest

Tubenoses

Shearwaters (family Procellariidae) differ from fulmars in having longer, narrower wings, narrower tails and longer, thinner bills. They fly with a series of rapid wingbeats and long glides, usually near the surface of the water. The wings, typically stiff and slightly bowed downwards, are held low in gliding flight. In stronger winds the wingbeats are dispensed with; they glide along and rear up over wave tops. They live on small fish and crustaceans. Active at night at the breeding sites. Lay only one egg.

Manx Shearwater *Puffinus puffinus* L 35, W 80. The commonest and most widespread of the European shearwaters. Large numbers breed on islands mainly off western Britain and in the Mediterranean Sea. Breeding takes place in colonies along the coast, in burrows in the earth. *Wholly dark upperside and pale underside* – looks black and white at distance – distinguish it from the larger shearwaters. The *mauretanicus* race, found in the W Mediterranean, has paler brown upperparts and darker underparts showing less clear contrast in colours. The E Mediterranean race *yelkouan* has brownish-black upperparts and pale dirty-white underparts. Flight swift, careening from side to side. Does not follow ships. Visits breeding colonies at night, when utters a variety of weird caws, screams and cooing noises. SP

Little Shearwater *Puffinus assimilis* L 28, W 63. Very rare visitor to European coasts, north to Denmark, mostly during the spring. Two rather similar races: *baroli* (Canary Islands, Madeira) with paler side of head (light colour reaches up around the eye), paler bases to primaries below, as well as white central undertail-coverts (difficult to see in the field); and *boydi* (Cape Verde Islands) with darker side to head, darker bases to primaries and tail-coverts below. Very like Manx Shearwater but differs in *small size, weak bill* and, in the race *baroli,* pale side to head. Flight very fast, differing from Manx by having *long series of fluttering wingbeats* interrupted by only short phases of gliding flight. SV

► **Great Shearwater** *Puffinus gravis* L 48, W 115. A large Atlantic shearwater with breeding period Nov–Apr on the Tristan da Cunha group of islands in S Atlantic. In May–June migrates north to the W Atlantic and in Sept-Oct southwards through its eastern sectors. *Black cap* and *white on the base of the tail* are conspicuous features. Distinguished from Cory's Shearwater by the cap contrasting with the white 'cheeks', often emphasised by *narrow pale nape band,* and by dark-tipped under secondary coverts (forming diagonal band). Dark patch on belly diagnostic. S

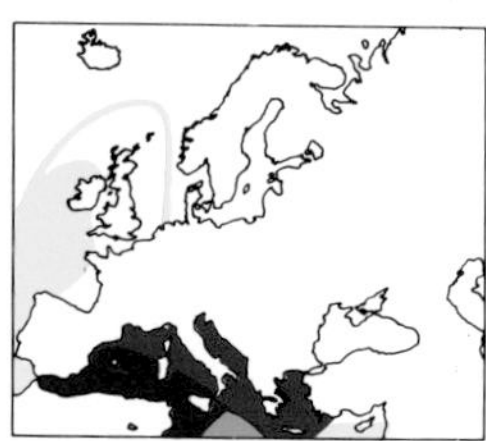

► **Cory's Shearwater** *Calonectris diomedea* L 50, W 118. Breeds on islands in the Mediterranean. Appears Aug–Nov in the N Atlantic. Largest of the Atlantic shearwaters. Some individuals have a small amount of white on the uppertail-coverts like Great Shearwater, but *never have black cap or pale nape band* also *underwing-coverts do not have markings* (apart from narrow brown border to wing). Flight slow, more albatross-like than in other shearwaters: usually *3–4 slow wingbeats and then glides for 6–7 seconds,* with the wingtips held slightly below the horizontal and distinctly angled backwards. The only Atlantic shearwater that can be seen flying high up and even soaring Sometimes follows ships, schools of small whales. P

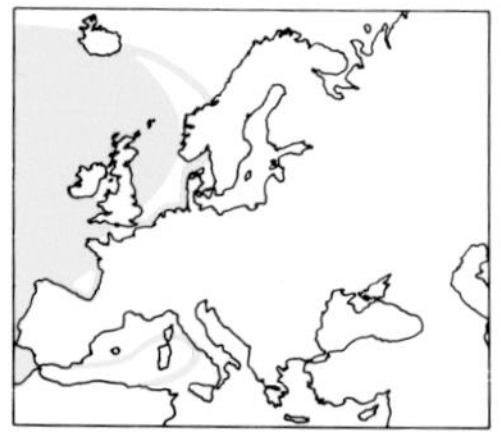

► **Sooty Shearwater** *Puffinus griseus* L 45, W 105. Breeds in the southern hemisphere, south of 30°S, in burrows on islands. Occurs in the Atlantic Jul–Feb, most abundantly in Aug–Nov, also annually in the North Sea. More tied to coastal waters than most shearwaters. Easily recognised by its *uniform greyish-brown plumage with poorly defined pale band under the wing* (at very long distance looks all-dark). Wingbeats faster than in Great Shearwater, with which it often occurs in W Europe. Wings longer and more pointed than in Manx Shearwater. In flight, normally holds wings more backswept than other *Puffinus* species. Follows ships only exceptionally. Often dives for food. P

■□□ **Manx Shearwater** in flight

□■□ **Manx Shearwater** flock from above

□□■ **Manx Shearwater** flock from below

■□□ **Little Shearwater** adult at nest burrow, race *baroli*

□■□ **Great Shearwater** in flight from above

□□■ **Great Shearwater** in flight from below

■□ **Cory's Shearwater**

□■ **Cory's Shearwater** in flight from below

■□ **Sooty Shearwater** in flight from below

□■ **Sooty Shearwater** in flight from above

Tubenoses

Storm-petrels

Storm-petrels (family Hydrobatidae) are small ocean-dwelling birds which feed on small fish, shrimps and plankton. Their flight is fluttering or bouncing over the waves, some 'patter along' on the surface with their webbed feet. Strong, hooked bills and tube-shaped nasal openings can be seen when close up. Lay one egg.

Wilson's Storm-petrel *Oceanites oceanicus* L 18, W 40. May be seen far out in the Atlantic, mainly Aug-Dec when returning to breeding sites in the S Atlantic. Dark brown plumage, with white rump, which extends down to the sides of the undertail-coverts. Rather indistinct pale wing patches above. Long legs, usually project just beyond tail. (When very close up, yellowish, not dark, webs between toes can sometimes be observed.) When looking for food, *dancing flight over the water's surface* with *wings held high, pattering along the water. The wings* are quite *rounded and held straight*, not angled at carpal joint. Lacks British Storm Petrel's obvious white wingbar below, has only diffuse paling effect. Often follows ships in loose flocks. V

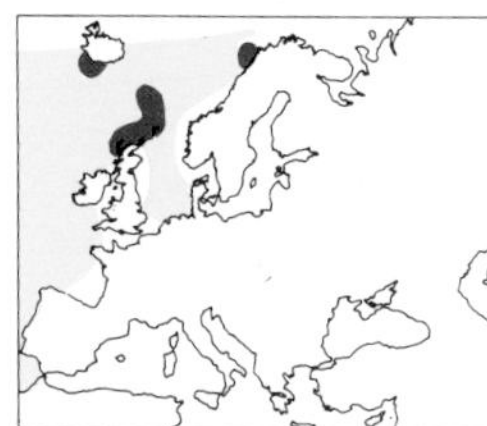

Leach's Storm-petrel *Oceanodroma leucorhoa* L 22, W 48. Dark with prominent white rump and pale grey wing panels above. The tail is forked, the feet dark. Distinctly larger than British Storm-petrel; distinguished from that species and Wilson's Storm-petrel by *hint of a grey stripe down centre of white rump*. Flight fast and jerky with deep wingbeats, sudden lunges and glides, on slightly depressed wings. *Wings rather long and pointed, often carried with marked angling at carpal.* Only rarely patters on water's surface (cf. Wilson's Storm-petrel). Bill heavier than British Storm-petrel's. Does not follow ships. SP

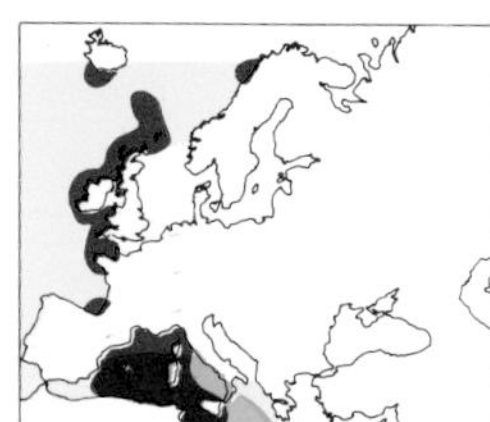

British Storm-petrel *Hydrobates pelagicus* L 15, W 37. The commonest storm-petrel in Europe, breeding in both N and W coasts and in Mediterranean. Occasionally in huge flocks after westerly autumn storms, when may also be encountered inland. *Smallest* storm-petrel with rather blunt-tipped wings which are generally held straight. *Darker* than Leach's, lacking pale upper wing-panel (only narrow trace), but having *prominent white band on underwing*. Rump pure white, tail square-cut. Flight recalling bat, *wingbeats rapid and fluttering* without the shearwater-like glides of Leach's. Follows ships. RSP

Madeiran Storm-petrel *Oceanodroma castro* L 20, W 45. Very rare visitor from breeding sites on Atlantic islands. Extremely similar to other storm-petrels but has *dark feet* (cf. Wilson's Storm-petrel), *pure white rump* (no grey central stripe as in Leach's) and is larger than British Storm-petrel. Flight shearwater-like, more so than in Leach's. Does not follow ships. (Not illust.) V

White-faced Storm-petrel *Pelagodroma marina* L 20, W 42. Very rare visitor from breeding sites on Atlantic islands. Short-winged and long-legged with pale feet, *face and underparts*. Looks like a winter-plumage phalarope, but not seen in flocks. Does not follow ships. V

Petrels

Petrels (family Procellariidae), placed between shearwaters and storm-petrels, are relatively small, fly more like shearwaters than like storm-petrels. Usually have shorter and heavier bills than shearwaters. Several species are markedly nocturnal and fish far out to sea.

Bulwer's Petrel *Bulweria bulwerii* L 28, W 70. A very rare visitor on NW coasts and in Mediterranean from breeding places on Atlantic islands (incl. Madeira and Canary Islands). Dark rump and *uniformly dark plumage* (but paler bar on wing-coverts) are best identification marks. Has quite a long, wedge-shaped tail and short pink legs. (Not illustrated) V

Soft-plumaged Petrel *Pterodroma mollis* L 35, W 88. Very rare visitor from breeding places on Atlantic islands (Madeira). As large as Manx Shearwater, from which immediately distinguished by *dark underwings, diffuse breast band* and *pale forehead*.

■□ Wilson's Storm-petrel
□■ Wilson's Storm-petrels feeding on scraps from Leopard Seal's meal

■□ Leach's Storm-petrel
□■ Leach's Storm-petrel

■□ British Storm-petrel
□■ British Storm-petrels

■□ White-faced Storm-petrel
□■ Soft-plumaged Petrel

Pelicans and allies

Pelicans and their allies (order Pelecaniformes) are large, aquatic and fish-eating birds with all four toes connected by webs (paddle-footed). Most species breed in large colonies and are silent outside the breeding season.

GANNETS (family Sulidae) are represented in Europe by the Northern Gannet, which dives vertically for fish like a giant tern. PELICANS (family Pelecanidae) have enormous bills with which they rake in fish, driving them by swimming in cordons. CORMORANTS (family Phalacrocoracidae) dive from the surface and swim under the water. They are often seen perched on posts and cliffs with their wings extended.

Northern Gannet *Sula bassana* L 92, W 175. Breeds on almost inaccessible precipitous rocky islands on Atlantic coasts, in immense colonies. Isolated colony on coast of NE England. Britain harbours the greater part of the world population, which has steadily increased over recent decades. Winters at sea. Very occasionally blown inland after severe autumn/winter storms. *Long pointed wings,* long wedge-shaped tail. *White with black wingtips* and *yellowish-buff head.* Immature is brown-speckled, acquires adult plumage by stages over 4–5 years. During the second autumn the head, belly and leading edges of the wings are pale. In the third autumn the first white secondaries appear interspersed among the remaining dark ones, and the crown and nape acquire the adult's yellowish tone. During the fourth autumn, dark central tail feathers and dark secondaries scattered among the new white ones are usually visible. Catches fish by vertical dives of up to c.40 m height like a gigantic tern, but usually completely disappears under the water (folds back wings on entry). On migration they fly close to the surface of the water, often in a line. Wingbeats vigorous but measured, gliding phases short. In stormy weather Gannets sweep up above the waves and down again like shearwaters, so that immatures can then be confused with, e.g. Cory's Shearwater. At breeding site makes loud gurgling calls. RS

White Pelican *Pelecanus onocrotalus* L 140-175, W 270-330. A rare species that is decreasing in numbers. Probably under 3000 breeding pairs in Europe. In summer found mainly in swampy areas and marshes of E Europe, in winter also on the coasts, in sheltered bays and river deltas. The two European pelican species are difficult to separate but in adults the markings on the *underwing* are characteristic: the white Pelican has *black flight feathers and white coverts,* roughly as in White Stork; in the Dalmatian Pelican they are grey. The immatures of both species are greyish-brown above and dirty-white below. *Immature White Pelican is considerably darker above* and has *yellow throat pouch*; the feathering on the forehead ends in a point; and the *legs are brownish-pink.* The immature Dalmatian Pelican is pale buffish-grey above, has a *faintly rosy-tinged throat pouch,* square-cut abutment of feathering on the forehead and lead-grey legs. When swimming, all pelicans float very high. Flight direct; a few, slow wingbeats are followed by gliding. Usually fly in a line. Often circle in flocks and *in formation* (soaring White Storks move in disorderly fashion when they gather in large flocks on migration). May ascend to high altitude. V

Dalmatian Pelican *Pelecanus crispus* L 160-180, W 310-345. Rare breeder on swampy ground and lakes in E Europe. Now probably no more than 250 breeding pairs in Europe. In winter often moves to sheltered sea coasts. Distinguished from White Pelican by *wholly pale underwing.* Even at a distance the *body feathers* are seen to be *greyish-white* (not yellowish-rosy). The eyes are yellowish-white (not red) and the *nape feathers curly. The immature is considerably paler above* than immature White Pelican – see also under that species. Gregarious, as White Pelican.

Gannet adult braking in flight

Gannet adult (right) and two 2nd-summers and one (partly hidden) 1st-summer in flight

Gannet part of breeding colony

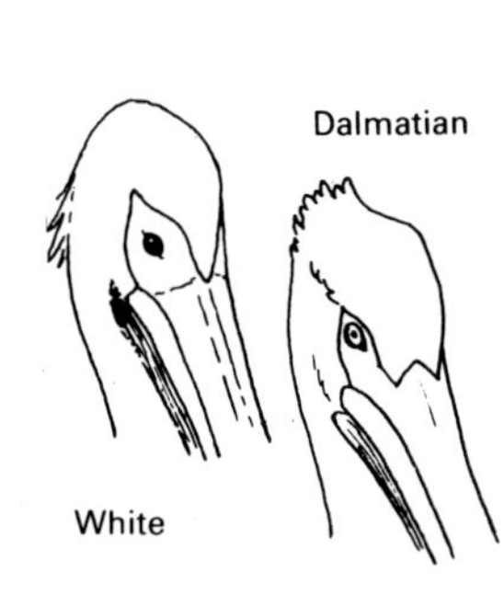

White Pelican adults

White Pelican imm.

Gannet juv. in flight

White Pelican adults in flight

Dalmatian Pelican adult in flight

Pelicans and allies

Cormorant *Phalacrocorax carbo* L 90, W 145. A widespread species, inhabits five continents. Nests colonially. Race *carbo* breeds along N Atlantic and Murman coasts, on rocky islands and cliff ledges (exceptionally in trees). Race *sinensis* breeds in central and S Europe (incl. Holland, Denmark, Sweden) in trees, often by fresh water, often in company of herons. The trees are killed by their droppings. In Britain mainly marine but avoids rough sea, prefers shallow coastal waters and estuaries, also visits reservoirs, rivers etc. *Large*, dark and reptile-like. In spring has white on chin and cheeks, a white patch on thigh and (for a short period) a varying amount of whitish hair-like plumes interspersed on hind parts of head. In *sinensis* these plumes are abundant and large, *much of head and upper neck looking white* in early spring. In autumn/winter almost all-dark; whitish on chin slight. Juveniles and immatures are brown-black, but *belly is whitish* with few exceptions (Atlantic juv. Shag: belly brown). All-dark birds can be difficult to tell from Shag, but *bill is heavier, head larger* and *more flat-crowned* and *angled at nape*. Swims low with neck erect, bill held up at an angle. Expert diver. Rests on rocky shores, sandbanks (often many in a long line, like bottles), piles, buoys etc, in upright posture, wings often typically held spread. Flight with goose-like wingbeats, at times interrupted by short glides. Usually flies several metres above sea (cf. Shag). When many fly together skeins are formed. Inland flights at a great height; then also soars. Deep guttural noise at nest, otherwise silent. RSW

Shag *Phalacrocorax aristotelis* L 70, W 100. Breeds in colonies on rocky coasts. Habits much as Cormorant but at home also in rough sea and avoids fresh water, rests on cliffs, only rarely perches on piles, buoys etc. Adult all-black, glossed green, with *bright yellow gape*; in early spring also a recurved tuft on forecrown. In winter Cormorant is similar (almost all-black too) but Shag has *slimmer neck, smaller and rounder head* with steeper forehead, *narrower bill* (note that occasional immature Cormorants have confusingly slender bill). Juveniles rather uniform brown below (juv. Cormorant: belly usually whitish) with well-marked whitish chin, but those of race *desmarestii* (Mediterranean and Black Sea) are extensively whitish below. Wing-coverts of juveniles and particularly of second-year birds are edged pale, giving *large pale wing panel in flight* (Cormorant: uniformly dark wings). Otherwise similar to Cormorant in flight; smaller size not obvious (and size of Cormorant varies a great deal), but *wingbeats noticeably faster*, slimmer *neck stretched out* (not slightly retracted and crooked), smaller head reaching upwards, *belly bulging*, all giving a somewhat tail-heavy look. Shag usually flies close to the water (Cormorant frequently higher up). R

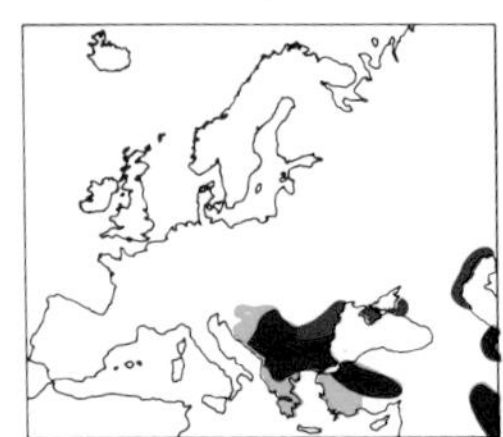

Pygmy Cormorant *Phalacrocorax pygmeus* L 50, W 85. Breeds locally in SE Europe, in colonies in bushes beside lakes and rivers with large reedbeds, often together with egrets and herons. Often fishes in quite small rivers and pools out in the swamplands. Immediately distinguished from Cormorant and Shag by *small size* – is smaller than a Red-breasted Merganser – and in addition has different proportions: *smaller head* and in particular *shorter bill* (looks 'baby-faced'), *longer tail*. In breeding plumage head and neck are dark chestnut-brown, the body glossy greenish-black with small white feather tufts which stand out like white droplets (both sexes). The feather tufts are soon lost and the chin becomes whitish, the breast reddish-brown. Juvenile is dark brown with whitish chin and belly. Swims low in the water and perches to dry out like its larger relatives, but may also use reed stems and thin branches as perches. Flies with same wingbeat rate as Eider, with short glides interspersed; at long range and at poor angles, therefore, Glossy Ibis is a confusion risk.

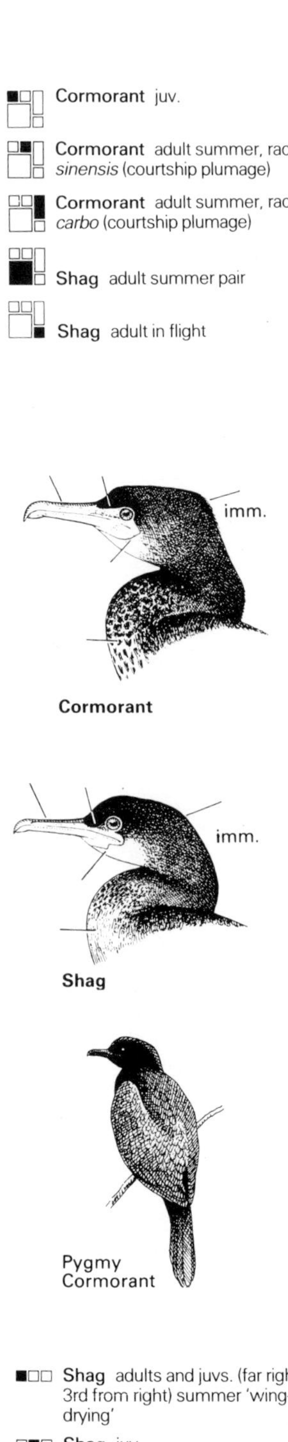

Cormorant juv.

Cormorant adult summer, race *sinensis* (courtship plumage)

Cormorant adult summer, race *carbo* (courtship plumage)

Shag adult summer pair

Shag adult in flight

Cormorant

Shag

Pygmy Cormorant

■□□ **Shag** adults and juvs. (far right, 3rd from right) summer 'wing-drying'

□■□ **Shag** juv.

□□■ **Pygmy Cormorant** adult in 'wing-drying' posture

Herons, storks and ibises

Herons, storks and ibises (order Ciconiiformes) are wading birds with long necks, legs and bills. Most live on smallish animals which they catch in shallow water. Some have long plumes (aigrettes) during the breeding season. Wings broad and rounded, tails short. Clutches 2–6 eggs.

Herons and their allies are divided into the following families:

HERONS AND BITTERNS (family Ardeidae), bills straight, flight slow with necks retracted. Most are colonial nesters. Partly nocturnal. Hoarse and muffled calls.

STORKS (family Ciconiidae), bills straight, flight with outstretched neck and slow powerful wingbeats. Soar readily. Plumages black and white.

IBISES AND SPOONBILLS (family Threskiornithidae), bills thin and curved or flat and spoon-shaped. Wingbeats fairly quick, necks outstretched.

Bittern adult

Bittern in camouflage posture ('bitterning')

Bittern *Botaurus stellaris* L 75, W 130. Breeds sparingly in scattered pairs in large reedbeds. Polygamous: one male may have several females in the reeds. Partly diurnal but keeps well concealed. Clambers about, clutching bunches of reed stems. If alarmed, it stretches its bill straight up in the air (the 'bitterning' posture). Easiest to see on early mornings in summer, when it flies to and from fishing sites. In flight has *retracted neck*, but the wingbeats are not sluggish and heavy like Grey Heron's but quick and even as in the smaller heron species. This, together with the *brownish-speckled appearance* and the ungainly shape, make it very owl-like in poor light. Immature Night Heron is a risk of confusion in southern Europe. The Bittern starts breeding activity early, in the north the first ones while the ice is still present, and the male's *booming night-time call* is uttered throughout spring and far into June; heard best at dusk and dawn. The powerful waves of sound, reminiscent of blowing into an empty bottle, audible over 5 km, are preceded by muffled intakes of breath; 'u u u u uh-POH, uh-POOMBH, uh-POOMBH, uh-POOMBH'. On dark autumn evenings far-carrying, hoarse 'kaau' calls are heard from flying Bitterns, at close range sounding like large gulls, at long range quite like the barking of a fox. RW

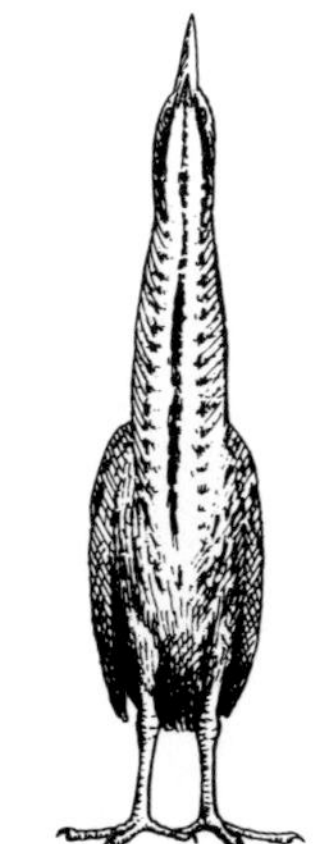

Bittern in camouflage posture

American Bittern *Botaurus lentiginosus* L 68, W 115. Very rare vagrant to W Europe during late autumn. Smaller than Bittern, has *reddish-brown crown* and long, *black 'whiskers'*. In flight the *dark flight feathers* are obvious. Like the Bittern, occurs in dense reedbeds. More diurnal than Bittern and seen more often in flight. V

American Bittern juv.

Little Bittern adult male (left) and adult female at nest

Little Bittern *Ixobrychus minutus* L 35, W 55. Shy and usually difficult to observe. Found in S and central Europe, overshooting spring migrants regular further north (has bred in England). Inhabits dense vegetation in swampy areas, preferably large reedbeds, where it breeds in single pairs. Easy to identify by size and colour. In flight the contrast between the *pale wing panels* and the *dark wing and back* is clearly visible. Male shows more contrast than female, has *black back* and *brilliant buff-white wing panels*. Female is *streaked brown* on the back and has dirtier wing panels and *more streaked breast*. Immature is spotted brown like Bittern but also shows the adult's pale wing panel in flight. Sometimes conceals itself by standing motionless as if paralysed ('freezing'). Avoids danger by running rather than flying. Flight characteristic with *Jay-like quick wingbeats and long glides*. Often flies very short distances, low over the reeds. Mating call is a quite muffled grunting 'grook' repeated rhythmically every two or three seconds and in very long series when the bird is in full song. Also has an excited, loud nasal 'kekekeke'. SV

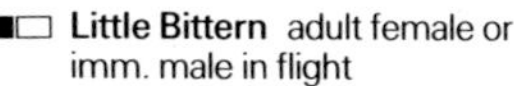

Little Bittern adult female or imm. male in flight

Little Bittern juv.

Herons, storks and ibises

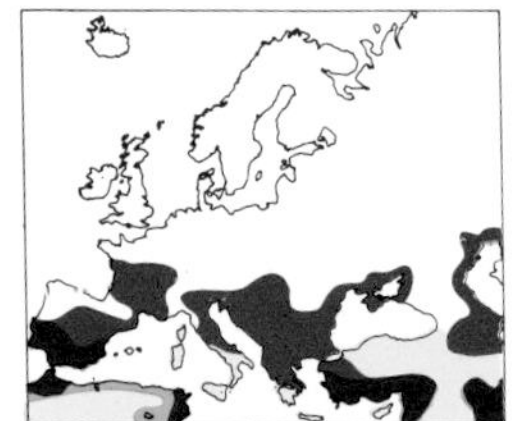

Little Egret *Egretta garzetta* L 60, W 92. Breeds in S Europe in colonies in marshes, river deltas and swamplands which have the necessary clumps of trees for nest-building. Regularly overshoots in spring. During rest of year seen beside all kinds of shallow water, but especially in swamps/marshes with salt or brackish water. Very gregarious. Reliable character is the *yellow toes* contrasting with the all-black legs. *Bill entirely black.* (The Western Reef Heron *E. gularis*, a rare visitor from coasts of W Africa, of which white form is extremely similar to Little Egret – and is regarded by some as a race of latter – is distinguished by shorter head plumes together with heavier bill, which turns brown or yellow outside breeding season.) Wingbeats in quick crow tempo. Shape and movements are more 'heron-like' than those of Cattle Egret and Squacco Heron. Captures its prey by standing in wait or by advancing slowly and stealthily. The elongated scapulars and nape feathers are worn only in summer. Great White Egret is much larger, has a differently coloured bill and legs, flies with more composed wingbeats and in flight legs project more than in Little Egret. Cattle Egret is more compact and has proportionately shorter wings. Call has ventriloquial effect, bubbling and frog-like 'gullagullagulla', also harsh raucous 'kark' calls. V

■□□ **Little Egret** adult summer (courtship plumage)
□■□ **Little Egret** adult winter in flight
□□■ **Little Egret** adult winter

▶ **Great White Egret** *Egretta alba* L 90, W 150. Scarce breeder in reeds in marshes, deltas and lagoons in SE Europe (has bred in Netherlands). During rest of year also found at other kinds of shallow water. Much larger than other white herons – *size of Grey Heron*. Lores blue-green, gape extends far behind the eye. *Yellow base of bill* (breeding period) or *all-yellow bill* (rest of year), dark toes and *reddish or yellowish-brown* (*breeding birds*) *tibia* separate it from Little Egret, which is also considerably smaller. Non-breeding birds have dark tibia, looking black-legged at distance. In flight the legs project farther behind tail than in Little Egret; wingbeats are also slower, like Grey Heron's. Like Little Egret, bears elongated scapulars, known as aigrettes, in summer plumage. The call is a harsh rolling 'krr-rr-rr-rra'. V

■□ **Great White Egret** adult winter
□■ **Great White Egret** adult winter in flight

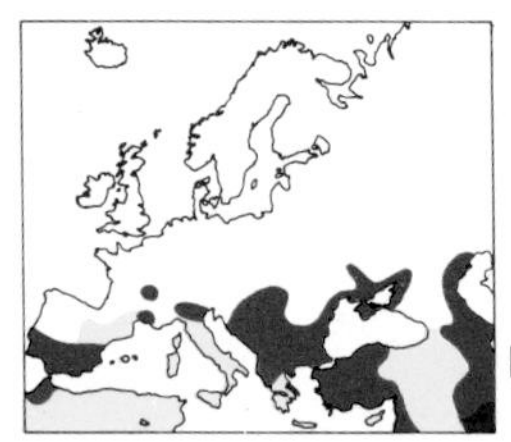

▶ **Squacco Heron** *Ardeola ralloides* L 45, W 87. Locally common in S Europe in swamps, lagoons and marshland, where nesting takes place in reeds or trees, most often forming a minority in colonies of other small herons. *Pale ochre on body and neck* with contrasting *snow-white wings and tail* are characteristic. In the field the effect is that a standing Squacco looks mainly brownish but is transformed into an almost completely white bird when it flies off. Distinguished from Cattle Egret also by bill colour (yellowish-green and blue with black tip when breeding, greenish during rest of year). Often spends the day perched in trees or shrubbery and searches for food at dusk; compared with Cattle Egret, is solitary, quiet and stealthy. Flight comparatively 'wobbly'. Call a harsh raucous 'krak', almost like Mallard. V

■□□ **Squacco Heron** adult summer
□■□ **Squacco Heron** imm.
□□■ **Squacco Heron** imm. in flight

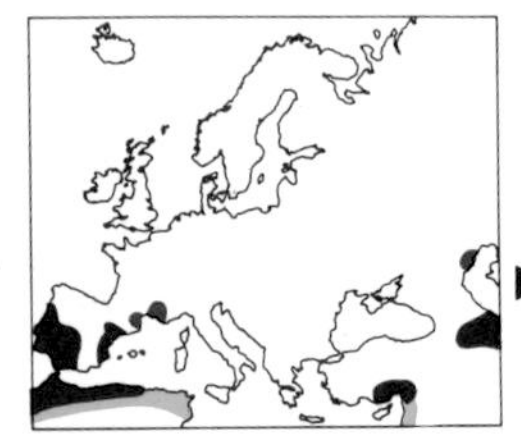

▶ **Cattle Egret** *Bubulcus ibis* L 50, W 95. An expanding species, is seen occasionally in many places in Europe. Usually breeds in colonies in clumps of trees and bushes together with other small herons. Gregarious. Seeks food in fields and dryer marshland, usually in flocks, often alongside cattle, normally in considerably dryer terrain than other herons. At a distance the *plumage* appears *all-white*; in breeding plumage and at closer range it can be seen that the crown, breast and lower back have a yellowish-brown tone. At close range the bill and leg colour should be noted: legs yellow or reddish during breeding season, grey-brown or blackish at other times; bill yellowish (red-toned at pairing time). Has strongly 'undershot jaw' (jowl), i.e. the *feathering on the lower mandible is conspicuous*. Migrates in long disorderly flocks at relatively low altitude. Flight silhouette in profile is markedly more distended, more *short-legged, short-billed and 'snub-nosed'* than Little Egret. Squacco Heron is smaller and flies more unsteadily, more like a Little Bittern. Calls quite subdued, slightly nasal, croaking, usually monosyllabic. V

■□□ **Cattle Egret** adult summer (courtship plumage)
□■□ **Cattle Egret** adult winter
□□■ **Cattle Egret** adult winter in flight

Herons, storks and ibises

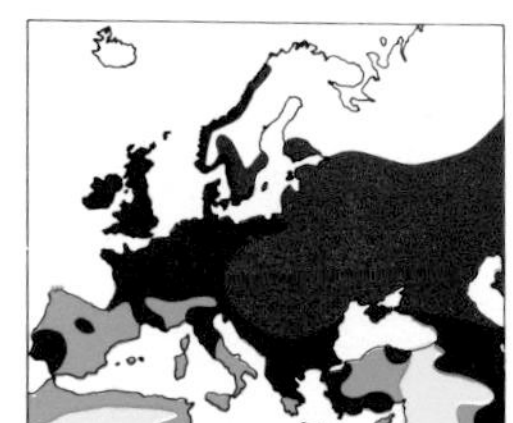

Grey Heron *Ardea cinerea* L 95, W 185. The most abundant and most widespread of Europe's herons. Found on food-rich lakes, rivers and most other fresh waters, also on sea shores. Nests usually in large, noisy colonies in trees near water. Stands motionless in wait for fish, which it captures with a lightning-fast bill stab. The patient watching behaviour and the stiffly held and often retracted neck are very characteristic of herons in general, and the Grey Heron is easily distinguished from other European herons by its size and the grey, white and black plumage. In flight the neck is always retracted; the heron then looks front-heavy. Over longer distances the Grey Heron flies at high altitudes, and can then be confused with large birds of prey because of its slow, heavy wing action. But even at long range the Grey Heron's particular characters in flight are obvious: *bowed wings* that *beat heavily and slowly*. Call a raucous 'kaark'. RWP

Purple Heron *Ardea purpurea* L 85, W 135. Locally common on marshy land and swamps in S and central Europe, spring migrants regularly overshoot. Nests in colonies, usually in reedbeds. Prefers denser vegetation than Grey Heron. The purplish-red elements in the plumage are difficult to see at a distance, when it looks generally *a little darker than the Grey Heron*. In flight the *forward-bulging crook of the retracted neck is less rounded than the Grey Heron*, forming a more pointed 'battering ram'. Head/neck more slender and snaky, bill more uniformly narrow, not dagger-shaped, and *toes are longer*, the hind toe sticking out more in flight. Adopts Bittern-like camouflage posture. P

Night Heron *Nycticorax nycticorax* L 60, W 112. Common in S and central Europe in swamps and marshes with fresh or salt water. Nests in clumps of trees in colonies with other small herons. Sturdy body and *black, grey and white* pattern distinguish adult. Gives rather pale general impression in flight. Immature is distinguished from Bittern by *large white spots on wing-coverts*; in flight by faster wingbeats and darker plumage. Often spends the day in trees or bushes. At times seen searching for food in daytime but mostly at dawn and dusk. In flight the body is held slightly raised, the bill pointing slightly downwards; moreover the *feet do not form a rectangular blob* as in other small herons, *but a slender point*. Call a soft frog-like 'kooark'. V

Glossy Ibis *Plegadis falcinellus* L 60, W 90. Found uncommonly in marshland or on mudflats. Breeds in SE Europe in colonies, usually in reeds, sometimes in trees. Immatures may straggle far outside breeding range in Sept-Oct. The *curved bill* and at a distance the *all-dark plumage* are good field characteristics. At closer range reddish-brown on head and body, a shimmering green wing patch and narrow white bill base can be seen. In winter plumage, head and neck brownish-black, spangled with small white spots. Immature resembles winter adult, but whitish spots less well marked and back and upperwing duller and browner. Flies in flocks in long lines, wingbeats quick like a curlew's, interspersed with short stages of gliding, roughly as Pygmy Cormorant (possible confusion at long range). *The neck is extended in flight.* Calls loud rumbling, belching and croaking. V

Sacred Ibis *Threskiornis aethiopicus* L 66. Very rare visitor to Caspian and Black Seas from more southerly breeding sites. *White plumage with black 'hind-bush'* (bushy tertials) together with dark neck and *dark head* make this species easy to recognise.

Bald Ibis *Geronticus eremita* L 75. Very rare vagrant in SW Europe from breeding sites in Morocco. A diminishing colony exists also in SE Turkey. Species threatened with extinction. (Nested in the 1500s as far north as Bavaria.) *All-dark plumage*, green with copper-red lesser upperwing-coverts; unfeathered *head together with long downcurved bill brownish-pink; neck* has long, lank, *bushy feathers*.

■□□ **Grey Heron** adult
□■□ **Grey Heron** 1st-year
□□■ **Grey Heron** 1st-years in flight

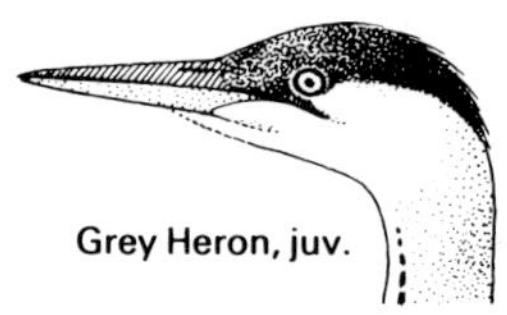

Grey Heron, juv.

■□□ **Purple Heron** adult
□■□ **Purple Heron** juv.
□□■ **Purple Heron** subadult in flight

■□□ **Night Heron** adult
□■□ **Night Heron** juv.
□□■ **Night Heron** adult in flight

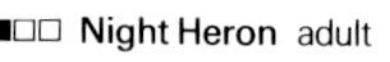

Glossy Ibis

Bald Ibis

■□□ **Glossy Ibis** imm. winter
□■□ **Glossy Ibis** flock in flight
□□■ **Sacred Ibis** adult in flight

Herons, storks and ibises

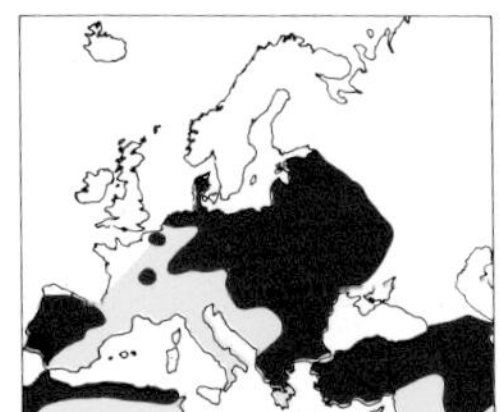

White Stork *Ciconia ciconia* L 110, W 165. Common except in northern part of breeding range, where it is decreasing in numbers (e.g. Denmark: 1200 pairs 1939, 35 pairs 1975). Prefers marshy land, wet meadows and grasslands where it feeds on frogs, snakes, grasshoppers, fish, etc. Typical bird of open agricultural districts. Nests on roofs of houses, often on carriage wheels put up for the purpose, and in big solitary trees, sometimes in small colonies. Easy to approach, seldom shy. Walks slowly and in dignified manner. Easily distinguished from Black Stork by the *white upperparts*. Flies with straight neck, is often seen soaring high up in good thermals. Winters in Africa. The western population leaves Europe over Gibraltar, the eastern one (far and away the largest) by the Bosporus. It can be seen in immense soaring flocks over Istanbul at the end of Aug. These soaring flocks are characterised by their *teeming disorder*. Pelicans, which may also appear in huge soaring glistening white flocks on migration, may be confused but they always maintain a certain order, individual groups moving in synchrony and formation. Communicates with characteristic bill-clappering. P

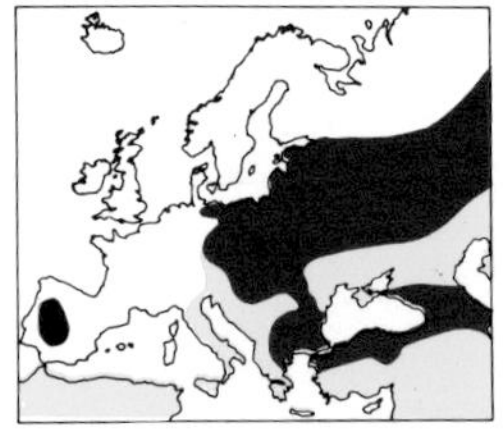

Black Stork *Ciconia nigra* L 100, W 155. Rare. Inhabits wooded regions, usually by lakes, rivers and swampland surrounded by trees (nests in trees). Easily distinguished from White Stork by *black upperparts with metallic sheen*. At long range and against the light, the colour of the upperparts and the neck can be surprisingly difficult to judge owing to the effect of the glossiness. The immature is identified by greenish colour on legs and bill, not red. Usually, but not always, shyer than White Stork and because of its small numbers, rarely seen in company (except at the Bosporus in migrating flocks, at the end of Sept). In contrast to White Stork, has a number of calls but seldom claps its bill. V

Spoonbill *Platalea leucorodia* L 88, W 130. Uncommon and with fragmented distribution. Found at shallow, open waters, reedy marshes and lagoons. Nests colonially in larger reedbeds, sometimes builds in trees and bushes. Distinguished on the ground from the white herons by the *broad and very long bill. Holds neck straight out in flight.* The long crest is worn only by adults in summer. Immature has black wingtips. Flies in flocks, usually in a line. Flies with very much faster wingbeats than the storks, if anything more like the rhythm of the Cormorant. Also glides and soars. *Sweeps head/neck from side to side when seeking food* in shallow water. Usually silent, but bill-clappering may be heard from birds when excited. Occasionally utters sound resembling clearing of one's throat. SP

White Stork adults at nest
White Stork group feeding on ploughland
White Stork adult in flight
Black Stork adult at nest with chick
Black Stork adults in flight

Spoonbill adults winter
Spoonbill juv. in flight
Spoonbill adults in flight

Flamingoes

(order Phoenicopteriformes) have extremely long legs and necks as well as heavy downward-bent bills. Nest in large colonies.

Flamingo *Phoenicopterus ruber* L 135, W 155. In Europe breeds in a few colonies but each containing many individuals. Occasional individuals may be seen anywhere in Europe, but are in most cases escapes from zoos. Lives and breeds in colonies on mud pans and banks with shallow, salt water. At long range flocks on the ground look like white stripes, flocks in flight like rosy-coloured clouds. Flies in a line over longer distances. *Neck and legs extremely long*, held *slightly drooped in flight. Bill short, thick and bent.* Immature is *brownish-grey-white without any pink*, has *dark legs* and *dark bill.* Seeks food by skimming in mud in shallow water with bill upside-down. Has various goose-like trumpeting and cackling calls, often given in flight. (Zoo escapes are often shown to be so by belonging to one of the two American forms, nominate *ruber* or closely related *Ph. chilensis*: *ruber* is strongly rosy-pink over the whole of its plumage; *chilensis* is appreciably smaller than European breeding form *roseus*, has greyish legs with gaudy pink 'knees' and more black on the tip of the bill – see fig.) V

Flamingo adults and young in nesting colony
Flamingo adults in flight

BV-52-27

Waterfowl

Swans

Swans (subfamily Cygninae). Very large, heavy, white long-necked birds. Sexes alike. Ungainly, waddling walk. Majestic on the water. Up-end like surface-feeding ducks in order to browse on the bottom. Build large nest of vegetable matter. Clutches of 3–5 (8).

Mute Swan *Cygnus olor* L 150, W 210. The most numerous and most widespread of our swans. Nests in reeds on lowland lakes, gravel-pits, sluggish rivers and canals (even in loose colonies), often close to human presence. Non-breeders gather in large flocks. In winter in flocks on the coasts. Fierce territorial combats in which dominant males drive off intruders with wing-splashing rushes and 'slides' along the water. Can behave rather aggressively, even towards man, more particularly so during the breeding season. Heavy, weighs on average 8–12 kg. When swimming it holds the *neck in a graceful S-shape* with the bill pointed downwards, often also with the wings raised in shape of a shield. The tail is long and sharply pointed. Adult's *bill orange-red with black knob*, immature's greyish-mauve with dark at the base. The immature is more variegated brown and white on the wings than immature Whooper and Bewick's Swans. Exceptionally, however, downy young as well as juveniles can have white plumage (so-called Polish swans). Comparatively *silent*. The adults give an explosive rumbling 'heeorr', the immatures a low 'bivivivi'. Hisses when using threat behaviour. *A loud singing buzz with each wingbeat* is heard from Mute Swan *in flight*. R

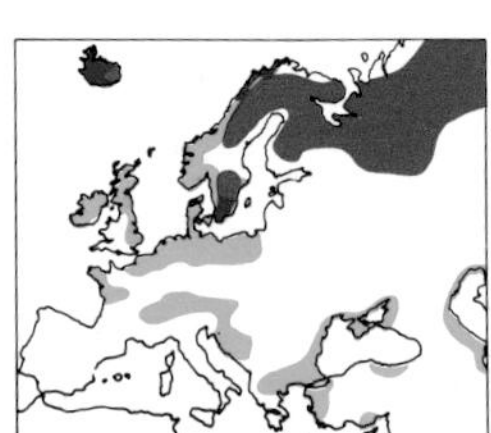

Whooper Swan *Cygnus cygnus* L 155, W 215. Nests in northernmost Europe on large tussocks in swamps and tundra lakes. In recent years has begun to nest, uncommonly and locally, further and further south. Habitually very shy at breeding site, but the recent new colonists in the south considerably more fearless than those in the north. In winter usually along the coasts as well as on larger lakes and watercourses, may often graze on land. Swims with *upright neck* and never raises its wings like Mute Swan. This makes both it and Bewick's Swan quite easy to distinguish from Mute, even at longer range. When it up-ends the shorter, blunter tail is obvious. At close range the *yellow on the bill*, more extensive than in Bewick's Swan, can be seen. Immature distinguished from immature Mute Swan by more even pale and cold grey coloured plumage; *paler bill* (largely grey-white) and by the silhouette, from immature Bewick's by size. Has *far-carrying call with melancholy tone, like blasts on a bugle*. The commonest flight call consists of three short blasts in rapid succession, 'klo-klo-klo'. When resting on the water, the Whooper often spins out the notes, sings. A chorus of large flocks is striking. *No singing noise from the wings* as in Mute Swan (only a slight and ordinary swishing). W

Bewick's Swan *Cygnus columbianus* L 122, W 185. Least common of the swans, but has increased somewhat recently. Nests on the arctic tundra. In winter and on migration frequents lakes, reservoirs, flooded grasslands and sometimes sheltered sea bays. A small version of the Whooper Swan but *the yellow on the bill is less extensive*, does not project forward in a wedge. *Neck proportionately shorter* than in Whooper Swan. Wingbeats slightly quicker than Whooper's. Often seen in family parties or large flocks, presumably representing whole populations. The immature has same plumage coloration as immature Whooper Swan, is more difficult than adult to identify by bill markings since the border between light and dark is indistinct. Calls are like Whooper Swan's but obviously higher-pitched. The singing chorus of drawn-out 'klah' notes is so clear that at a distance the flock sounds like clamouring Cranes. The loud cackling flight call is not only much clearer but also bent into a diphthong 'kläu', not straight like the Whooper Swan's. Neither does it have latter's tendency to three syllables but is monosyllabic (or disyllabic), thereby acquiring a yelping character, can recall geese. In quieter mood gives a muffled Whooper-like 'kokokoko'. WP

Mute Swan adult male swimming with wings arched

Mute Swan juv.

Mute Swan flock of adults, with Goosanders behind

■□□ **Whooper Swan** close-up of adult head to show extent of yellow on bill (many have more yellow)

□■□ **Whooper Swan** adults with (behind) two 1st-years, with two male Pochards in background

□□■ **Whooper Swan** adult (lower left) with two imms. in flight

■□□ **Bewick's Swan** close-up of adult head to show extent of yellow on bill

□■□ **Bewick's Swan** adults

□□■ **Bewick's Swan** adults with (centre) imm. in flight

Waterfowl

Geese (subfamily Anserinae) are large birds with long necks. They feed on seeds, grass and aquatic plants. Indefatigable fliers. Wingbeats composed. Fly in V-formation or in diagonal line. Have curious habit of half-rolling and pitching when flying in to land. Sexes alike. Pair for life. Long lived.

Canada Goose *Branta canadensis* L 90–100, W 165–180. N American species, split into several races of various sizes. Introduced to Europe. Also spontaneous vagrants claimed in Britain. Breeds at inland waters, preferably large and open ones, also in forest districts. English population mainly sedentary, large Swedish one migrates to S Sweden and down to Netherlands. Feeds much in shallow water, like a swan, but also on pasture and arable fields. Not unlike an *Anser* goose at a distance, neck appearing dark, *pale breast striking,* but is larger and *longer-necked*; flight more majestic. Call a loud dissonant honk, 'rhot', at times in see-sawing duets; in flight disyllabic, second note in falsetto, 'rho-ÜT' (can also be rendered 'gah-HONK'). R

■□□ **Canada Goose** adult
□■□ **Canada Goose** adults and juvs.
□□■ **Canada Goose** flock in flight and one White-fronted Goose (centre)

Brent Goose *Branta bernicla* L 62, W 125, Dark-bellied race *B. b. bernicla* breeds in large and increasing numbers on coastal tundras in Siberia, winters along North Sea coast incl. SE England. Pale-bellied race *B. b. hrota* of arctic Canadian islands, NE Greenland and Svalbard is much sparser, winters in Ireland, NE England and Denmark. Main winter food is eel-grass (*Zostera*) found on tidal mudflats. In shallow water feeds by up-ending like a duck. Rests on sea when tide is up. Sometimes also grazes on coastal meadows. Flocks usually unmixed. *Small, grey-black* goose with *gleaming white 'stern'*. Note rather light upper flank of dark-bellied Brent and brown tone on back of pale-bellied. Juveniles acquire *white half-collar* in first autumn but retain white edges to wing-coverts into spring. In flight beats noticeably *narrower wings* at much quicker pace than other geese (like swinging flexible rulers), almost like Eider; immediate goose impression caused mainly by length of wings. Migrating flocks often huge, sometimes enormous (Gulf of Finland, late May), arranged in systems of irregular, wavering bow shapes with long trailing lines. Call a gargling 'r-rot'. W

■□□ **Brent Goose** adult, race *bernicla*
□■□ **Brent Goose** feeding flock, mostly race *bernicla*, with (foreground, far right) one adult of race *hrota*
□□■ **Brent Goose** juv., race *bernicla*

Barnacle Goose *Branta leucopsis* L 64, W 140. Breeds on fox-proof cliff ledges and offshore islets, in three well-separated populations, in E Greenland, Svalbard and Novaya Zemlya (greatest numbers), wintering in W Scotland/Ireland, the Solway Firth and in the Netherlands, respectively. A small Baltic population on Gotland. Grazes on coastal meadows in large flocks (usually unmixed). Juveniles recognised by tendency towards black area connecting eye and crown and, better, by lack of distinct crescentic barring on flanks typical of all adult geese. Migrating flocks often large, usually fly in Brent-like bow formation rather than in regular V, but with markedly *slower wingbeats than Brent*, equal to White-fronted Goose. In flight, at a distance, white head is difficult to discern, *breast-belly contrast* being a better character. Call a nasal, monosyllabic yelping 'gak', merging into a loud roar in large flocks. W

■□□ **Barnacle Goose** adult in breeding habitat
□■□ **Barnacle Goose** flock in flight with six corvids
□□■ **Brent Goose** flock in flight, migrating

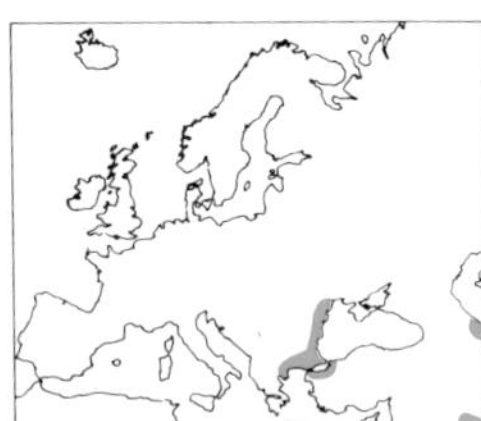

Red-breasted Goose *Branta ruficollis* L 60, W 120. Breeds on Siberian tundra, in groups on steep river banks, preferably close to nest of Peregrine or Rough-legged Buzzard for protection. Winters mainly in SW Asia, but odd birds join flocks of other geese and migrate to W Europe. Small, with *rather thick neck* and *very small bill. Broad white flank stripe on black body* is a better fieldmark at a distance (also in flight) than chestnut-red breast. Juvenile has a smaller chestnut cheek patch than adult. Call a shrill, staccato 'ki-kwi' V

■□□ **Red-breasted Goose** adult
□■□ **Red-breasted Goose** adults
□□■ **Red-breasted Goose** two 1st-winter (upper right) in flight with eight half-year old White-fronted Geese (no black on belly, white fronts not complete)

Waterfowl

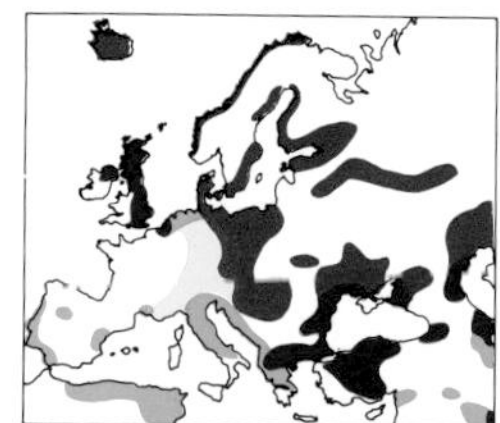

Greylag Goose *Anser anser* L 75–85, W 147–170. The most widespread goose in Europe, nests chiefly in swamps and on reedy lakes but also e.g. on small islands on the sea coast, often in small colonies surrounded by loafing flocks of non-breeding immatures. Largest, *heaviest Anser* goose. Wings comparatively broad and blunt. Rather *large bill*. Pale pink legs. Greylag has, like Pink-footed Goose, *pale panels on forewings*, but Greylag's panels are paler, almost silvery-white, and contrast more sharply with secondaries and back. Also, *Greylag's wing is bicoloured below*: pale grey lesser and median coverts, and dark grey greater coverts and flight feathers (all other *Anser* geese have uniformly dark underwings). On the ground, Greylag never appears pale-backed like Pink-foot. On the other hand *head and neck are characteristically pale*. Individuals flying directly away from observer can be distinguished from other geese by grey lower back, which is in pale contrast to browner scapulars. Juveniles have dark nail to bill. Like other *Anser* geese is gregarious and readily mixes with other species. Pitches and freewheels in flight even more than Pink-foot when landing. Has, like other *Anser* species, a wide repertoire of calls, incl. really shrill ones, but the most typical is a nasal, cackling 'kyang-ung-ung', the first syllable typically higher-pitched and more stressed. (Calls identical to those of domestic goose, of which Greylag is ancestor.) RWP

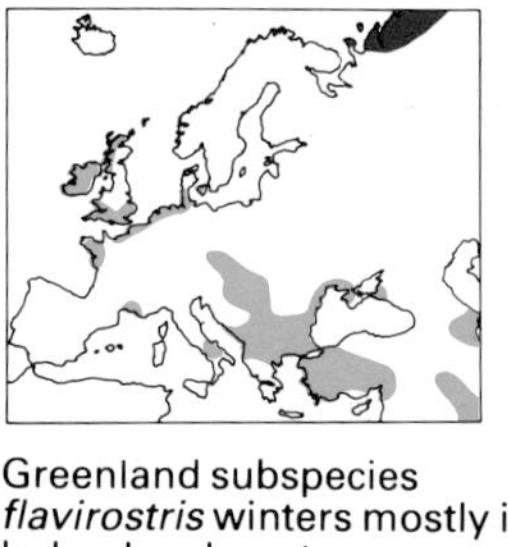

Greenland subspecies *flavirostris* winters mostly in Ireland and western Scotland

White-fronted Goose *Anser albifrons* L 60–73, W 130–160. Breeds on arctic tundra. A western population (race *flavirostris*; rather big, bill long and yellow-orange, plumage fairly dark) breeds in W Greenland and winters in NW Britain (numerous), an eastern one (race *albifrons*; slightly smaller than *flavirostris*, bill weaker and predominantly pink, plumage somewhat paler) breeds along the Russian arctic coast and winters from England (uncommon) diagonally across Europe to Turkey and eastwards. Adult White-front has *white blaze on forehead* and *black markings on belly*, can be confused only with Lesser White-front. Distinguished from latter by generally perceptibly larger size, larger bill, by fact that *forehead blaze is straight in side view and does not extend so far up on the forehead*, also by *lack of yellow eye-ring*. Juvenile distinguished from juvenile Lesser White-front mainly by lack of yellow eye-ring, slightly paler plumage and larger size. Since white forehead blaze is absent during first autumn and nail of bill is dark, juvenile can at distance be confused with Bean Goose, but is told from latter by *paler cheek with swarthy forehead and area around bill base* together with slightly narrower white feather edges on upperparts. Flight much as in other *Anser* geese. Does not appear pale-winged like Greylag and Pink-foot, but nevertheless has slightly paler wing-coverts than Bean Goose. Commonest call is characteristically high-voiced 'double yelp', 'kya-ya', almost laughing; other calls deeper. W

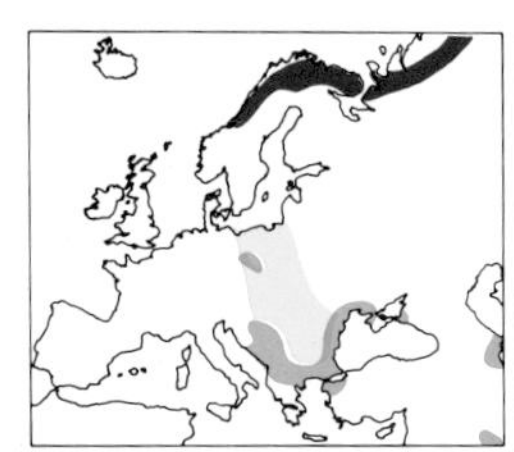

▶ **Lesser White-fronted Goose** *Anser erythropus* L 53–66, W 120–140. Very rare breeding bird in northernmost Fenno-Scandia, in willow and upper birch zone. Has decreased dramatically in recent decades. Expert at concealing itself at breeding site. In winter on pastureland and arable fields in SE Europe; only occasional individuals are seen in W Europe. Reintroduction attempt in Swedish Lapland with birds programmed to migrate southwest (colour-marked). Looks like a *small* version of White-fronted Goose, but distinguished from that species by *small bill* and peaked forehead, *larger white blaze* (angular in side view), *yellow eye-ring* which is visible even at distance, and also on average slightly darker plumage. Yellow eye-ring present also in juvenile. (Note that some White-fronts can have a narrow, indistinct yellow eye-ring.) Folded wingtips project beyond tail, only rarely the case in White-front. Despite being as small as a Brent Goose, still looks first of all like an *Anser* goose. Great practice and skill required to distinguish a lone flying bird at great distance from larger *Anser* geese. Calls resemble White-front's, but typical flight call is clearly higher and clearer in voice, 'kyee-yee'. V

Greylag Goose adult on nest

Greylag Goose new arrivals joining flock on water

White-fronted Goose adult, race *albifrons*

Greylag Goose adults

White-fronted Goose adults, race *flavirostris*

White-fronted Goose adult in flight (right) with Bean Goose

Lesser White-fronted Goose adults with (centre) juv.

Waterfowl

Bean Goose *Anser fabalis* L 68–80, W 142–165. Breeds on the tundra (race *rossicus*) and by taiga bogs (race *fabalis*) in N Europe. Intermediate forms occur. (See below for the appearance of the two types.) Winters on the Continent; rare in Britain (race *fabalis*). Closely related to Pink-footed Goose. Is, however, clearly darker and (especially *fabalis*) larger, longer-necked, larger-headed and longer-billed. Diagnostic character is Bean Goose's *orange legs and bill markings*. Tail has narrower white terminal band than in Pink-foot, looks generally darker from behind in flight. At longer range best told from Pink-foot by darker back (as dark as flank area) and wings – together with Lesser White-front has darkest wings of all *Anser* geese (though forewings with blue-grey tone and can appear fairly pale in slanting light). Note that many *fabalis* have white rim at bill base, though never as White-front. Can be confused with juvenile White-front, but *whole of head dark* (not only forehead and area around bill base), and colour of legs and bill different. When grazing (dark head and neck hidden) can be difficult to pick out among Greylags, since both species are equally dark on back and almost the same size. Race *rossicus* is distinguished by heavy (in particular deep) bill with predominantly black markings, also short neck and tarsus; *fabalis* has narrower and usually predominantly orange bill and also longer neck and tarsus. Variations, however, exist; racial identification requires experience and observation of standing birds at close range. Commonest call is a deep, nasal, disyllabic, jolting 'ung-unk', with more of a base tone than Pink-foot's. W

Pink-footed Goose *Anser brachyrhynchus* L 63–73, W 135–160. Breeds in Greenland, Iceland and Svalbard, the first two populations wintering in Britain (large numbers). By day grazes on arable fields, roosts on lakes and in estuaries. Mass movements between night and day sites spectacular. Characterised by short and *dark bill with pink markings near tip*. Dark head, pale, *blue-grey lustre on upperparts* ('frosted', upperparts thus paler than flank area) and pink legs. *Upperwings pale as back*, considerably paler than in Bean Goose, though not so pale as in Greylag (and lack latter's contrast between silvery-white and mid-brown). From below distinguished from flying Greylag by *uniformly dark underwings* and dark head, from behind by darker and browner rump. Juveniles distinguished (as in other *Anser* geese) from adults by more indistinct 'wet-combed' effect on neck and more rounded feather tips on upperparts and flanks; also more indistinct pale edgings on covert feathers. Commonest call is a short trumpeting 'ang-ank'. W

Snow Goose *Anser caerulescens* L 65–80, W 135–165. In some cases a genuine visitor from North America, but most cases probably escapes from zoos and collections. Most Snow Geese have been observed during autumn and winter. Usually seeks the company of *Anser* geese. Easily recognised by the *pure white plumage with black wingtips*. Immatures are so pale that they cannot be confused with immatures of other European geese. (The dark variety, the Blue Goose, has head and upper part of neck white and body and all the flight feathers grey and blackish respectively.) The call is a harsh monosyllabic cry, 'keeh'. Very noisy, a very loud cackling is heard from large flocks. V

Bar-headed Goose *Anser indicus* L 75. Escapes of this species from zoos are sometimes seen in the company of grey geese. Nests in highlands of central Asia, crosses Himalayas on migration to and from lowland India. Easily distinguished from other geese by *white crown with two black transverse bands*. The immature lacks the black markings but is very light grey. Looks whitish in flight. The dark on the upperwings is restricted to the outer parts of all the flight feathers.

■□ Bean Goose adult
□■ Bean Goose flock in flight

■□ Pink-footed Goose adult
□■ Bean Goose adult

■□ Pink-footed Goose
□■ Pink-footed Goose flock on wintering grounds

■□ Snow Goose adults with (centre) imm.
□■ Bar-headed Goose adults

Waterfowl

Surface-feeding ducks

Surface-feeding ducks (dabbling) are often found in shallow water. They feed by 'up-ending' or by skimming the water surface with bill. Strong fliers, often rising almost vertically. Most can dive, but seldom do. The sexes are very different in plumage.

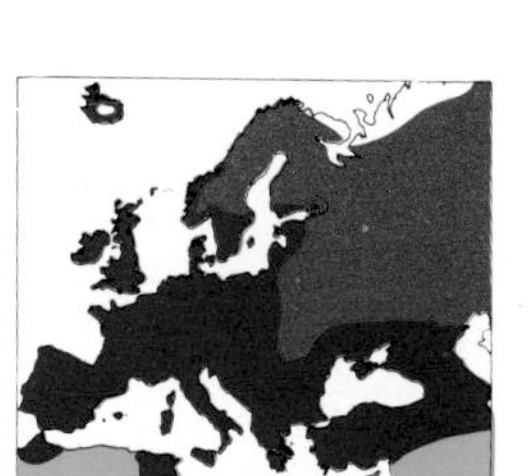

Mallard *Anas platyrhynchos* L 56, W 95. Commonest and most widespread of the surface-feeding ducks, also the largest and heaviest. Identified in flight by *size, robust body, slightly rounded wings, moderately quick wingbeats. Wing whistle characteristic of species.* Found in parks and on city canals, on rivers, ponds, lowland lakes, woodland swamps, upland waters etc. Very active at night, not least on migration in N Europe. Versatile in choice of nest site, readily accepting 'duck-baskets'. The males gather in flocks before the summer moult. In winter found in large flocks on the sea along northern coasts, elsewhere commonly inland. Males court females in winter when he gives a short weak whistle 'piu'. Female has a loud quacking call; drake a one-syllable, quieter, nasal and confident 'vehp'. RWP

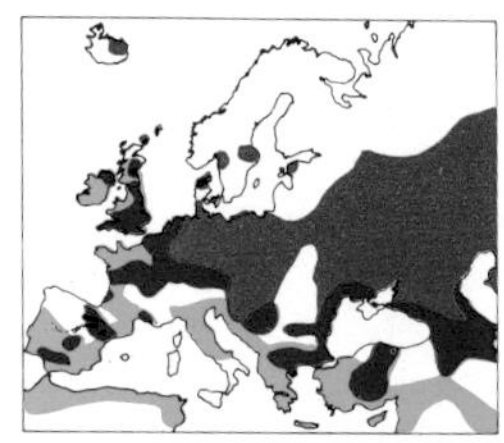

Gadwall *Anas strepera* L 51, W 89. Uncommon but widespread in Europe. Breeds mostly on shallow open freshwater lakes and pools with reed cover or small overgrown islands. In winter also on reservoirs, gravel-pits, floodland – tends to avoid salt water. Shy, flies far away when put up. The male is comparatively *dull grey*, but on the water shows a characteristic *black stern.* In flight it is distinguished by a large *white, dark-framed speculum.* Female very like Mallard. When swimming her white belly is not visible, then look for *orange along the sides of comparatively thin bill.* In flight she has a characteristic white speculum, which is smaller and with a less prominent border than the male's (see fig). The male has a fairly low, slightly Corncrake-like 'rrep' call and a shrill 'pyee' in pursuit flight and courtship. Female's call is slightly higher than Mallard's. RW

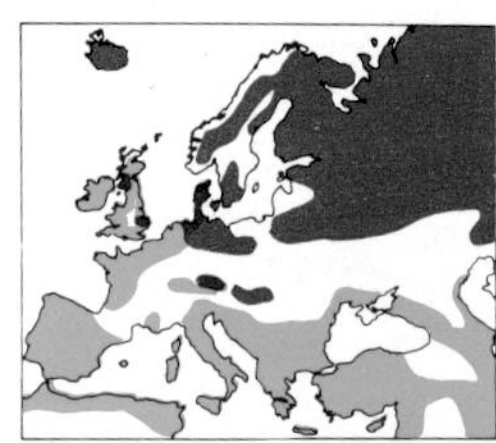

Pintail *Anas acuta* L ♂ 71, ♀ 56, W 89. Rather scarce as a breeding bird, mainly on upland pools, lowland marshes and lagoons. In winter on sheltered estuaries, floodlands and nearby lakes. *Long-necked,* generally *slim build,* 'greyhound-like'. Characteristic *white rear edge to the brown speculum.* Both sexes have *grey bill.* Male has a long pointed tail in breeding plumage. On spring migration seen mostly in individual pairs. Shy. Upstretched neck of alert male glistens among the aquatic vegetation. His spring call is a short whistle, 'kree', like Teal's but lower pitched. In autumn often joins flights of Wigeon (with which commonly associated in winter). RWP

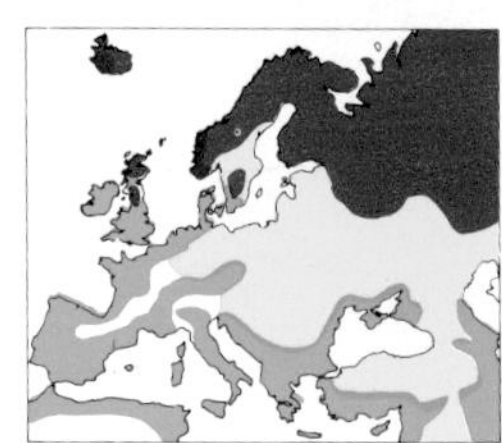

Wigeon *Anas penelope* L 46, W 81. Not an uncommon breeder in north (taiga zone) on shallow, open fresh waters. On migration and in winter often in large flocks, mainly on coasts and on flooded grasslands. Migrating flocks form long lines. Fairly *long wings,* compact body, *pointed tail, short neck, slightly rounded head.* Younger males lack white wing panels, otherwise plumage like adults'. Female's wing markings rather insignificant, but because of the whitish innermost secondary (see fig.) can be confused with female Gadwall. All Wigeon plumages show *sharply offset snow-white belly.* Grazes on grassy banks, on coasts, eats eel-grass. Male has typical loud whistle, 'wheee-oo'. Night-migrating flocks give a yapping 'wip, wee-wee'. Female's call is a Goldeneye-like 'karr-karr-. . .'. In autumn a snorting 'ra-karr' is heard. RWP

American Wigeon *Anas americana* L 51, W 87. The American counterpart of our Wigeon. Rare visitor to W Europe. Male typical with *white band on crown* and *green panel on side of head,* female very like female Wigeon but has paler and greyer head and more rosy tinge to flanks (field identification still usually impossible). *Underwing-coverts and axillaries white* (not brownish-grey as in Wigeon). The male has a whistle like Wigeon's but weaker and of three syllables, 'whee-whee-whew'. V

■□□ **Mallard** males and females resting

□■□ **Mallard** female in flight

□□■ **Gadwall** female (left) and male

Gadwall, adult ♂

■□□ **Pintail** male

□■□ **Pintail** female

□□■ **Gadwall** female (left) and male in flight

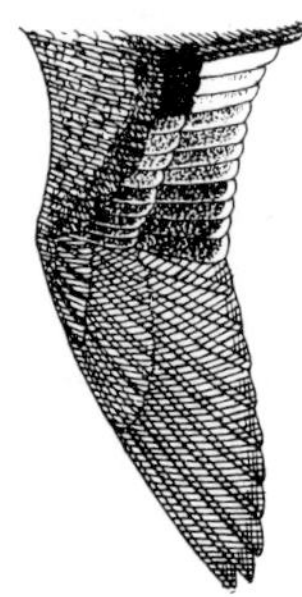

Gadwall, ♀

■□□ **Wigeon** male

□■□ **Wigeon** males and females in flight

□□■ **Pintail** female in flight

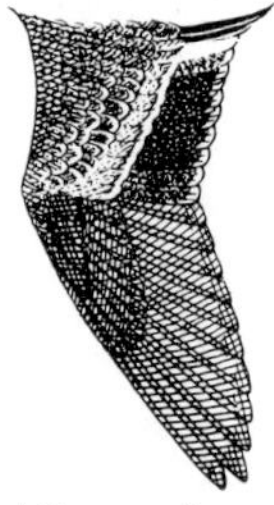

Wigeon, ♀

■□□ **Wigeon** young male

□■□ **Wigeon** males and females feeding

□□■ **American Wigeon** males, the right one in partial eclipse

Waterfowl

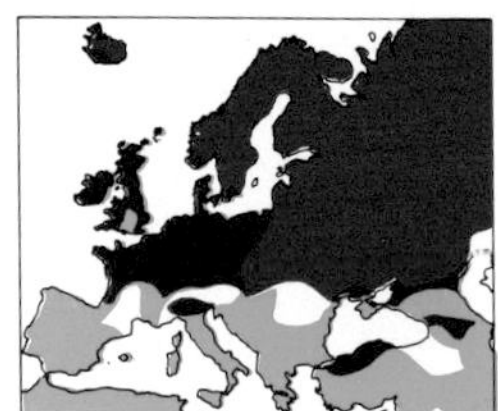

Teal *Anas crecca* L 36, W 61. Fairly common and widespread, breeds on smaller usually fresh waters in uplands, lowland and coastal areas. In winter on shallow estuaries, saltmarshes, lakes and reservoirs. Mainly a nocturnal migrant. Gathers in large flocks. Drake very colourful in spring plumage but looks (like the female) generally dark at a distance, when characterised (apart from small size) mainly by *whitish-yellow patches on side of rump*. Female like female Garganey but has more evenly coloured side of head, a slightly *shorter bill*, usually with *a little yellowish-red at the base*, and *light patch on side of tail base*. See also wing pattern and under Garganey. Readily takes to the wing and manoeuvres to and fro above reeds and marshes in tight flocks with smooth flight like waders. It may then be further distinguished by *white wingbar in front of speculum*. The pale belly not very conspicuous. The male's call is a *far-carrying ringing whistle as clear as a bell*, 'kreek'. Female has a shrill and feeble croak, considerably more nasal than female Mallard's. RWP

Green-winged Teal *Anas crecca carolinensis* L 36, W 61. The North American race of Teal is a rare visitor to W Europe. The male has a *vertical*, not horizontal, *white stripe on the side of the body*. The female is indistinguishable from the European Teal. Behaviour and call as Teal. V

Blue-winged Teal *Anas discors* L 38. Rare visitor from North America. The male has *white crescent on side of head*. The female resembles female Teal but has light spot at base of bill and is darker and has *bright blue forewing* as well as longer bill. V

Baikal Teal *Anas formosa* L 38. Rare visitor from breeding sites in Asia. The male's head pattern unmistakable. The female has green speculum and a distinct white mark with dark surround at base of bill. V

Falcated Teal *Anas falcata* L 51. Very rare vagrant to E Europe from breeding grounds in E Siberia. The male's head is reddish-brown and glossy green. Female like female Gadwall but speculum is dark green and the narrow bill entirely grey.

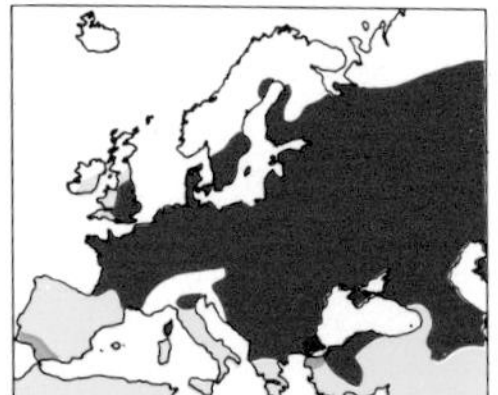

Garganey *Anas querquedula* L 38, W 63. Scarce on lowland lakes, mainly on small pools in marshy and flooded meadows. *Small* as Teal. In flight the male's wings appear whitish blue-grey at long range. Younger males have dark grey wings (pattern otherwise like older males). The female's *forewing panel not dissimilarly pale* (or blue), but she differs from female Teal in that the *rear white band bordering the speculum is obviously thicker than the front one* (as in Pintail) instead of the other way round, and by pale wing quills which give a slightly paler general look to the wing in flight. On the water female distinguished from female Teal by a *light stripe* below the dark eye-stripe (widened in front into a pale patch at bill base), *bordered below by dark cheek markings*. (See also under Teal.) The male's call is a *drawn-out dry crackling* with a hollow wooden ring: 'knerrek'; female's a Teal-like shrill and feeble croak. SP

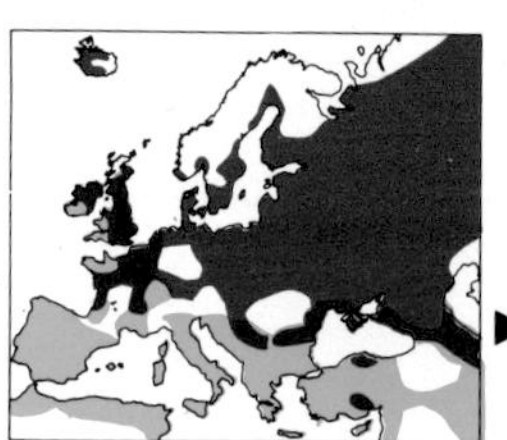

► **Shoveler** *Anas clypeata* L 51 W 79. Fairly common on very shallow lowland waters with surrounding cover. Usually in small flocks, often hidden out of sight. On water has 'front-heavy' appearance with the *long spoon-shaped bill* lowered. Also front-heavy in flight. The wings have large blue-grey panels (but not so pale and striking at long range as in male Garganey). The Shoveler is usually identified immediately in flight by the long bill. The female in flight shows an *all-dark belly* contrasting with white underwing-coverts. (Wigeon and Gadwall have white belly, while Mallard and Pintail are somewhere in between.) On rising, male's wings make a rattling noise. The male's spring call is a nasal double-note 'sluck-UCK', heard mostly in the evenings. The female quacks at the same time broadly with the same rhythm and emphasis: 'pe-ETT'. RWP

■□□ **Teal** male
□■□ **Teal** female
□□■ **Green-winged Teal** male

Teal, ♀

Blue-winged Teal ♀

■□□ **Blue-winged Teal** male (left) and female
□■□ **Baikal Teal** male
□□■ **Falcated Teal** male

■□□ **Falcated Teal** female
□■□ **Garganey** male
□□■ **Garganey** female

Garganey

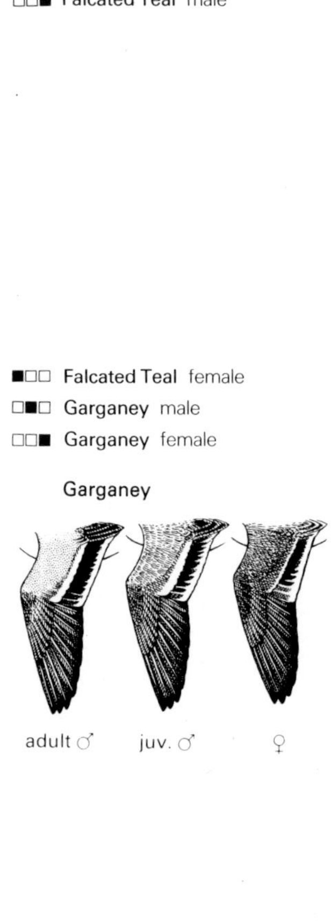

adult ♂ juv. ♂ ♀

■■□ **Shoveler** female (left) and male
□□■ **Shoveler** male in flight

Waterfowl

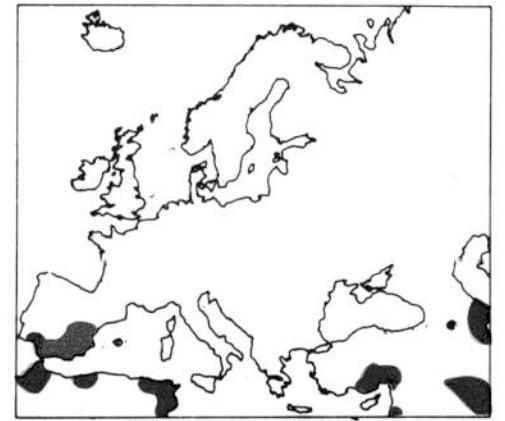

Marbled Duck *Marmaronetta angustirostris* L 40. Rare and local breeder in S Europe. Prefers sheltered ponds and marshland with rich vegetation. Both sexes similar, light brown and with no very obvious distinctive features. Between Garganey and Wigeon in size. Best characteristics on swimming bird are striking *pale overall impression*, long pale tail, long neck and rather large round head with *dark area around the eye* and *dark*, quite long and *narrow bill*. In flight *long-winged* and can recall female Pintail. Lacks speculum. Stays hidden away and is difficult to approach. Seen mostly singly or a few together. The male's call is a quiet, high nasal 'jeeb', the female's similar, a double whistle 'pleep-pleep'.

Mandarin *Aix galericulata* L 46. Escaped birds have established feral populations in parts of England. Prefers ponds surrounded by trees, breeds in holes in trees. The beautiful male is unmistakable. The female is less strikingly coloured but note the characteristic head pattern. She is distinguished from the similar female Wood Duck *Aix sponsa* (in Europe found only in bird collections) by the absence of green on the rear crown and the different line at the base of the bill (see fig.). Usually feeds on land. R

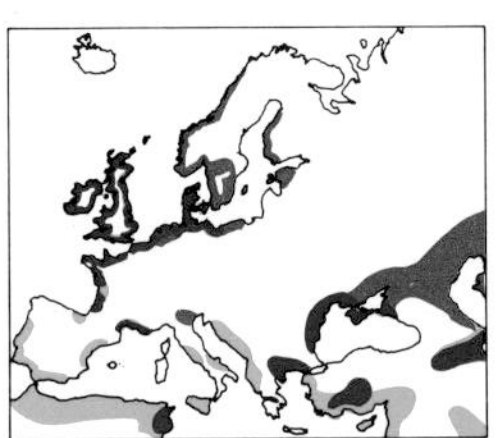

Shelduck *Tadorna tadorna* L 60, W 110. Fairly common breeder in NW and SE Europe on flat, shallow coasts, locally also on inland lakes. Nests in burrows and under bushes near the shore. Male and female are similar in plumage, which is *white, reddish-brown and black with a green gloss*. Male has a large *red knob on the bill*, female a small pale red one. Immatures are considerably paler than adults, among other things lacking the rust-brown breast band, and have white chin and cheeks. Normally flies low over the water with arched wings moving in a rhythm half-way between duck and goose. During moulting they often form very large flocks, while at the same time the young on the breeding grounds which are still not able to fly also gather in flocks and are attended by only a few older birds. The male's spring call a high whizzing whistle: 'sliss-sliss-sliss-. . .'. The female's call is a characteristic straight whinnying 'geheheheheheh', and when nervous a nasal intense 'ah-ang', usually uttered in flight. Silent outside the breeding season. RS

Ruddy Shelduck *Tadorna ferruginea* L 60. Breeds in S and SE Europe. Escapes from captivity also appear regularly outside the normal range. More terrestrial than Shelduck. Fairly long-legged. Nests in hollows in the ground as well as in trees. Found in winter along rivers, by sandy lakeshores and on fields and steppes. The *orange-brown body* and the pale head are characteristic, *white panel on the wing striking in flight*. The male has narrow black neck band. Resembles Shelduck in build and behaviour. Flight also exactly like Shelduck's. Call a trumpeting 'galaw', somewhat like Canada Goose but more nasal and not so powerful (can recall plaintive cry of a donkey). Also has sonorous gurgling 'porrr'. V

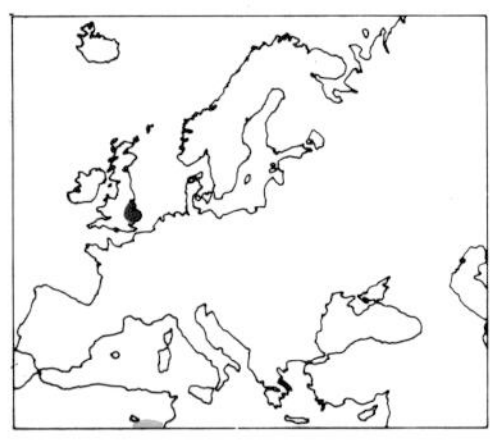

Egyptian Goose *Alopochen aegyptiacus* L 70. Very rare vagrant to southeasternmost Europe from nesting sites in Africa. Escaped individuals turn up in some places in England. Note *large white wing panel*, both above and below, and the long legs. Both sexes identical in plumage. Feeds mainly up on dry land, as geese habitually do. Harsh trumpeting calls. R

■□ **Marbled Duck** adults
□■ **Marbled Duck** adult in flight

Mandarin, ♀

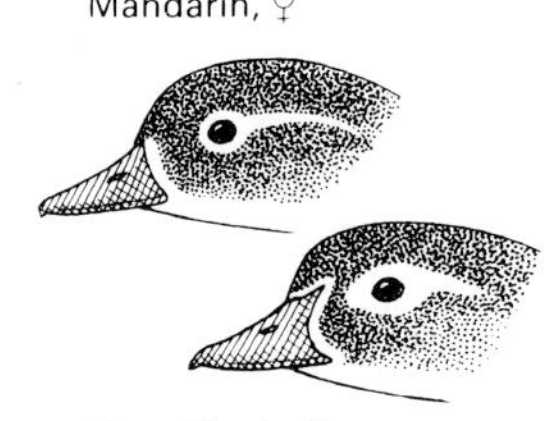

Wood Duck, ♀

■□ **Mandarin** adult male
□■ **Mandarin** female flying to nest

■□□ **Shelduck** adult male
□■□ **Shelduck** juv.
□□■ **Shelduck** adults in flight

■□ **Ruddy Shelduck** adult male
□■ **Egyptian Goose** adult female (foreground) and male

Waterfowl

Diving ducks (subfamily Aythyinae) nest by lakeshores, on islands and in swampy areas. In winter they occur in flocks in sheltered bays, on larger lakes and in river mouths, but also further out to sea where several species feed on crustaceans and other small animals. They dive from the surface of the water, swim underwater, and run along the surface to take off.

Red-crested Pochard *Netta rufina* L 56. Breeds uncommonly and locally in S and central Europe on brackish lagoons and reedy lakes. Escapes not uncommon. *Large.* Male has rather brilliant colours: *flanks are gleaming white,* head is yellowish-brown, crown feathers form an erectile crest, *bill is red* (even in female-like eclipse plumage). Female is superficially like female Common Scoter but paler, larger, sits higher on water, has *pink band across outer bill,* like male has *very broad snow-white wingbar.* Behaviour resembles that of surface-feeding ducks. WP

Scaup *Aythya marila* L 46, W 79. Uncommon to scarce breeding bird on northern coasts (in Scandinavia on upland lakes in birch and willow zone). Most easily confused with Tufted Duck. The male however has *pale grey back,* which at a distance produces shining white 'amidships' appearance. Female has broad white band (sometimes tinged brown) around bill base and *in summer also a pale mark towards the back of the cheek* (see fig.), and is slightly paler than female Tufted, more reddish-brown (breast) and grey-washed (back). The Scaup is slightly larger, *at all times lacks crest on head* and has *less peaked forehead* (gives rounder head profile) and has slightly larger bill. Only nail of bill is black. WP

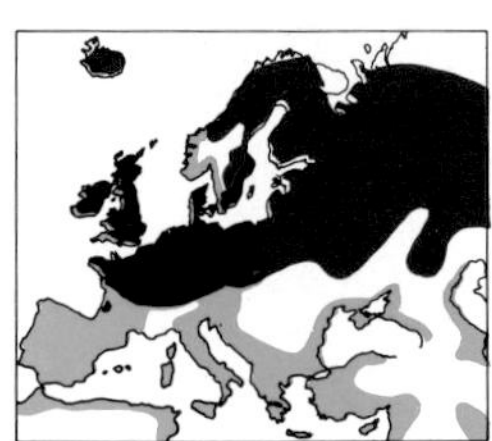

Tufted Duck *Aythya fuligula* L 42, W 70. Common. Breeds on wide variety of lowland waters, incl. park lakes. Outside breeding season in large flocks on lakes, reservoirs, gravel-pits and sheltered coasts. Male characteristic, *black with white rectangle at the side* and *drooping crest.* Female has shorter crest and often has narrow white band at bill base (sometimes broad one: see Scaup). Belly brown during the nesting period. Often white under the tail (cf. Ferruginous Duck). Both sexes have yellow eye. Whole tip of bill black. Female's call is a repeated lively 'kerrb', male's spring call a giggling 'bheep-bhibhew'. RW

Ring-necked Duck *Aythya collaris* L 43. Very rare winter visitor to W Europe from North America. Male easily told from male Tufted by head shape and vertical white stripe on sides level with front edge of wing. Female is more difficult to identify, but head shape and *grey* (not white) *wingbar* in both sexes is characteristic. V

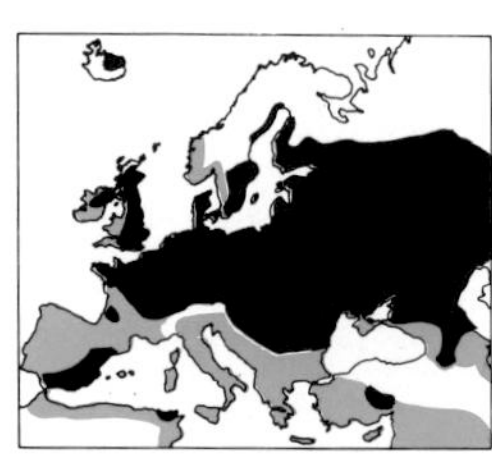

Pochard *Aythya ferina* L 46, W 79. Breeds fairly commonly on well-reeded marshy lakes. In winter on lakes, reservoirs, gravel-pits, sometimes sheltered estuaries. Male characteristic. Lacks whitish 'amidships' appearance of Scaup. Female more non-descript but has diffuse dark cheek patch between pale eye-stripe and pale chin. *Head shape triangular* with hefty bill and *flat forehead. Wings greyish-brown in flight,* palest in male. In breeding parties, males often outnumber females. Court female with hoarse 'bhee-bhee-. . .', also utter nasal, rising whistle (which may be cut short with a wheeze). Female's call is a harsh 'krrah, krrah'. RSW

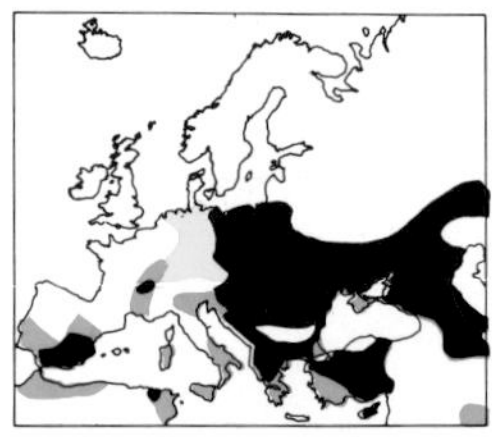

Ferruginous Duck *Aythya nyroca* L 40, W 66. Breeds in S and central Europe on reedy lowland lakes. Rather unobtrusive. Slightly smaller than Tufted Duck, and *white wingbar is noticeably broader* and brighter in flight. Male is rich dark red-brown with *white eye* and gleaming *white undertail. White area of belly is smaller and completely enclosed by dark colour.* Female is dark greyish-brown with dark eye, has white undertail. Note *flat forehead and high crown,* and *rather long bill,* which with brilliant white wingbar are safest distinguishing marks compared with female Tufted. Female's call is a repeated, burring 'karr', with particular, high, almost ringing tone, quite different from female Tufted. W

■□□ **Red-crested Pochard** adult male
□■□ **Scaup** adult males, females and imms. in winter
□□■ **Tufted Duck** adult female (foreground) and adult male

■□□ **Red-crested Pochard** female
□■□ **Scaup** 1st-winter male in autumn (female-like plumage)
□□■ **Tufted Duck** adult male in flight

Scaup, ♀ summer

Ring-necked Duck

■□□ **Ring-necked Duck** adult male
□■□ **Pochard** adult male
□□■ **Pochard** males (upper left two) and females in flight

■□□ **Ring-necked Duck** adult female
□■□ **Pochard** female
□□■ **Ferruginous Duck** adult male

Waterfowl

Goldeneye *Bucephala clangula* L 45, W 79. Fairly common breeder on waters in northern forests. Nests in Black Woodpecker holes and in nestboxes. In last 20 years has increased markedly, probably mainly because of provision of nestboxes. Hardy species, the last ones move south only to escape the ice. Winters along coasts, also on reservoirs and gravel-pits. Has tendency to disperse in smaller groups, does not pack together in large dense flocks like, e.g. Tufted Duck. Decidedly shyer than most other diving ducks. *Big head* with characteristic shape: *'triangular' with peak in centre of crown.* Male's *white loral patch* is visible at long range; flanks brilliant white, like drake Goosander but rear black. Both sexes have white wing panels like sawbills, but obviously *dark underwings.* Immature lacks the female's yellow eye and white neck ring, looks generally dark grey-brown but has white speculum (though smaller than in adult female) and the characteristic head shape of the species. Downy young are white-cheeked. For distinguishing marks in comparison with Barrow's Goldeneye, see latter. The male has a *musical whistling wing noise* – a well-known phenomenon of early spring in the northern countries is the characteristic paths of sound drawn across the night sky by migrating Goldeneyes. Migrants often rest on lowland lakes. When displaying, the male tosses his head backwards on to the back, splashes his feet and utters piercing rasps 'be-beeezh' (accompanied by a low, hollow, Garganey-like rattle). The female gives a grating 'berr, berr . . .' when she circles over the breeding territory. WP

▶ **Barrow's Goldeneye** *Bucephala islandica* L 48. Very rarely observed outside Iceland, its sole breeding area in Europe. Nests along streams and beside lakes in the lava regions, which afford suitable hollows. Male in breeding plumage distinguished from Goldeneye by *crescent-shaped white loral patch, which reaches above the eye,* and by fact that the *black on the back* is more extensive and *reaches far down onto the sides of the breast.* More difficult to discern is the different head shape (more drawn-out in length, steeper forehead, peak less obvious and situated well forward on the crown), that the bill is slightly shorter and that the head has a violet, not green gloss. Note that young male Goldeneyes can have brownish-black heads with, depending on moult, quite noticeable crescent-shaped loral patches. Females and immature males are extremely difficult to distinguish from Goldeneye in the field. The female's bill is sometimes all-yellow (never so in Goldeneye).

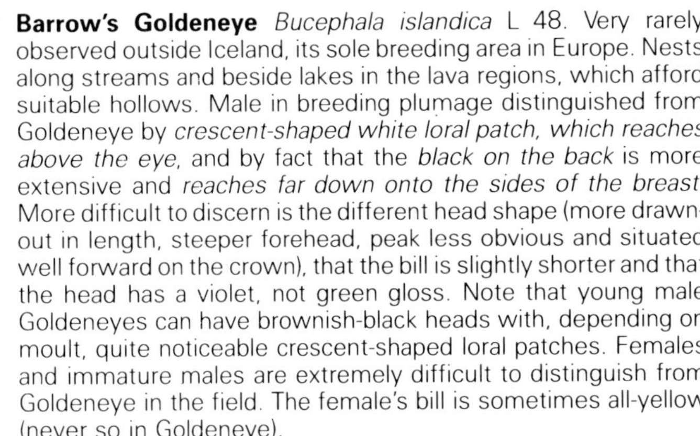

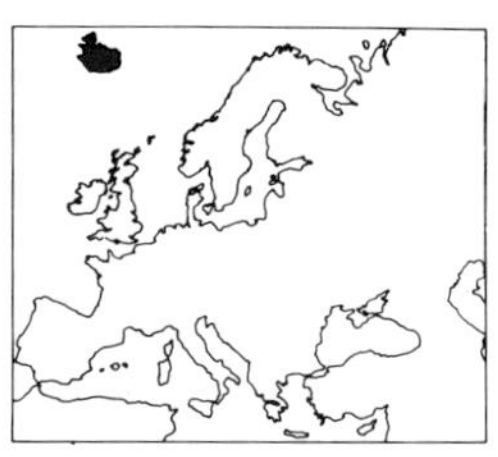

Bufflehead *Bucephala albeola* L 36. Very rare vagrant to W Europe from North America. Only *as large as a Teal,* pattern basically as Goldeneye but with *large white head patch which crosses the rear crown* like a doctor's ice-bag. Eye dark. Female resembles female Goldeneye, but the head is brownish-black and has *a large horizontal white patch on the cheek.* Rises from water like a surface-feeding duck, without running. V

▶ **Harlequin Duck** *Histrionicus histrionicus* L 40, W 65. Like Barrow's Goldeneye an Icelandic (and American) species, rarely seen in the rest of Europe. Nests on islands in fast-flowing watercourses. In winter resorts to heavy surf off the rocky coast. Male easily identified by the light and dark pattern (at a distance the blue and red colours appear all-dark), the small size and the long tail, which is usually held slightly cocked. Female is smaller and darker than female Goldeneye, lacks white wing panels and has *three prominent white patches on the head* (beware confusion with some juvenile female Long-tailed Ducks, see fig. but note that latter has white, not brown-washed belly). Rarely mixes with other ducks. Often *swims with head nodding* in pace with leg strokes; sits high in water. Flight swift, actively pitches to and fro. Usually silent. The male sometimes gives a soft whistle, the female an agitated nasal jarring sound. V

■□□ **Goldeneye** adult male
□■□ **Goldeneye** adult female
□□■ **Goldeneye** female (left) and male in flight

Goldeneye, imm. ♂ moulting

■□□ **Barrow's Goldeneye** adult male
□■□ **Barrow's Goldeneye** adult female
□□■ **Bufflehead** adult male

Bufflehead, ♂

Harlequin Duck adult male
Harlequin Duck adult female
Harlequin Duck adult male in flight

Harlequin, ♀

Long-tailed Duck, ♀

Waterfowl

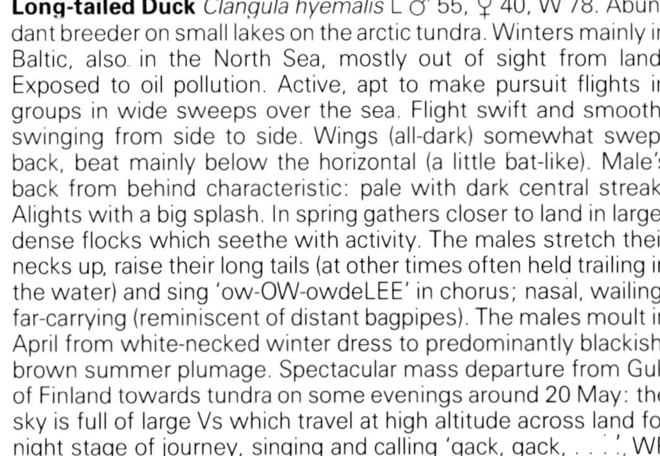

Long-tailed Duck *Clangula hyemalis* L ♂ 55, ♀ 40, W 78. Abundant breeder on small lakes on the arctic tundra. Winters mainly in Baltic, also in the North Sea, mostly out of sight from land. Exposed to oil pollution. Active, apt to make pursuit flights in groups in wide sweeps over the sea. Flight swift and smooth, swinging from side to side. Wings (all-dark) somewhat swept back, beat mainly below the horizontal (a little bat-like). Male's back from behind characteristic: pale with dark central streak. Alights with a big splash. In spring gathers closer to land in large, dense flocks which seethe with activity. The males stretch their necks up, raise their long tails (at other times often held trailing in the water) and sing 'ow-OW-owdeLEE' in chorus; nasal, wailing, far-carrying (reminiscent of distant bagpipes). The males moult in April from white-necked winter dress to predominantly blackish-brown summer plumage. Spectacular mass departure from Gulf of Finland towards tundra on some evenings around 20 May: the sky is full of large Vs which travel at high altitude across land for night stage of journey, singing and calling 'gack, gack, ...', WP

■□□ **Long-tailed Duck** adult male summer

□■□ **Long-tailed Duck** adult male winter

□□■ **Long-tailed Duck** adult female winter

Velvet Scoter *Melanitta fusca* L 55, W 92. Breeds mostly in taiga zone but also well above tree line; also in Baltic archipelagos. In winter marine like Common Scoter but keeps nearer to land and in smaller flocks. Males migrate to Danish waters as early as July to moult. Return very late to breeding grounds. Clearly larger than Common Scoter (half way between it and Eider), tail shorter, forehead more sloping. The orange on male's bill is striking even at a distance, but white spot at eye is not and white secondaries often hidden. Female's whitish face patches very variable; the front one especially can be absent in old birds. Younger females often have whitish belly. The large white wing patches conspicuous in flight, make wings look narrow when above horizon, at distance. Looks heavier in flight than Common Scoter and holds head lower. Usually migrates in well-ordered bands of moderate size. When the pair circles over the breeding grounds the female calls a coarse, jolting 'pa-a-ah', otherwise silent. WP

■□□ **Long-tailed Duck** adults males (top left and bottom right) and females winter in flight

□■□ **Velvet Scoter** adult male

□□■ **Velvet Scoter** adult females, late autumn, fresh plumage

Surf Scoter, juv.

Surf Scoter *Melanitta perspicillata* L 50, W 85. Irregular visitor from arctic America. Male unmistakable: has *large, brightly coloured bill* and *white patches on nape* (largest) and forehead. Female usually has two whitish spots on cheek as female Velvet (one or both may be missing) but sometimes also a smaller one on nape. Moreover, head profile is different, *bill* being *deep and wedge-shaped*, feathering reaching down onto bill, forehead practically missing. Equivalent of male's *black patch on base of bill* (sides) *is discernible*. Juvenile similar to adult female but belly usually much paler, and bill lacks black patch; also never has pale spot on nape. In flight Common Scoter is main confusion risk owing to size and *all-dark wings* (though male does not have brown primaries as male Common Scoter). RSWP

■□□ **Velvet Scoter** adult female summer in flight

□■□ **Surf Scoter** adult male

□□■ **Surf Scoters** adult males in flight, four without white nape patch, due to moult

► **Common Scoter** *Melanitta nigra* L 50, W 85. Rare breeder in Scotland and Ireland, abundant breeder on lakes of N taiga zone, also on tundra. Large-scale migration by males in July to moulting waters west of Denmark. Females and juveniles follow in late autumn. Winters in large dense flocks (rafts) along N Atlantic coasts, well out to sea but in shallow waters. Exposed to oil pollution. Male looks all-black when swimming but shows *medium-brown primaries* in flight (striking in sunlight). Female dark brown with *dark cap* and *pale cheeks*. Juvenile even paler on cheeks, also pale on belly. Rounder head and longer tail (often raised) than Velvet Scoter and characteristically *keep very close together* also when in quite small parties. Migratory flocks often huge, fly low over the sea in scythe-shaped formation, side projection of which looks like a toy kite: crowded 'head', long snaking 'string'. Spring migration overland by night at great height, announced by call of males: a mellow, piping 'pew, pew, pew, . . .', slurred but amazingly far-carrying. Male has whistling wing noise, but only at take-off. RWP

Common Scoter, ♀
Showing faint division of pale cheek

■□ **Common Scoter** adult male

□■ **Common Scoter** adult female

Waterfowl

Eider *Somateria mollissima* L 60, W 100. Breeds abundantly along coasts of N Europe, mostly resident in areas where ice allows, migrant (considerable migratory movements) in Arctic Ocean and Baltic Sea. A big and heavy diving duck. *Male for the most part white* (in eclipse in late summer brown-grey with element of white on back), *female uniformly brown-mottled. Bill wedge-shaped and pointed,* pale greyish. *Heavier wingbeats* than other ducks, holds the *head low* in flight. Courtship in flocks, when the males fight and utter far-carrying, deep 'a-OOH-e' calls, while the females give a clucking 'kok-ok-ok-. . .', like a throbbing motor engine, which often forms dense sound effects during calm spring nights. The young broods hatch early, join up together and are attended collectively. The males gather in large flocks at sea from the end of May, after which they move along to Danish waters and North Sea coast, to moult in July and Aug. Females and juveniles follow in autumn. Juveniles darker than adult female, young male darkest, has pale supercilium. RW

Spectacled Eider *Somateria fischeri* L 55. Rare vagrant to arctic coasts, mostly in winter. *Pale green head* and *large white patch around the eye* characteristic of male, which otherwise resembles male Eider. Female is separated from female Eider by suggestion of 'spectacle markings' and greyer neck and head.

King Eider *Somateria spectabilis* L 55, W 92. Common in arctic regions, where like Long-tailed Duck nests mainly beside tundra meres. Otherwise maritime. Rare visitor south of Arctic Circle. Behaviour more or less as Eider, with which it often flocks. Adult male unmistakable, has a *deep* sideways-flattened, *orange-red bill shield* (though this shrinks back after breeding season, when also a rather drab dark brown eclipse plumage is assumed). In flight *black back* and *large white wing panels* are visible at long range. When swimming, shows two black fins on the back. Female resembles female Eider, but has clearly different shape to head and bill (*feathering on forehead* reaches considerably *further down towards the nasal openings*) and besides has a *rusty tone in the plumage,* the *markings* of which are a shade bolder, *sparser and more U-shaped* (especially mantle and flanks) than in Eider, which is more finely barred. Often also *'happy-looking' corners of bill* appear to stand out against rather *pale area around bill base.* Immatures during their first winter are treacherously similar to Eider in plumage, greyish-brown and without U-shaped markings; identified only by *small bill* and by the *feather abutment.* On male King Eiders in obscure plumage, the *rounded nape* should be noted and also that bill is pink, not dirty yellow or grey. V

Steller's Eider *Polysticta stelleri* L 45, W 75. Arctic species, in W Europe rare winter vagrant. Seems not to be at home on open sea, often stays close in beneath cliffs, enters shallow rocky shore waters and feeds by up-ending, but certainly dives too in deeper water. Size as Goldeneye. Male unmistakable (in eclipse plumage, however, drab dark brown apart from white wing panels). Female difficult to identify; has much of a small Eider about her in plumage pattern and behaviour, but the head (rather large) has a totally characteristic profile with *rather long bill,* low but convex forehead, *flat crown* and *sharply angular crown/nape.* A diffuse pale ring around the eye visible at least at certain angles. *The speculum is framed by conspicuous white edges* (otherwise no features in common with Mallard). Tips of the downcurved elongated tertials in the adult female are usually pale, forming then a *pale transverse pattern* at stern. Immature *lacks* this character, is further *usually slightly paler* brown, especially on belly but the difference is not always easy to see. Furthermore, immatures *lack blue speculum* (have dull brownish-grey one) and have *distinctly narrower white bands framing the speculum* than in adult female. Young male has dark-shaded chin, forehead and nape. Flight like Common Scoter's. Pronounced wing noise, like something between Goldeneye and Mallard. V

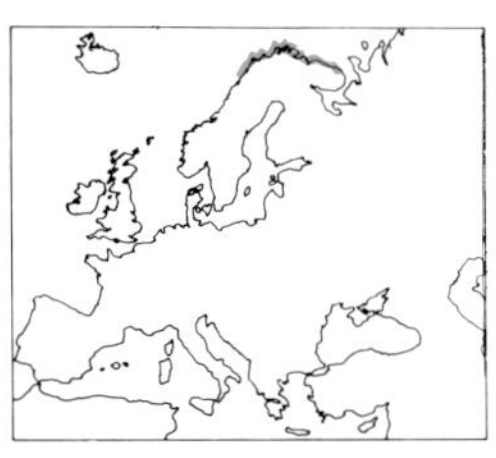

■□ **Eider** adult male
□■ **Eider** raft on sea, incl. adult males, females and imm. males

Common Eider

■□□ **Eider** adult female
□■□ **King Eider** adult female (n.b. the bright rufous colour of the head is due to the light)
□□■ **Steller's Eider** adult female

Spectacled Eider

King Eider

■□ **King Eider** adult male
□■ **Steller's Eider** adult males, some in partial eclipse

Steller's Eider, juv. ♂

■□□ **King Eider** imm. male
□■□ **King Eider** adult male in flight
□□■ **Spectacled Eider** adult male

Waterfowl

Sawbills

Sawbills (subfamily Merginae) are fish-eating, diving waterfowl with saw-toothed edges to the bill. All have white wing panels.

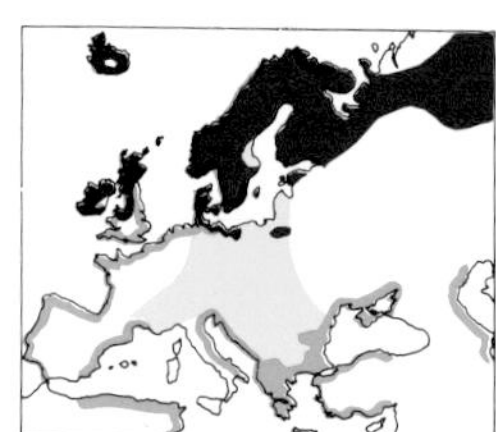

Red-breasted Merganser *Mergus serrator* L 55, W 85. Breeds fairly commonly in N Europe along coasts but also beside larger clear inland waters and rivers, particularly in upland regions. Nest is on the ground, under bushes. Late breeder. In winter almost exclusively coastal. The male is characteristic (but moulting and immature males with brown head like female are a common sight). Female resembles female Goosander but distinguished by *darker*, more brown-toned grey *back, paler brown head* (cinnamon-brown rather than chestnut-brown), *thinner and more pointed crest* (not thick and drooping), *less sharply contrasted pale chin*, more grey-spotted breast and above all *much less sharp division between brown neck and grey body. The white speculum patch is divided by a narrow dark stripe.* Further, in flight appears to have clearly more slender head. The male displays with strange curtseying body movements. The female gives 'prrak, prrak' calls in circle flight over land. RW

Goosander *Mergus merganser* L 64, W 95. More widespread breeder than Red-breasted Merganser, fairly common on clear waters, also on coast in far north. Nests in tree holes and nestboxes. In winter on open lakes and reservoirs. Male in winter has splendid *pinkish-buff underparts*, fading to white in Apr (the same applies to female's belly). Female's distinguishing features compared with rather similar female Red-breated Merganser are: greyer back, *darker, reddish-brown on head*, thick drooping nuchal crest, *sharply contrasted pale chin* and *sharp division between brown neck and grey body. The white speculum is not divided* (or has barely a hint of a half-stripe – see fig.). Displaying males in winter utter a murmuring frog-like 'oorrp, oorrp . . .'. In spring a related more penetrating, metallic ringing 'drruu-drro' is heard. The female utters a 'skrrak, skrrak . . .' in flight. Nests early. Males fly to N Norway for wing moult. In autumn gathers in N Europe in thousands at favoured lakes, fishes collectively in driving cordons, eagerly attended by gulls. RW

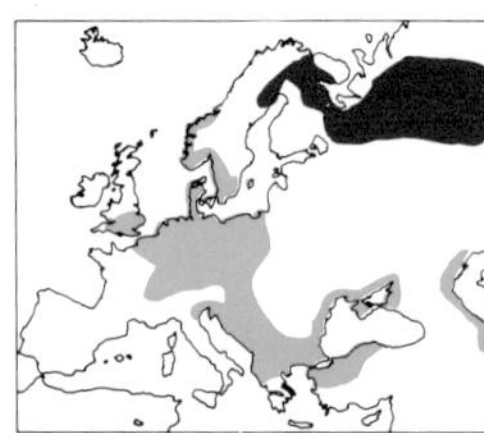

Smew *Mergus albellus* L 40, W 65. Breeds in the northern taiga in tree holes and nestboxes beside small lakes. In habits resembles Goldeneye (with which can interbreed). The male displays by raising the crest on his forehead and drawing back his head on to the back, though with bill still pointing forward. Male characteristic (but does not lose female-like eclipse plumage until Nov). Female and juvenile distinguished by *white cheeks*. Rests on lowland lakes and on coasts, often with Goldeneye and Tufted Ducks, and fishes in shallow water. In winter on reservoirs, lakes, occasionally sheltered bays. Poor flock unity, inclined to make aerial excursions. Flight swift and agile. W

Stifftails

Stifftails (subfamily Oxyurinae) are small with short, thick necks and large bills. Tails markedly long and stiff, hence the name. Often swim with tail cocked. Dive smoothly.

White-headed Duck *Oxyura leucocephala* L 46. Rare breeder in S Europe on freshwater swamps and brackish lagoons. Male has strikingly large and *heavy bill*, a beautiful *pale blue* in colour. *The head* is largely *white*, with black markings only on crown and hind nape, occasionally also chin. The neck is black, and *the body* if anything *chestnut-brown*. Recognised in flight by *short, rounded uniform-coloured wings* and *long tail*. Female told from female Ruddy Duck by *shade deeper bill* and *more distinctly marked dark band on cheek*. Rarely takes wing, dives all the more frequently.

Ruddy Duck *Oxyura jamaicensis* L 41. This American species breeds locally in England, originally escaped from captivity. Male reddish-brown with *white undertail-coverts*. Note head markings and bill shape. Female is distinguished from female White-headed Duck by *weaker bill* and *only* faint *dark cheek bar*. R

■□□ **Red-breasted Merganser** sub-adult male
□■□ **Red-breasted Merganser** adult male
□□■ **Red-breasted Merganser** adult female

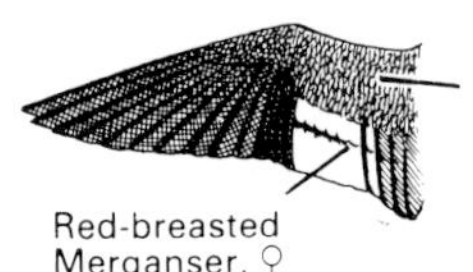

Red-breasted Merganser, ♀

■□ **Goosander** adult male
□■ **Goosander** adult female with chicks

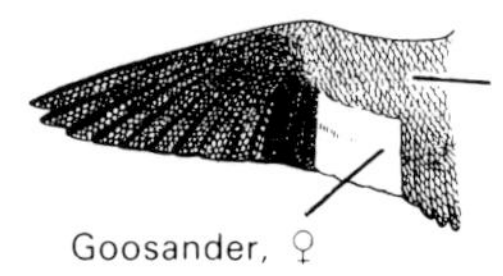

Goosander, ♀

■□□ **Smew** adult male
□■□ **Smew** adult female
□□■ **White-headed Duck** female

■□□ **White-headed Duck** adult male
□■□ **Ruddy Duck** male
□□■ **Ruddy Duck** female

Birds of prey

Vultures

Vultures are very large and powerful birds which live principally on carrion and refuse. Their wings are very long. The vultures are for the most part seen soaring in circling flight, at times very high up, now and then making a very deep embracing wingbeat. Plumage of the sexes alike. The short-tailed species lay one egg, the wedge-tailed ones one or two. Eggs are incubated for a good seven weeks in the large species, six weeks in Egyptian Vulture.

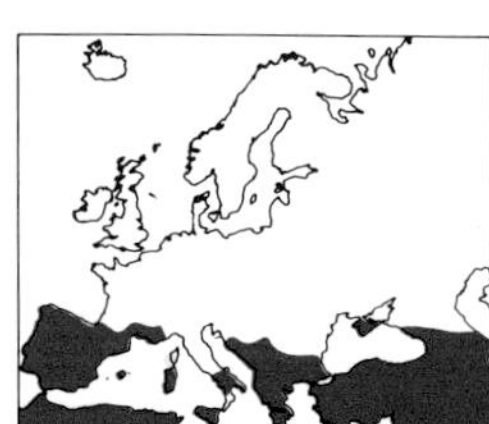

Egyptian Vulture *Neophron percnopterus* L 55–65, W 155–170. Smallest and commonest of Europe's vultures. Found in S Europe in most habitats, but most often in mountain areas. Nests in mountain crevices or small caves. Often visits refuse tips. Easily distinguished from other European vultures by small size and the *white plumage with black flight feathers* (though secondaries greyish-white above). Wings moderately broad and only a little 'fingered'. At long range the adult can be confused with light-phase Booted Eagle, but note the *small, pointed head*, the *long, quite thin bill* and the *wedge-shaped tail*. First-years are dark brown with buff-white feather tips, especially on wing-coverts, uppertail-coverts and tail feathers, which form fair-sized bars and panels (see illustration). Immatures may also be seen which are all-dark apart from the pale face (older, worn immatures?, individual variation?). Usually seen soaring, but on migration can show persistent active flight. Roosts mostly on mountain crags. Very silent. V

Griffon Vulture *Gyps fulvus* L 95–105, W 230–265. Breeds locally in some numbers in mountain regions in S Europe. Nests on ledges or in small caves in mountain face. *Very big*, moves in slow motion in flight. Tail and head protrude only slightly beyond the wing edges, the *long, strongly upward-flexed 'fingers' at the wingtips* give a characteristic silhouette, especially at oblique side angles. Immatures have markedly lighter underwing-coverts than adults, while the body feathers are about equally dark brown in both. The adult's white neck collar is not always visible; the immature's collar is brown. Mostly seen soaring, sometimes several together. *The wings are then held like Golden Eagle's, raised* above the horizontal; in gliding, the wings are slightly angled at the carpal. Roosts on mountain crags, often in numbers and at certain established ledges. A variety of unmusical clucking sounds and whistles are sometimes heard. V

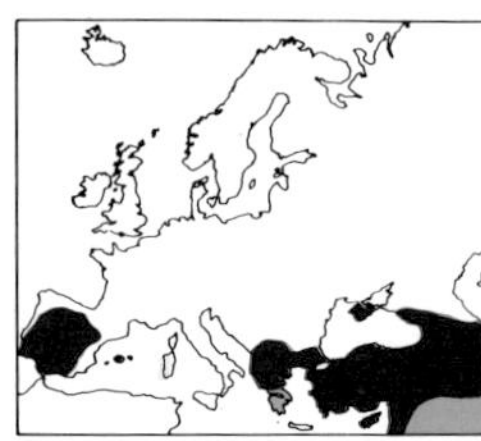

Black Vulture *Aegypius monachus* L 100–115, W 250–285. Very rare breeder in S Europe. Usually lives in regions with desolate mountains and plains. Nests in trees. Distinguished from the eagles by size and the strongly splayed 'fingers', from the rather similar Griffon Vulture by slightly longer, more rounded tail together with (and most safely) *all-dark plumage* and *horizontal or even slightly downward bowed wings in gliding flight*. Underwing-coverts almost black in the immature, becoming a shade paler with age. Solitary, but is seen together with Griffon at carcases and then occupies the highest rank in the pecking order.

Bearded Vulture *Gypaetus barbatus* L 105–125, W 230–285. Very rare breeding bird in S Europe – in total only 50–100 pairs exist. Found almost exclusively in wild mountain regions. Nests in caves in inaccessible mountain faces. Easily identified by its *considerable size, long, narrow wings* held slightly bent, and *long, wedge-shaped tail*. From below the contrast between pale yellowish-brown body and dark wings and tail is clearly visible. Immature is dark on head and breast, grey on the belly. Solitary in behaviour. Patrols the sides of mountains in tireless soaring flight, on the look-out for carrion. Prefers flesh from freshly killed animals; drops bones on to a rock to break them into pieces small enough to swallow, strong gastric juices melt the bone and the marrow is thus ingested. Usually silent, but at breeding sites gives noisy loud whistles.

■□□ **Egyptian Vulture** adult
□■□ **Egyptian Vulture** imm.
□□■ **Griffon Vulture** juv.

■□□ **Black Vulture** adult
□■□ **Black Vulture** juv.
□□■ **Egyptian Vulture** adult in flight from below

■□□ **Egyptian Vulture** imm. in flight from below
□■□ **Griffon Vulture** adult in flight from above
□□■ **Griffon Vulture** adult in flight from below

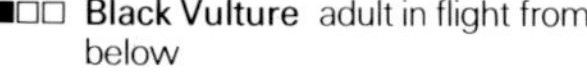

■□□ **Black Vulture** adult in flight from below
□■□ **Bearded Vulture** adult in flight from below
□□■ **Bearded Vulture** imm. in flight from below

Birds of prey

Eagles

Eagles have many features in common, even though all species are not closely related. They are big, broad-winged raptors with 'fingered' wing-tips and powerful bills. Often soar. The change in plumage from immature to adult takes place over several years. Sexes alike in plumage, but the female larger.

White-tailed Eagle *Haliaeetus albicilla* L 77–92, W 200–245. Rare breeder in coastal regions and by lakes and rivers rich in fish. Recently re-introduced to W Scotland. Their enormous stick nests are built on cliff ledges, in tall pines or other large trees. A quite sluggish eagle, spends hours perched on the look-out. In suitable weather scans while soaring, from very high altitude. Lives on fish and seabirds, often carrion. Frequently robs large gulls. Adult has *white tail, yellow bill* and *pale brown head, neck and breast.* Immature looks generally all-dark at a distance with lighter (rusty-brown) panel on median upperwing-coverts and with pale bill base (actually loral spot). At closer range head/neck are seen to be dark brownish-black like the lesser wing-coverts. The tail feathers have dark edges but are usually whitish in the centre, translucent. At close range a pale axillary patch is often visible. First-year has black-spotted rust-brown breast, 2–3 year-olds brown underside with irregular white spotting, may also show obviously pale upper back. Occasional strongly pale-marked younger birds can cause problems. Often soars, on slightly raised, slightly bowed wings. Then easily identified by *enormous size, broad, rectangular dark wings*, rather narrow and long neck together with *big bill* and short *wedge-shaped* tail. More vulture-like than other European eagles. Appears very heavy. Active flight with long series (typically) of slow, shallow wingbeats relieved by sporadic short glides on straight or slightly arched wings. Call 'klee klee klee klee klee', strongly reminiscent of Black Woodpecker's spring call. RV

Reintroduced on Inner Hebrides in 1970s

Pallas's Sea Eagle *Haliaeetus leucoryphus* L 70–84, W 180–205. An eastern species that prefers open steppe country near rivers or lakes. Adult characteristic: *head and neck buffish-white* and *white tail with black terminal band,* as immature Golden Eagle. *Legs grey, bill dark.* Immature is like immature White-tailed, but has pale yellowish-brown median underwing-coverts, strongly contrasting with dark flight feathers and darker brown lesser wing-coverts. *Large pale panel on inner primaries,* unlike White-tailed Eagle. Tail feathers virtually all-black. *Dark brown stripe through eye.*

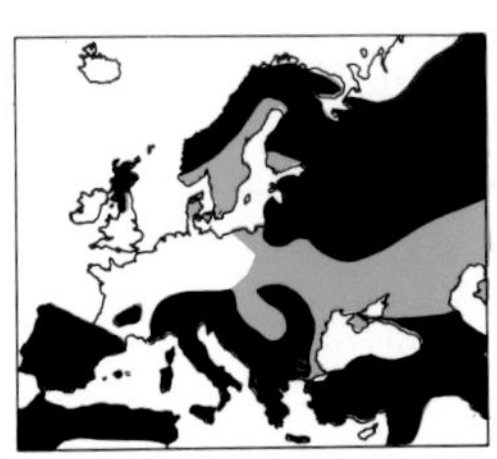

Golden Eagle *Aquila chrysaetos* L 75–86, W 190–230. Rare breeder in mountain districts, locally also on sea cliffs and in pine forests. Nests on cliff ledges or in crown of trees. Adults predominantly resident, but immatures and some older birds, especially in north and northeast, move south in winter when sometimes found in cultivated country with scattered woodland. Often hunts low along mountainsides or wood edges. Lives mainly on rabbits, hares, grouse and other birds, and carrion. Foxes draw attention to eagle's presence in vicinity by walking with their tails in the air. Easily distinguished from White-tailed Eagle by *longer and evenly rounded* (not wedge-shaped) *tail,* narrower wings and shorter, broader neck. Flight powerful, usually 6–7 wingbeats followed by long glide of 1–2 seconds in typically regular succession. *In soaring flight,* and more often than not when gliding, *the wings are held raised* (like a very shallow V). *White wing patches* and *white tail with black outer band* make immature easy to identify. Amount of white in wing varies individually, is not an age characteristic. The white becomes dark-barred grey when adult plumage is acquired within 5–7 years. At all ages *golden-brown nape shawl.* Birds more than one year old have *pale brown panel on upperwing-coverts.* The two spotted eagles are clearly smaller, hold their wings bowed downwards and have noticeably shorter tails. Imperial and Steppe Eagles have proportionately shorter tails and are smaller (see also those species). R

White-tailed Eagle juv.

White-tailed Eagle adult

White-tailed Eagle juv. in flight from below

Golden Eagle adult

Golden Eagle subadult in flight from below (outer four primaries reveal age to be 5 years)

White-tailed Eagle adult in flight from below

Golden Eagle juv. in flight from below

Pallas's Sea Eagle juv. in flight from below

Pallas's Sea Eagle adult

Golden Eagle, adult

Birds of prey

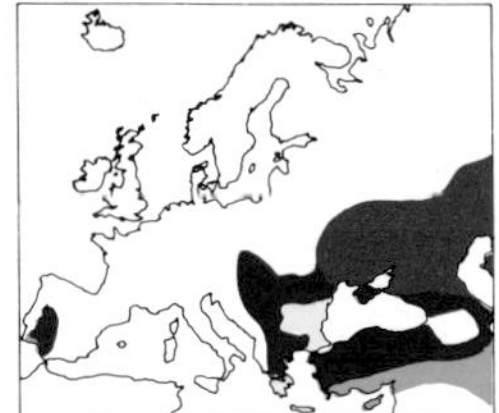

Imperial Eagle *Aquila heliaca* L 70–80, W 175–210. Inhabits steppe and open plains (prey includes sousliks and rabbits). Nests in solitary tree or group of trees, also in woods at foot of mountains. Two races: Spanish *adalberti* extremely few in number, and southeastern *heliaca* very rare. Adults are particularly dark, *black-brown, with pale buffish-yellow nape shawl, snow-white scapulars* and *grey inner tail.* Spanish race also has white leading edge to wing. Immatures are pale brown with *dark-streaked breast* and characteristically *pale, creamy-white lower back.* Inner primaries typically pale, contrasting with remaining dark flight feathers. Lack immature Steppe Eagle's *broad* white wingbar below. Immature *adalberti* have a redder tint than the more yellowish-brown *heliaca* and lack latter's breast streaking. In *variegated* transitional plumage often identified by pale nape shawl. Silhouette like Golden Eagle's but *tail distinctly shorter* (often closed when soaring), and wings held horizontally when gliding. Call scolding, a little like Raven's.

Steppe Eagle *Aquila rapax* L 63–74, W 160–200. Very rare breeder on steppe in SE Europe. Adult dark brown with diffuse pale nape patch and hint of pale patch at base of upper primaries. *Flight feathers usually markedly barred* (Eurasion ssp.), in adult with broad trailing band. Immature pale brown with dark flight feathers, basically like immature Imperial Eagle. Differs in broader and purer *white rear edge on tail and wings,* and in *broad white bar along middle of wing* (greater underwing-coverts) below. Differs above also in broad pale bar along tips of otherwise dark greater coverts and large pale patch at base of primaries. Immature further lacks Imperial's large pale area on lower back, has *only uppertail-coverts white. Bill heavy, yellow corners distinctive.* Quite long neck and tail, long deeply fingered wings. Soars on horizontal wings, glides wings slightly bowed.

Spotted Eagle *Aquila clanga* L 60–69, W 155–180. Very rare breeder in NE Europe in extensive forest regions, often near lakes, river, marshes. Hardy, winters in SE Europe with a few in France. Size between buzzard and large eagle. Stability of flight path and broad, fingered wings give immediate eagle impression. Short tail in many gives ungainly silhouette quite like White-tailed Eagle. Wingbeats quick, almost as in a buzzard. Wings typically *downward-bowed* when gliding. Silhouette very similar to Lesser Spotted but slightly more deeply fingered wings and broad hand of typical birds creates specific jizz to the experienced eye. In all plumages best told from Lesser Spotted by *brownish-black underwing-coverts, darker than flight feathers.* Adult is rather uniform dark brown, often with a little pale on uppertail-coverts and diffuse pale patch at base of primaries above. In worn, faded plumage may have paler, mid-brown coverts above and below (cf. Lesser Spotted), but fore edge proper of wing (lesser coverts) is usually brownish-black. *Immature is almost black* with white spots on tips of wing-coverts and scapulars (varying in extent, form one or more wingbars) and distinctly white uppertail-coverts. Narrow pale bar (tips of greater secondary coverts) along middle of dark upperwing, intermediate plumages. V

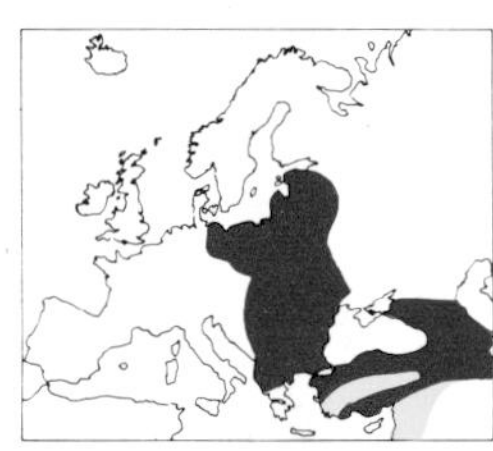

Lesser Spotted Eagle *Aquila pomarina* L 57–64, W 145–170. Breeds not uncommonly in E Europe in forest associated with level country and marshes. Leaves Europe end of Sept. Adult dark brown with *contrasting, distinctly lighter brown,* even greyish-yellow-brown *upperwing-coverts* (lesser and median), light brown head, a *pale patch above at base of inner primaries* and a little pale colour on uppertail-coverts. Immature slightly darker, especially on head, but has similar contrast between upperwing-coverts and rest of wing. Also has very thin bar along tips of wing-coverts. *Small pale patch on nape* (seen only at close range). Silhouette and flight similar to Spotted Eagle's. *Underwing-coverts* colour of milk chocolate, normally *paler* and never darker *than flight feathers* (cf. Spotted Eagle). Lacks bushy 'trousers'.

■□□ **Imperial Eagle** adult race *heliaca*

□■□ **Imperial Eagle** juv. in flight from above

□□■ **Imperial Eagle** juv. in flight from below

Imperial Eagle, adult

■□□ **Steppe Eagle** juv.

□■□ **Steppe Eagle** adult in flight from below

□□■ **Steppe Eagle** adult in flight from above

Spotted Eagle, adult

Steppe Eagle juv. in flight from below

Spotted Eagle juv. in flight from below, note heavily abraded tail

Spotted Eagle juv.

Lesser Spotted Eagle adult in flight from below

Lesser Spotted Eagle juv. in flight from above

Spotted Eagle, light variety (*fulvescens*)

Birds of prey

Bonelli's Eagle *Hieraaetus fasciatus* L 60–66, W 140–165. Scarce breeder in S Europe. Prefers open mountain regions, in winter also seen in other open terrain. Often soars in pairs along mountainsides, when generally perhaps most like Golden Eagle in behaviour and silhouette. Distinctive, however, with rather broad but comparatively not very fingered wings, with carpals projecting but rear edge fairly straight like Honey Buzzard, as well as *relatively long tail.* Wingbeats surprisingly quick (but shallow). Adult characteristic with *whitish belly* and generally *dark underwings* (lesser underwing-coverts are whitish, bases of flight feathers light grey, but underwings still appear dark at a distance, in contrast to belly). Tail greyish-brown with *broad dark terminal band.* Upperparts dark brown with *white patch on upper back* (like athlete's shirt number). Immature is very pale below; rosy-buff belly and coverts, greyish-white flight and tail feathers (closely and finely barred, no thick terminal band) with contrasting black 'fingers'. Usually there is a dark 'comma mark' around the primary coverts. In slightly older immatures often a darker diagonal border across underwing, between coverts and flight feathers.

Booted Eagle *Hieraaetus pennatus* L 42–49, W 110–135. Fairly common in Spain, rare elsewhere in S and central Europe. The smallest of Europe's eagles, similar in size to a Buzzard but still very much an eagle – hands markedly fingered. Inhabits deciduous forest with clearings and glades, usually in lower mountain regions but also in plains country. Hangs motionless in air for long periods, but does not hover. Then dives with closed wings from considerable height vertically towards ground at terrific speed (with legs extended forwards). Occurs in two colour phases, a more common pale one and a less common dark one. Rarely, intermediate types are seen. Pale phase sometimes confused with extremely pale variants of Buzzard and Honey Buzzard but differs from these and all other raptors (except Egyptian Vulture) by underwing having *all-dark flight feathers* behind whitish coverts. Median upperwing-coverts are, in both phases, usually so pale that they form a *characteristically pale V on upperparts,* as in Red Kite, but in addition *uppertail-coverts are pale.* Dark phase is dark brown below (with blackish greater coverts) but with slightly paler tail, can be confused with Marsh Harrier (juv.) and Black Kite. Both phases have slightly paler, more *transparent inner three primaries* as well as *smaller white patch at front edge of each wing join* (against sides of the body – 'landing lights'), well visible from in front. Calls shrill, clear, chattering.

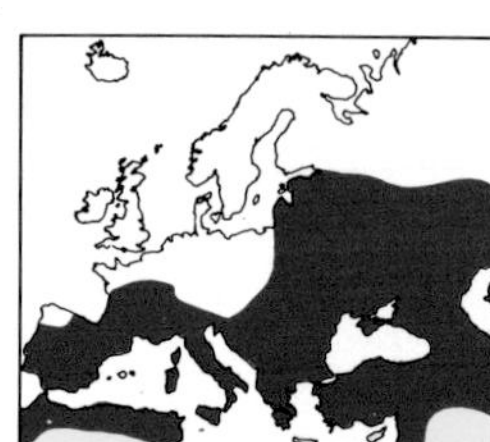

Short-toed Eagle *Circaetus gallicus* L 66–70, W 160–180. Rather uncommon in S and E Europe but some numbers in Spain. Inhabits both mountain regions and lowland. Requires open terrain, for lives on snakes and lizards. A *very pale, long-winged eagle.* Upperparts greyish-brown with paler wing-coverts. Plumage variations: common type has quite *dark head and breast forming sharp border with whitish, narrowly cross-streaked belly,* rarer form is almost all-white below. *Never shows dark carpal patches.* The tips of the flight feathers noticeably 'washed-out', merely grey-edged in very pale individuals (pale Buzzards have solid black tips to flight feathers). Tail quite long and narrow with sharp corners; it has *three distinct, dark bars* (rarely a fourth is indistinctly visible at base). The wings are held horizontally in soaring flight (or very slightly raised); in gliding flight inner wing is raised and outer wing drooped with 'fingers' flexed well upwards. From below the carpal joints are seen to project pronouncedly forward. Head large, but modest in proportion to large wings. Distinguished from Osprey by larger size, broader wings and absence of dark carpal patches below. *Hovers* regularly. Majestic, thoroughly eagle-like wingbeats in normal flight. Melodic, melancholy whistle 'PEEH-o' often heard.

■□□ **Bonelli's Eagle** juv. in flight from below

□■□ **Bonelli's Eagle** adult in flight from below

□□■ **Booted Eagle** adult light phase in flight from below

Bonelli's Eagle, adult

■□ **Short-toed Eagle** adult at nest with chick

□■ **Booted Eagle** light phase adult at nest with chick

Booted Eagle, head-on

'landing lights'

■□□ **Booted Eagle** dark phase adult at nest with chicks

□■□ **Booted Eagle** dark phase adult in flight from below

□□■ **Booted Eagle** dark phase adult in flight from below

■□□ **Short-toed Eagle** hovering

□■□ **Short-toed Eagle** adult in flight from below

□□■ **Short-toed Eagle** adult in flight from below

Birds of prey

Buzzards

Distinctly bigger than crows. Often seen in soaring flight. Wings broad, only moderately fingered. Take small animals on the ground.

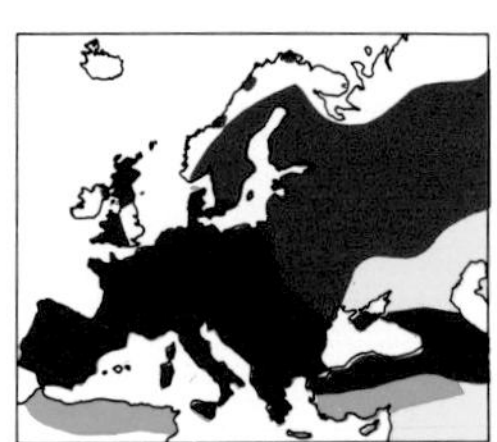

Buzzard *Buteo buteo* L 43–50, W 100–125. Quite common in forest and woodland, often near farmland, bogs etc. The raptor seen most often in much of N Europe. Migratory in far north. Uses fence posts and telegraph poles as look-outs, flies off with slow wingbeats and often circles in sky and hovers. Like Honey Buzzard but has *thicker neck, shorter tail* with straight sides, glides on flatter wings, has faster, shallower, stiffer wingbeats. Plumage very variable. Dark forms predominate in most of Europe. In all dark plumages in Europe characteristic *pale breast band* is apparent. Particularly on the Continent, white-variegated individuals exist which can be confused with Rough-legged Buzzard, Booted and Short-toed Eagles, but these Buzzards often have large snow-white wing patches above, dark comma-shaped carpal marks below. Eastern races more rusty, sometimes resemble Long-legged Buzzard. Tarsi bare. Call a mewing 'peeeeoo'. RP

■□□ **Buzzard** adult at nest with chick

□■□ **Buzzard** juv. in flight from below

□□■ **Buzzard** pale phase in flight

Rough-legged Buzzard *Buteo lagopus* L 50–60, W 125–145. Fairly common breeder in northern mountains, during vole years also in adjacent forests. Winters in open flat country. Hovers more frequently than Buzzard, which it otherwise most resembles. Typical is *white on inner part of tail, black carpal patches* and pale head. The gleaming white tail/dark wings of upperparts are characteristic (pale Buzzards tend to have white also on the upperwings). Immatures are most characteristic: much yellowish-white on breast and underwings, contrasting with dark carpal patch and belly. Adult males dark on throat/breast, belly patch usually paler, tail with several bars, can be exceedingly Buzzard-like. Adult females are intermediate. Longer, narrower wings and tail than Buzzard (occasionally give impression of harrier), *slower, more flexible wingbeats*, and in gliding flight a *head-on silhouette showing characteristic wing kink*. Tarsi feathered. Calls like Buzzard but more mournful. W

■□□ **Rough-legged Buzzard** juv.

□■□ **Rough-legged Buzzard** juv. in flight from below

□□■ **Rough-legged Buzzard** adult male in flight

Long-legged Buzzard *Buteo rufinus* L 55–62, W 130–155. Nests in SE Europe on dry steppes and in mountain districts. Large and long-winged. When gliding, wings are held slightly raised, kinked at carpal joints as in Rough-legged Buzzard. Pale head and leading edge of wing above, *pale breast, belly darkening backwards*. In adult *tail is very pale rusty-coloured without barring* (can appear white at a distance). Tail of immature pale grey-brown, barred at tip. Markings often very like eastern races of Buzzard, but difference in size and flight usually obvious to experienced observer. N African population (separate species?) is, however, small.

■□□ **Long-legged Buzzard** juv.

□■□ **Long-legged Buzzard** adult in flight from below

□□■ **Honey Buzzard** dark juv. in flight from below

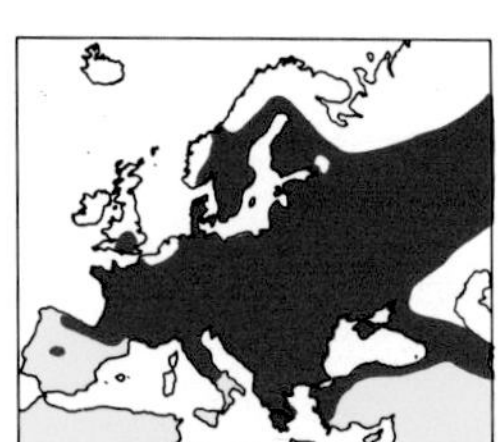

A few pairs breed in southern England

Honey Buzzard *Pernis apivorus* L 51–58, W 125–145. Breeds fairly commonly in secluded forests with clearings. Long-distance migrant. Arrives May, returns mainly Aug/Sept. Brownish, broad-winged, often seen soaring, at a glance very like Buzzard. Silhouette, however, very different: *narrower neck* (head projecting like Cuckoo's), *longer tail* (when gliding, tightly closed, with slightly convex sides, rounded corners) and characteristic combination of carpals held forward/rather straight rear edge of wing. Wingbeats a little deeper and more fluid. *Wings are depressed when gliding*, often faintly so also in soaring flight. Never hovers. Adult male above *greyish*-brown, head ash-grey, eye Cuckoo-yellow, below heavily barred red-brown (sometimes densely, appears all-black; sometimes insignificantly, appears Osprey-white), has little black on the 'fingers' with sharp division. Female browner above and on head, has more dark on 'fingers' with diffuse division. *Tail has wide dark bars, one at tip, two at base* (typical), flight feathers likewise. Immatures even more variable: most are dark brown (bright yellow cere, dark eye) – very like Buzzard; others are rusty-coloured or white (streaked) below. Even dark individuals can have white faces. Dark eye patch. Typical of immatures are dark secondaries, dark 'fingers' (adult: only the tips dark) and more even tail barring (narrow). Call a clear, musical, melancholy 'PEEE-lu'. SP

■□□ **Honey Buzzard** adult female in flight from below

□■□ **Honey Buzzard** adult male in flight from below

□□■ **Honey Buzzard** pale juv. in flight from below

Birds of prey

Hawks

Hawks Medium-sized raptors with fairly short, rounded wings and long tails. Swift active flight, manoeuvre agilely. Gifted bird-catchers. Clutches 3–6 eggs. Nest in dense wood in fork 5–20m up.

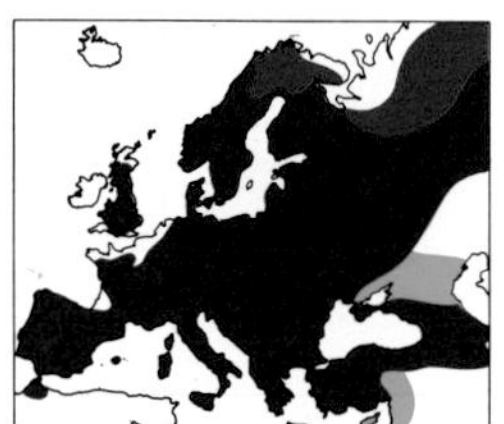

Goshawk *Accipiter gentilis* L 48–60, W 85–115. Scarce breeder in tall coniferous forests. Partial migrant in far north (immatures most prone to move). Widely persecuted. Takes pigeons, crows, gamebirds, thrushes etc, often by surprise but also in very swift pursuit. Manoeuvres agilely in dense forest. Mostly, however, sweeps low over trees, crosses fields on same level in purposeful flight (rapid wingbeats, straight swift glides), often waits on concealed perch (though sometimes in very top). In brighter weather often soars high up, hard to detect. From there launches impressive strike against distant quarry. Female much larger than male, has shorter wingspan than Buzzard but appears more robust. Male usually considerably larger than Carrion/Hooded Crow, in extreme cases only barely equal. Nevertheless treated with great respect by the crows: dive-bombing, but pulling out as if to avoid getting burnt, with frantic yells (not with boldness and snoring calls shown towards Sparrowhawk). Exceptions quite few. Male easily confused with female Sparrowhawk. Best told by noticeably heavier, *looser wingbeats* (quick-winged in squalls and when beginning long-range attack) and *heavier body* (belly distended). Also proportionately slightly smaller head, *longer neck*, shorter tail (long enough!) with bevelled corners, longer inner wing, shorter and more pointed outer wing. *White undertail-coverts bushy*, can be spread. *Immature* heavily *streaked below* (immature Sparrowhawk barred). Display flight with slow-motion wingbeats like harrier. On perched bird profile characterised by width at 'hip' level. Alarm a loud cackling 'kyekyekye . . . ', begging call a wild, melancholy 'PEEE-leh'. Both calls heard in nesting wood on early mornings in March. Mimicked by Jay. Race *buteoides* from N Russia whiter below and paler and bluer-grey above when adult; immatures have paler ground colour, show more pale mottling on upperwing. R

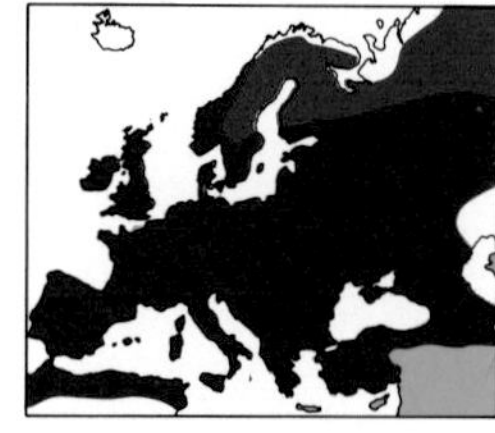

Sparrowhawk

Sparrowhawk *Accipiter nisus* L 30–39, W 58–77. Widespread, quite common in dense woods (open country with clumps suffices). British breeders sedentary; northern ones, especially young, often move south. Takes mostly birds up to thrush size. Often flies swiftly at low level, under cover of curtains of trees etc, to make surprise attack. Drawn-out cheeps from tits often give advance warning. Quite often, however, is high up, soaring, then stoops on prey. Normal flight is *short series of quick wingbeats alternating with short descending glides*. Display with slow wingbeats (also hunting flight at times). Female much larger than male, approaching male Goshawk, but has quick, easy wingbeats, looks much *slimmer, lighter, longer-tailed* (narrow where tail meets body). When perched shows slim body, 'padded shoulders', head drawn down. Size and dashing flight recall Merlin, size and tail length recall Kestrel, but wings rounded. Adult male slate-blue above, finely barred reddish-yellow below. Immature resembles female, but is warmer brown above (males especially have rusty fringes, most obvious on lesser wing-coverts), has slightly sparser, thicker barring below, upper breast almost spotted. Alarm 'kyikyikyi . . . ', slower and jerkier than falcon. Begging call 'PEEE-ee', thinner than Goshawk. RWP

Levant Sparrowhawk

Levant Sparrowhawk *Accipiter brevipes* L 32–39, W 63–76. Inhabits open dry country in SE Europe. Feeds largely on lizards (has short, thick toes), grasshoppers etc. Tropical migrant. Migrates *in flocks* (10-30 birds, sometimes 100s). Very like Sparrowhawk. Male, however, has *sooty wingtips* contrasting with *white underparts* and lighter blue-grey upperparts (pigeon-coloured, incl. cheeks). Female also pale below with sooty wingtips. Immature told by *large drop-shaped spots* in vertical rows on breast. Also silhouette is slightly *shorter-tailed, with longer and more pointed wings*, thus markedly falcon-like. Iris brown.

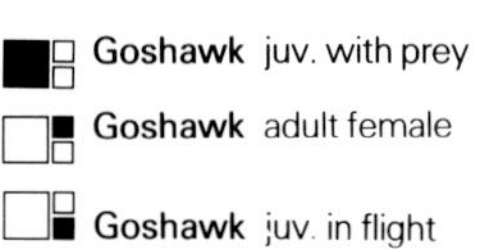

Goshawk juv. with prey

Goshawk adult female

Goshawk juv. in flight

Sparrowhawk adult male at nest

Sparrowhawk juv. male

Sparrowhawk juv in flight from below

Levant Sparrowhawk, adult ♂

Levant Sparrowhawk flock on migration soaring in thermals

Levant Sparrowhawk adult male

Levant Sparrowhawk adult male in flight

Levant Sparrowhawk adult male in flight

Birds of prey

Kites

Kites are medium-sized, long-winged and long-tailed raptors that are often seen gliding. They twist their tails and manoeuvre skilfully above trees and fields. Feed on fish and refuse. The nest is built in trees, often near water.

Red Kite *Milvus milvus* L 60–70, W 140–165. Breeds in well-wooded districts, often near lakes, fairly common in some regions in S and central Europe but rare and extremely local in N Europe. Distinguished from all other raptors by *long, deeply forked tail*, which, like the *belly, is rusty-red above.* The wings have *large white 'windows' below*, and a broad pale brown bar across inner wing above. Young have pale streaking on breast. Distinguished from Black Kite by proportionately longer tail (more deeply forked) as well as by paler and rustier plumage. Specialist in soaring and gliding flight, appears very buoyant, holds wings slightly bowed and slightly angled with projecting carpals, *turns and twists tail* continuously. In flight profile looks *stooped* with tail and head hanging down slightly. Call a thin piping whistle, rising and falling: 'peeeoooh, pee-oo-ee-oo-ee-oo'. RSP

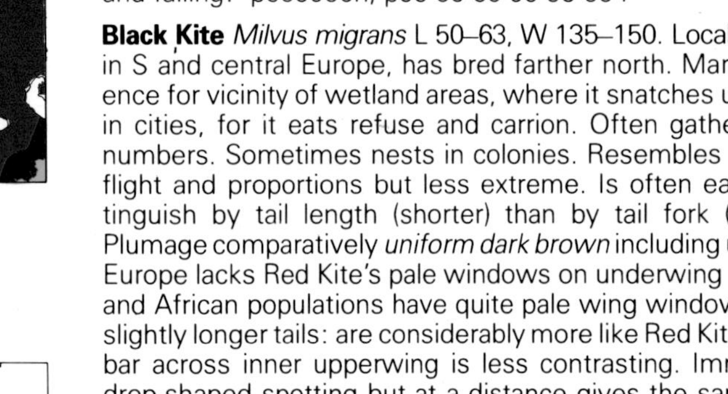

Black Kite *Milvus migrans* L 50–63, W 135–150. Locally common in S and central Europe, has bred farther north. Marked preference for vicinity of wetland areas, where it snatches up fish, also in cities, for it eats refuse and carrion. Often gathers in large numbers. Sometimes nests in colonies. Resembles Red Kite in flight and proportions but less extreme. Is often easier to distinguish by tail length (shorter) than by tail fork (shallower). Plumage comparatively *uniform dark brown* including uppertail, in Europe lacks Red Kite's pale windows on underwing (but Asiatic and African populations have quite pale wing windows and also slightly longer tails: are considerably more like Red Kite). The pale bar across inner upperwing is less contrasting. Immature has drop-shaped spotting but at a distance gives the same impression. Call resembles an immature Herring Gull's, 'PEEe-errr'. V

Black-winged Kite *Elanus caeruleus* L 33, W 78. Breeds very scarcely and locally in dry, cultivated regions in south-westernmost Europe (recent local increases and range extension). Slightly bigger than Kestrel. Head unusually large and forward-projecting like an owl's, tail short, wings long and pointed. Adult unmistakable, white, pale grey and black. Immature brown-tinged on breast, neck, head and upperparts. Active flight with owl-like swift, soft wingbeats, *glides with harrier-like raised wings, often hovers.*

Osprey

Osprey (family Pandionidae) Only a single species in this family. Widespread in many parts of the world. Threatened by environmental pollution because its diet is exclusively fish.

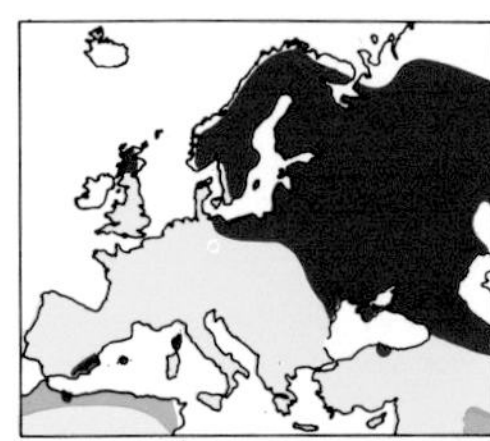

Osprey *Pandion haliaetus* L 53–61, W 140–165. Fairly common by freshwater lakes in N Europe and Fennoscandia, in Britain confined to Scottish highland lochs, in Mediterranean strictly coastal. On migration widespread inland and on coast. Builds a large stick nest on exposed site on top of an old pine, for instance, out on a small island (cliffs in Mediterranean). Lives entirely on fish, for which it searches while *hovering* at height of 10–40 m and catches in a headlong dive (feet first at the strike), during which it almost completely disappears in a cascade of water. Upperparts brown with white crown, *below whitish* with a very constant wing pattern in which *carpal is always dark.* Also the secondaries appear rather dark in most lighting conditions. Female has a more obvious *breast band* than male. The Osprey is big and heavy, but the wings are neither particularly broad nor 'fingered', at long range often gives impression of large gull, especially as wings are usually held slightly bowed. In spring the male flies on strongly undulating course with dangling feet and whistles a mournful 'yeelp-yeelp- . . .'. The contact call is a short loud whistle, 'pyep'. Alarm call a hoarse, sharp 'kew-kew-kew-kew'. SP

■□□ **Red Kite** juv.
□■□ **Red Kite** adult in flight from below
□□■ **Black Kite** adults

■□□ **Black Kite** juv. in flight from below
□■□ **Black Kite** juv. in flight from above
□□■ **Black Kite** juv. in flight from below

■□□ **Black-winged Kite** adult
□■□ **Black-winged Kite** juv.
□□■ **Black-winged Kite** adult in flight

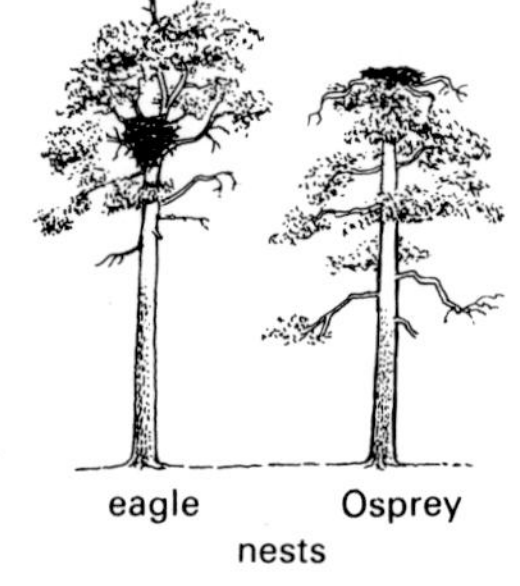

nests

■□ **Osprey** juv. at nest
□■ **Osprey** in flight

Birds of prey

Harriers

Harriers Medium-sized, long-winged, long-tailed raptors. Inhabit open country. Hunt low over ground (or reeds) with slow wingbeats alternating with glides on raised (shallow V position) wings. Nest on ground.

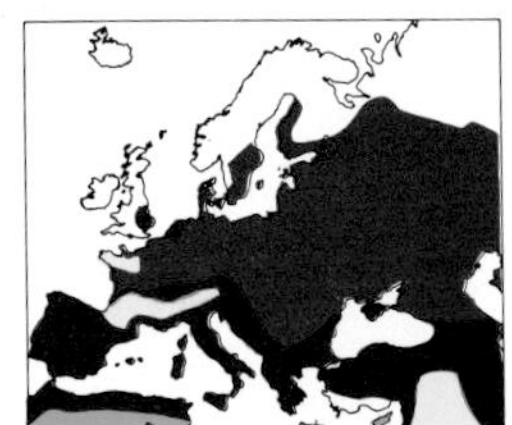

Marsh Harrier *Circus aeruginosus* L 48–55, W 115–140. Widespread, generally uncommon but locally abundant. Nests in larger reedbeds. Usually seen flying close above reeds with steady wingbeats alternating with glides on raised wings. Also hunts over fields and farmland. Heavier and has *broader wings* than other harriers. Male silver-grey on wings and tail (hint of white at tail base), at times appearing so clean and shining as to be confused with Hen Harrier, but has *rusty belly*. Female and immature dark brown (buzzard-like) with respectively yellowish-white or rusty-yellow elements. Some immatures practically all dark brown. In spring male displays high in sky on deeply undulating course, light and dancing, uttering shrill Lapwing-like 'vay-ee'. In early autumn immatures often soar like Buzzards. RSP

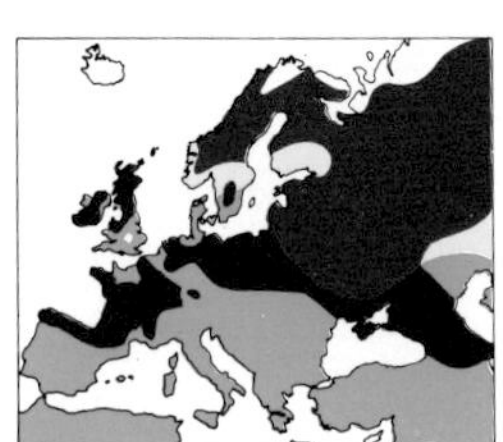

Hen Harrier *Circus cyaneus* L 45–52, W 100–120. Breeds in N and W Europe in open terrain, moorland, young conifer plantations, often near bogs. On migration and in winter over arable fields, moors, coastal marshes and marshy meadows. Flight like Marsh Harrier's, though not infrequently attacks small birds as they flush. Male fairly characteristic: note especially *snow-white rump*. Younger males mangy brown on back. Female and immature brownish with white rump, resemble Pallid and Montagu's Harriers but flight not so light and bouncing, are not so slim, have noticeably *shorter, more rounded wings*, 2nd–5th primaries forming wingtip (female gliding over high can look very like Sparrowhawk). Adult female has on average more white on rump than Pallid and Montagu's in same plumage. Narrow pale neck collar. Immature streaked on breast like female, though warmer in tone, and some streaked only on upper breast. RWP

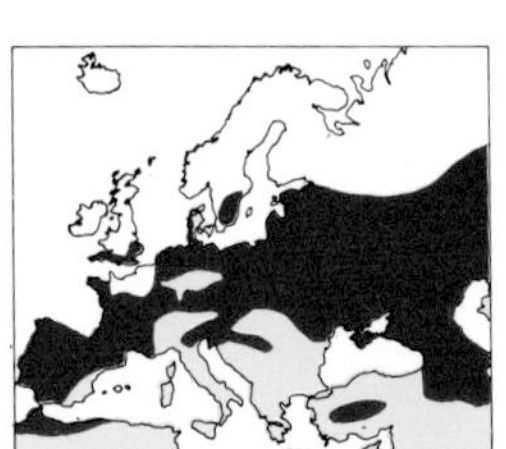

Montagu's Harrier *Circus pygargus* L 41–47, W 100–116. Nests on lowland moors/heaths, in cornfields and in young conifer plantations. Flight buoyant, elegant, tern-like (especially male's). *Wings long, pointed* (2nd–4th primaries form wingtip), producing silhouette recalling Kestrel in gliding flight. Male darker grey than Pallid and Hen Harriers, furthermore has one *black bar* (two below) *across secondaries*, as well as (close range) chestnut streaking on belly. Female (streaked below, narrower white rump patch) and immature (rusty-brown below, fuller rump patch) extremely like Pallid, but collar faint or absent. Adult female has more white at back of eye than female Pallid. First-year male has pale neck collar like Pallid, but is usually distinguished by grey breast shield and cheeks. Adult female has *dark bar across upperwing* (bases of secondaries), discernible at fair range. Below, *the hindmost pale bar across secondaries is broad and equally pale up to body. Dark bar across middle of secondaries is darker than trailing edge* (see fig.) and is *always broad*. SP

Pallid Harrier *Circus macrourus* L 43–52, W 100–119. Nests on dry plains in SE Europe, also visits marshes. Rare vagrant to N and W Europe (mostly early summer and Sep). Very like Montagu's Harrier in silhouette and flight, but in each case the adult birds (and particularly the female) have slightly broader wing base and shorter hand; male appears slightly longer-tailed and more falcon-winged, has stiffer, quicker wingbeats than Montagu's, not so tern-like and elastic. Male *greyish-white on breast* and otherwise shining white below, has paler back than relatives (but small pale rump), has smaller black patch (narrowing like *wedge*) at wingtip (most obvious below). 1–2-year-old male grey-brown above (wing wedge hard to see), whitish below (wedge obvious). Female (streaked below, narrower white rump patch) and immature extremely like Montagu's. Immature (always wholly unstreaked below) has *pale neck-collar*, further enhanced by *uniform dark brown neck sides*, the typical 'boa'. Adult female has *unbarred brown secondaries above*; below, the *pale bars on the secondaries darken towards body*; underwing-coverts fairly dark. V

■□□ **Marsh Harrier** adult male
□■□ **Marsh Harrier** subadult male in flight
□□■ **Marsh Harrier** juv. in flight from below

■□□ **Hen Harrier** adult male
□■□ **Montagu's Harrier** adult male
□□■ **Hen Harrier** adult female

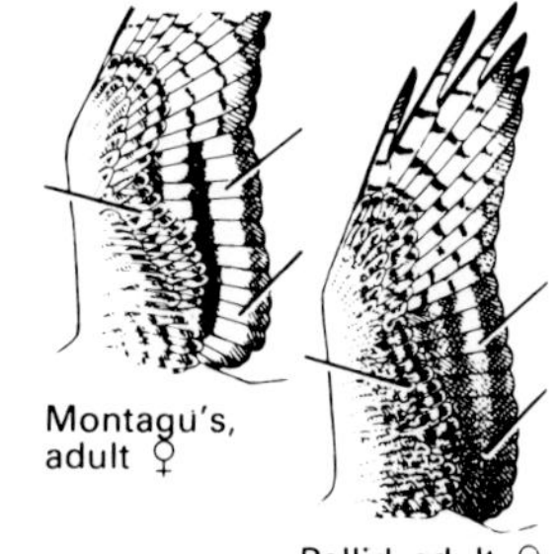

Montagu's, adult ♀

Pallid, adult ♀

■□□ **Hen Harrier** adult male in flight
□■□ **Montagu's Harrier** adult male in flight
□□■ **Hen Harrier** adult female in flight moulting flight feathers

Pallid Harrier, adult ♂

■□□ **Pallid Harrier** juv. in flight
□■□ **Pallid Harrier** adult female in flight
□□■ **Montagu's Harrier** adult female in flight

Birds of prey

Falcons

Falcons (order Falconiformes). Small to medium-sized raptors with pointed wings. Flight often dashing. Female often much larger than male.

Gyrfalcon *Falco rusticolus* L 53–62, W 105–130. Uncommon breeder on cliff crags in mountains. Grouse form basic food. Adults remain in the mountains all year, some immatures resort to coasts and flat country in winter. Largest and most powerful falcon. Can be confused with Goshawk (which however has shorter, more rounded, stiffer wings). Where immense mountains reduce impression of buzzard size, similarity to Peregrine is emphasised – though tail noticeably longer, *wings broader towards tips*, wingbeats slower (but can certainly move rapidly). Greyish above with *weak moustache* (more distinct in immatures) and *dirty cheeks*. Underside in adults extensively but faintly patterned, barred lower down; in immatures heavily streaked, often on yellowish-brown tinted ground colour. This is the usual colour pattern in Scandinavia; in Greenland a very pale, almost all-white one predominates, in Iceland it is usually between the two. A wide range of intermediates exists, however. Young in same brood can be of different colour phases, Alarm a gruff, scolding, nasal 'GEHe-GEHe-GEHe. . .', more drawn-out than Peregrine. V

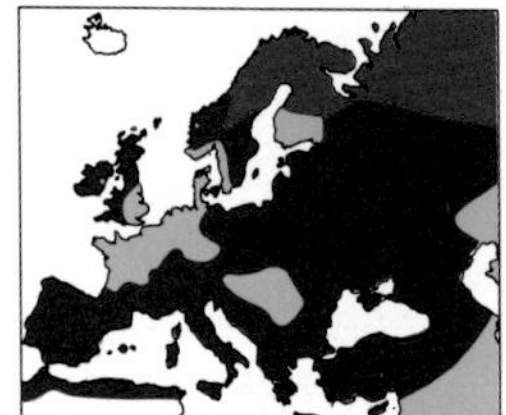

Rare throughout the whole of its European range

Peregrine *Falco peregrinus* L 40–52, W 85–110. A widespread species which since 1950s has declined dramatically, mainly because of habitat pollution but also theft of young (for falconry) and eggs. Now on verge of extinction in many areas (but increasing again in Britain). Breeds mainly on cliff faces. In winter also on moors and estuaries. Lives on medium-sized birds caught in flight. Most impressive of various methods are the several-hundred-metre-long diagonal downward stoops with closed wings, in which the falcon appears as a blurred blob and a howling noise is created. On impact knocks out prey with its feet. Normal flight not very remarkable: quick and fairly shallow wingbeats, moderate speed. Is distinctly smaller than Gyrfalcon and Saker, and has characteristic compact silhouette with *fairly short tail* and *broad-based but sharply tapering wings*. Female markedly larger and heavier than male; male requires more than a glance to separate from Hobby. Adult is characteristic: black and white head, dark blue-grey upperparts, *gleaming white breast*. Immature brown above like Lanner and Saker, but has full moustache and *darker crown*. Alarm a scolding 'rek-rek-rek-. . .'. RP

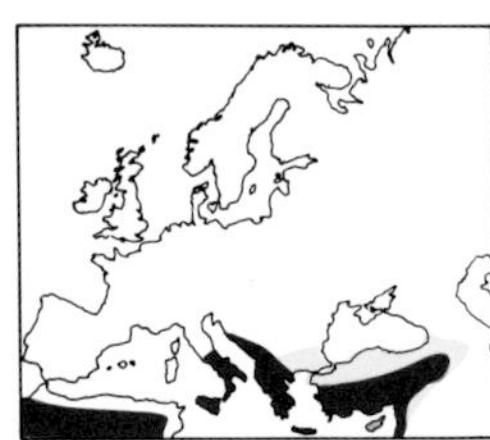

Lanner Falcon *Falco biarmicus* L 43–52, W 95–115. Principally an African species. Adapted to plains, deserts. Nests on cliffs. Five races, of which European (*feldeggii*) is declining. Larger than Peregrine but generally takes smaller prey. Adult *feldeggii* has greyish-brown back, paler head, whitish underparts, thus resembles Saker. Usually, however, greyer and more barred pattern on back, more distinct tail barring (incl. central feathers), *darker and rust-coloured crown*, more prominent moustache and *tendency towards barring on flank feathers*. Some Sakers can, however, approach Lanner in any one and sometimes several of these respects. *Immature extremely like immature Saker*, but clearly smaller, more often resembles Peregrine than does Saker (but slimmer, longer-winged than Peregrine).

► **Saker** *Falco cherrug* L 47–55, W 105–125. Uncommon in SE Europe, found mostly in steppe country. Lives largely on sousliks but also on birds. Often nests in heronries. Most easily confused with Lanner. Adult Saker can usually be identified by *colour of upperparts almost like female Kestrel, pale crown, weak moustache* together with unbarred central tail feathers. Occasional individuals, however, are, like Lanner, brownish-grey and barred above – including on centre of tail. *Flank feathers are streaked*, not cross-barred. Immature has darker brown back and is heavily streaked below, *is extremely like immature Lanner* (both have unbarred tail centre). Saker, however, is impressively large, *near size of Gyrfalcon*. In active flight appears considerably larger and heavier than Peregrine (rarely so with Lanner). V

Gyrfalcon adult dark phase

Gyrfalcon adult light phase

Peregrine adult

Peregrine adult female in flight from above

Peregrine adult female in flight

Peregrine adult in flight from below

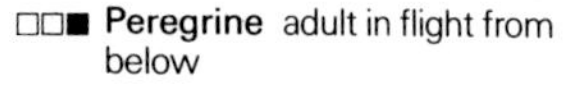

Lanner, adult

Saker, adult

Lanner Falcon imm.

Lanner Falcon adult in flight, race *erlangeri* of NW Africa

Saker juv.

Birds of prey

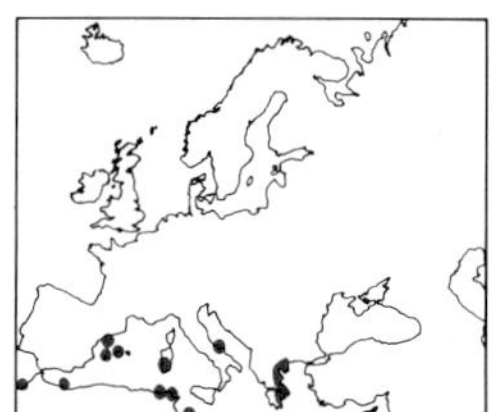

Eleonora's Falcon *Falco eleonorae* L 36–42, W 85–105. Named after a medieval princess who put a protection order on Sardinia's birds of prey. Inhabits isolated rocky islands in the Mediterranean Sea and in the Canaries. Principally a migratory bird which winters in Madagascar, but some remain during winter in the eastern Mediterranean region. Size between Peregrine and Hobby, but distinguished by *extremely long wings*. Very fast and agile flier, catches small birds and insects in flight like Hobby. Often indulges in a skua-like relaxed flight. Often hunts in flocks, often late in the evening. May hover. Nests in colonies on coastal cliffs. Returns to nesting colonies at end of Apr, but in spite of this puts off nesting to the autumn in order to take advantage of the passage of small flight-weary migrant birds, which are captured during the morning hours. Lays up prey reserves. Two colour phases. Dark phase (25% of population) is easily separated from Red-footed Falcon by larger size, longer and darker wings, more supreme aerial ability and *lack of red thighs*. Light phase resembles Hobby and immature Peregrine but distinguished by *dark underwing-coverts*, contrasting with pale bases of flight feathers, as well as by *belly having rusty-brown ground colour*. Juvenile less distinctive; underwing-coverts barred and paler than adults, but trailing edge of underwing noticeably dark. Belly paler than in adult. Call a nasal, slightly grating 'kje-kje-kje-kjah'. V

Hobby *Falco subbuteo* L 32–36, W 73–84. Breeds uncommonly in open, mainly lowland country with scattered woods and often some moist terrain. Nests in old nests of crows. Characteristic flight silhouette with long pointed wings and relatively short tail, resembles a large Swift. Extremely swift and agile hunter, often chases swallows and can even catch Swifts. Chorus of alarm is given by House Martins ('pree pree') and Swallows ('glitt, glitt'). Often dashes low over ground, when long wings are beaten in typically spaced and powerful clips. Feeds to large extent on dragonflies, which are hunted in late afternoon/evening in more relaxed flight. Never hovers. Long-distance migrant, arrives in May and disappears in Sept. Plumage characteristic with *slate-grey upperparts* and densely streaked underparts (breast and belly look uniform dark at a distance), *rusty-red thighs and under-tail-coverts, white throat and cheeks, pronounced moustache.* Juvenile lacks the rusty-red, is generally more rusty-yellow in tone, often has rather pale forehead, in extreme cases so much as to create superficial resemblance to Red-footed Falcon. Silhouette, too, is just like Red-footed's, but larger size and powerful flight often reveal the species at once. When excited, screams, long, rapid, 'over-energetic', series of notes: 'jijijijijijiji. . .'. Begging call 'YEEE(eh)-YEEE(eh)-. . .', identical with Merlin's. SP

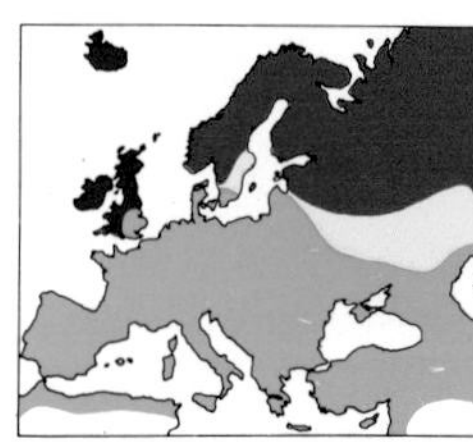

Merlin *Falco columbarius* L 25–30, W 55–65. In Britain breeds uncommonly (declining) in open hilly, mountain or moorland regions in old stick nest in tree or on cliff face, also on ground. Not uncommon in NE subarctic region. Smallest of Europe's raptors. Male clearly smaller than female, blue-grey above, rust-coloured below. Female is brownish above, immature also. In all plumages *diffusely marked face* with faint, indistinct moustache. Lives mainly on small birds, captured in flight after vigorous close pursuit. Often dashes low over ground, flight becoming gently bouncing (tendency towards thrush-like series of wingbeats) in final phase of attack. 'Thrush flight', however, also at low speed when new target is picked out – thus a camouflage tactic. Relatively long tail and relatively *short but pointed wings* as well as *small size* are characteristics of the flight silhouette. When the Merlin is circling very high up Peregrine is actually a perfectly possible confusion risk, since there is then nothing to compare the size with; the proportions are like Peregrine's, including obviously sturdy breast area. Alarm call fairly short, rapid, accelerating series of shrill, piercing notes (the male's more rapid, shriller). Begging call very similar to Hobby's. RWP

Hobby adult with young at nest

Hobby adult in flight

Hobby juv.

Eleonora's Falcon adult dark morph in flight

Merlin adult female at nest with young

Merlin adult male in flight, moulting flight-feathers

Merlin adult male

Merlin female

Birds of prey

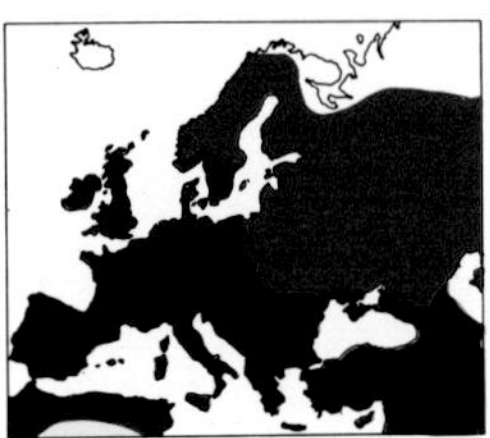

Kestrel

Red-footed Falcon *Falco vespertinus* L 28–33, W 67–76. Fairly common in SE Europe on steppes and in open cultivated land with groups of trees. Nests colonially, usually in Rook nests. Resembles Kestrel in behaviour but has proportionately longer wings and shorter tail and can therefore appear surprisingly Hobby-like when it flies directly overhead fairly high up when size comparison is not possible, but has proportionately slightly longer tail than Hobby. Lives mostly on insects. Often uses telephone wires as look-out posts. Also hovers. Catches flying insects in Hobby fashion, often at dusk, hunting in flocks. *Male is slate-grey* with distinctly *paler flight feathers* together with *rusty-red 'trousers'* and undertail-coverts. *Female is barred slate-grey on back* but pale and unmarked rusty-yellow below, and the head is pale with contrasting dark area around eye. Base of bill and feet are orange-red in adults. Red-footed Falcons which overshoot north and west during very hot weather at the end of May are usually first-years, some already moulted to adult-like plumage (the males slate-grey with Cuckoo-like barring on underwings and yellow feet), others not (the males with juvenile head markings and grey belly with rusty-yellow patches). Birds of the year have dark brown back and streaked underparts (like Merlin) but have the same head pattern as adult female. V

▶ **Lesser Kestrel** *Falco naumanni* L 28–33, W 63–72. Fairly common in Spain, scarce around the Mediterranean and further east. Lives in open country. Nests colonially on cliffs and city buildings (tiled roofs, cathedrals). Lives mostly on insects, caught in flight. Usually hunts in flocks. Hovers less often. Very gregarious. Very like Kestrel but slightly smaller, has weaker bill and *pale claws* (Kestrel's are black) and now and then beats wings more quickly (as fast as Swift). Adult male is in addition unmarked reddish-brown on back and wings, has *blue-grey greater upperwing-coverts* (between dark brown flight feathers and reddish-brown lesser wing-coverts), *lacks dark moustachial streak* (but shadow effects can be deceptive) and has practically unbarred grey-tipped flight feathers below and paler underwing-coverts (which may lack dark drop-shaped spots completely) than Kestrel. Female has on average more grey on uppertail-coverts than female Kestrel, but this of little use in the field, though it may be possible to make out the pale claws, for the Lesser Kestrel is a quite fearless bird. Markedly vocal at breeding site. Gives Kestrel-like (but often more rapid and more chattering) series of notes, 'kikikiki . . . ', also a species-specific *three-syllable, rasping 'chay-chay-chay'* with a cracked, hoarse tone. The young beg with drawn-out, trilling screams, exactly like young Kestrels. V

Kestrel *Falco tinnunculus* L 32–38, W 68–78. Commonest and most widespread of the falcons, both in Britain and throughout Europe, familiar raptor along motorway verges. Found in almost all types of open country, from cultivated lowlands to upland moors. Frequently nests in an old crow nest in a clump of trees but also on cliff ledges, often even on buildings in town and city centres. Lives mainly on voles but also on insects. Scans the ground by *hovering* at height of 7–12m, remaining stationery in the air with fluttering wings and fanned, depressed tail. Is not particularly fast, seldom attempts to catch flying birds. Flight silhouette characteristic with long rather pointed wings and *very long tail.* Male is reddish-brown (with small dark spots) on back and wing-coverts, has dark brown flight feathers, grey-blue head as well as grey-blue tail with a broad black terminal band. Can be confused only with Lesser Kestrel, see that species. Female and immature have *reddish-brown upperparts*, and tail with pronounced blackish-brown barring, and are almost impossible to separate from Lesser Kestrels in corresponding plumages. The most usual call is a piercing but not very harsh 'kee-keekeekeekeekee' (in shorter series than in the other small falcons). The young beg with a drawn-out, trilling 'keerrrl, keerrrl, keerrrl . . . '. RWP

■□□ **Red-footed Falcon** 1st-summer male

□■□ **Red-footed Falcon** adult male

□□■ **Red-footed Falcon** juv. in flight

■□□ **Lesser Kestrel** adult male

□■□ **Lesser Kestrel** adult female

□□■ **Red-footed Falcon** juv. in flight from below

Kestrel adult male by motorway

Kestrel adult female in flight from above

Lesser Kestrel female in flight

Kestrel juv. hovering

Kestrel female in flight from below

Gallinaceous birds

Gallinaceous birds

(order Galliformes). Terrestrial. Have plump bodies and short bills. Short, broad, stiff, bowed wings. Have strong feet and can run quickly. Fly with series of rapid wingbeats, alternating with long glides.

Grouse

(family Tetraonidae). Medium-sized or large. Nostrils and feet feathered. Several species have elaborate courtship displays. 5–12 eggs.

Willow Grouse *Lagopus lagopus* L 40. Numbers vary periodically, but quite common in taiga zone near boggy terrain and, most abundantly, in mountains, mainly in birch forest near overgrown brooks but also in damp willow sections on otherwise barren hillsides. In winter in small flocks in birch and coniferous woods of valleys. In the *white winter plumage* both sexes resemble Ptarmigan (though *never has black loral streak*), but altitude found usually distinguishes the two. During summer, male especially, recognised by *chestnut-brown elements* in plumage. In late spring, male is white with head, neck and upper breast deep reddish-brown; in summer and autumn plumage is mottled reddish-brown with belly and wings white, resembling the hen, which is quicker to moult the winter plumage. Grouse fly in characteristic manner of game birds: rapid wingbeats alternating with long glides on rigid, bowed, slightly depressed wings. The cocks, often many gathered loosely together, display at night in the spring, and utter both the barking *laugh usually given on rising* (far-carrying, nasal, choking) 'KEH-uk, KEH-hehehehehehe-eHEH-eHEH, eHEH', and ventriloquial 'go-BEK, go-BEK', and, for display, an evenly accelerating 'ka, ke ke-ke-ke-ke-kekekekeke-rrr'. Short aerial excursions an integral part of display. The cock will come up if the hen's 'nyow' call is imitated. Silent in winter.

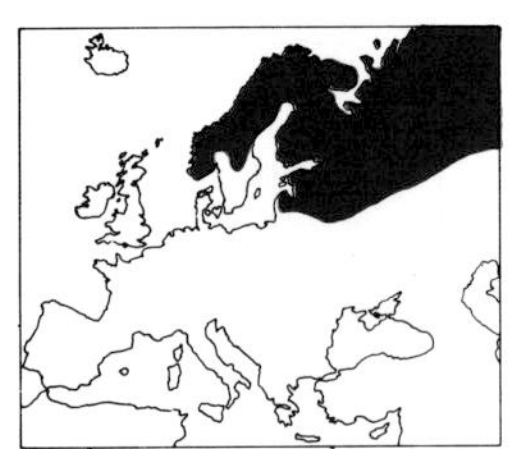

Red Grouse *Lagopus l. scoticus* and *L. l. hibernicus*. L 38. The British and Irish Red Grouse are two races of the Willow Grouse very closely related to each other and not separable in the field. Previously considered together as a separate species. Inhabit upland heather moors. Throughout the year chestnut-brown (hen less reddish) with *dark wings* (darker than hen Black Grouse). Call and general behaviour same as Willow Grouse. R

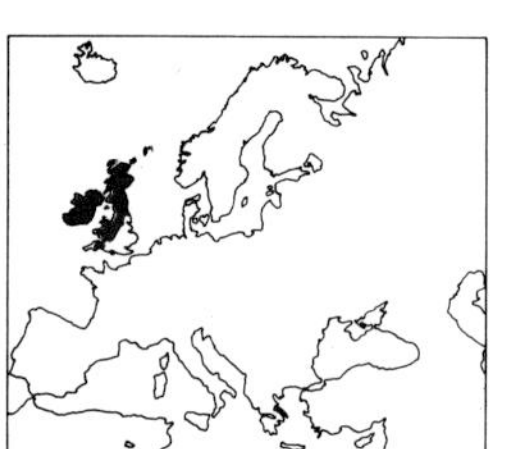

Ptarmigan *Lagopus mutus* L 35. Breeds in higher mountains in numbers that vary periodically. Less abundant than Willow/Red Grouse. In summer lives high up in lichen region, often near boulder ridges, i.e. as neighbour of the Snow Buntings, above the Dotterels. Winters, sometimes in large flocks, lower down on the bare mountain, often in upper birch forest, where Willow/Red Grouse also found. Differentiated from latter in *white winter plumage* by *black loral streak in male*, sometimes an ill-defined one also in female. Call, when uttered, is species-specific. In late spring male becomes *blackish-grey on head/neck*, in summer gets brown-grey over whole back, then acquires autumn plumage, which is more *grey-blue vermiculated*. Therefore very different from reddish-brown male Willow/Red Grouse. To separate the drab grey-brown (wings of course white) hen from hen Willow Grouse is much more difficult, but ground colour is more buffish-yellow, not so rusty-red; altitude where found a guide. Cock's call *very hard crackling*, belching 'arrr arrr' with variations, different from Willow/Red Grouse's burst of laughter. R

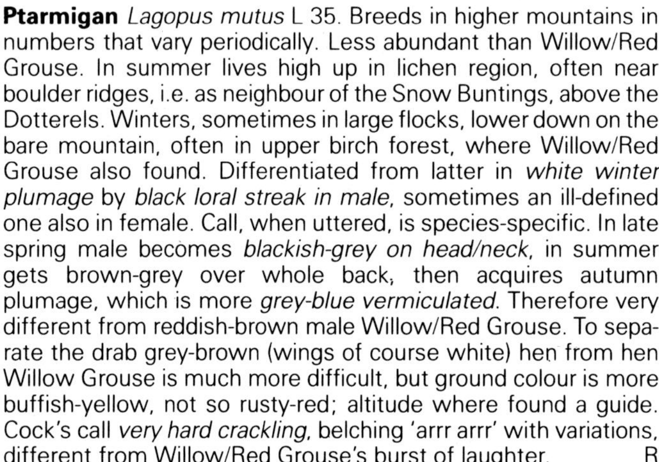

Caucasian Snowcock *Tetraogallus caucasicus* L 58. Sedentary in Caucasus in rocky terrain above tree line. Larger than Black Grouse, almost Capercaillie size with very heavy build. Grey with much white on head. Flanks have *rusty-brown* and yellowish-white *stripes. Flight feathers whitish*. Has bare tarsi like pheasants. More closely related to *Alectoris* partridges than to grouse.

Caspian Snowcock *Tetraogallus caspius* L 65. Sedentary in E Turkey and Iran. Like Caucasian Snowcock although larger, darker and less reddish-brown in the plumage.

Willow Grouse female summer
Willow Grouse male spring
Willow Grouse winter

Red Grouse male spring
Red Grouse flock flying over moorland
Red Grouse female summer on nest

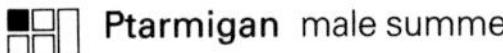

Ptarmigan male summer
Ptarmigan female (left) and male spring
Caspian Snowcock adult male calling
Ptarmigan females winter
Ptarmigan male winter

Caucasian Snowcock

Gallinaceous birds

Capercaillie *Tetrao urogallus* L ♂86, ♀61. Re-introduced to Scotland in 19th century. Occurs mainly in larger coniferous forests with some taller trees. Favourite winter foods are pine needles (droppings characteristic: 12mm-thick, curved cylinders), in summer bilberries, in autumn aspen leaves. In the early mornings picks up gravel from forest roads. Walks through the forest but is quick to take flight (characteristically loud wing noise); then cock easily identified by immense size and *big black tail*, while hen can be confused with hen Black Grouse but has larger and *dark chestnut-red tail*. Longer flights with fast wingbeats varied with long glides. Rigid wings appear short in proportion to long thick neck and long tail (closed). In April the cocks display in a loose group at established area within the forest. At evening gatherings belching, bellowing calls are heard. Display in tree begins in dawn silence, consists of clicks (double, with dry, wooden ring), gulps (a violent 'cork-popping', audible up to c.300m) and whetting sounds (ecstatic grinding). In ground display (when the forest is awake) the whetting calls may be exchanged for crashing leaps into the air. The surrounding hens give a slow cackle, 'krok, krok, krok'. Polygamous. The hen alone guards the chicks. R

Black Grouse *Tetrao tetrix* L ♂53, ♀41. Uncommon, much diminished in Britain. Inhabits coniferous forest, but attracted to bogs, clearings and meadows, also to heather moors. Birch buds are favoured winter food. Rather shy. Cock is noticeably smaller than cock Capercaillie, also shows *white wingbars on (noisy) rising*. The hen differs from hen Capercaillie in smaller tail and *darker brown, less rusty plumage*. Lyre or fork of tail on the other hand difficult to make out. Flight: series of wingbeats varied with long glides, and shows a considerably smaller head/neck than the Capercaillie. Has collective display ('lek') in spring. The cocks gather at dawn out on an established bog or moss, frozen lake or forest clearing – somewhere exposed. Often 8–10 cocks in one lek, sometimes considerably more. Display posture is crouched and inflated with white 'water lily' at the rear (gleams in the darkness) and bulging red combs above the eyes. Plenty of conflict, even fights. Makes leaps into the air showing white underwings. Display call is a *bubbling cooing* and resounding hisses 'choo-EESH'. Later (in morning sun) solo display from bog pines, cooing then much louder, audible for a couple of miles. The hen has a fast cackle, ending with a nasal slide: 'kakakakakaKEH-ah'. Polygamous. The hen alone guards the chicks. R

'Rackelhahn' Hybrid between hen Capercaillie and cock Black Grouse. Well known on Continent from time when gamebird populations were strong but cock Capercaillies were severely reduced through shooting displaying birds. The males emerge on Black Grouse leks. Has 'shrunken' cock Capercaillie tail and head like cock Black Grouse.

Caucasian Black Grouse *Tetrao mlokosiewiczi* L 50. Inhabits meadow and bush land in the Caucasus. Like Black Grouse but cock *lacks white wingbars*, and tail is longer, *lyre smaller*. Undertail-coverts are *all-black*. Hen's tail is square-cut.

▶ **Hazel Grouse** *Bonasa bonasia* L 35. Sedentary and local in central and eastern half of Europe in coniferous forests, preferably damp, dense and tangled spruce with birch and alder beside the streams. Occur in pairs. Difficult to see but not shy, can be called up by whistling its call. Rather *greyish-brown*, the sexes relatively similar, though hen's throat brown, smudgily bordered white, cock's brownish-black with more distinctly defined white border. *Crown tuft*, twitches when nervous. On rising, lower back and tail appear uniform lavender-grey. Characteristic noise from series of wingbeats: 'boorr, boorr'. Usually lands in trees. Advertising call thin like Goldcrest's but drawn-out, sucking: 'tseeuu-EEE titititi'. Alarm a very rapid twitter, 'pyittittittittitt-ett-ett'. Chicks only a few days old can fly up into the trees, distinguished by dark line through eye; tended by the hen alone.

Capercaillie female

Black Grouse female on nest

Capercaillie male in ground display to group of females

Black Grouse males displaying at lek

Rackelhahn

Caucasian Black Grouse, ♂

Hazel Grouse adult male

Hazel Grouse female

Gallinaceous birds

Partridges and pheasants

Partridges and pheasants (family Phasianidae) live in open country such as arable land, heaths or sunny mountain slopes. Often run, rather reluctant to take flight. Large clutches.

Chukar *Alectoris chukar* L 33. Breeds in open barren mountainous country, in Europe in Thrace (Greece) and bordering parts of Bulgaria. Very like Rock Partridge, but *bib is creamy-white* (not snow-white) and its black upper border touches only uppermost part of bill base. Call: nervous series of nasal, cracked clucks in falsetto, e.g. 'kakakakakachuckAR-chuckAR-chuckAR- . . . .

Rock Partridge *Alectoris graeca* L 33. Common in S Europe on very steep mountainsides above 1200m, essentially with plenty of rocks and boulders, preferably also southward-facing and with mosaic of meadow and bush vegetation, but forest is often also accepted (in Balkan peninsula deciduous forest) if conditions otherwise right. In winter often goes up to exposed windblown areas. Runs very ably (especially uphill), reluctant to fly. Very like Chukar but has *snow-white bib*, and its black upper border follows upper mandible down to corners of bill. Differs from Red-legged Partridge mainly in that *black lower border of bib is distinct*, not broken up. Call: repeated series at galloping pace of quite deep and hollow clucks, e.g. 'CHEkore-CHEkore- . . . ', accelerating and increasing in intensity towards end.

Barbary Partridge *Alectoris barbara* L 33. Breeds on dry bushy mountainsides, in Europe on Sardinia and Gibraltar. *Blue-grey bib framed with chestnut-brown.* Brown crown/central nape shows up well on rising, resembles mohican hair-cut. Call: series of shrill, broken monosyllabic clucks with interposed double notes (trotting rhythm with 'stumbling steps'), e.g. 'krett krett krett kretERRR krett krett . . .'.

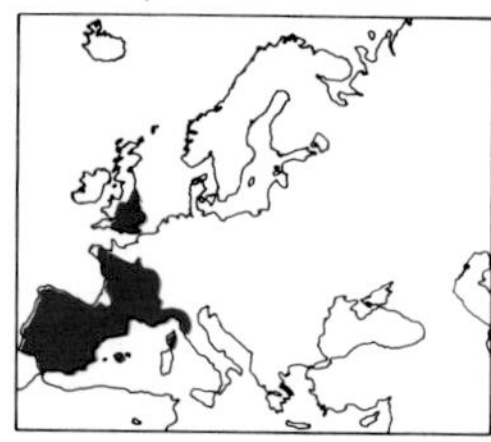

Red-legged Partridge *Alectoris rufa* L 35. Common in agricultural country, on dry bushy heaths and also in rocky mountains. Like Grey Partridge, but small black-framed bib is striking. At closer range note that *lower area of the black frame is broken up into small black patches* (species-specific) and that bill and legs are gaudy red. On rising none of this is visible, Red-legged is then very like Grey Partridge with its rust-red tail. But even directly from behind one can see some *orange*, not present on Grey Partridge. Immature very like Grey Partridge, does not have red legs (but greyish-pink, immature Grey brownish-yellow), but has diffuse dark vertical bars on flanks instead of yellowish-white lengthways streaks. More inclined to run away than the Grey; differs also in habit of perching on fence posts and even up trees. Call: rhythmically repeated of notes in hoarse broken voice (rather like Grey Partridge), 'kuchek-CHER-kuchek-CHER- . . . ' R

Grey Partridge *Perdix perdix* L 30. Commonest and most widespread of Europe's partridges. Found in open country, especially farmland with hedgerows. Numbers fluctuate. Completely terrestrial. Cock and hen together tend the chicks. The coveys keep very close together, squat firmly. All rise at same time with wing noise and loud 'grrree-grrree- . . . '. Clearly smaller than Pheasant (but beware of vaguely similar-looking half-grown Pheasant chicks). Rather grey-brown, but rusty-red tail conspicuous on rising. *Head orange.* Cock has large *dark brown patch below*, hen usually a less obvious patch. On spring evenings cock's creaky 'kiERRR-ik, kiERRR-ik' (=Perdix!) is heard. R

Black Francolin *Francolinus francolinus* L 33. Breeds in Turkey and south of the Caspian Sea in dense scrub and grassland (agricultural fields in Israel). Male *black below* with white cheek patches and reddish-brown neck band and undertail-coverts; both sexes dark with paler 'cloven-hoof' marks. Crown, back and wings brown-spotted. Rarely seen but *easily spotted by call*, a strong and rhythmic, slightly hoarse 7-syllabic 'kok, KEEEK kee-kee-kah kee-kEEK'.

■□ Chukar
□■ Chukar

Chukar

Rock Partridge

■□□ Red-legged Partridge
□■□ Red-legged Partridge
□□■ Grey Partridge male

Barbary Partridge

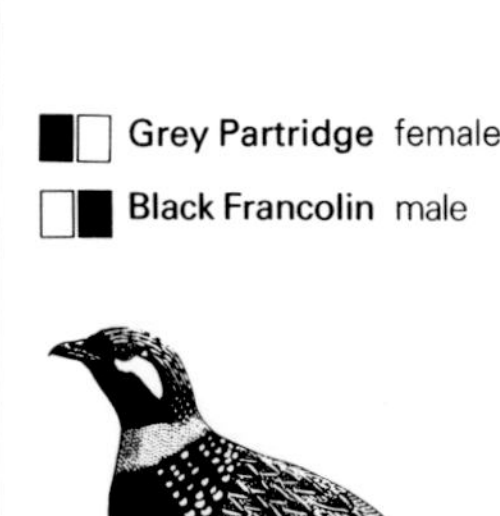

■□ Grey Partridge female
□■ Black Francolin male

Black Francolin, ♂

Gallinaceous birds

Pheasant *Phasianus colchicus* L ♂85, ♀60. Originally introduced from SW Asia. Common in open wooded terrain and agricultural land with copses, hedges, reeds etc. Often seen on open fields. Both sexes have *long, pointed tails* and short, rounded wings. The cock is very colourful, with bright red cheek patches contrasting with greenish-black head and neck. Plumage varies depending on the origin of the introduced stock. Usually distinct *white ring around the neck*. The hen is more nondescript pale brown with dark markings but the long tail is characteristic. Note that half-grown but fully fledged Pheasant chick has red-tinted short tail, can therefore be confused with Grey Partridge. Takes flight in rapid noisy climb when put up. Flies rapidly, but only short distances. Spends the night in trees, often in small flocks. Feeds on spilled grain, seeds and berries. The cock's loud, explosive, two-note hacking call is followed by a series of noisy wingbeats. R

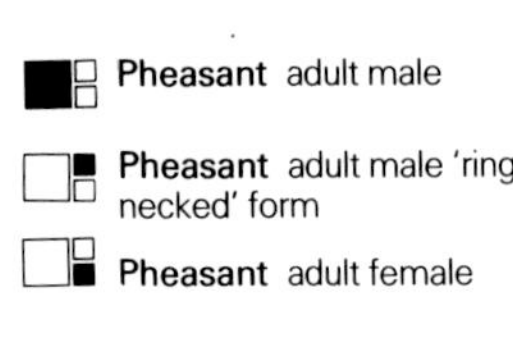

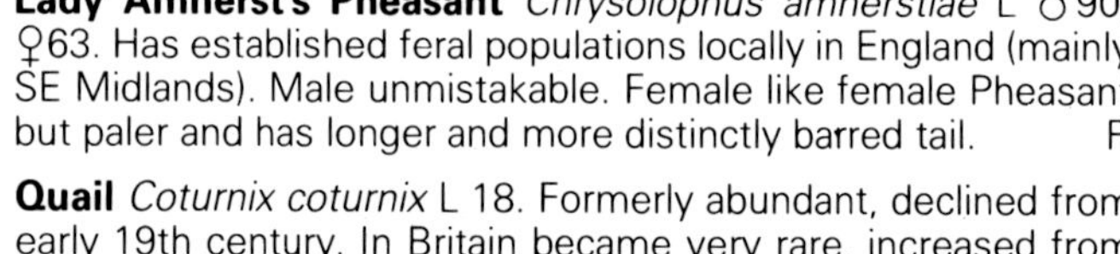

Lady Amherst's Pheasant, ♂

Lady Amherst's Pheasant *Chrysolophus amherstiae* L ♂90, ♀63. Has established feral populations locally in England (mainly SE Midlands). Male unmistakable. Female like female Pheasant but paler and has longer and more distinctly barred tail. R

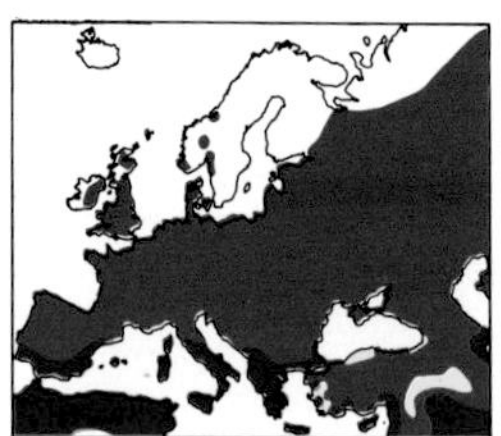

Quail *Coturnix coturnix* L 18. Formerly abundant, declined from early 19th century. In Britain became very rare, increased from mid 1940s, but still very uncommon and irregular. Inhabits large open fields of corn and grass and clover pastures, keeps well concealed in the vegetation. Long-distance migrant, arriving in May and returning in Oct. Much smaller than other gallinaceous birds: *size of a barely ⅓-grown Grey Partridge chick*. Has *no rust-red on the tail*. Is a washed-out brown with paler streaking on back and sides. Adult male has dark on the throat, unlike female. In size and appearance similar to Andalusian Hemipode (see below). Very difficult to flush (and one is seldom given the chance, since it lives mostly in crops). Flies low and markedly slowly, hunched up with retracted head, appears round-backed. Wings are surprisingly long and narrow (relatively speaking), held bowed with very fast, shallow beats. Glides between series of wingbeats almost negligible. In flight does not resemble a small Grey Partridge but rather a snipe, albeit a straight- and slow-flying one. Attracts attention mostly by its call, a far-carrying, trisyllabic whistle like dripping water, 'KWIC, kwic-ic' (often written 'wet-my-lips'), which is repeated persistently. (But beware confusion with Curlew's distress call, 'kyoi-yoi-yoi', which is often heard during the night in early summer.) May be heard for a large part of the summer (June-July), both day and night but mostly at dusk. S

Quail adult female

Quail adult male

Lady Amerherst's Pheasant adult male

Hemipodes

(order Gruiformes, family Turnicidae) are small, quail-like birds related to cranes and rails. Males take care of the young, and female has the more colourful plumage. (The species is illustrated here for easier comparison with the rather similar Quail.)

Andalusian Hemipode *Turnix sylvatica* L 15. Very rare and local breeder in SW Europe in dense ground vegetation. Very shy and unobtrusive. For the most part inhabits dense thickets and grasslands. Very like Quail, but has *pale, orange patch on the breast* and brownish-black spots on the sides. More closely related to cranes and rails than to gallinaceous birds. Usually seen singly or in pairs and family groups. Very difficult to flush. When seen if flight, note *smallness* and *very short tail*. Wings produce whirring noise. Call a characteristic muffled and reverberating 'hoo-hoo-hoo', heard particularly often at dusk and dawn on clear nights, uttered by female, which also has the brightest plumage. (Not illustrated)

Cranes and allies

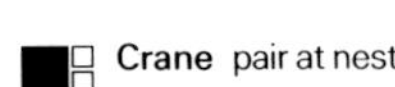

Crane pair at nest

Crane adults in flight

Demoiselle Crane adults in flight

Cranes and allies

(order Gruiformes) are a diverse group of birds. All are swampland birds with long legs. Other characters are very variable.

CRANES (family Gruidae) are tall, stately birds with long legs. The long neck is extended in flight. Gregarious outside the breeding season. Have a peculiar dancing display. Clutch 2 eggs. p. 90
BUSTARDS (family Otididae) are large or medium-sized, long-legged and long-necked birds. They are terrestrial and prefer extensive, open plains. Gait is slow and deliberate. Very wary. Clutches 2–5 eggs. p. 92
RAILS (family Rallidae) may be divided into two subfamilies: *Rails and crakes* are primarily wading birds, medium-sized to small, with compact bodies, long legs and long toes. Spend most of their life hidden away in tall vegetation, rather shy. Attract attention mainly by their calls. Clutches 5–15 eggs. p. 94
Coots are chiefly swimming birds, duck-sized with lobed toes. Bills short and thick. Gregarious outside the breeding season. Clutches 5–12 eggs. p. 96
HEMIPODES (family Turnicidae). see p. 88

Crane *Grus grus* L 115–130, W 185–220. Breeds rather sparsely on watery bogs and in reed marsh in forests, mainly in deserted regions, sometimes unsuspected near farms; is unobtrusive. On migration rests on arable fields, at favoured sites in some numbers. Spends the night in marshes. *Big*, silvery-grey, on the ground at great distance can look like grazing sheep; looks 'bushy' at the rear, the 'bush' being formed by the elongated tertials which cover the short tail. Breeding Cranes are rusty-brown on the back owing to their being washed with bog water. The immature lacks contrast in the face (Ostrich-like). Unlike herons, cranes fly with *extended neck*. The silver-grey can flash whitish in slanting light and recall White Stork. Migrating flocks form V or oblique line, usually fly high, glide while gaining height by soaring (leisurely progress; goose Vs appear to be in a hurry). The pair has a mating dance in spring: deep bows, high fluttering leaps; more peculiar than attractive. Very attractive by contrast are the Crane pair's duets, e.g. 'krrookrraw/kaw-kaw-kaw, . . .', with pure *horn sound and extremely far-carrying*. In summer the breeding pair leads a secretive life, often leaves the breeding bog and leads the young to pure wooded land. Non-breeding Cranes move south as early as late summer, breeders not until September. In the adults' chorus of trumpeting, jarring 'krraw' sounds can then be heard the juveniles' remarkable 'cheerp, cheerp' (like a small bird).

Siberian White Crane *Grus leucogeranus* L 135. Extremely rare, threatened with extinction. Breeds in Ob area and in NE Yakutsk; attempts are in progress to build up new stock by transferring eggs to Cranes, which then become foster parents. Wintering areas include NE India (Bharatpur). A few are seen at staging post in Volga delta, on route to and from winter sites which probably lie in Iran. Tied to marshes, shuns fields. Wholly *white plumage* with *black primaries*, *red legs* and red face. Calls soft, not so far-carrying as Crane's.

Demoiselle Crane *Anthropoides virgo* L 97–107, W 170–190. Breeds on steppe and dry high plateaux in central Asia and, sparsely west to S Russia. Winters, often with Cranes, on fields and in marshes, the majority in India but also with a population in NE Africa. The latter can be seen at staging posts in Cyprus, in August (autumn passage thus a whole month earlier than Crane). Differs from Crane in smaller size, *long white ear tufts, elongated black breast feathers* and in elongated tertials not being 'bushy'. In flight, when size difficult to judge and ear tufts 'plastered down', is remarkably hard to tell from Crane, but *the black on the neck extends to below the crop*. Calls resemble Crane's but are slightly shriller and flatter.

Demoiselle Crane

Siberian White Crane three adults, with Coots and Gadwall in background

Siberian White Crane in flight

Cranes and allies

Great Bustard *Otis tarda* L ♂100, ♀80, W ♂230, ♀180. Rare and local breeder on large open plains (steppe or cultivated land). Formerly widespread in England, last bred in 1832 (Suffolk); attempts at re-introduction unsuccessful. In cold winters may find its way far from its normal range. Feeds mainly on vegetable matter, but also on insects, frogs etc. Very shy and difficult to approach. The male is Europe's heaviest bird (normal weight 8–16 kg); the females are considerably lighter (3.5–5 kg). When walking on the ground the bustard may be taken at first for a roe deer or sheep. Gait deliberate. In flight looks like a giant goose with eagle wings (legs not protruding). *The wing action is powerful* and uninterrupted (no tendency to soaring flight as in the relatively light Crane). In flight *the large white wing patches* are very conspicuous. Usually occurs in flocks. On spring mornings the males display – a spectacular sight. They begin by raising the tail and drawing the neck towards the back, then continue by inflating the neck like a balloon (the head is almost swamped), at the same time as displaying the long bristly moustaches straight up in the air. Large 'water lilies' of snow-white coverts under the tail and on the wings are turned forwards, and the climax is reached when the whole bird seems to be buried in a white foam bath. Usually silent, but during the breeding season occasionally gives a raucous barking call. V

Little Bustard *Tetrax tetrax* L 43, W 90. Rather scarce on grassy plains or in open agricultural country in S Europe. Shy but not as unapproachable as Great Bustard. The male discards his striking black-and-white neck pattern in winter and then resembles the female. Flies away with relatively *quick* (like Black Grouse) but not very propulsive *wingbeats*. Wings are hunched and rigid which adds to the impression of a gamebird. *The wings appear almost completely white* – only the four outermost primaries have much black. The 4th primary is stunted in the male and shaped in such a way that it produces a characteristic high whistling wing noise in flight. Often seen in small flocks. During the display in spring the cock stretches itself up with raised tail and every 8–10 seconds throws back its head (with raised neck feathers, so that the white neck markings sparkle even more) and utters the display call, a dry 'prrrt' (which sounds about as loud at 50m as at 500m range). It also makes fluttering leaps into the air from time to time. V

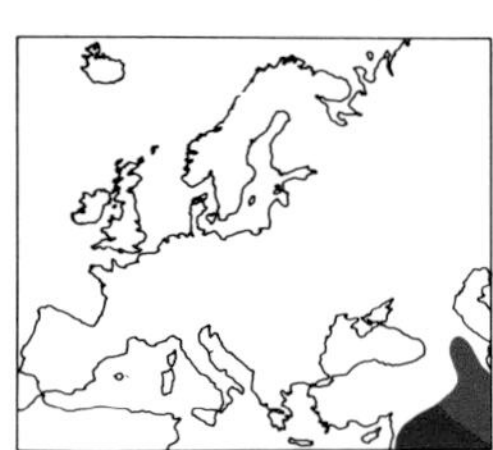

Houbara Bustard *Chlamydotis undulata* L 63, W 150. Very rare vagrant (mostly in autumn) from Asia or Africa. Prefers steppes and semi-deserts but may occur in agricultural country. The favourite quarry of the Arabs when hunting with Sakers. Very gregarious where abundant. The cock is nearly as big as female Great Bustard. Distinguished from other bustards by *black line down the neck* (elongated feathers) and *smaller, restricted white wing patch*. Has a short crest, most obvious in the cock. Expert at sneaking away unseen and without taking wing. Very alert and difficult to approach on foot. V

Great Bustard male in full display to female

Great Bustard male at start of display

Great Bustard, full display

Great Bustard ♂

Little Bustard male giving fluttering leap in display

Great Bustard Group taking off

Little Bustard male

Little Bustard ♂

Houbara Bustard ♂

Little Bustard female

Houbara Bustard

Houbara Bustard in flight

Cranes and allies

Water Rail *Rallus aquaticus* L 28. Common in reedbeds (and in sedge bogs with tall tufts). Fairly dark in plumage, dark-spotted brown above, beautiful blue-grey below with belly area striped in black and white. Short tail, often held cocked, when shows white undertail-coverts with touches of pinkish-buff and black. *Long bill, largely gaudy red.* Legs long, pale brown. Difficult to see but makes presence known by its voice. Most active at dusk and dawn. Calls are more loud than musical, usually uttered at night or when it is disturbed. In spring male utters a pounding 'kipp, kipp, kipp, kipp . . . ' in long rhythmic series. Easily recognised is an *explosive (pig-like!) squealing,* which rapidly dies away, 'grruueeit, grruit, groo, gru'. Associated with this is a half-stifled groaning 'uuugh'. On spring nights a soft rumbling 'piirrr' (also the squealing call) is heard from rails flying high in the air. Female's courtship song is an associated 'piip-piip-piirrrr', like female Little Crake's call in structure but still distinct in its high-pitched tone and unmistakable Water Rail voice. RSW

Spotted Crake *Porzana porzana* L 23. Uncommon breeder on lakes with sedge and horse-tail marsh. Extremely rare in Britain, less so on passage. Very difficult to see. Resembles Water Rail, both when it scampers past and when it flutters away, but has fairly short bill. Fore edge of wing snow-white. Undertail-coverts buff-white. Its call carries widely on spring and early summer nights: *sharp, rhythmically repeated whistles,* 'whitt, whitt, whitt, . . . ' (at very long range sounds like dripping water), with rhythm of just over one whistle per second. SP

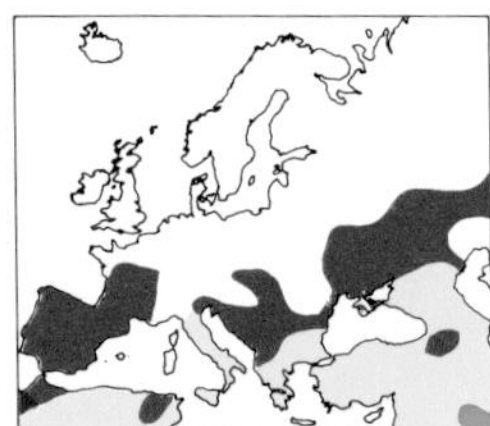

Baillon's Crake *Porzana pusilla* L 18. Breeds in S Europe, very rare vagrant further north. Prefers marshy meadows, swamps and pools overgrown with sedge. Secretive. Adults (sexes alike) differ from male of Little Crake in heavily barred flanks, greyish-pink legs and lack of red spot at base of bill. The immature resembles immature Little Crake, but is a trifle more heavily barred and has *irregularly scattered ring-shaped white spots on the wing-coverts* (not white spots arranged in rows as in Little Crake). *The call is low* and unmusical, *reminiscent of call of both male Garganey and several frog species,* a 2–3 second long dry rattle 'trrrr-trrrr-trrrr- . . . ' audible over 200–300m. V

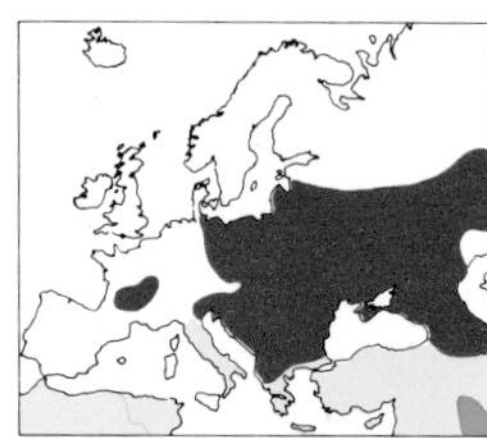

Little Crake *Porzana parva* L 19. Breeds mainly in eastern half of Europe, rare vagrant north and west. Found in reedy swamps and ponds. Secretive. The male differs from Baillon's Crake in less strongly marked barring on the side, green legs and red spot at base of bill. Female is pale sandy-buff below, not blue-grey, has green legs and red at base of bill. Immature resembles immature Baillon's – see latter for differences. The male's courtship call is a *far-carrying series of clucks,* the voice recalls barking of a small dog. Notes maintain a low tempo for a long time but then accelerate, at same time falling in pitch, and merge into a rapid stammer, 'kuAK . . . kuAK . . . kuAK, kuAK, kuAK kuAK-kwa-wa-a-a-a-a-a'. Female (also male?) calls 'kuek-kuek-kwarrr'. V

Now very rare breeder in N. of range

Corncrake *Crex crex* L 26. Breeds in moist thick grass, clover and damp meadowland. Has decreased markedly over most of range. In Britain and Ireland familiar bird in 19th century, before mechanised farming, now restricted mainly to Ireland and west Scotland (but still decreasing). Suffers from grass mown early. Arrives from middle of April. Size similar to a small, slender Grey Partridge. Brownish plumage and prominent *rusty-red on the wings,* especially conspicuous in flight. Very difficult to catch sight of; runs away, concealed in the vegetation, even when driven. Can be called up by imitating its voice and may then show itself briefly. If flushed, after all, the wings glisten rust-red. Flight excursions short, low and clumsy. Gives away its presence by its *loud, creaky and rasping, two-syllable 'rerrrp-rerrrp'* (like grating a comb on a matchbox), repeated almost once a second for hours during early summer nights (more sporadically in the daytime). SP

■□□ **Water Rail** adult
□■□ **Spotted Crake**
□□■ **Spotted Crake**

■□□ **Baillon's Crake** adult
□■□ **Baillon's Crake** adult from in front
□□■ **Baillon's Crake** adult from behind

Corncrake male calling in spring
Little Crake imm.
Corncrake in breeding habitat

Cranes and allies

Purple Gallinule *Porphyrio porphyrio* L 48. Breeds rarely in SW Europe in marshes with dense vegetation, especially larger reed-beds. Easy to identify by *chicken size, large red bill* and *long red legs.* Immature is best identified by size and bill shape. Shy in behaviour, but more inclined to leave shelter of clumps of rushes in autumn. Very noisy, making deep tooting calls.

Allen's Gallinule *Porphyrula alleni* L 25. A very rare visitor to the Mediterranean countries, also ocassionally further north, from breeding sites in Africa. Lives in swamps with dense vegetation. *Small size, red bill* with *green-blue frontal shield* and *red legs* together with *shimmering green upperparts* easily distinguish this species from other gallinules. (Not illustrated.) V

Moorhen *Gallinula chloropus* L 33. Common in swamps, ponds and lakes with shore vegetation. Often seen in parks, where it walks about on grass. Places its nest in dense vegetation in or near the water. Swims readily with vigorous nodding movements. Adult easily recognised by sooty-black body colour, *red base to the bill, greenish legs,* white line along the side, and *white undertail-coverts* with a black central line. The white side line and the undertail pattern also distinguish the immature from young Coot. The tail is held high, and is jerked both when swimming and when walking. Short flights are low and with dangling legs; looks unstable but likes to make circular flights on spring nights, calling. Large repertoire of calls, e.g. a very characteristic sudden, bubbling 'pyurrrrk' and a sharp 'KIKack'. May sit all night or fly around at night calling with a fast clucking 'kreck-kreck-kreck . . .kreck-kreck-kreck . . .', an alternative being a rapid, shrill, nasal 'kekeke . . . kekeke . . .'. RW

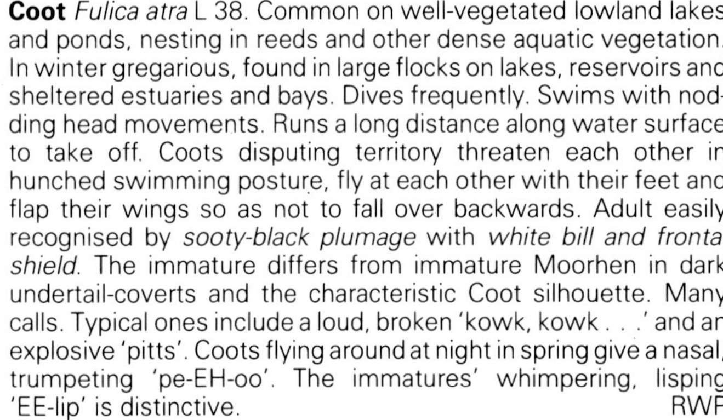

Coot *Fulica atra* L 38. Common on well-vegetated lowland lakes and ponds, nesting in reeds and other dense aquatic vegetation. In winter gregarious, found in large flocks on lakes, reservoirs and sheltered estuaries and bays. Dives frequently. Swims with nodding head movements. Runs a long distance along water surface to take off. Coots disputing territory threaten each other in hunched swimming posture, fly at each other with their feet and flap their wings so as not to fall over backwards. Adult easily recognised by *sooty-black plumage* with *white bill and frontal shield.* The immature differs from immature Moorhen in dark undertail-coverts and the characteristic Coot silhouette. Many calls. Typical ones include a loud, broken 'kowk, kowk . . .' and an explosive 'pitts'. Coots flying around at night in spring give a nasal, trumpeting 'pe-EH-oo'. The immatures' whimpering, lisping 'EE-lip' is distinctive. RWP

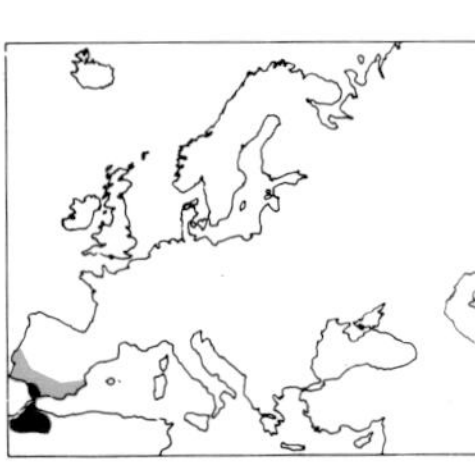

Crested Coot *Fulica cristata* L 40. Small European population has decreased, now uncertain as a breeder. Very like Coot, but the two red knobs above the white frontal shield distinguish them during breeding season; the knobs are, however, difficult to see at longer distances, and they are duller and much smaller after nesting. Note instead the *blue-tinted bill* (Coot's is yellowish-white) and the *shape of the feathering at the base of the upper mandible* (see fig.). *Wings are pure black* without the white rear edge that can be seen on the Coot's wing in flight. Resembles Coot in behaviour, but is more shy. Call two-toned, deeper than Coot's, 'keruck'.

■□□ **Purple Gallinule** adult

□■□ **Purple Gallinule** adult picking food

□□■ **Moorhen** adult

■□□ **Moorhen** adult

□■□ **Moorhen** adult feeding chick

□□■ **Moorhen** juv.

■□□ **Coot** adults

□■□ **Coot** adult taking off from water

□□■ **Coot** adult on nest with chicks

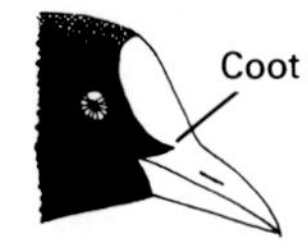

winter

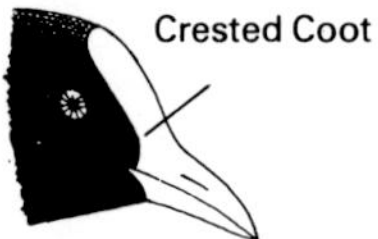

■□□ **Coot** juv.

□■□ **Crested Coot** adult summer breeding

□□■ **Crested Coot** adult summer flock after breeding

Waders, gulls and auks

Waders, gulls and auks (order Charadriiformes). Oystercatchers (family Haematopodidae) are large shorebirds with bright red bills and black heads. Plovers (family Charadriidae) are small to medium-sized, with long legs and short bills.

Oystercatcher *Haematopus ostralegus* L 43. Breeds commonly along coasts, on islands and coastal meadows, locally also inland. Shorebird, which can open large bivalves with skilful incisions, but also does a lot of feeding on fields. Heavy build, unmistakably pied *black and white*, noisy. *Bill coral-red, legs pink*. A white bar across the throat in winter plumage and some juveniles. Flies low over the water, announcing itself with a shrill 'ke BEEK, keBEEK'. The bowed wings are beaten quickly and shallowly, and flight therefore closely resembles that of duck. Migrating flocks, usually in an arc shape. Flight display has slow, stiff wingbeats like the plovers. In spring often runs around in circles in groups with the neck held forwards and downwards and open bill pointing downwards, uttering trilling 'beek, beek, beek, birrrrrrrrr-iBEEK-iBEEK . . .'. Alarm a shrill, short 'beek'. RWP

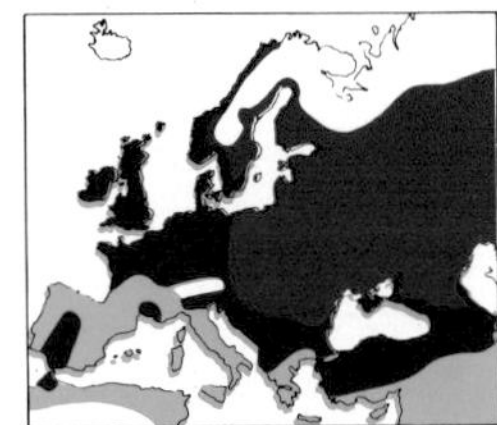

Lapwing *Vanellus vanellus* L 30. Breeds commonly on coastal meadows, lakeside marshy meadows, fields, arable land, moors and bogs. Breeding numbers in Britain have recently declined enormously. Easily recognised by *long thin crest*, black and white markings (black green-glossed) and *uniquely broad, rounded wings* – males in particular have veritable 'frying-pans'! Female spotted white around bill base and on throat. Immatures have shorter crest and lack black on the throat. Early nester. Display flight of males remarkable: after a slow-motion start with deep, heaving wingbeats, the Lapwing steps up to full speed; travels along close to the ground with muffled droning wing noise ('engine throb'), fiercely pitching from side to side, suddenly to shoot up in the air with a shrill 'chay-o-wee'; then utters one or two short 'eVIP-eVIP' calls in normal level flight, only to dive promptly head-first towards the ground with acrobatic rolls and a drawn-out 'cheew-o-wee'; then continues with the frenetic zigzag flight. On breeding grounds mobs intruding humans, foxes (active at night) etc with a shrill 'WEEW-ee, WEEW-ee'. Adult Lapwings migrate from the north during the summer. Migrating flocks relatively disorderly. Flight is with clipped wingbeats but leisurely for a wader. Juveniles gather in autumn in large flocks on the fields, feed on worms in plover fashion. RWP

Spur-winged Plover *Hoplopterus spinosus* L 28. Occurs rarely and locally in SE Europe. Frequents marshlands, sandy beaches on saltwater lakes and irrigated fields. Black and white markings make the species easy to identify. In flight distinguished from Sociable Plover by *black secondaries* and from White-tailed Plover by *black tail*. Has a hint of a crest. Behaviour like Lapwing. Wings blunt but not broad-tipped and rounded as Lapwing's. The *dark grey legs* are proportionately *longer* than in Lapwing. Alarm call is a loud, rapid 'chip-chip' and similar. Display call a fast, harsh, sonorous 'charadee-deeoo', superficially reminiscent of Golden Oriole's song.

Sociable Plover *Chettusia gregaria* L 30. Breeds (in declining numbers) on steppes. Very rare vagrant to W Europe. At a distance appears grey-brown, but in flight *white secondaries* and white on tail are conspicuous. Black crown, *white supercilium*, dark eye-stripe. *Belly black and chestnut-brown* in summer, white in winter. *Legs greyish-black*. The flight is Lapwing-like but the wing shape more normal. The calls are mostly harsh chatters, often trisyllabic, e.g. 'kretsch-kretsch-kretsch'. Also gives thick, scratchy, nervously rapid chuckle 'greckreckreckreck . . .'. V

White-tailed Plover *Chettusia leucura* L 28. Very rare vagrant from W Asia (mainly in late autumn). Like Sociable Plover but *legs much longer* and *yellowish*, head and belly pale. Differs from Spur-winged Plover in pale head, *white tail* and long yellow legs. V

■□□ **Oystercatcher** adult summer on nest
□■□ **Oystercatcher** imm.
□□■ **Oystercatcher** flock in flight

■□□ **Lapwing** adult male on nest
□■□ **Lapwing** juv.
□□■ **Lapwing** flock in flight with several Black-headed Gulls

■□□ **Spur-winged Plover** adult
□■□ **Spur-winged Plover** in flight
□□■ **Sociable Plover** adult spring (moulting from winter plumage, chestnut and black on belly still missing)

Spur-winged Plover

■□□ **White-tailed Plover** adult
□■□ **White-tailed Plover** adult in flight
□□■ **Sociable Plover** adult winter

Waders, gulls and auks

Ringed Plover *Charadrius hiaticula* L 18. Quite common, breeds along coasts on sandy and shingle beaches and short-grass shore meadow, also locally inland on heaths, by gravel-pits etc. Common on migration, alone or in small flocks, often among Dunlins. In winter common on mudflats. Appears longer-winged and flies with rather more clipped wingbeats than Dunlin. Runs very quickly ('rolling gait'). Seeks food in manner typical of small plovers (and some other plovers): alternatively trundling forward and standing dead still, suddenly bowing to pick up something. Always *white wingbar* and *pale legs* (bright orange-yellow in adults). Adult's bill orange-yellow with black tip, juvenile's dark. Call a gentle 'TOO-eep'. During display flight (wavering, with slow stiff wingbeats) a rapid murmuring 'TOO-widee-TOO-widee- . . .' is heard, alternating with differently stressed 'too-weDEE-too-weDEE- . . .'. RSWP

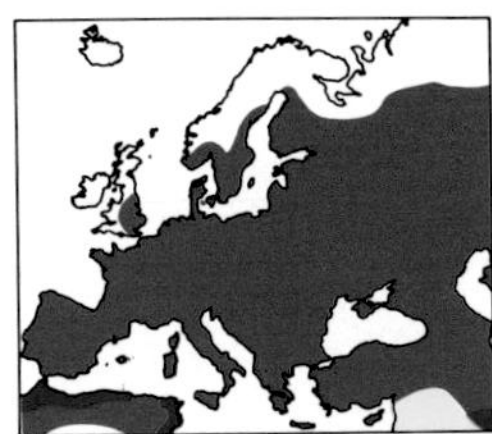

Little Ringed Plover *Charadrius dubius* L 16. Nests locally and sparsely on sand and gravel shores of inland waters (rarely coasts), and clay-pits and gravel-pits. Scarce even on passage. *Lacks wingbar*, always has pale legs and *dark bill. Yellow ring around eye* very conspicuous in the male, generally less so in the female, negligible in the juvenile. The juvenile is best distinguished from juvenile Ringed Plover by lack of white patch behind/above the eye and by yellowish-brown zone between brown crown and pale forehead (as well as by call and all-brown wings). When flying away, flight is jerkier than Ringed Plover's (rather like Common Sandpiper's). Voice relatively loud and ringing. Common call 'p(i)ew' (almost monosyllabic). In wavering, slow-beating display flight (mostly at night) rapidly pounding 'pree-pree-pree- . . .', Sand Martin-like 'rrerererere . . .' and drawling 'prrrEE-aw, prrrEE-aw' are heard. S

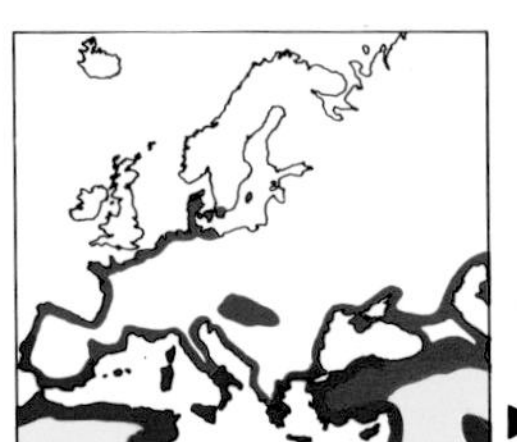

▶ **Kentish Plover** *Charadrius alexandrinus* L 16. Nests on sandy shores in SE Europe, also on saline steppe lakes. Rare on passage in S and E Britain. Even at long range appears *obviously pale* and white. Always *dark legs* typical of species (though immature's sometimes grey-brown). *Wingbar.* Head markings black in male, brown in female. The male's touch of orange colour on the crown and on the nape is visible at close range. Calls are a hoarse 'BEE-it' (funnily like distant human wolf-whistle), 'bip, bip', which can turn into giggly 'bibibibi . . .', as well as rapid, hoarse 'rrerererererere . . .', surprisingly similar to Dunlin display call. P

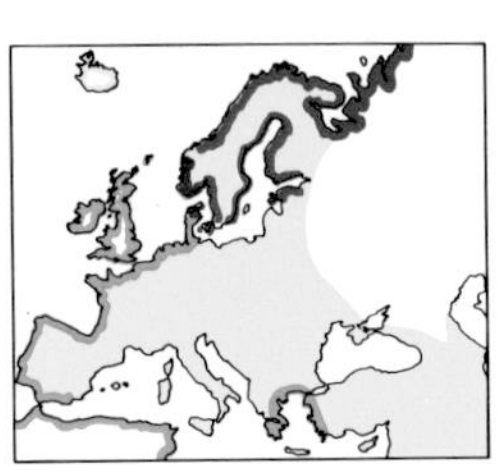

Turnstone *Arenaria interpres* L 23. Breeds on bare rocky, stony coast, also on shore meadows with boulders. On migration and in winter also found on sandbanks, mudflats and among seaweed, usually in small numbers. Unusual inland. Large as a Knot. Unmistakable *black, white and variegated red-brown pattern in summer plumage.* When a pair is seen together at breeding site, male is distinguished by slightly brighter colours. Winter plumage is considerably duller in coloration, blackish-grey and whitish. Juvenile like adult in winter plumage but has evenly buff-edged feathers above and also is finely spotted grey-brown on breast, not sooty-black. Feeds at water's edge, roots about, turns over stones and seaweed by pushing with bill or head. Sits guard on elevated rocks, gives alarm with strident, shrill accelerating series of notes: 'KYE-hwee-KYE-hwee-kyewee-wetetetetet'. Other calls include short 'kew' and chuckling 'tuk-e-tuk'. WP

■□□ **Ringed Plover** adult summer
□■□ **Ringed Plover** 1st-winter
□□■ **Ringed Plover** adults in flight

■□□ **Little Ringed Plover** adult male summer
□■□ **Little Ringed Plover** adult female summer
□□■ **Little Ringed Plover** juv. (a drop of mud makes the bill look thick)

■□□ **Kentish Plover** adult male
□■□ **Kentish Plover** adult female on nest
□□■ **Turnstone** adult male summer

■□□ **Turnstone** juvs.
□■□ **Turnstone** adult winter group
□□■ **Turnstone** flock (mostly adult summer) in flight

Waders, gulls and auks

Greater Sand Plover *Charadrius leschenaultii* L 23. Breeds in W and S Asia in stony deserts and on saline clayey steppes, appears in winter and on passage on sandy sea shores and saltpans. Rare vagrant in Europe. In summer plumage has rusty-orange breast band (of varying width; usually without black border) and black loral and forehead bands (some with completely black forehead, just as some Lesser Sand Plovers). Female's breast band weaker in colour than male's. In winter and juvenile plumages very like Lesser Sand Plover and Caspian Plover; is bigger than Lesser Sand but better distinguished from that species by *longer and more powerful bill* (proportionately bigger even than Grey Plover's), *bigger head, longer legs* (even project a little beyond tail in flight) which also are *paler, greenish-grey*; distinguished from Caspian Plover, apart from by bill size, by white underwings, pure white outer tail feathers, *obvious white wingbar*, incomplete greyish-brown breast patch (adult almost white in centre of breast) and also by fact that the pale supercilium is indistinct behind eye. The usual call is a fairly low, soft, rolling 'trrri' or 'trritrrit'. V

Lesser Sand Plover *Charadrius mongolus* L 20. Very rare vagrant to Europe from alpine region in central and E Asia. In winter season seen on grassland more often than Greater Sand Plover, but frequently joins it on mudflats and shorelines. Very similar to Greater Sand Plover but is *smaller*, has *shorter, stubbier bill, shorter legs* which are *dark grey*, generally darker than in Greater Sand Plover; white underwings, white wingbar and narrow white outer edges to tail. In summer plumage has broad rufous breast-band and black cheeks and forehead, in some with a small white spot above bill. Females apparently more variable than in Greater Sand and Caspian Plovers, some closely resemble males, others have clearly duller head pattern. In winter and juvenile plumage breast is white with grey-brown sides (may recall Kentish Plover when size is not evident); face and supercilium off-white. Cf. also Caspian Plover. Call similar to Greater Sand Plover's, but is shorter, harder and less rolling, 'chitik' and similar.

Caspian Plover *Charadrius asiaticus* L 20. Breeds on steppes, appears in winter quarters and on passage on savanna and other open grasslands. Very rare vagrant to W Europe. In manner and posture recalls Dotterel rather a lot. Male in summer plumage has a broad rusty-orange breast band with thin black lower border, female has a considerably weaker-coloured and mainly greyish-brown breast band. At this time distinctions from rather similar Greater Sand Plover and Lesser Sand Plover include whiter head (*lacks black lores and bar on forehead*). In winter and juvenile plumages very like Greater and Lesser Sand Plovers, but has *thin* medium-long *bill*; grey underwings; almost wholly grey tail; *wingbar short*, confined to centre of wing; almost invariably a *complete and broad, grey-brown breast patch* as well as distinct whitish supercilium, distinct also at rear of eye. Flight call 'chep', often repeated on rising, in tone rather reminiscent of Turnstone. V

Killdeer *Charadrius vociferus* L 25. Rare vagrant to W Europe from North America, where it breeds on fields, preferring same habitats as the Lapwing in Europe. *Double black breast band* and size distinguish this species on the ground. In flight recognised by distinct white wingbar, *long tail and reddish-brown rump*. Call a high 'kill-dee' (with same tone as young Long-eared Owl). V

■□□ **Greater Sand Plover** adult male summer, western race *columbinus*

□■□ **Greater Sand Plover** juv.

□□■ **Greater Sand Plover** juv.

■□□ **Lesser Sand Plover** adult male summer, race *atrifrons*

□■□ **Lesser Sand Plover** adult winter, moulting into summer, probably female

□□■ **Lesser Sand Plover** juv.

■□□ **Caspian Plover** adult male summer

□■□ **Caspian Plover** adult winter

□□■ **Caspian Plover** juv.

■■□ **Lesser Sand Plover** (left) with Greater Sand Plover winter

□□■ **Killdeer**

Waders, gulls and auks

Grey Plover *Pluvialis squatarola* L 29. Breeds on arctic tundra. Common winter visitor to coastal mudflats and sandy shores of W Europe and NW Africa. Usually seen singly or in small groups, often well spaced out (on spring migration often in big flocks). Rare inland. Adults in summer plumage have more highly variegated appearance than Golden Plover: more white on forehead and sides of breast, black of belly reaches up under wings. As in Golden Plover, female is less contrasty than male. Juvenile resembles winter adult, has grey patterning with pale yellow tinges but does not have golden-brown appearance as juvenile Golden Plover. In flight *conspicuous white tail/rump* and *pale wingbar* are distinctive, *black axillaries* unique. The call is a three-note, plaintive whistle; two variations in stress; 'pee-ooEE' and 'plee-OOee' WP

■□□ **Grey Plover** adult male summer
□■□ **Grey Plover** juv.
□□■ **Grey Plover** flock (five adults and one juv.) in flight summer

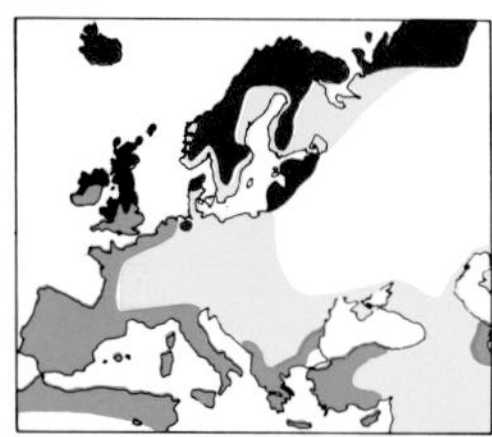

Golden Plover *Pluvialis apricaria* L 27. Breeds rather commonly in upland areas on moors, heathlands, bogs and peatlands, less common in south of range. On migration and in winter mostly on ploughed fields, meadows and pasture, permanent open grassland and occasionally mudflats, usually in compact flocks (can be very large), often with Lapwings. Flies rapidly and powerfully, on migration in blunt V formation. Northern populations in summer plumage are on average more contrasty and cleaner than the southern ones. Both lack black below in winter. Juvenile is yellow-toned brown. The Golden Plover has discernible pale wingbars but *no pale colour on tail/rump. White axillaries.* Gives a *monotone* melancholy whistle at different pitches; 'peeh' and pluuh'. During display flight (stiff slow-beating wings) a piping, melancholy, rhythmically pumping 'pleu-EEH-u, pleu-EEH-u . . .'. This often followed by a repetitive 'perPUUrlya-perPUUrlya- . . .' (normal flight; also heard on migration). RWP

■□□ **Golden Plover** adult male summer
□■□ **Golden Plover** juv.
□□■ **Golden Plover** winter flock in flight

Pacific Golden Plover *Pluvialis fulva* L 24. Very rare vagrant from arctic Asia and NW Alaska. Very like Golden Plover in plumage and behaviour but slightly smaller and *slimmer-bodied, longer-legged* and *narrower-winged.* Adult in summer plumage resembles northern Golden Plover, thus has undertail-coverts and flanks mostly white (cf. American Golden Plover); juvenile too like Golden Plover, but in all plumages distinguished by *grey axillaries* and *pale grey underwing-coverts,* not white underwing. Insignificant wingbar. Bill fine, legs thin. Difficult to separate from American Golden Plover, which see (earlier treated as conspecific). Calls similar to Golden Plover, e.g. a monosyllabic plaintive 'peeh', but include differing 'dlu-eep' (recalling Spotted Redshank). V

■□□ **American Golden Plover** juv.
□■□ **Pacific Golden Plover** winter
□□■ **Pacific Golden Plover** juv. in flight

American Golden Plover *Pluvialis dominica* L 26. Very rare vagrant from N America. Resembles Pacific Golden Plover (which see) in having *grey underwing,* but differs in following respects: slightly larger, proportionately *longer-winged* with *shorter legs and bill,* in adult summer plumage *more extensive black on flanks* (as in Grey Plover) *and undertail-coverts,* in juvenile plumage more grey appearance with darker back and crown, not so brightly spangled with golden spots, and with duskier, less white belly, often a shade *paler forehead and supercilium* above dark, narrow eye-stripe (in *P. fulva* usually yellowish supercilium and diffuse dark ear patch). Whether certain calls are species-specific and differ from Pacific Golden Plover's is not yet clarified. V

Dotterel *Charadrius morinellus* L 23. Breeds on high-lying mountain moors with lots of lichen and scree, at the upper levels for Golden Plovers. Scarce on migration (traditional sites on fields, occasionally coast). Female more clearly marked and a shade larger than male, does the courting. Juveniles lack the black on the belly, and dark orange coloration above it is faint, but they have the *white bands below the crown and upper breast.* The back in the juvenile is patterned in rusty-yellow on brownish-black background. The incubating male is renowned for his fearlessness. Females fly around high up, calling a high, indefatigable 'pwit, pwit, pwit, pwit . . .'. A Dunlin-like 'keerrr' on rising. SP

■□□ **Dotterel** adult male brooding chicks
□■□ **Dotterel** adult male
□□■ **Dotterel** juv.

Waders, gulls and auks

Small sandpipers (family Scolopacidae) are small in size, rather podgy, short-necked, short-legged waders. Most are Arctic breeders. Northward migration in Apr–May, southward passage mainly in July–Oct. Often occur in large mixed flocks (which regularly include Ringed Plovers), mostly along coasts.

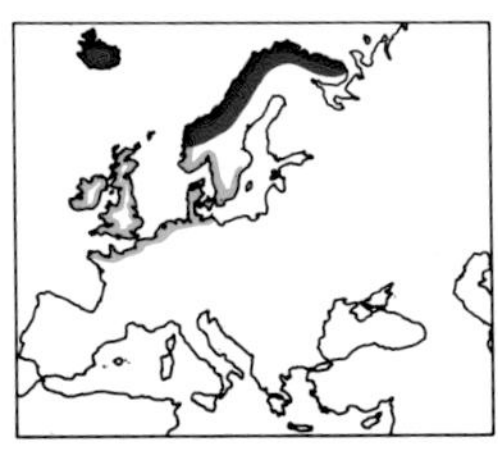

Purple Sandpiper *Calidris maritima* L 20. Uncommon breeder on high mountain plateaux, in Arctic down to sea level. Winters locally in small flocks on rocky islets and shores. Clearly larger than Dunlin. *Darkest* of the smaller sandpipers: *uniform slate-grey* in winter plumage with *orange-yellow legs* (*short*) and *bill base* (conspicuous at long range); in summer plumage rather more vividly marked in dark grey and rusty-brown, with grey-brown legs. Commonest call is a full, loud 'kuit', and lower 'kwit-it, kwit'. Alarm a laughing 'puhuhuhuhu'. During display flight a Dunlin-like droning 'trrüee-trrüee-trrüee-. . .'. A stuttering 'kevikevikvikvikvi' is also heard in association with display. WP

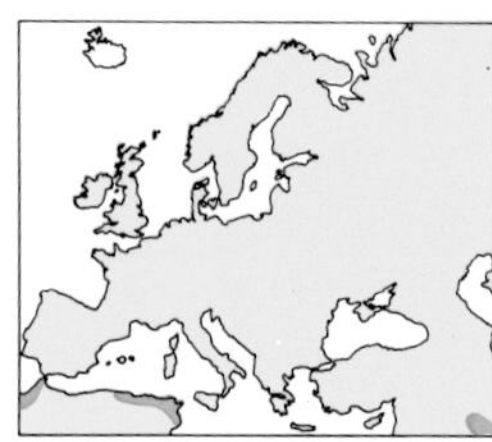

Curlew Sandpiper *Calidris ferruginea* L 19. Breeds on the Siberian tundra. On southward migration fairly uncommon but regular, usually among Dunlins or Little Stints. On northward migration (from Africa) a more easterly route is chosen, is rare in W Europe in May. Adults in summer plumage unmistakable brownish-red (darker colour than Knot's), but complete summer plumage not usually seen south of the tundra; in May it is partly hidden by white fringes, and in late summer face/neck have already been moulted to grey-buff, with only breast and belly brownish-red. Juvenile (most frequently seen) resembles juvenile Dunlin but is a shade bigger, slightly longer-legged, slimmer, with longer and more decurved bill, has paler and only faintly *marked sides of neck/breast* (orange-tinted), more distinct *pale supercilium*, prominent scaling on upperparts. Pure white rump is the feature by which species is picked up in flying Dunlin flocks. Lone Curlew Sandpipers in flight often appear slightly longer-winged and with more Reeve-like clipped wingbeats than Dunlin's. Call 'kürrlT', more twittering than Dunlin's. P

Dunlin *Calidris alpina* L 18. Uncommon and local breeder on grassy moorland with pools, lowland mosses and saltmarshes (race *schinzii*). Large flocks come from tundras in the far north-east (mainly the race *alpina*). On southward migration in large tight flocks along coastal flats, also quite common inland (muddy areas, sewage-farms, reservoirs etc). Adults in summer are *black on the belly*, in winter insipidly grey-brown above, white below, but *fairly long, slightly decurved* (outer half) *bill* is characteristic. Juvenile rather contrastingly brown-patterned above (almost like Little Stint), distinguished by *heavily grey-spotted flanks*. In Sept acquires rows of grey winter feathers interspersed in the wings. Call a wheezy whistled 'keeerrr', but call heard from feeding flocks at close range is entirely different: high 'beep-beep, beep . . .'. Flight display begins with gloomy 'uerrp, uerrp, . . .', changes to rising, strained 'rrÜee-rrÜee- . . .', ends in a falling and slightly decelerating 'rürürürürürürü'. RSWP

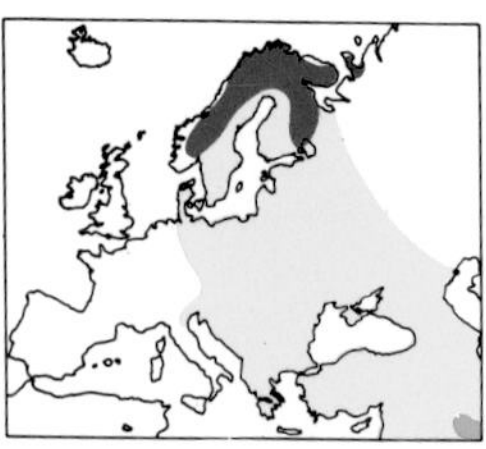

Broad-billed Sandpiper *Limicola falcinellus* L 16.5. Breeds sparsely on quagmires of Lapland bogs. Rare on southward as well as northward passage. Quiet and unobtrusive. Most reminiscent of a juvenile Dunlin but slightly smaller and darker. *Narrow snipe-like stripes* run down markedly *dark back. Dark stripes on head* even more striking; supercilium forked (in front of eye). *Bill rather long, downward-kinked at very tip.* Wingbar rather faint. Tail and rump as Dunlin. Juvenile resembles adult in summer plumage but has broader pale edges above and lacks V-shaped marks on flanks. Winter plumage like Dunlin with greyish-brown upperparts and dark carpal area but still characteristic head pattern. Call a buzzing whistle, more biting, dryer, more rasping than Dunlin's, a little like Sand Martin's: 'brrrEEit'. Voice also revealed in the rhythmically buzzing display. Alternative flight call 'tett', quite distinctive. V

■□□ **Purple Sandpiper** adult summer
□■□ **Purple Sandpiper** 1st-winter
□□■ **Purple Sandpiper** juv.

■□□ **Curlew Sandpiper** adults moulting, almost in full summer plumage
□■□ **Curlew Sandpiper** juv. with (left) juv. Dunlin
□□■ **Curlew Sandpiper** winter in flight

■□□ **Dunlin** adult summer
□■□ **Dunlin** adult winter
□□■ **Dunlin** juv. moulting to 1st-winter plumage

■□□ **Dunlin** flock joining others at winter roost, with Grey Plovers in background
□■□ **Broad-billed Sandpiper** adult summer
□□■ **Broad-billed Sandpiper** juv.

Waders, gulls and auks

Knot *Calidris canutus* L 25. Arctic species. Winters on large sandy or muddy estuaries, sometimes in huge flocks at favoured localities. On migration regular in small flocks along coast (rare inland), often with Dunlin. Much larger than Dunlin (body size as Redshank's) but typical *Calidris* in behaviour. Body almost disproportionately big and stout (long-distance flier, powerful 'engine'), *bill rather short*. Adults in summer plumage beautiful *copper-red below*. In winter plumage *pale grey* with delicate *scaly pattern* (fine black and white feather edges). Juveniles resemble adult in winter plumage, but darker grey upperparts have more distinct *scaly pattern* and breast tinged buff. *Pale grey* (vermiculated) *rump* in all plumages. Call a hoarse, nasal, squeaky 'wett-wett' (softer than Bar-tailed Godwit's). WP

■□□ **Knot** adult summer
□■□ **Knot** adult winter flock in flight
□□■ **Knot** juvs.

Sanderling *Calidris alba* L 18. In winter found on sandy shores, often in single-species flocks. Specialist in dashing to and fro beneath the large breakers. Most migrate through western half of Europe (May, July-Oct), stopping off at favoured localities. *Conspicuously active, constantly darting about.* Slightly bigger and stockier than Dunlin. Winter plumage extremely *pale* with *dark at bend of wing.* Juvenile also much whiter than other *Calidris*, though back vividly marked in black and rusty-yellow. Small speckled 'neck boa'. *Bill straight and relatively short. Black legs.* Appreciably *broader white wingbar* than, e.g. Dunlin. Summer plumage rusty-brown apart from white belly. In May, however, usually still has pale feather edges, giving grey and 'untidy' rather than rusty-brown impression. Call a short 'klit'. WP

■□□ **Sanderling** adults summer
□■□ **Sanderling** adult winter flock in flight
□□■ **Sanderling** juv.

Little Stint *Calidris minuta* L 14. Breeds on tundras in the north-east. Rare on northward migration in W Europe (chooses easterly route), fairly common on southward migration, on mudflats, sandy beaches, saltmarshes, also inland (muddy lakes, reservoirs etc), usually among Dunlins. Differs from latter not only in *small size* and short bill but also in more *active and scampering* behaviour. Temminck's Stint is roughly as small but behaves differently (see below). The two are also very different in appearance. Juvenile Little Stints (the ones most often seen on migration) are characteristic: have *rather a lot of white on face*, some rusty-brown on sides of breast, and *richly coloured back* (rusty-brown and black) *with two white longitudinal lines* which join to form a V. The Little Stint has *blackish legs*. Adults are more rusty on face and breast (cf. Sanderling). When they pass south in autumn they are faded: face and breast pale yellowish-brown, on upperparts blackish centres of scapular feathers fairly striking. Call a very thin and high 'tit', quite different from Sanderling's similarly transcribed call. Display call (on ground or in flight) a weak 'svee-svee-svee- . . .' recalling distant Arctic Tern courting and (above all) 'bibbling' Great Snipe. When sexually agitated, a silvery 'svirrr-r-r' (actually very Temminck's Stint-like) may be heard. P

■□□ **Sanderling** adult winter flock at high-tide roost with (right) adult Royal Tern *Sterna maxima*
□■□ **Little Stint** juv.
□□■ **Little Stint** juv.

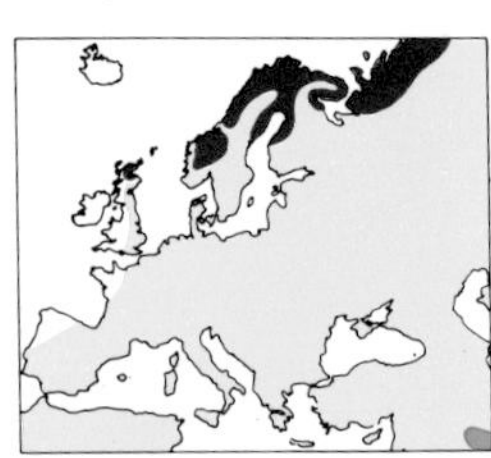

Temminck's Stint *Calidris temminckii* L 13.5. Breeds fairly commonly to sparsely on sandy shores of lakes and rivers in northern mountain districts, mostly above tree line (a few breed N Scotland). Not uncommon on migration, seen as often in spring as in autumn. Often rests in small single-species groups and in less open sites than other *Calidris*, e.g. by small muddy pools on pasture meadows. Quiet and unobtrusive. Moves in slightly more crouched posture than Little Stint, appears to have longer body. Plumage recalls Common Sandpiper's: grey-brown upperparts, neck and upper breast. *Legs brownish-grey* (Little Stint: blackish). Adult has scattered but large black blotches on back; juveniles lack these. Unlike Little Stint, climbs high after rising, and when flushed, has more erratic flight with more clipped wing-beats. Call a high rolling 'tirrr-r-r'. In display flight male hangs still in air (5-10m) on fluttering, high-raised wings and gives 'interminable', high, rapid, twittering reeling, 'tititititi . . .'. P

■□□ **Little Stint** adult winter
□■□ **Temminck's Stint** adult summer
□□■ **Temminck's Stint** juv.

Waders, gulls and auks

Accidental small sandpipers

Least Sandpiper *Calidris minutilla* L 13. Very rare vagrant from N America. *The true dwarf of the genus.* Apart from size, also recognised by short, very *thin and all dark bill* (thin also at the base; tip faintly down-curved), *dark crown* and *dark back* without clear scaly pattern but with faint pale lines (the upper ones sometimes forming V as in Little Stint) and *dirty-yellow to greyish-green legs.* Lores markedly dark. Supercilium faintly forked. Dark colour extends far down on forehead but does not reach bill. Poorly marked wingbar. Found in about same terrain as Temminck's Stint. Call a distinct high 'prreep' or a disyllabic 'krrü-eep', not unlike Temminck's Stint. V

Long-toed Stint *Calidris subminuta* L 13.5. Very rare vagrant from E Asia. Small, has *pale legs*, usually olive-yellow, like Temminck's Stint and Least Sandpiper. *Tibia and toes very long*, giving moderate tempo of gait. Base of lower mandible sometimes slightly paler than rest of bill. *Brownish-grey of the forehead reaches right to the bill.* Nape rather pale, sets off the dark cap. *Vivid rusty-brown edges on crown, mantle and tertials.* Call shrill, rolling 'cherrrp'. V

Semipalmated Sandpiper *Calidris pusilla* L 14.5. Very rare vagrant from N America. Like Little Stint but a shade larger, has equally short but slightly *heavier bill* (deep base, 'blob tip' viewed head-on), has *darker lores and cheek patches*, whiter supercilium (not distinctly forked as in Little Stint). Back is not as rusty-brown in colour as in juvenile Little Stint, *lacks prominent white V marks*, is rather evenly 'scaly'. In juveniles scapulars do not have such extensively dark centres as in Little Stint, dark colour consists more of dark shaft streaks and dark crescent just before the tip (form an 'anchor'). Breast sides marked on grey-buff ground colour, occasionally the whole breast marked on warm buff ground (cf. Baird's Sandpiper). Legs blackish. Web right in between the bases of the toes (which otherwise only Western Sandpiper has). Call *short*, thin, *humming* 'chruup'. V

Western Sandpiper *Calidris mauri* L 15. Very rare vagrant to Europe from N America or E Asia. Biggest of the small 'stints', between Little Stint and Broad-billed Sandpiper. *Blackish legs.* Shares with Semipalmated feature of having *partial webbing between the toes. Long bill,* generally down-curved at tip, separates most from Semipalmated (but a few overlap and can be very difficult to distinguish). Rather short-winged and front-heavy. Juveniles are brightly coloured, have *rufous upper scapulars* and sometimes back, contrasting with plainer and greyer lower scapulars and wing coverts. *Pale-faced*, dark lores narrow and not prominent. In winter pale and clean grey, *streaks of head and breast sides neat and distinct.* Call a thin, high-pitched 'cheet', recalling White-rumped Sandpiper but shorter. V

Red-necked Stint *Calidris ruficollis* L 14. Very rare vagrant from E Asia. Very like Little Stint (size, black legs, general patterning) but has a shade *shorter legs*, more *attenuated body shape* with fuller ventral area as well as more *horizontal stance*. In summer plumage *bright orange-brown on head and neck, without dark streaking*; a sparse band of spots across breast, beneath the brown. In winter and juvenile plumages exceedingly like both Little Stint and Semipalmated Sandpiper (though has no trace of webbing like latter), but can be distinguished in favourable cases. Juvenile has *paler wing-coverts and tertials* than juvenile Little, without latter's dark and contrasting feather centres. *Breast sides with weak, fine streaks.* Poorly defined pale V on back. Call a slightly impure 'treet'.

White-rumped Sandpiper *Calidris fuscicollis* L 18. Rare vagrant from N America. Size and behaviour as Dunlin, but bill shorter and straight (exceptionally the tip slightly down-curved), wingbar faint, *rump white*, body slightly more slender and *wings clearly longer* (reach beyond the tail in resting position). In winter plumage generally grey above, in summer plumage and juvenile plumage warm brown with pale feather edges, the breast streaked grey-brown. Legs dark greyish-green ('blackish'). Flight call a characteristic, thin, squeaky 'tzeet'. V

Baird's Sandpiper *Calidris bairdii* L 17. Very rare vagrant from N America. Slightly smaller than Dunlin, has shorter, straight and rather narrow bill. *Wings characteristically long* (reach beyond tail at rest), posture/body shape horizontal and elongated. Upperparts have white (juvenile in autumn) or pale brownish-grey (adult) feather edges, giving *unusually scaly impression*, especially on the scapulars. *Cheeks and breast sandy-brown* with dark spotting. Rump dark. Faint wingbar. Blackish legs. Toes short. Call a rather 'frothy' 'kreep'. V

■□□ **Least Sandpiper** summer

□■□ **Least Sandpiper** juv.

□□■ **Semipalmated Sandpiper** juv.

■□□ **Semipalmated Sandpiper** juv.

□■□ **Long-toed Stint** juv.

□□■ **Red-necked Stint** juv.

■□□ **Western Sandpiper** juv.

□■□ **White-rumped Sandpiper** adult moulting from summer to winter plumage

□□■ **White-rumped Sandpiper** adult moulting from summer to winter plumage

■□□ **Baird's Sandpiper** adult summer

□■□ **Baird's Sandpiper**

□□■ **Baird's Sandpiper** juv.

Waders, gulls and auks

Long-billed Dowitcher *Limnodromus scolopaceus* L 30. Vagrant from N America. Compact build with *bill as long as Snipe* and medium-long legs. Wavy barring on rump with white patch on back as in Spotted Redshank. Pale colour on secondaries. Very similar to Short-billed Dowitcher, and in winter plumage may sometimes be impossible to distinguish in the field. Usually slightly bigger and with longer bill. Dark bars on tail feathers are usually wider than white ones in between. In summer, plumage brick-red on whole of underparts with heavy wavy barring on both neck sides and flanks. In winter, plumage fine differences in tail barring and also sometimes bill length are the only clues as regards appearance. In juvenile plumage is distinguished from the Short-billed species by *cleaner grey tone on underparts* together with *uniformly dark tertials and greater coverts with narrow pale border* (cf. Short-billed species). Best feature is considered to be one of the calls, a thin piping, Oystercatcher-like 'keek', uttered singly or several in series. Vagrants prefer Snipe habitat and muddy shores. V

Short-billed Dowitcher *Limnodromus griseus* L 29. Very rare vagrant from N America. Extremely similar to Long-billed Dowitcher. Usually slightly smaller and with shorter bill. Dark bars on tail feathers are narrower than white ones in between, or at most equal in width. In summer, plumage pale orange-red on underparts but whiter on the belly. Markings below are considerably more sparing than in Long-billed species, often only scattered spots. In winter, plumage fine differences in the tail barring and sometimes bill length are the only clues as regards appearance. In juvenile plumage it is distinguished from the Long-billed species by *warmer tone of the underparts* (buff-coloured, pale greyish-brown) together with coarsely *barred tertials* and inner greater coverts (cf. Long-billed species). The best feature is the call, a rapid slightly slurred 'tururu', somewhat recalling Turnstone (not always trisyllabic). Prefers sandy beaches but sometimes also found in Snipe habitat. V

Stilt Sandpiper *Micropalama himantopus* L 21.5. Very rare vagrant from N America. Summer plumage characteristic with *entire underparts barred* and a *rusty-red patch behind the eye.* Winter and juvenile plumages distinguished by white rump which does *not* extend in a wedge up the back, greyish-green fairly long legs, as well as *downward-kinked tip to bill* (underparts then pale, not barred). Most like dowitchers in behaviour. Call a low, quite hoarse, single-note whistle. V

Pectoral Sandpiper *Calidris melanotos* L 21. Rare but regular vagrant from N America and Siberia. Clearly bigger and shorter-billed than Dunlin. When alarmed, recalls a small Reeve in shape and posture (long-necked). Upperparts patterned like Little Stint. *Breast heavily streaked* on pale grey-brown ground colour, typically *sharp demarcation against white belly. Legs greenish- or brownish-yellow.* Bill often has paler brown base. Wings rather long, wingbar faint. Found in Snipe habitat. When rising often pitches like Snipe, wingbeats comparatively clipped. Call a rich 'drrüp', rather like Curlew Sandpiper's. V

Sharp-tailed Sandpiper *Calidris acuminata* L 20. Very rare vagrant from NE Siberia. Like Pectoral Sandpiper in appearance and behaviour but lacks latter's sharp border between streaked breast and white belly, has *diffuse transition.* In summer plumage has crown vividly rufous-brown streaked dark, *distinct white supercilium* and *dark line behind eye* (more contrastingly patterned head than Pectoral Sandpiper's), neck streaked, *breast and flanks richly patterned with arrowheads* on rusty-yellow ground; in winter plumage both patterning and ground colour are considerably weaker. Juvenile has only a narrow zone of streaks over lower part of neck and on breast sides on yellow-ochre ground. Bill dark. *Legs dirty-yellow.* Call soft, metallic 'weep'. V

■□□ **Long-billed Dowitcher** adult late summer

□■□ **Long-billed Dowitcher** juv.

□□■ **Short-billed Dowitcher** adult winter

■□□ **Short-billed Dowitcher** juv.

□■□ **Short-billed Dowitcher** juv. in flight

□□■ **Short-billed Dowitcher** adult winter flock in flight with (far right) Dunlin

■□□ **Stilt Sandpiper** winter

□■□ **Stilt Sandpiper** winter

□□■ **Sharp-tailed Sandpiper** juv.

■□□ **Pectoral Sandpiper** adult

□■□ **Pectoral Sandpiper** juv.

□□■ **Pectoral Sandpiper** in flight (far right) with two Dunlins

Waders, gulls and auks

Snipes and Woodcock (family Scolopacidae). Live in marshland and in damp wooded areas. Short legs, bills very long.

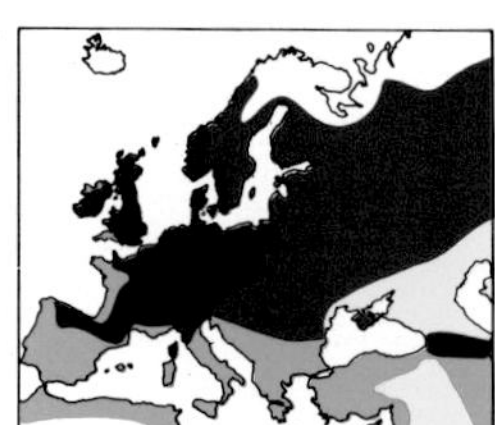

Woodcock *Scolopax rusticola* L 36. Common in damp woodland with open rides, also upland birchwoods in the north. On ground appears *round and short-legged* like a game bird. Rises with slight wing noise; one glimpses something *reddish-brown* among trees. Migrates at night. Male performs display flight ('roding') at dusk and dawn in spring and partly in summer. Then flies immediately above treetops with *slow wingbeats* but good speed with muffled grunting 'oo-ort, oo-ort, oo-ort', followed by explosive 'piss-p', *long bill* pointing obliquely down. Two males often hotly pursue each other giving almost twittering 'plip, plip-plip' calls. When female is put up from young, she flutters away with rear of body drooping heavily and with Jay-like scream. Can air-freight the young squeezed tight between the legs. RSWP

Great Snipe *Gallinago media* L 29. Breeds uncommonly on soggy ground on mountainsides near tree line in N Europe, and at lower levels in E Europe. Has declined greatly (much hunted). Arrives May, returns Aug-Sept. Migrants use slightly dryer ground than Snipe. Flushes at 4–6m, sometimes with muffled, hoarse 'ehtch-ehtch-ehtch- . . . ' (nothing like Snipe's call). *Flight more composed and straight* with clipped wingbeats, does not climb, drops fairly soon. Appears much *heavier* than Snipe, has much more *white on outer tail feathers*. When flying past, *more distended profile*, proportionately *slightly shorter bill, more profuse barring below* are distinctive, as well as more obvious wingbar (*white edging* also *along tips of primary coverts*, lacking in Snipe) but *hardly any white at all on trailing edge of wing*. On early summer nights displays in groups: stands erect, moves breast up and forward, opens bill wide, displays white areas of tail, all while uttering rising and falling series of rapid, high chirps ('bibbling') and a string of clicking notes (table-tennis ball!) which run into high whining 'whizzing' sounds (audible at 300m). V

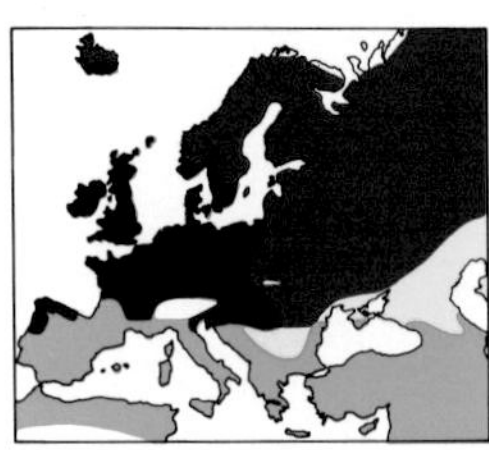

Snipe *Gallinago gallinago* L 25. Common in marshy areas and bogs. Most active at night. Hides in the vegetation, often in loose groups. Often rise at 10–15 m distance. As they fly up rapidly as if catapulted up, a few scraping 'catch' notes are given. Wing action violent, flight course *pitching in zigzags*. *Belly and trailing edge of wing (arm) white*. Climbs to a good height, flies far away. Often sits on fence posts or similar and calls loudly 'TIK-a TIK-a . . .' (rapid 'yik-yak-yik-yak- . . .' notes also occur). During display flight male dives steeply with a loud humming, the so-called drumming. Sound is produced by the spread outer tail feathers, which vibrate in rapidly pulsating air current caused by wing-fluttering during the steep dive. Male also has silent display flight at lower height, in which short wing flaps are succeeded by acrobatic 'somersaults' on end or even half on its back. RSWP

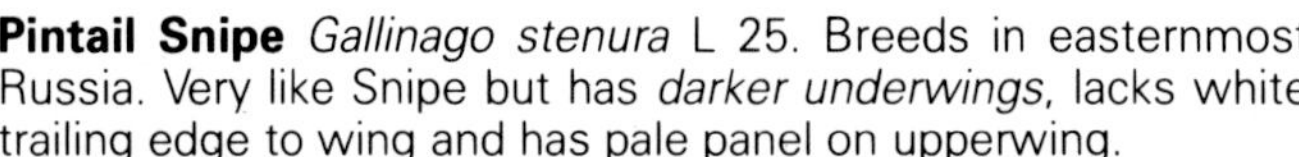

Pintail Snipe *Gallinago stenura* L 25. Breeds in easternmost Russia. Very like Snipe but has *darker underwings*, lacks white trailing edge to wing and has pale panel on upperwing.

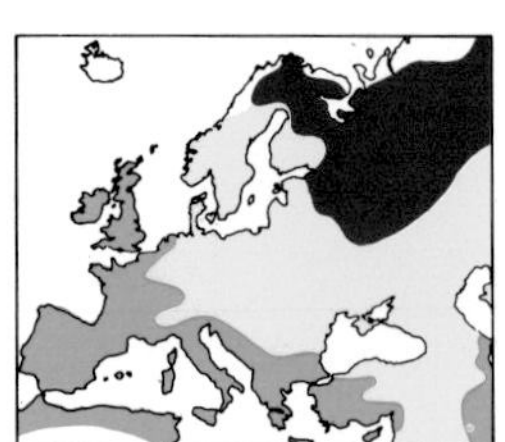

Jack Snipe *Lymnocryptes minimus* L 20. Not uncommon breeder on vast Lapland bogs and locally elsewhere in far north. On passage and in winter on tussocky swamps, often on dryer ground in winter. Extremely hard to flush, *rises at about 1m distance*. Flight then relatively fluttering, not so explosive and erratic as in Snipe. Additionally, on rising, neck more erect and tail pointed, is clearly smaller and has *considerably shorter bill*. Usually silent (but may utter a quiet 'catch'). Often drops down again quite quickly. Pronounced stripes on back but lacks pale central crown-stripe. Gives flight display in the light of the Lapland nights: moves widely around high up in shallowly undulating rising and falling flight, suddenly performs long steep dive in which a high rattling 'kolloRAP-kolloRAP- . . . ' (as from a galloping horse) is produced. WP

■□ **Woodcock** with young at nest

□■ **Great Snipe** displaying

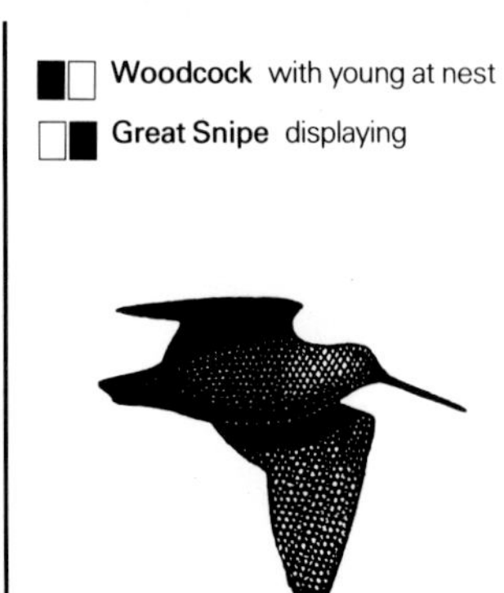

Woodcock, roding

Great Snipe,

young

■□□ **Snipe**

□■□ **Snipe**

□□■ **Snipe** in display flight

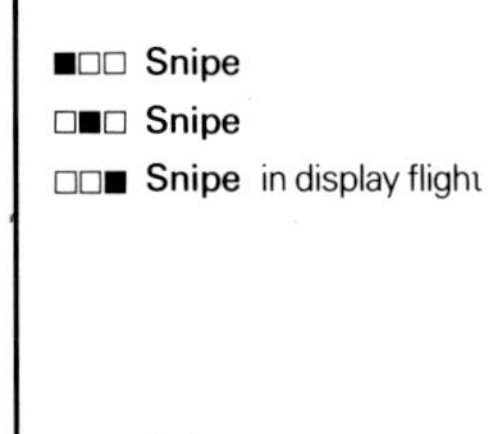

Snipe

maximum white

■□ **Pintail Snipe** in flight

□■ **Jack Snipe**

Waders, gulls and auks

Curlews and godwits

Curlews and godwits (family Scolopacidae) occur in two distinct groups: the genera *Numenius* and *Limosa*. Large, long-legged and long-billed waders in brown or grey. *Numenius* species have downcurved bills, are mainly brownish-grey. *Limosa* species have straight or very slightly upturned bills, reddish-brown in plumage during the breeding period, grey in winter. Sexes similar.

Curlew *Numenius arquata* L 56. Breeds fairly commonly on extensive, dry coastal dunes, lowland fields and pastures, moors and open bogs. On migration and in winter on open mudflats and shores and on coastal fields. Large as Common Gull in body and wings. Slender and tall, *long downcurved bill* (female has a noticeably longer bill than male, juvenile has relatively short bill). Drably *mottled grey-brown* with *whitish wedge-shaped rump*. Lacks eye-stripe and crown-stripes of Whimbrel, only faint suggestion is discernible. In display flight makes steep fluttering climb (silently), then glides down with 'gloomy', restrained 'oo-OHP, oo-OHP . . . ' notes which gradually rise in pitch and tempo and merge into clear, full, exultant, rhythmically rippling trill. Fairly shy. Alarm call intense, rather hoarse 'KWUwuwuwu'. Wingbeats composed, the neck retracted, in flight at a distance recalls Common Gull. Call a far-carrying, melodic, drawn-out whistle, 'KUur-lee', on migration a more eager 'KUee-KUee-KUH'. RSWP

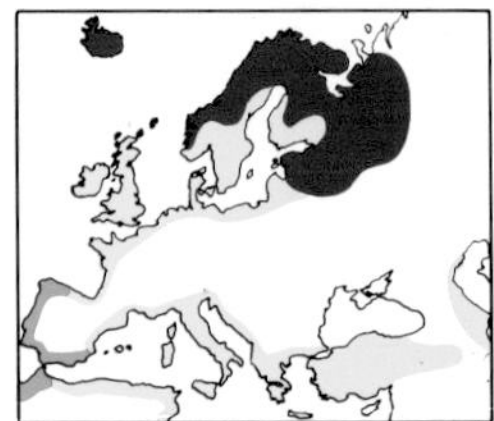

Whimbrel *Numenius phaeopus* L 40. Breeds in mountainous districts on cloudberry bogs and scrubby moors, most commonly in far north. Passes through quickly on northward migration in Apr–May, returns July–Sept, migrants found on mudflats, rocky shores, fields, moors (eats berries!), often with Curlews. Considerably smaller than latter, noticeably faster wingbeats, shorter bill and *brown crown with pale central stripe* together with fairly distinct dark eye-stripe. Call a shrill, *whinnying* whistle, 'puhuhuhuhuhuhu'. Display call has Curlew-like beginning ('oo-OHp') but breaks into a whinnying trill, straight and even, not pulsating: 'buurrrrrrr'. SP

▶ **Slender-billed Curlew** *Numenius tenuirostris* L 40. Scarce breeder on wet steppes in W Siberia. Very rare vagrant to W Europe. General coloration as Curlew, size and bill length as Whimbrel but bill narrower. Is, however, slightly *paler*, especially on tail and secondaries, and more distinctly marked than both these, has characteristic *heart-shaped spots on the flanks* (lacking in juveniles). Call like Curlew's (but higher in pitch). (Not illust.)

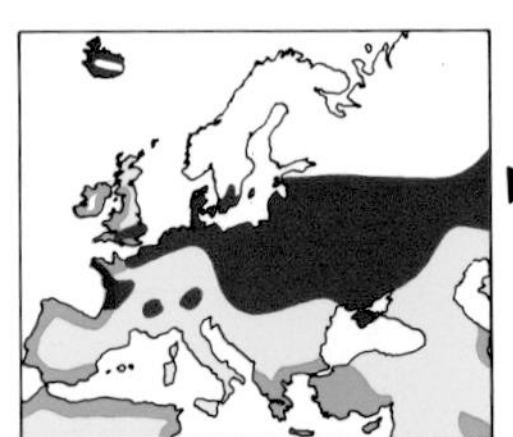

▶ **Black-tailed Godwit** *Limosa limosa* L 40. Breeds on extensive marsh-meadows, very local in distribution. On migration and in winter found along coasts and estuaries and in small numbers inland. Nervous and noisy. Flight rapid and energetic. *Long, straight bill* and *broad white wingbars* and *white tail base* above *black tail* characteristic. Female has less rusty-red in the plumage. In winter both sexes grey-brown above, pale below. Juvenile is buff on neck and breast, resembles juvenile Bar-tailed Godwit but buffer, less grey, lacks streaking on breast, has lighter bill. All calls are nasal, creaking and nervously repeated: 'ketteKAY', 'WIwiwi', 'WEH-ee' (Lapwing-like), 'KEHwee-weeit, KEHwee-weeit . . .' (display). RWP

▶ **Bar-tailed Godwit** *Limosa lapponica* L 38. Nests on tundra and bogs in the extreme north. Migrants found in Apr–May on coasts, and large flocks also pass through English Channel; in autumn and winter mostly small flocks seen in shallow coastal bays. Rare inland. In summer male is rusty-red on entire underparts, female is just orange-buff and distinctly larger and longer-billed. Juveniles and winter adults rather like Curlew in markings. Bill not quite so long as Black-tailed Godwit's and also *more clearly upturned*. White wedge on back and white tail base, *tail narrowly barred dark*. *Lacks white wingbars*. Calls creaking, nasal. On migration 'ke-ke', at breeding site drawling or rapid series of notes: 'kuWAY-kuWAY- . . .' or 'kuWEkuWEkuWE . . .'. WP

■□□ **Curlew** adult female
□■□ **Whimbrel** in flight
□□■ **Curlew** in flight

■□□ **Whimbrel**
□■□ **Black-tailed Godwit** adult female summer
□□■ **Black-tailed Godwit** adult female summer

■□□ **Black-tailed Godwit** juv.
□■□ **Black-tailed Godwit** adult female winter
□□■ **Black-tailed Godwit** adult male summer in flight

■□□ **Bar-tailed Godwit** adult male summer
□■□ **Bar-tailed Godwit** adult male summer in flight
□□■ **Bar-tailed Godwit** 1st-winter flock with (top) one adult and (centre foreground) Dunlin

Waders, gulls and auks

Larger sandpipers

(family Scolopacidae). Medium-sized, slender waders with fairly long narrow bills and long legs. Nervous, bobbing behaviour. Often identified by their calls.

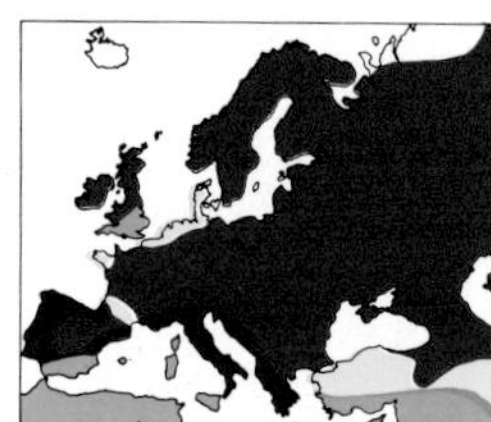

Common Sandpiper *Actitis hypoleucos* L 20. Prefers rocky shores poor in vegetation, is generally common breeder beside lakes, rivers and streams and on islands. Widespread on migration, both inland and on coast. Stands in characteristic, horizontal, crouched posture with *continuously rocking rear body*. Flight particularly characteristic: close above the water with *rapid, shallow wingbeats, releaved by short glides on rigid, diagonally downward-slanted wings*. Grey-brown above with white wingbars, white below with fairly pronounced grey-brown breast. Extremely reluctant to leave the vicinity of water, though often heard high over land on nocturnal migration. Passage individuals usually singly or in quite small groups. Call a thin, high 'hee-dee-dee'. Display call series of rapid rhythmic 'hideeDEEdeedi-hidiDEEdeedi- . . .'. Alarm 'heeep, heeep'. SWP

Spotted Sandpiper *Actitis macularia* L 19. Vagrant from N America. In winter plumage extremely like Common Sandpiper, but has *more distinct light transverse barring on wing-coverts* (mantle on other hand *less* barred than Common Sandpiper), *shorter wingbar*, yellow legs (though juveniles sometimes more greyish) and *whiter underparts*, as well as shorter tail. In summer plumage easily recognised by large dark spots on underparts and yellow-toned bill base. Calls quite like Common Sandpiper's but usually shorter and lower on scale and slightly rising, 'peet-weet-weeit', sometimes even resembles Green Sandpiper. Sometimes utters species-specific monosyllabic 'peet'. V

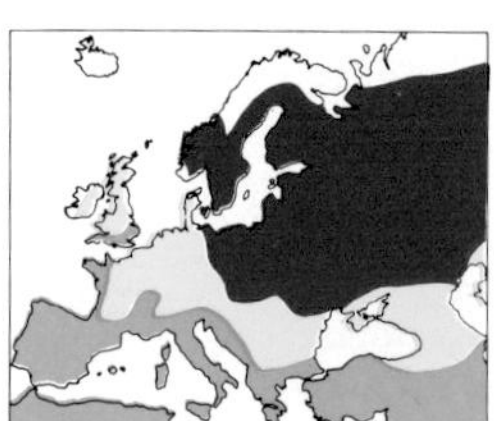

Green Sandpiper *Tringa ochropus* L 23. Breeds in NE Europe, widespread but never abundant, in secluded forests with small pools and marshes. Uses old thrush nest. Arrives early in spring, with the thaw. Females migrate south very early, in June. Migrate usually singly or 2–3 individuals together. Stops besides ponds and streams, in gullies and on watercress beds, but normally not on sedge swamps (and when it does, then e.g. by marginal pool). Resembles Wood Sandpiper but is a shade larger and broader-winged and more contrasting dark brown/white. Back *darker brown* (quite small pale spots) and *conspicuously white rump/tail*, underparts white with sharper border against speckled breast. *Brownish-black underwings*. Legs greyish-green, not quite as long as Wood Sandpiper's, feet project insignificantly beyond tail in flight, looks cut off at rear (Wood Sandpiper: comes to a point). Call a thin but clear and ringing 'TLUeet-wit-wit'. Display call a ringing stream of shrill notes, 'TLUeeTUee-TLUeeTUee-TLUee-TUee- . . .' or 'teeTUee-teeTUee-teeTUee' with introductory and interspersed alarm calls 'tit-tit-tit-tit'. WP

Solitary Sandpiper *Tringa solitaria* L 21. Vagrant from N America. Similar to Green Sandpiper (almost as dark underwings) but is long-winged, has *rump and central tail dark*. *Lacks wingbar*. Also has *distinct white eye-ring*. Call a thin, often two- or three-syllable whistle, 'peet-weet-weet' like Common Sandpiper's. V

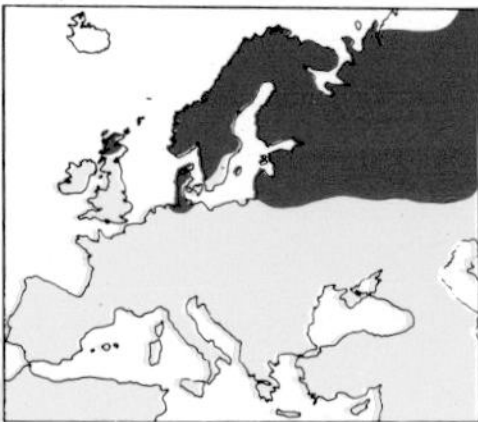

Wood Sandpiper *Tringa glareola* L 22. In the north quite common in sedge bogs, also in upland birch forests; in N Scotland very rare breeder near lochsides. Normally nests in sedge tussocks (exceptionally in old thrush nest). Passage Apr-May (scarce) and in Jul (fairly common), e.g. on marshy edges of lakes, usually singly but occasionally small flocks. Basically not as solitary as Green Sandpiper. Most closely resembles Green Sandpiper, but *back is not so dark brown* and is also densely and quite heavily pale-spotted, rump tail not so pure white, breast spotting fades out on flanks, and *underwings comparatively pale*. *Legs olive-yellow*. The call is an excitedly repeated mellow whistle, 'chiff-chiff-chiff', display call a rapid and pleasantly ringing yodel, 'LEELtee-LEELtee-LEEL-tee- . . .'. Alarm 'kip-kip- . . .'. SP

■□ **Common Sandpiper** adult
□■ **Common Sandpiper** juv.

■□□ **Solitary Sandpiper** adult autumn
□■□ **Spotted Sandpiper** juv.
□□■ **Spotted Sandpiper** adult moulting into summer plumage

■□□ **Green Sandpiper** juv.
□■□ **Green Sandpiper** adult
□□■ **Green Sandpiper** in flight

■□□ **Wood Sandpiper** adult
□■□ **Wood Sandpiper** juv. wing-stretching
□□■ **Wood Sandpiper** in flight

Waders, gulls and auks

Greenshank *Tringa nebularia* L 31: Breeds fairly commonly in the north on bare, boggy moorland and open upland forest. On migration regular visitor to inland lakes and reservoirs and to shallow coastal shores and marshes (not selective), but usually only in small groups. Can be seen running after fish fry in shallow water. Our largest and most robust *Tringa*. *Bill relatively heavy, slightly upturned.* Neck rather pale, wings dark grey-brown, *tail/rump brilliant white*, the white continuing up the back in a broad wedge. Call is a powerful ,three-note whistle,'tew-tew-tew'. Song, given on wing and high up, a rhythmic 'tewhü-tewhü-tewhü- . . .' (at close range overhead sounds fuller 'clewhü-. . .'). Alarm 'kyukyukyukyu . . .'. SWP

■□□ **Greenshank** adult summer
□■□ **Greenshank** adult winter
□□■ **Greenshank** adult in flight

Greater Yellowlegs *Tringa melanoleuca* L 34. Rare vagrant from N America. Recognised by large size (at least as big as Greenshank), *bright yellow legs* and white rump (*without wedge up back*). Distinguished from Lesser Yellowlegs (apart from size) by rather long, *slightly upturned bill as heavy as Greenshank's* together with often darker back and barred flanks. Juvenile has pale base to bill. Call a characteristic, sharp three- or four-syllable whistle, similar to Greenshank's but faster, more 'volatile' and often with final syllable dropping in pitch, 'chu-chu-cho'. V

■□□ **Greater Yellowlegs** juv.
□■□ **Lesser Yellowlegs** juv.
□□■ **Lesser Yellowlegs** adult

Lesser Yellowlegs *Tringa flavipes* L 25. Rare vagrant from N America. Very like Wood Sandpiper, but slightly larger, with longer wings and longer *yellow legs*. Bill all dark. Has off-white rump (*without wedge up back*). Distinguished from Greater Yellowlegs by smaller size, shorter, *straighter and thinner bill* and also, usually, paler back. Distinguished from Marsh Sandpiper by light spots on upper parts, yellow (not greyish-green) and proportionately shorter legs together with lack of white wedge up back. Call a soft, very Redshank-like monosyllabic 'chu'; when flushed often a two- or three-syllable whistle. V

Marsh Sandpiper *Tringa stagnatilis* L 23. Breeds in marshes on steppes or in taiga of E Europe. Passes through SE Europe on migration. Stops off mostly in inland areas, by pools, water meadows etc. Slightly larger than Wood Sandpiper. Slender. *Legs conspicuously long*, project a good way behind the tail in flight. *Bill markedly thin*, rather long as well as straight (very slightly upcurved in some). Markings roughly as Greenshank's: rather *pale neck*, brownish back/upperwing (without Wood Sandpiper's light spots, but in summer with black blotches like Reeve), white on rump and in a wedge up the back. In winter forehead white, upperparts grey and plain. Call a rather unobtrusive whistle, 'tew' (sometimes a Greenshank-like 'kew-kew-kew' but weaker). V

■□□ **Marsh Sandpiper** adult summer
□■□ **Marsh Sandpiper** juv. moulting to 1st-winter plumage
□□■ **Marsh Sandpiper** adult summer in flight

Terek Sandpiper *Xenus cinereus* L 23. Nests along lowland rivers and lakes in Russo-Siberian taiga, up to the tundra (Oulu coast, Finland, is western outpost). Frequents shallow, muddy shores. Sporadic visitor to W Europe. Size between Common Sandpiper and Redshank. Usually stands in horizontal, crouched posture like Common Sandpiper, even bobs rear body. Quick and active when feeding, running among boulders and on driftwood, picking insects from surface. Usual flight is straight with even wingbeats, resembling Knot; at times, low over water, wing action is shallow and quick, rather like Common Sandpiper. *Bill long, rather thin and noticeably upturned. Legs fairly short, yellowish or orange.* Rather a *pale grey above*, white below. In flight white bar is revealed *along trailing edge of wing* (not so broad as Redshank's and less contrasting, since back is paler). Note that *rump and tail are grey*. On migration utters trills which resemble Whimbrel's but are softer and more melodic, as well as trisyllabic 'chududu', which is like Redshank but faster. Display call is a slow, repetitive but sonorous 'klü-rrrüh, 'klü-rrrüh-. . .', somewhat recalling Stone-curlew display. V

Terek Sandpiper, adult summer

■□□ **Terek Sandpiper** adult summer
□■□ **Terek Sandpiper** 1st-winter
□□■ **Terek Sandpiper** in flight with (right) Grey Plover

Waders, gulls and auks

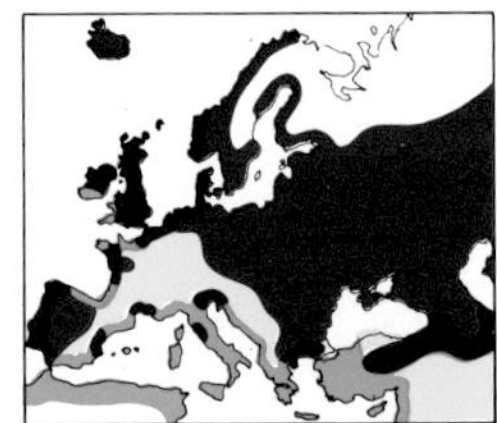

Redshank *Tringa totanus* L 27. Typical coastal bird, commonest wader on estuaries and coastal marshes, on passage and in winter often in large flocks. Breeds in wet meadows, also inland on bogs and upland moors. Rather uniform grey-brown with *red legs* (more orange-red in juvenile; cf. female Ruff, immature Spotted Redshank). In flight instantly recognised by *broad white bars along rear edges of wings*, conspicuous at long range also is white rump/tail. Ringing, mellow, melancholy call 'TEU-hu, TEU-huhu', song a loud 'TOOle-TOOle-TOOle- . . . chu-chu-chu- . . . -weelYO-weelYO-weelYO'. Alarm an irritatingly persistant 'kip-kip-kip- . . .', pressing on the intruder. RSWP

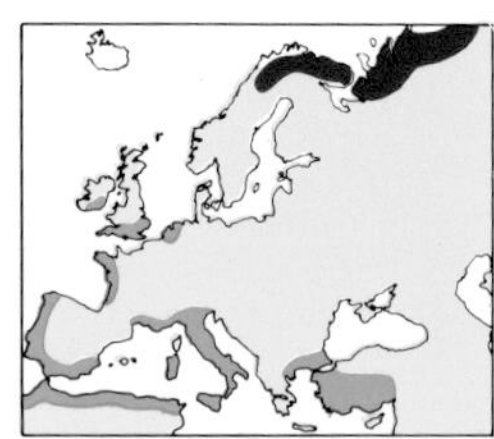

Spotted Redshank *Tringa erythropus* L 30. Breeds chiefly in open coniferous forest in the far north. On migration and in winter found on flooded lake margins, muddy reservoirs, coastal marshes. Wades far out into the water, sometimes swims. Flight rapid with vigorous wingbeats. Summer plumage sooty-black, legs blackish. Immatures brown and red-legged like Redshanks, but larger, slimmer, have *longer legs* (project beyond tail, but may sometimes be held retracted) *and bill* (rather thin, straight with a *hint of a downward kink at the very tip*), are more active in behaviour. *In addition lack wingbar*, have typically narrow white 'slit' on back above a darker tail (applies to all plumages). Also more contrasting face (white line in front of eye) as well as more vermiculated flanks. Winter plumage similar but more greyish-white. Call a *shrill whistle*, 'chu-it'. On rising, occasionally gives a chuckling 'chu, chu'. Song 'trruEEh-e trruEEHe', repeated. Alarm a rapid, dry, hard 'kekeke . . .'. WP

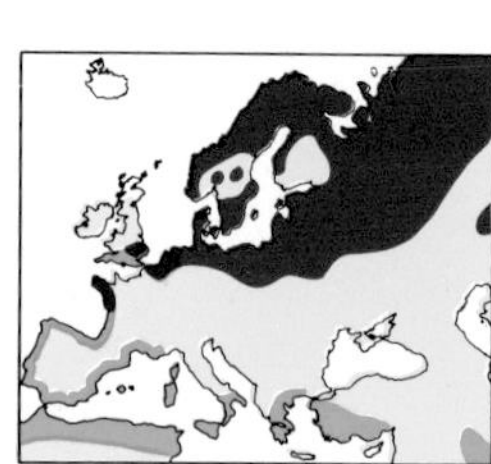

Ruff *Philomachus pugnax* L ♂30, ♀23. Breeds in sedge swamps in upland areas, most abundantly on northern tundra, in E Britain also locally on wet grassy meadows. On migration fairly common on marshy meadows, also on arable fields and open grassy areas. Often tight, fairly large flocks which perform flight manoeuvres. Males (Ruffs) much larger than females (Reeves), flocks appear to consist of two different species. In May-June the males have large *ruffs and ear tufts* in different colour combinations, and faces covered with yellow-brown or reddish warts. Gather at established sites, leks, for their remarkable display, in which at one moment they come to blows with flapping wings and the next appear to 'freeze' in deep, courtly bows. Females are light brown with big black 'diamonds' above, *legs orange-red, yellow-brown or greenish*. In late summer, young are yellowish-brown on neck, dark brown on back (pale feather-edges produce scaly pattern). Distinguished from large *Tringa* by narrow wingbars, *dark central band and wihite sides of rump, hunch-backed silhouette in flight* and well-spaced wingbeats, often including long stretches of gliding. Often stands upright; head then looks small, and bill (slightly down-curved) short in comparison with long neck. Almost *silent* (rarely, a muffled croak). SWP

Buff-breasted Sandpiper *Tryngites subruficollis* L 20. Rare vagrant from N America. Resembles small Reeve with *short bill*, small head and habit of *standing erect with extended neck*, but is *rusty-coloured buff on whole of underparts* in all plumage. In flight, reveals *white underwing* with little dark patch on leading edge (primary coverts dark grey). Upperparts scaly like Ruff, as is rump, thus lacking white sides. No wingbar. *Hint of pale eye-ring*. Sides of head and neck unmarked buff. *Pale legs*. Prefers short-grass meadows, airfields etc, but also along beaches. Attempts to zigzag away from intruders. Call a quiet 'grreet'. V

Upland Sandpiper *Bartramia longicauda* L 28. Rare vagrant from N America. As big as a Redshank. Brown-spotted. Very long tail and long, pointed, *finely barred wings. Narrow neck, small head* and straight, rather short bill. Flight swift, often alights on posts, holds wings straight up for a moment after landing. Behaviour like plovers, often rests on airfields and golf courses. Call a fast bubbling trill like Little Grebe's, 'puhuhuhuhu'. V

■□□ **Redshank** adult summer
□■□ **Redshank** winter
□□■ **Redshank** adult summer in flight

■□□ **Spotted Redshank** adult summer
□■□ **Spotted Redshank** juv.
□□■ **Spotted Redshank** adult winter

Spotted Redshank, adult summer

■□□ **Ruff** adult males displaying in spring
□■□ **Ruff** adult male winter
□□■ **Ruff** female in flight

■□□ **Ruff** juv. male
□■□ **Buff-breasted Sandpiper** juv.
□□■ **Upland Sandpiper** juv.

Waders, gulls and auks

Avocets and stilts

Avocets and stilts (family Recurvirostridae) are elegant white and black waders with very long legs and long, thin bills. Loud calls.

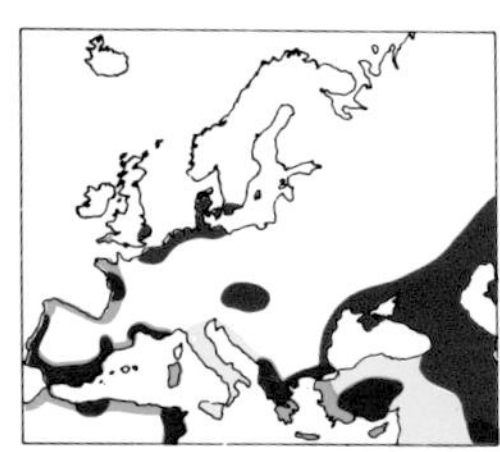

Avocet *Recurvirostra avosetta* L 43. Breeds uncommonly, though locally in fairly large, loose colonies, beside shallow sea bays, coastal lagoons and steppe lakes. *Shining white with black markings.* Slender and delicate build. Legs very long, blue-grey. *Bill thin, strongly upcurved,* is swept from side to side under the water when searching for food. Swims freely. Flies with rather fast wingbeats, not clipped, not particularly progressive. Noisy and restless. The usual call is a short, rich fluting, which is repeated with great energy, 'kluit kluit kluit . . .'. When young are threatened, parents give a biting and whining shriek, 'grreet', and perform injury-feigning with unusual intensity. RSWP

■□□ **Avocet** adult
□■□ **Avocet** juvs. feeding
□□■ **Avocet** adult in flight

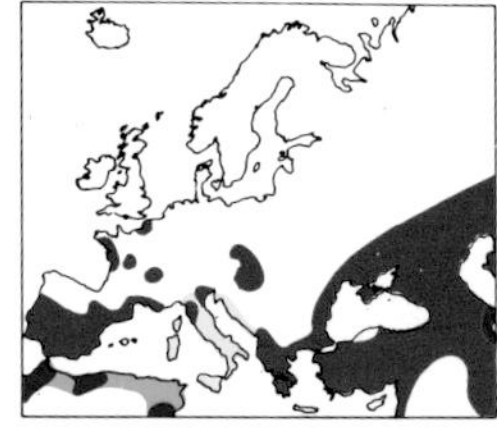

Black-winged Stilt *Himantopus himantopus* L 38. Nests in S Europe in shallow marshes and lagoons in small, loose colonies. Seen in small groups. Unmistakable with *improbably long, pale red legs* and *thin, straight bill,* shining white plumage with dark wings and back. Male has black back, female brown-toned. Head markings vary considerably in both sexes. Has many calls, incl. a persistently repeated, Avocet-like 'klit-klit-klit- . . .' as well as 'krre', almost like Black-headed Gull and 'kye' or 'kyee' like Black Tern. V

■□□ **Black-winged Stilt** adult female

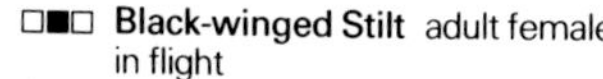

□■□ **Black-winged Stilt** adult female in flight
□□■ **Black-winged Stilt** part of large flock in flight

Stone-curlews

Stone-curlews (family Burhinidae). A family with several similar species. Only one in Europe, but quite a number found in Africa. Large yellow eyes (adaptation for nocturnal habits), rather short heavy bills, long yellow legs and highly developed camouflage pattern.

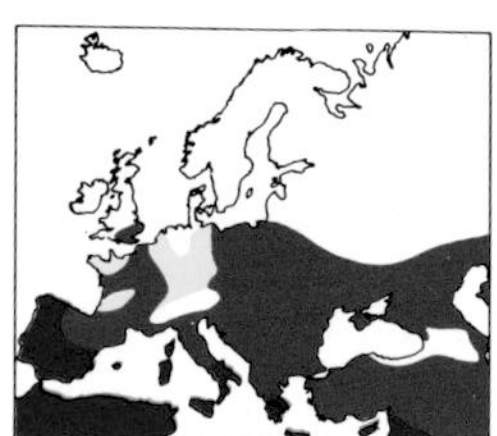

Stone-curlew *Burhinus oedicnemus* L 40. Occurs sparsely in S and central Europe on dry heaths with sandy or stony areas. Now rare in Britain, confined to S and E England. Feeds on worms, insects etc, but may also take mice. Mainly nocturnal, has *large yellow eyes.* Difficult to see, runs away with head retracted and body held horizontally. Stands very erect to scan around; also tends to rest in a 'sitting' position with whole length of tarsi resting on ground but tibia vertical. When taken by surprise may flatten itself against ground with neck extended. Often seen flying away low, the size of a large Whimbrel. Flight similar to Oystercatcher's: bowed wings, beaten rather quickly, shallowly and low. *White bars and patches on the wings* show up well. At and after dusk gives its melancholy, rolling whistle, a little reminiscent of Curlew's (and Terek Sandpiper's), 'pü PÜrrr-ü PÜrrr-ü PÜrrr-ü . . .'. Also thin 'TÜ-lee' calls like shrill Curlew, an excited 'küwüWI-küwüWI-küwüWI-küwüWI- . . .' like Curlew alarm call, and a 'kuBEEK-keBEEK-keBEEK . . .' like a furious outburst from an Oystercatcher. S

Stone-curlew

Coursers and Pratincoles

Coursers and Pratincoles (family Glareolidae). Fairly small waders of open country. The *coursers* are plover-like, breeding on arid ground. Expert runners. Only one species regularly found in the area. The *pratincoles* are short-legged, have long, pointed wings, deeply forked tails and short bills. Often seen in flocks, hunt insects in flight. Clutches of 2-3 eggs.

Stone-curlew female (left) and male at nest site
Stone-curlew male displaying
Cream-coloured Courser adult

Cream-coloured Courser *Cursorius cursor* L 23. Breeds in the Canary Islands and in the desert belt from Morocco to Pakistan. Runs extraordinarily quickly with sudden halts in manner of plovers. Usually endeavours to run away from an intruder. *Sandy-coloured* with black and white eye-stripe. Down-curved bill. Legs yellowish-grey, appearing white. In flight *black primaries* and *black underwings* are very striking. Utters frog-like croaking. V

Cream-coloured Courser

Waders, gulls and auks

Pratincole *Glareola pratincola* L 25. Breeds in S Europe in loose colonies in dry areas (e.g. sunbaked mud) in extensive marshy land. Spends large parts of day on the wing. Chases winged insects in elegant, fast flight (also at dawn and dusk), often many in loose party and at fairly low level. At long range appears brown with pale belly and *shining white rump/tail. Underwings reddish-brown* (also in juveniles), but this often difficult to see in the southern sun because they become shadowy black. Distinguishable from Black-winged Pratincole by narrow but distinct *white band along tips of secondaries* (can be abraded or indistinct in a few) as well as by generally slightly paler back and upperwing-coverts, which give some contrast against dark flight feathers. Can run quickly with its small, frail legs. Calls shrill, nasal, commonest flock call a five-syllable one in 'simmering', jerky rhythm, 'KEERR-ek-ek Kit-IT', recalls Little Tern in pitch. Also shorter conversational 'kik'. V

► **Black-winged Pratincole** *Glareola nordmanni* L 25. Very like Pratincole in appearance, habits and habitat (considered by some authors to be a race of Pratincole). Has, however, *jet-black underwings*, generally darker upperwings, and *lacks narrow white trailing edge on inner wing* (which should be a better distinguishing mark in the strong sunshine). Call like Pratincole's. V

Phalaropes

(family Scolopacidae) look like the smaller sandpipers but have lobed toes and are excellent swimmers.

Wilson's Phalarope *Phalaropus tricolor* L ♂21, ♀24. Rare vagrant from N America. In summer plumage unmistakable. In winter general pattern like a Wood Sandpiper with white tail base and *lack of wingbar*, but paler (especially on head and neck) and more uniformly grey above; has *long, straight and very thin bill*, long and *strikingly thick legs* (yellowish in winter plumage, blackish in summer). Distinctions from Marsh Sandpiper include *lack of white wedge up back* and thicker and shorter legs. Very active, in contrast to congeners, *runs* or steals, often on muddy shores and in shallow water, crouched, 'stabbing' insects with its bill. Usually silent on migration, occasionally a low, nasal 'vit'. V

Grey Phalarope *Phalaropus fulicarius* L 19. Circumpolar breeder in Arctic, also in coastal lagoons in Iceland. Winters in South Atlantic. Sporadic visitor to coasts of W Europe, usually in autumn and winter, sometimes in hundreds after gales. Behaviour and habits like Red-necked Phalarope, fearless and almost always seen swimming. In summer plumage unmistakable. In winter plumage like Red-necked, but distinguished by *thicker and very slightly shorter bill*, which often (but not always) has pale, yellowish-brown base, and by *uniform blue-grey back*. In juveniles and adults in autumn, grey back often partly variegated black, therefore resembles Red-necked more than adult in full winter plumage. Call a distinct, high 'kit', also a softer 'dreet'. P

Red-necked Phalarope *Phalaropus lobatus* L 16.5. Rather common breeder in far north, in Britain rare breeder (very local) in boggy areas with small pools. Winters in large numbers in middle of Arabian Sea. Very rare on passage. Almost always seen swimming: holds neck slanting forwards like Black-headed Gull, nods in pace with swimming motions, is fussy in actions. Stirs up small animals by spinning around while swimming. Female, more showy in plumage, does the courting, leaves incubation etc to notoriously fearless male. Summer plumage unmistakable. (At distance appears dark with white chin/throat.) Juvenile white with dark patch on crown and behind eye, and *dark back with two pairs of rusty-yellow longitudinal stripes* (like adult in summer plumage but unlike Grey Phalarope). *Distinct white wingbar*. Winter plumage (rarely seen in Europe) like juvenile's but greyer back with white stripes. Call a short, hard 'kett' like a violin string being plucked; variations include a 'kereck', like a Coot in miniature. SP

■□□ **Pratincole** pair at nest site

□■□ **Pratincole** juv.

□□■ **Pratincole** adult summer in flight from below

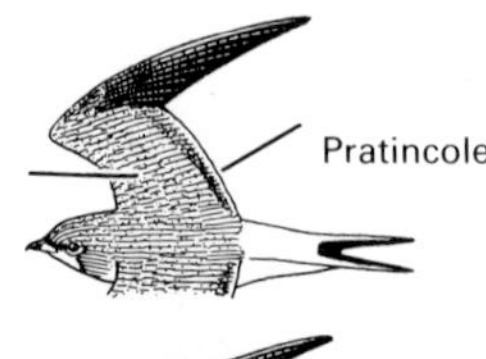

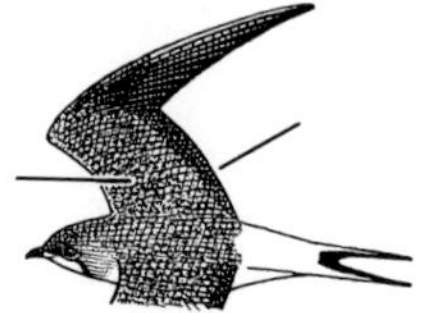

Black-winged Pratincole

■□□ **Black-winged Pratincole** 1st-winter

□■□ **Wilson's Phalarope** adult female summer

□□■ **Wilson's Phalarope** 1st-winter

Wilson's Phalarope, winter

■□□ **Wilson's Phalarope** flock in flight

□■□ **Grey Phalarope** adult female summer

□□■ **Grey Phalarope** adult winter

■□□ **Red-necked Phalarope** juv. in flight

□■□ **Red-necked Phalarope** adult male summer

□□■ **Red-necked Phalarope** juv.

Waders, gulls and auks

Skuas

Skuas (order Charadriiformes, family Stercorariidae) resemble gulls but are superior in flight, feeding methods include robbing gulls and terns. In winter at sea. Central tail feathers slightly or markedly elongated.

Great Skua *Stercorarius skua* L 59. Breeds on islands in N Atlantic, incl. N Scotland, often in colonies on upland moors near rocky coasts. Defends nest with impressive head-on attack. Steals fish from seabirds (often Gannet) but eats carrion and offal to greater extent than do other skuas, follows fishing craft. Rather recalls dark large gull (beware confusion with oiled gull), but has much *heavier body* and *broader wing bases*, and weightiness and stability in direct flight are quite outstanding, in contrast to great agility in pursuit flight. *Large snow-white wing flashes (above as well as below)* prominent even at longest ranges. SP

Pomarine Skua *Stercorarius pomarinus* L 51. Inhabits arctic tundras. In winter at sea, incl. off W Africa. Passes British coasts mainly May and Sep–Nov. Adults have *broad tail projections, which are twisted a full 90°* so that tail tip looks thick in profile (but fairly thin overhead). Two phases, one all-dark and one pale. Commonest is pale phase, with or without breast band. Immature extremely like immature Arctic Skua: larger size (= small Herring Gull; Arctic = Common Gull) often discernible, but Arctic too looks big in smooth steady migration flight; proportionately *larger bill* with heavier base can be judged at close range; *bill pale with dark tip* like Glaucous Gull (appears more uniform in most Arctic); central tail feathers only very little elongated, blunt, do not form sharp double point (often do in young Arctic). Adults in winter (Oct–Apr) and sub adults have 'half-length' tail projections, blunted, not fully twisted, also breast band and barred flanks. Much white on base of under primary coverts indicates Pomarine. Experienced observers go for bulk, size and flight. Width of arm just exceeds length of tail. P

Arctic Skua *Stercorarius parasiticus* L 46. Breeds in scattered pairs or loose colonies on barren rocky islands on Atlantic, arctic and Baltic coasts, incl N and W Scotland, on coastal and upland moors. Arrives in Apr, Arctic breeders pass in May, return mainly Aug–Sep. Two colour phases, dark commonest in south, pale in north. Intermediates occur. Both light phase and intermediates may have dark breast band. *Central tail feathers elongated, pointed.* Generally gull-like but always appears strikingly *dark* (even the light phase), and superior flying ability obvious. Forces gulls and terns to disgorge fish, then displaying magnificent speed and aerobatics. Even normal flight strikingly fast considering relaxed wing action. Lands on water with peculiar caution, after long glide. Commonest call a nasal mewing like a cat on the tiles, 'EH-glaw, EH-glaw, . . . '. Immature brown (variable), has mere hint of elongated tail feathers, in field scarcely distinguishable from immature Pomarine (which see); width of arm equals length of tail, or less. On perched bird at close range, however, *bill delicate like Common Gull's*, not like the large gulls'; bill usually rather uniform in colour. SP

Long-tailed Skua *Stercorarius longicaudus* L 53. Breeds on upland moor and tundra, not dependent on water. Breeding numbers vary with vole and lemming cycles (basic food). Does not parasitise other birds, except in summer in poor lemming years and in winter at sea. Rare on passage (especially so in spring). Colour pattern constant (occurrence of all-dark individuals negligible). *Tail projections very long,* 15–20cm. Smallest and slimmest of the skuas, *wings proportionately longer and narrower,* flight more buoyant, more playful. Often hovers. Catches winged insects. Call in close display chases a gull-like 'klee-aah', alarm a loud 'krepp-krepp-krepp'. Immature similar to immature Arctic but smaller (body Black-headed Gull size), proportionately longer- and narrower-winged, often quite obviously *greyer* brown, has short (and rather heavy) two-coloured bill and only 2 outermost primary shafts white (Arctic and Pomarine 3–5). P

■□□ **Great Skua** adult harrying 2nd-summer Gannet

□■□ **Great Skua** juv.

□□■ **Great Skua** adult in flight

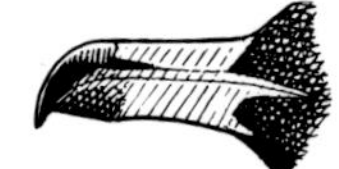

Pomarine Skua, juv.

■□□ **Pomarine Skua** adult summer pale phase in flight (tail projections virtually absent on this bird)

□■□ **Pomarine Skua** adult winter in flight, moulting primaries

□□■ **Pomarine Skua** imm. in flight, starting to moult

adults of

Pomarine Skua Arctic Skua

Arctic Skua, juv.

■□□ **Arctic Skua** adult summer pale phase in flight

□■□ **Arctic Skua** adult dark phase at nest

□□■ **Arctic Skua** juv. dark individual in flight

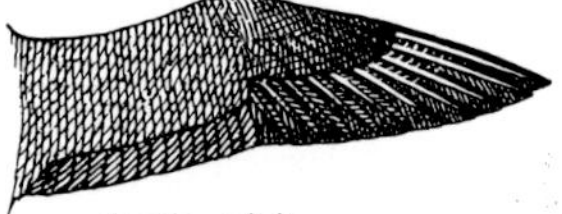

Arctic, adult

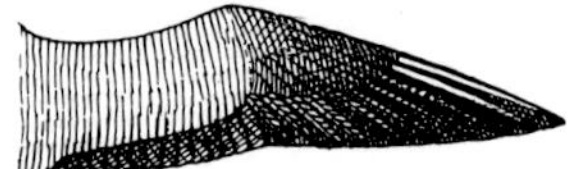

Long-tailed, adult

Long-tailed Skua, juv.

■□□ **Long-tailed Skua** adult summer in flight

□■□ **Long-tailed Skua** juv. dark individual in flight

□□■ **Long-tailed Skua** juv. dark individual in flight

Waders, gulls and auks

Gulls (order Charadriiformes, family Laridae) are robust birds with webbed feet, long, rather narrow wings, powerful bills, fairly short tails. Generally white, grey and black. Sexes similar. Immatures usually mottled grey-brown. Larger species gain adult plumage only after several years. Versatile, eat fish, carrion, bivalves, earthworms, birds' eggs and young etc. Nest colonially. Clutches of 2–3 eggs.

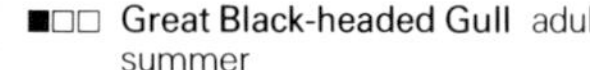

■□□ **Great Black-headed Gull** adult summer

□■□ **Great Black-headed Gull** 1st-winter/1st-summer

□□■ **Great black-headed Gull** 1st-winter/1st-summer in flight

Great Black-headed Gull *Larus ichthyaetus* L 63, W 154. Breeds SE Europe on steppe lakes, coastal marshes. Rare visitor to W Europe. In summer plumage adult identified by Great Black-backed Gull *size* and *black hood*, in winter plumage by *yellow bill with black transverse band* and dark head markings. Mantle and scapulars fairly rich grey, darker than e.g. Black-headed Gull. At very long range black spots on wingtip can be difficult to see. Juvenile told from other young large gulls by *sharply outlined, broad black outer band on clean white tail* and *mottled grey breast sharply divided from white belly*; the wing feathers are usually all-dark. As early as the first autumn breast and upperwing-coverts become lighter; acquires adult colours almost as quickly as Common Gull, despite its size. In 1st-winter and 1st-summer plumage rather like a Herring Gull in 2nd-summer plumage, but *larger*, and *greyish-yellow and black-tipped bill* appears *longer*; white 'eye-lids' (all plumages); *greyish-black mark behind eye*; legs have a green tinge; still a *sharp border between black terminal band and white base of tail*; pale panel on upperwing-coverts. In flight *wings strikingly long and pointed*, seen head-on often appears more arched than in Herring. Call hoarse and crow-like. V

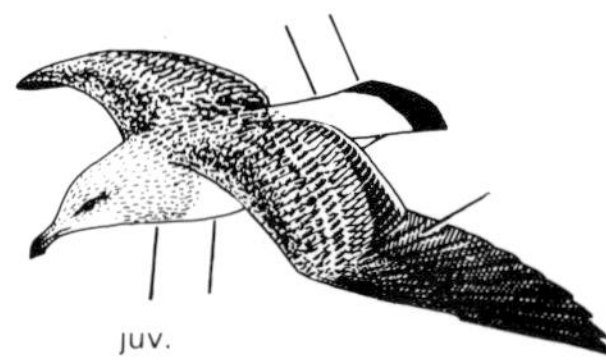

Great Black-headed Gull

■□□ **Great Black-headed Gull** adult summer in flight

□■□ **Glaucous Gull** adult summer

□□■ **Glaucous Gull** adult winter

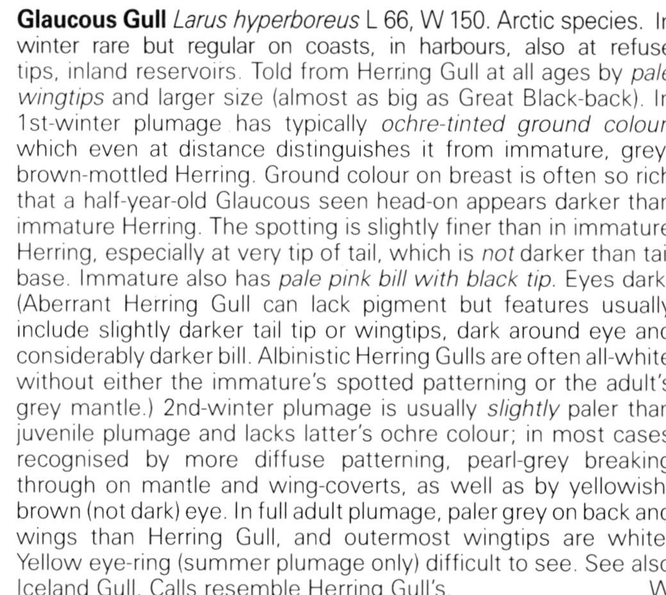

▶ **Glaucous Gull** *Larus hyperboreus* L 66, W 150. Arctic species. In winter rare but regular on coasts, in harbours, also at refuse tips, inland reservoirs. Told from Herring Gull at all ages by *pale wingtips* and larger size (almost as big as Great Black-back). In 1st-winter plumage has typically *ochre-tinted ground colour*, which even at distance distinguishes it from immature, grey-brown-mottled Herring. Ground colour on breast is often so rich that a half-year-old Glaucous seen head-on appears darker than immature Herring. The spotting is slightly finer than in immature Herring, especially at very tip of tail, which is *not* darker than tail base. Immature also has *pale pink bill with black tip*. Eyes dark. (Aberrant Herring Gull can lack pigment but features usually include slightly darker tail tip or wingtips, dark around eye and considerably darker bill. Albinistic Herring Gulls are often all-white without either the immature's spotted patterning or the adult's grey mantle.) 2nd-winter plumage is usually *slightly* paler than juvenile plumage and lacks latter's ochre colour; in most cases recognised by more diffuse patterning, pearl-grey breaking through on mantle and wing-coverts, as well as by yellowish-brown (not dark) eye. In full adult plumage, paler grey on back and wings than Herring Gull, and outermost wingtips are white. Yellow eye-ring (summer plumage only) difficult to see. See also Iceland Gull. Calls resemble Herring Gull's. W

■□□ **Glaucous Gull** 1st-summer/2nd-winter

□■□ **Glaucous Gull** 1st-summer/2nd-winter

□□■ **Glaucous Gull** adult winter in flight from below

▶ **Iceland Gull** *Larus glaucoides* L 57, W 133. Breeds Greenland. In winter uncommon on coasts of NW Europe, in Britain also inland at refuse tips, reservoirs etc. Like Glaucous Gull in all plumages (gradual transition from pale brown to grey-white) but smaller (if anything smaller than Herring Gull), has proportionately *smaller and rounder head* (crown peak immediately behind eye; in Glaucous crown flatter, and peak far behind eye), *shorter bill*, therefore appears more delicate and more like Common Gull, has *shorter legs* and *longer wings*, tips of which often project far beyond tail (Glaucous Gull's usually project less beyond). Often holds wings slightly drooping. *Bill in 1st-winter plumage darker than Glaucous Gull's*: more black at tip, often blends into paler base. In 2nd-winter plumage, bill pattern identical with Glaucous. Looks rather broad-winged and short-necked in flight. For confusion with miscoloured Herring Gulls, see Glaucous Gull. Adult has (summer plumage only) red eye-ring, but difficult to see. W

Iceland Gull

■□□ **Iceland Gull** 1st-winter (unusually coarsely patterned)

□■□ **Iceland Gull** 1st-winter/1st-summer

□□■ **Iceland Gull** 1st-winter in flight

Waders, gulls and auks

Great Black-backed Gull *Larus marinus* L 69, W 155. Breeds quite commonly on coasts, also sporadically at larger inland waters, in isolated pairs or small colonies, often together with other gulls. Distinguished from rather similar Lesser Black-backed Gull by *larger* size, *more powerful bill, greyish-pink legs* and slightly *broader wings* with *more white on the tips above*. Adult Great Black-backs in W Europe also have blacker upperwing and back than Lesser Black-backs breeding in the area, while in the Baltic the comparison is the other way around. Immature is distinguished from immature Lesser Black-back by paler inner primaries than outer, heavier bill and narrower black tail band, from immature Herring Gull (with some difficulty) by larger size, *heavier bill* and often paler head and tail. Birds of the year during the first two or three months, however, are in practice very like immature Herring Gulls in plumage; head and neck do not become lighter until their first winter or spring, and even then the difference can be subtle. One-year-old bird is like juvenile, but with whiter head and tail. Dark back (not wings) acquired in second winter. Flies with quite *slow, powerful wingbeats*. Feeds on fish, offal and eggs and young of birds, can also kill full-grown birds of some size. Calls are *very deep and low-pitched*, gruff 'klaow', 'ga ga ga' etc. RSW

Lesser Black-backed Gull *Larus fuscus* L 53, W 127. Breeds quite commonly in colonies on coast, locally also at inland waters. British race *graellsii*, which is partly resident, partly migratory, is pale slate-coloured on back and inner upperwings. Baltic race *fuscus* is strongly migratory, passes overland across Europe to winter in the Mediterranean Sea and E Africa; this race is much darker, black on back and upperwings. (An intermediate race *intermedius* breeds in SW Scandinavia.) Distinguished from Great Black-back by *smaller* size, *thinner bill, yellow legs* and slightly *narrower and more pointed wings*, which have *merely a white spot at the very tip* above. Immature Lesser Black-backs are recognised in N and NW Europe by fact that *all flight feathers are almost uniformly brownish-black*. (Immature Herring Gulls of S and SE Europe also have rather uniform dark flight feathers.) Other marks are *darker general impression* (created above all by *dark upper greater coverts*), darker underwings, and very broad dark outer edge to tail. Dark back is acquired at about 1 year of age. Calls not quite so gruff as Great Black-back's, but *deeper* and *more nasal* than Herring Gull's. RSWP

Herring Gull *Larus argentatus* L 54–60, W 123–148. Breeds commonly in colonies or in isolated pairs along sea coasts but also by inland lakes. Often seen in harbours and at rubbish tips, present in winter and in large numbers. Adult distinguished from Common Gull by larger size, slower, lazier wingbeats, *yellow eyes* and *bright yellow bill with red spot* near tip, from adult Great and Lesser Black-backs from below in flight by lack of dark grey panel along rear edge of wingtip. Legs are greyish-pink, but yellow in races in E Europe and the Mediterranean (*cachinnans* group; species status suggested by some). Immature is distinguished from immature Lesser Black-back by *paler inner primaries than outer* (though many immatures in S and SE Europe have uniformly dark primaries, exactly as in Lesser Black-back), from immature Great Black-back (with some difficulty) by smaller size, weaker bill and in most cases slightly darker overall impression and broader dark tail band. Pearl-grey back is acquired in second autumn. Often seen high in the sky, circling in loose flocks, or in direct flight (often in V formation), purposeful but with lazy beats of the gently bowed wings, on route to feeding or roosting site. Often hangs in the wind above the surf, follows fishing boats. Lives on fish and offal as well as birds' eggs and young. Sometimes seen diving clumsily from lower height. The usual calls are loud 'kleow', triumphant, crowing 'klaOW-klaOW-klaOW- . . .' and also short whinnying 'ge-ge-ge'. RSWP

■□□ **Great Black-backed Gull** adults displaying

□■□ **Great Black-backed Gull** subadult winter (4th-winter or possibly advanced 3rd-winter)

□□■ **Great Black-backed Gull** 1st-summer

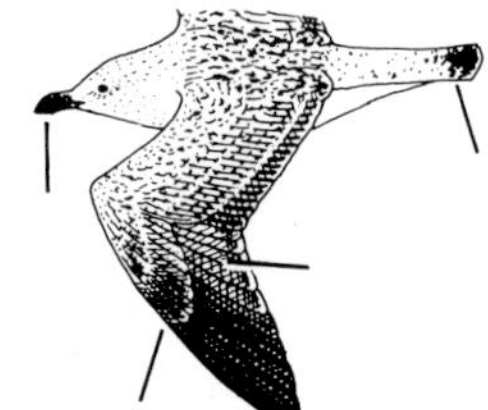

Great Black-backed Gull 1st-winter

■□□ **Great Black-backed Gull** 1st-winter in flight

□■□ **Lesser Black-backed Gull** adult summer race *graellsii*

□□■ **Lesser Black-backed Gull** adult in flight race *fuscus*

Lesser Black-backed Gull, 1st-winter

■□□ **Lesser Black-backed Gull** juv.

□■□ **Lesser Black-backed Gull** juv. in flight race *fuscus*

□□■ **Herring Gull** adult race *michahellis* (Mediterranean)

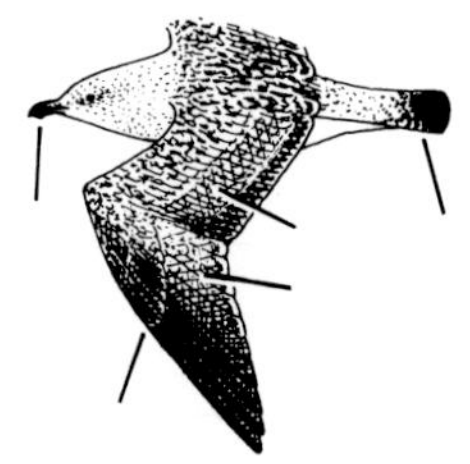

Herring Gull, 1st-winter

■□□ **Herring Gull** juv.

□■□ **Herring Gull** 2nd-winter/2nd-summer

□□■ **Herring Gull** 1st-winter in flight

Waders, gulls and auks

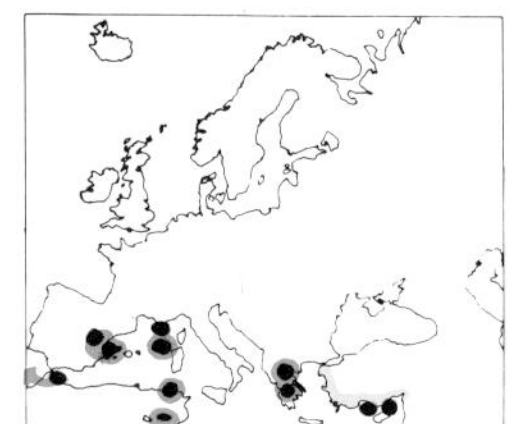

Audouin's Gull *Larus audouinii* L 48, W 122. Uncommon and local in occurrence, breeds in small colonies on islands in the Mediterranean Sea. Distinguished from the most similar Herring Gull by slimmer build and characteristic bill and *black outer primaries with only the very outermost tips white.* At a distance the dark red *bill looks black.* Note also that the grey of the back fades into white nape and tail without sharp division. Only indistinct white trailing edge on secondaries. Juvenile has whitish face and crown, *all the flight feathers are almost evenly dark* as are greater coverts. In 2nd year acquires plumage recalling immature Mediterranean Gull with *distinct dark terminal band on white tail* and along inner wing. Immature Herring Gulls in Mediterranean usually have whiter tail base and darker terminal band on tail than those in W and N Europe, so confusion risk can arise, but Herring Gull is slightly larger. Call weak, hoarse and nasal.

■□□ **Audouin's Gull** adult in flight
□■□ **Audouin's Gull** 1st-summer in flight
□□■ **Ring-billed Gull** 2nd-winter

Ring-billed Gull *Larus delawarensis* L 48, W 120. Rare visitor from N America, now annual in Britain (sometimes in small groups). Like a large Common Gull or small Herring Gull. Adults yellowish *bill with distinct black band across.* Legs (greenish) yellowish, *iris pale.* First-winter similar to first-winter Common Gull but is larger, has heavier, *pink bill with black tip,* paler grey mantle, *more distinct spots* (some crescent-shaped) *on lower neck, breast and flanks,* and tail pattern differs: *dark subterminal tail band broken up* by paler narrow bars, especially distally (not all-black and clear-cut as in Common Gull); upper- and undertail-coverts rather prominently spotted. Legs pinkish. Second-winter told from Common Gull of same age by generally retained prominent dark spots on lower neck, and *remnants of narrow dark subterminal tail band,* pale iris, and by bill and legs rather like in adult. V

■□□ **Ring-billed Gull** 1st-winter
□■□ **Ring-billed Gull** 2nd-winter
□□■ **Common Gull** adult summer

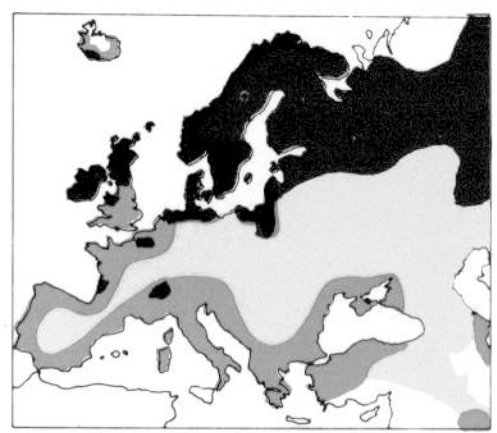

Common Gull *Larus canus* L 43, W 109. Breeds commonly (in Britain locally) in isolated pairs or colonially, by coastal and inland waters, mainly in N Europe. Preferred nest site is high up, e.g. on large boulders sticking up out of the water (also on piles, even house roofs). Picks up worms on fields in flocks. Adult like Herring Gull, but smaller and narrower-winged, flies with quicker and more vigorous wingbeats, and has *dark eyes* and *weaker, greenish-yellow bill without red spot.* Distinguished from Kittiwake by prominent white patches on the otherwise black tips of the primaries. Juvenile has *sharply defined black band on the tail,* brown back which is moulted to blue-grey as early as the autumn, brown wing-coverts which are retained during the winter. Calls are higher and weaker than Herring Gull's, are loud, heard often, e.g. high cackling 'kakaka . . . ', falsetto scream 'kleee-a', and also persistent alarm call 'klee-UU-klee-UU- . . . '. RSWP

■□□ **Common Gull** 1st-winter
□■□ **Common Gull** 1st-summer in flight
□□■ **Common Gull** adult in flight

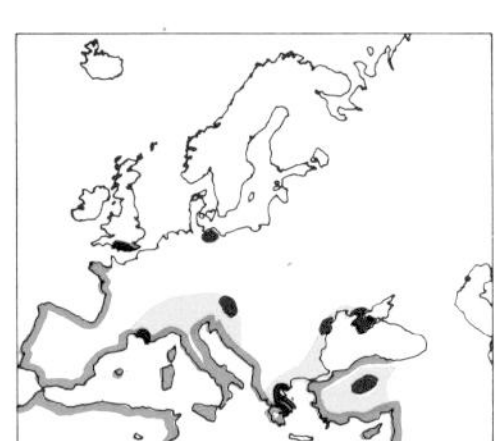

Mediterranean Gull *Larus melanocephalus* L 37, W 98. Nests colonially on steppe lakes, coastal marshes etc in SE Europe. Range expanding towards NW; occasionally breeds S England (hybridises with Black-headed Gull), increasing in winter/on passage. Slightly larger and heavier than Black-headed Gull but smaller and shorter-winged than Common Gull. Adult distinguished from Black-headed and *heavier, more obtuse bill* (dark band near tip), by *pure white primaries,* as well as in summer plumage by hood which is *black* (not brown) and extends far down onto nape. When the hood is lost in late summer, the bird looks generally *very white.* Immature very like paler examples of immature Common Gull but is slightly smaller, has *heavier bill,* has *greyish-white, not so dark grey back* (back brown in the very first plumage but is soon moulted to greyish-white), and more contrasty wings with brownish-black outer primaries (showing diagnostic *whitish subterminal spots* when fully spread), *whitish inner primaries* together with distinct brownish-black bar across the secondaries, bordered in front by pale *greyish-white greater coverts* (lesser wing-coverts spotted brown); also has *dark behind eye.* Call nasal, shrill, a little like skua, 'jeeah'. SWP

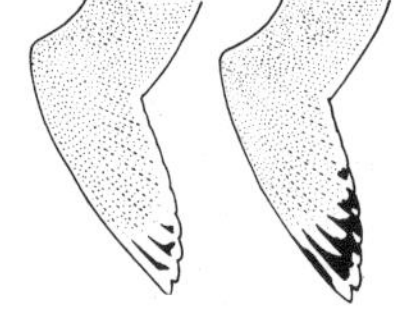

Mediterranean Gull, 2nd summer (variation)

■□□ **Mediterranean Gull** moulting to adult summer plumage
□■□ **Mediterranean Gull** adult winter in flight
□□■ **Mediterranean Gull** moulting to 1st-winter in flight

Waders, gulls and auks

Slender-billed Gull *Larus genei* L 40, W 96. Breeds by lakes and coastal lagoons (often among terns), in small numbers and locally in S Europe, in large colonies from the Black Sea and eastwards. Resembles Black-headed Gull, mainly through wings having the same pattern, but Slender-billed Gull is larger and slightly slimmer in build: bill, neck, tail, wings and legs are proportionately longer than in Black-headed Gull; also tail more fully rounded, *forehead has a flatter slope merging evenly into the long* (but not slender!) *bill*, which appears a shade down-curved. Bill and legs in adult red, at a distance in the field 'dark', in immature dirty-yellow, the bill with darker tip. *Iris* in adult *pale*. Immature, which like some adults outside the breeding season has Black-headed Gull's dark patch behind the eye (though paler), is recognised by shape, by the slower, more vigorous flight (larger wingspan, proportionately longer inner wing). Nevertheless, long-billed immature Black-headed Gulls are occasionally seen – confusingly. Call nasal, deeper than Black-headed Gull's. V

■□□ **Slender-billed Gull** adult summer

□■□ **Slender-billed Gull** 1st-winter (right) with adult winter Black-headed Gull (left)

□□■ **Slender-billed Gull** 1st-winter dipping to water

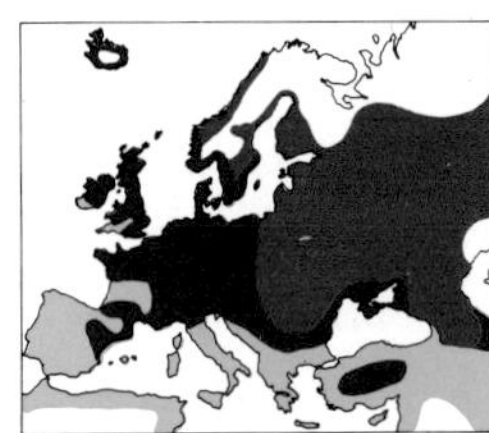

Black-headed Gull *Larus ridibundus* L 38, W 91. Nests commonly in colonies, which can sometimes become huge (thousands of pairs), on reedy lakes and marshes both inland and coastal, also on low islands. Often found in cities and harbours, as well as on farmland. Seen together with Common Gull in large flocks following the plough. Catches winged insects in flocks high in the sky during the day, low over the reeds in the evening (in cities occasionally by artificial lights). The only common gull in Britain with *dark hood* (chocolate-brown). *Upperwings* in all plumages *have a triangular white panel* formed by the outer 4–5 primaries. *Underwings* are always *partly dark grey with a broad white fore-edge*. Adult has feet and bill dark brownish-red, in summer plumage brown hood leaving the nape white (a little white also at the eye), in winter plumage white head with dark spot at the ear. Juveniles are reddish-brown on back, nape and crown, soon moult this to grey and white, respectively, but retain brown wing-covert bar and dark tail band. Feet yellowish-brown, bill yellowish-brown with black tip. Slender-billed Gull is very similar in winter and immature plumages (see that species). Call a screaming, rolling 'krreeay', 'krre' etc. RSWP

■□□ **Black-headed Gull** adults at breeding colony

□■□ **Black-headed Gull** 1st-winter

□□■ **Black-headed Gull** adult winter in flight

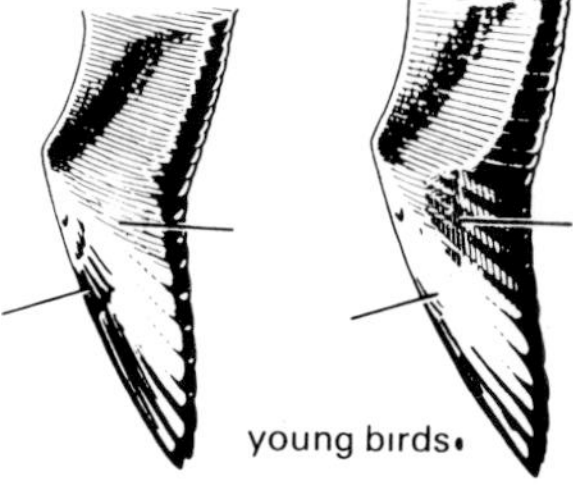

Bonaparte's Gull *Larus philadelphia* L 33, W 82. Breeds in desolate coniferous forests in North America, in isolated pairs with the nests up in spruces. Rare vagrant to W Europe, most often in winter, often among Black-headed Gulls. In summer, adult is distinguished from Black-headed Gull by *sooty-black* (not brown) *hood* and *all-black bill*. Legs bright red. In all plumages *undersides of primaries are pale greyish-white*, not largely dark as in Black-headed. Smaller and more elegant than Black-headed Gull, especially in flight, which is buoyant and resembles Little Gull's. The immature resembles immature Black-headed, but the leading, longest primaries and especially the primary coverts have more black (see fig.); as in the full adult it lacks dark grey patch on underside of primaries. Bill grey-black, legs yellowish. Call a low, almost Coot-like cackle. V

■□□ **Black-headed Gull** adult summer calling

□■□ **Black-headed Gull** juv.

□□■ **Black-headed Gull** 1st-winter in flight

■□□ **Bonaparte's Gull** adult winter (far right) with three adult winter Black-headed Gulls

□■□ **Bonaparte's Gull** adult winter in flight

□□■ **Bonaparte's Gull** adult winter

Waders, gulls and auks

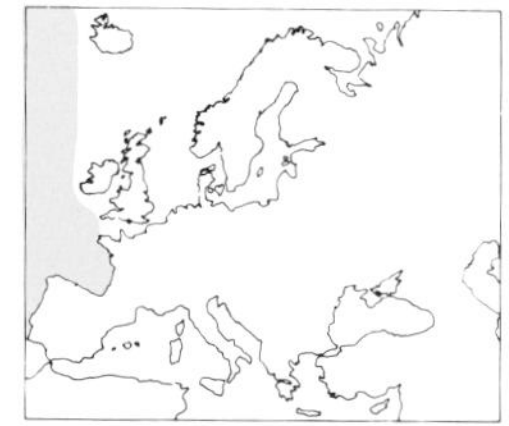

Sabine's Gull

Sabine's Gull *Larus sabini* L 33, W 84. Breeds in the Arctic. Winters usually far out to sea off S Africa and S America. On migration (adults first, juveniles later) may be blown in to W European coasts by heavy storms. Adult in summer is typical with *slate-grey hood* and black bill with yellow tip. In all plumages note characteristic *black, white, and grey* (ad.) *or brown* (juv.) *triangles on wings*. Tail more obviously forked than in Kittiwake. *Juvenile rather uniform brownish on forewing and on crown to back, incl. sides of neck*, leaving forehead, 'eyelids' and throat white. At distance can be confused with young Kittiwake, whose dark diagonal band across inner wing behind pale grey lesser wing-coverts can look like uniform brown-grey panel. See also 1st-summer Kittiwake. Versatile feeding habits: runs, spins (phalarope), dives (clumsy tern). Flight light and tern-like. Call grating and tern-like. P

■□□ **Sabine's Gull** juv.
□■□ **Sabine's Gull** adult summer in flight
□□■ **Sabine's Gull** juv. in flight

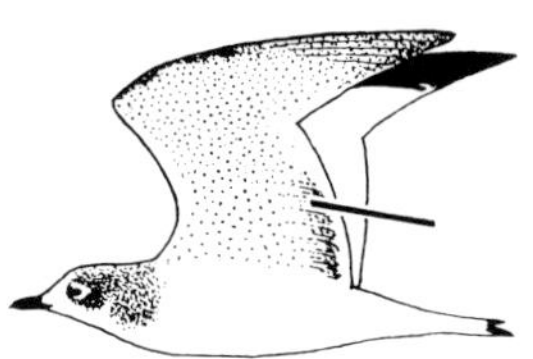

Sabine's Gull, juv.

Kittiwake *Rissa tridactyla* L 40, W 95. Breeds Atlantic coast in large colonies on precipices of bird cliffs (the nests sited like swallows' on diminutive projections), sometimes also on conveniently situated building. Outside breeding season found mostly at sea. Swarms around fishing boats. Regular on passage, large numbers sometimes blown in to coasts in storms in autumn and winter. Flight noticeably lighter and more elegant than Common Gull's, in rough weather the action is more like Fulmar's. Tail square or shallowly forked. *Legs black* and rather short. Adults resemble Common Gulls but have *all-black wingtips* and wings more uniform in width ('fuller' hand), and upperside tricoloured: black wingtip, pale grey outer wing, darker grey inner wing and back (Common Gull is bicoloured: the grey is uniform). Immature with its black diagonal bar on upperwing recalls immature Little Gull and others but differs in broad, *distinct black nape band*, Common Gull size and also always *white crown* and pure white secondaries. 1st-summer generally lacks nape band and has smudgy dark markings on wing-coverts, can be confused with Sabine's. Call, 'kittiweelK', in nasal falsetto. RSWP

■□□ **Kittiwake** 1st-winter in flight
□■□ **Kittiwake** adult summer in flight
□□■ **Kittiwake** adult winter

Little Gull *Larus minutus* L 26, W 63. Breeds in E Europe, occasionally in Britain, in rushy marshes and reedy lakes, usually among Black-headed Gulls. Sometimes in large numbers on passage. Maritime in winter. *Smallest* of Europe's gulls. In the evenings hunts winged insects over the reeds as Black-headed Gull, but flight considerably more rapid and elegant. Also snatches insects from surface of water. All year round, adults appear to have *rounded wings* with greyish-white upperside and *blackish underside with conspicuous white trailing edge*, in summer also a jet-black hood which extends far down onto nape. Juveniles have more pointed wings which are pale below and have a *black angled band above*. Back, mantle and crown are blackish-brown. Back is moulted to grey during first autumn, but dark upper mantle is retained somewhat longer, producing *Kittiwake-like look*. However, is markedly smaller, has darkish secondaries and often sooty-grey crown. Following spring/early summer black hood develops, angled wing pattern still shown. Calls loud and nasal, e.g. 'kep', often repeated in series. Display call 'ke-KAY ke-KAY ke-KAY . . .' uttered with wings beating low down and neck upstretched. WP

■□□ **Little Gull** juv. in flight
□■□ **Little Gull** adult winter in flight
□□■ **Little Gull** adult summer in flight

Ross's Gull *Rhodostethia rosea* L 30, W 77. Breeds on rivers in easternmost Siberia, but scattered breeding records known from Greenland, Svalbard and Canada. Encountered in the pack-ice zone in winter and summer too. Very rare visitor to coasts of W Europe. As small as Little Gull (major confusion possibility), but has *longer and more pointed wings*. That tail is wedge-shaped (unique among Europe's gulls), is not so easily seen, but *the tail appears long*. Adult has *strong pink tone below* in summer and often a hint also in winter. Narrow black necklace diagnostic Wing markings essentially as in Little Gull, incl. *grey undersides with broad white rear edge*. Young has markings like young Little Gull. Flight light, tern-like. Silent outside breeding range. V

Ross's Gull, adult summer

■□□ **Little Gull** 1st-winter
□■□ **Ross's Gull** adult winter in flight
□□■ **Ross's Gull** adult winter

Waders, gulls and auks

Laughing Gull *Larus atricilla* L 39, W 105. Very rare visitor from N America. Size of Common Gull but has *longer, more pointed wings*. Rather short-legged, gives long-bodied, slim impression on the ground. *Bill powerful and long, culmen curved down* giving 'drooping' look. Can be confused only with Franklin's Gull. Adult has black hood with white crescents above and below eye, sooty-grey mantle and upperwing (inner wing with white trailing edge) and *black wingtips without white*. First-winter is sooty-brown above, on breast and on the head (apart from pale forehead, chin and eye-ring), has very *dark flight feathers* (inner wing with white trailing edge), white uppertail-coverts and *grey* tail feathers with broad black terminal band. Underwing-coverts heavily patterned grey. Blackish legs. Second-winter told from adults by more extensive black on wingtips and by traces of tail band remaining. V

Franklin's Gull *Larus pipixcan* L 34, W 87. Very rare visitor from North America. Slightly smaller than a Black-Headed Gull and has more rounded wings. A distinctive species, the only risk of confusion being Laughing Gull. In all plumages has *prominent white crescents above and below eye* ('swollen eyelids'), more so than in Laughing Gull. Bill rather heavy, but not so long and 'drooping' as in Laughing. Adult has black hood, *dark grey mantle and upperwing*, prominent white trailing edge, and *white area inside black and white wingtip*; centre of tail is light grey. First-winter has, like adult winter, a *dark half-hood* (darker and more clear-cut than in other winter gulls), rather *narrow dark tail band* leaving the outermost tail feathers light (first-winter Laughing has wider tail band running across all tail feathers), and pale underwing (Laughing has rather dark pattern on wing-coverts). Unlike other gulls has two complete moults a year, the second in early spring prior to northward migration: meaning that first-summer birds return with a more adult type of wing, though lacking the white area between dark wingtip and rest of upperwing; leading edge of primaries blackish, and dark hood is half or almost complete. V

Ivory Gull *Pagophila eburnea* L 44, W 107. Arctic species. Breeds in loose, small colonies, mainly on cliff precipices (even on drifting ice). Builds nest (larger and untidier than Kittiwake's) on ledge. Patrols vast expanses of pack-ice and edges of ice, seldom seen south of ice zone. Feeds on fish, excrement from seal and polar bear, prey remains, carrion and offal. Snatches food from the water's surface, and will also alight on the water. Markedly fearless, readily resorts to camp bases. Said often to fly to places where guns are being discharged. Size of Common Gull. Adult *white, with yellowish bill with blue-grey base*. Immature is sparsely *spotted black above*, has darker bill and *'dirty' face*. The *short legs are black in all plumages*. The Ivory Gull gives a relatively long-winged impression, and its flight is light and elegant. Call recalls drake Wigeon's, 'pfEEoo' or with an 'r' sound, 'frrEEay'. V

■□□ **Laughing Gull** 1st-winter
□■□ **Laughing Gull** adult winter
□□■ **Laughing Gull** juv. in flight

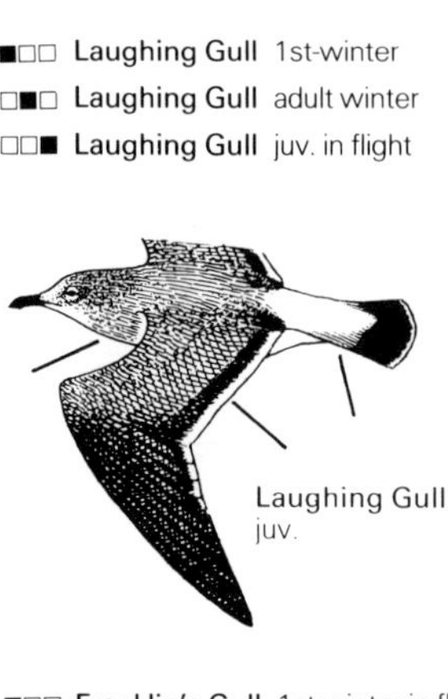
Laughing Gull, juv.

■□□ **Franklin's Gull** 1st-winter in flight
□■□ **Franklin's Gull** 1st-winter in flight
□□■ **Ivory Gull** adult summer

Ivory Gull 1st-winter
Ivory Gull 1st-winter in flight
Ivory Gull 1st-winter in flight

Waders, gulls and auks

Terns

(order Charadriiformes, family Sternidae). Slender build. Long narrow wings. Forked tails. Pointed bills. Small legs.

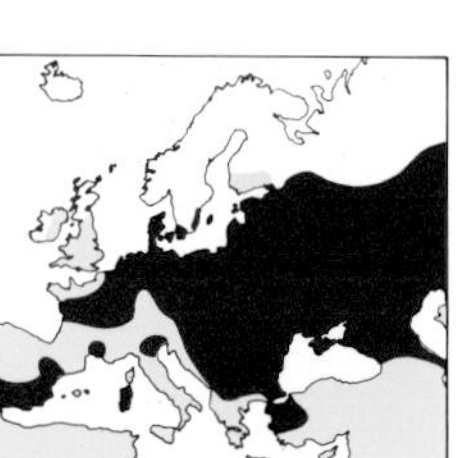

Black Tern *Chlidonias niger* L 24. Nests colonially in quagmire marshes and fens. Outside breeding season found mainly along coasts. Passage migrant in Britain, incl. inland. Feeds mainly by snatching insects from surface of water while moving about in graceful and playful flight. Often hangs fluttering few inches above aquatic vegetation. Also catches flying insects. Does not dive like the white terns, at least not during the breeding season. Unmistakable in summer plumage, which is *wholly dark* (dark grey, head and breast almost black) except for *pale grey underwings* and *white undertail-coverts*. Distinguished in winter and immature plumages from White-winged Black Tern mainly by *dark patch on sides of neck*, slightly *darker upperwings*, and as a rule grey, not whitish, uppertail-coverts (beware: occasional juveniles are paler here and in the field can appear almost white), as well as evenly grey tail. In addition the crown shawl is practically uniform dark grey. The commonest calls are a short, sharp, nasal, shrill 'kyeh' and a conversational 'klit'. SP

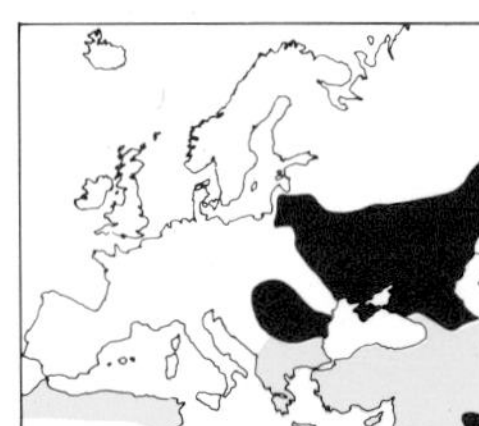

White-winged Black Tern *Chlidonias leucopterus* L 24. Breeds in SE Europe in swamplands. Seen on passage along sea coasts. Very like Black Tern in behaviour. Adult in summer plumage easily recognised even at long range by *jet-black body and underwing-coverts, gleaming white on the tail area and whitish on upper-wing-coverts*. Compared with Black Tern usually has slightly shorter bill, broader wings and shorter tail – is slightly more compact, but the difference is subtle. Distinguished from Black Tern in winter and immature plumages by *lack of dark patch on sides of neck*, slightly *paler upperwings*, generally (but not always obviously) paler, whitish rump/uppertail-coverts, *whitish outer sides of tail* which contrast with otherwise light grey tail, and by paler crown shawl (front part is just dark marks on white background). In juveniles there is also *greater contrast between sooty-brown back* ('saddle') *and pale wings and tail*. (Winter plumage adults have rather pale grey back.) In winter plumage very like Whiskered Tern (which see). Call dry and harsh, 'kesch', like Grey Partridge in tone. Short conversational notes, 'kek'. V

Whiskered Tern *Chlidonias hybridus* L 25. Breeds in swamps in S Europe. On migration on sea coasts. Similarity to Black Tern immediately revealed by restless, acrobatic flying around, usually low over the quagmire and flooded meadows, from which aquatic insects are snatched up (also dives from air). Plumage (adult, summer) appears at a distance whitish like *Sterna* terns, and in strong sunlight dark colour on underparts can be taken for effect of shadow. Still distinctive: *sooty-grey on whole of underparts* from belly to neck. *Head appears white except for the black tern-cap*. In winter plumage very like White-winged Black Tern, but can sometimes be distinguished by slightly *larger size, longer and heavier bill*, and no white wedge projecting up behind ear-coverts. Juvenile very like juvenile White-winged Black, but white *nape band narrow or broken* and white wedge projecting up into dark on ear-coverts is merely suggested. Mantle/back sooty-brown, feathers broadly tipped buffish-white (moulted early to pale grey first-winter feathers). *Wings pale* as in juvenile Common Tern. Note *lack of markedly dark fore-edge of arm*. Rump/uppertail-coverts whitish, tail pale grey with narrow dark subterminal band. Commonest call is a short, loud, almost Corncrake-like 'krsch'. V

Sooty Tern *Sterna fuscata* L 40. Breeds in gigantic colonies on small oceanic islands in the tropics. Fishes very far out at sea. Does not dive but snatches fish from surface in flight. *Large* as a Sandwich Tern. Forked tail, long tail streamers. At all times white below and *sooty-black above* (back as dark as crown) and *white forehead* reaching the eye (but not further). Immature entirely sooty-brown. Voluble, including shrill, nasal 'wehde-wehk'. V

■□□ **Black Tern** pair at nest
□■□ **Black Tern** adult spring in flight
□□■ **Black Tern** juv. in flight

■□□ **Black Tern** juv. in flight
□■□ **White-winged Black Tern** adult summer (centre right) with 1st-summer birds
□□■ **White-winged Black Tern** adult spring in flight

White-winged Black Tern, juv

Whiskered Tern, juv.

■■□ **White-winged Black Tern** flock in flight incl. adult winter, 1st-winter and some late juvs
□□■ **Whiskered Tern** adult summer

■□□ **Whiskered Tern** adult summer in flight
□■□ **Whiskered Tern** winter in flight
□□■ **Sooty Tern** adult in flight (moulting primaries)

Waders, gulls and auks

Sandwich Tern *Sterna sandvicensis* L 40. Nests in colonies locally on coastal islands, usually on sandy coasts. On migration wholly tied to sea. Fishes further out at sea, plunges from greater height than other terns. Often noticed by *call* and recognised by *general paleness, long, narrow wings,* short tail, powerful flight with deep rather hurried wingbeats, *long slender black bill* (with yellow tip) and, on ground, by suggestion of crest and black *short legs.* In winter plumage (often from July) forehead is white (not the whole crown as in Gull-billed, from which also distinguished by long slender bill and narrow wings). Juvenile usually has all-dark bill, little white on forehead (less than juvenile Gull-billed) and dark-patterned back and fore wing-coverts. The adults, which in late summer accompany their offspring during fishing, have contrastingly darker grey outer primaries and often different wing shape owing to moult. Species often revealed by its call, a loud, penetrating, grating 'kee-yek' (like amalgam being pressed into a tooth). Immatures' call is clearer, more ringing, 'kee-e' SP

Gull-billed Tern *Gelochelidon nilotica* L 38. Nests in colonies, uncommonly and locally in W and S Europe, also Denmark, on coastal marshes and sandy shores. Less tied to the sea than other terns, hunts mainly over land, coastal marshes and pasture meadows. Food consists mostly of insects – grasshoppers and crickets, beetles and dragonflies – but also of frogs, reptiles, mice and small crabs. Main species characteristic is the *gull-like, thick, black bill.* Leisurely, steady flight recalls Caspian Tern, but wings are very long, narrow and pointed, much as Sandwich Tern. No contrast between dark outer and pale inner primaries as in Sandwich. Dark trailing edge below to outer primaries narrow and distinct. Tail is short and shallowly forked. When standing, Gull-billed Tern shows characteristic *long black legs.* Rump and upper-tail pale grey. In winter plumage there is only very little black behind the eye (Sandwich Tern has black on the nape), *head* is therefore *almost all-white.* Juvenile very like juvenile Sandwich Tern but has *more white on forehead,* shorter and thicker bill together with different wing shape. Call a distinctive, nasal 'kayWEK'. Alarm a rapid series of nasal, almost laughing notes, 'kevee-kevee-kevee-kevee', quite different from relatives (but resembling displaying Bar-tailed Godwit). The young beg with squeaky 'piuu' notes. V

Caspian Tern *Sterna caspia* L 53. Breeds in the Baltic Sea, in large or small colonies on the outermost skerries of the archipelagoes, and feeds particularly in inner island groups and larger inland lakes (therefore flies daily tens of miles to and fro). Baltic Caspian Terns migrate partly across the Continent to the Mediterranean Sea on route to African winter quarters, do not avoid land like the Sandwich Tern. Dives for fish, but not too daringly like, e.g. Sandwich Tern. Very big, *almost as large as Herring Gull.* Large, gleaming red bill ('carrot'), visible even at long range, is, together with *the call* and the almost *gull-like leisurely flight,* the best field character. In flight the head area appears strikingly large, *neck long and thick, projecting well forward,* and *tail short.* Legs black. Wing is pale grey above but has black wedge at tip below. Juveniles distinguished from adults by *more orange bill* with dark tip, *brown-and-white-speckled cap* which reaches farther down than on adult, varyingly dark *scaly pattern* on back and wings and also *pale legs* (which are the age character visible at greatest range on standing birds). Call very deep, loud and heron-like in harshness, 'kraay-ap'. Begging call of young often given on late-summer migration is a squeaky 'slee-wee'. V

Sandwich Tern breeding colony

Sandwich Tern adults at nest (left bird moulting into winter plumage)

Sandwich Tern adult winter

Gull-billed Tern, winter

Sandwich Tern 1st-winter

Gull-billed Tern adult summer in flight

Gull-billed Tern 1st-winter in flight

Caspian Tern cuddling nestling

Caspian Tern adult summer in flight

Caspian Tern winter in flight

Waders, gulls and auks

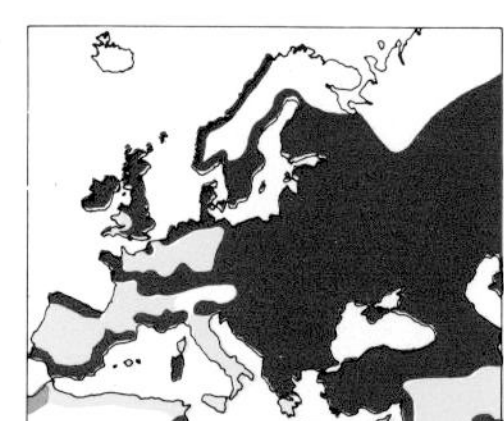

Common Tern *Sterna hirundo* L 35. Breeds in isolated pairs or smallish colonies on coastal marshes and islands, also on shores of inland lakes (incl. those with murky water). Frequently dives for fish. Best distinguished from rather similar Arctic Tern by following: *shorter tail streamers*, broader wings, *faster and more rigidly clipping wingbeats* (yet quite elegant, and when displaying exquisitely slow, elegant wingbeats, exactly like displaying Arctic Tern), larger head (*longer neck and bill*), longer legs. *Outer primaries above are slightly darker grey than inner ones*, and the transition looks like a *'nick' in the rear edge of wing* (Arctic Tern uniformly pale grey). Wings not so transparent when seen from below (mostly only the inner primaries). The *dark orange-red bill nearly always has a black tip*. Juvenile has *grey secondaries* (with white tips; not all-white) and clearly marked *dark grey leading edge of wing* above. Back normally with heavy, sooty, wavy barring. *Inner part of bill usually orange-toned* (not all-dark bill as in Arctic Tern). Voice often noticeably deeper than Arctic Tern's. Usual calls while fishing, courting and squabbling are short sharp 'kitt', rapid 'kyekyekyekye . . .' and also characteristic 'kirri-kirri-kirri . . .'. Alarm against humans a drawn-out 'kreee-eh' against, e.g. crows a sharp 'ktchay'. SP

▶ **Arctic Tern** *Sterna paradisaea* L 38. Breeds in colonies on islands, grassy dunes etc on clear-water coasts and also by small upland tarns. Shows less bias towards diving for fish than Common Tern, more inclined to snatch small animals from the surface of the water and to catch insects in flight. Best distinguished from similar Common Tern by following: *longer tail streamers*, narrower wings, even more elegant flight with *leisurely, springy wingbeats*, small head (*short neck and bill*), *very short legs*. Upperwings uniformly light grey, *without 'nick' in edge*. On wing seen from below against the light *all the flight feathers appear transparent*. *Blood-red bill*, normally without black tip. Grey-toned throatside of neck, separated from black cap by broad white band. Juvenile is recognised by *almost white secondaries* (grey with white tips in Common Tern) and also *not such dark grey leading edge of wing* above; back has only hint of wavy grey barring; *bill all-dark*. Several calls rather like Common Tern's, but in courting and squabbling they have respectively squeakier and clearer ('pee-pee-pee-pee', clear ringing 'pree-e') or harder and rattling calls ('kt-kt-kt-krrr-kt-kt-') than latter. Alarm call against humans a dryer and more rasping scream than Common Tern, 'kree-ERRR', against e.g. crows a loud, sharp 'kIEEu'. SP

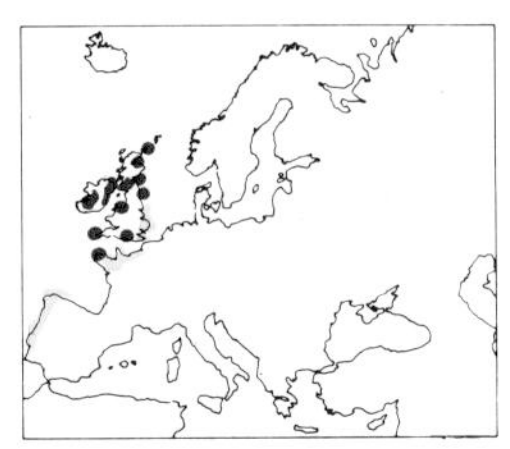

▶ **Roseate Tern** *Sterna dougallii* L 38. Breeds sparsely and locally in W Europe along coasts, often with Common and Arctic Terns. *Paler above* than both its relatives, appears strikingly *whitish*. Wings proportionately shorter, and *tail streamers* normally *very long and pure white*. *Bill long and black with red only at base*. *Legs longer* than in Common Tern. At close range pink tinge visible on breast during breeding season. In winter plumage like Common Tern, but general impression is whiter, and long tail streamers are retained. Juvenile has restricted white on forehead, pattern of back as juvenile Sandwich, primaries without dark on tips, legs black. In flight resembles Sandwich Tern, in spite of long streamers, looks light and rather 'front heavy'. *Calls characteristic*, a rapid soft 'chuWIK' and a broad, hoarse rasping 'zraaaach'. S

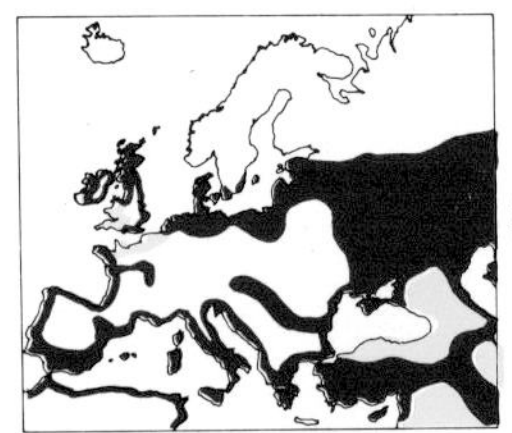

▶ **Little Tern** *Sterna albifrons* L 23. Breeds sparsely to uncommonly in small colonies on flat, sandy or shingle coasts (on the Continent also at shallow, sandy inland lakes). *Smallest* of Europe's terns. *White forehead* in all plumages, *black-tipped yellow bill* (in spring and early summer) and *yellow legs* (all year). Juvenile is recognised chiefly by small size. Short-tailed. Flies quickly with fast wingbeats (rather like ringed plovers when it rushes about over the water). Gives butterfly-like impression when hovering above the water. Often dives excitedly over and over again, in rapid succession. Active and noisy, call a hoarse, shrill 'pret-pret'. S

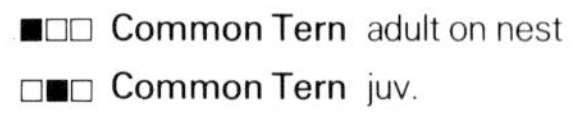

■□□ Common Tern adult on nest
□■□ Common Tern juv.
□□■ Common Tern adult in flight

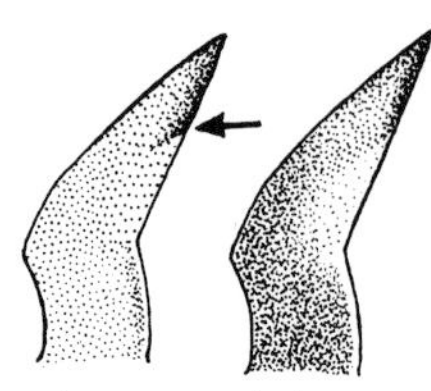

Common Tern, adult

■□□ Arctic Tern adult summer
□■□ Arctic Tern juv.
□□■ Arctic Tern adult summer in flight from below

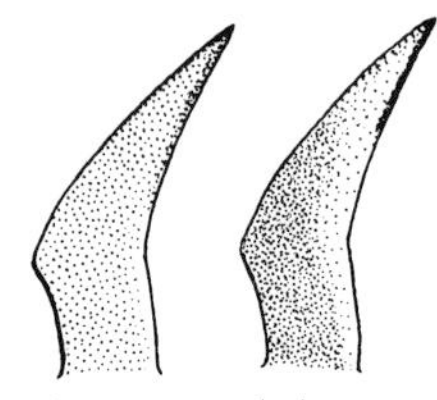

Arctic Tern, adult

■□□ Roseate Tern adult summer pair
□■□ Roseate Tern juv.
□□■ Roseate Tern adult summer in flight

■□□ Little Tern pair at nest
□■□ Little Tern juv.
□□■ Little Tern adult summer hovering

Waders, gulls and auks

Auks (order Charadriiformes. family Alcidae) are black and white, ocean-dwelling birds with short tails and narrow wings. Flight swift, close above the sea, wingbeats fast as propellers. Silent outside breeding season. Come ashore only to breed. Nest in large colonies on sea cliffs (which look like gigantic bee-hives). Swim underwater using the wings, feet serve as rudder. Different winter and summer plumage. Immatures resemble the adults. Clutches, 1-2 eggs.

Razorbill *Alca torda* L 38. Nests in cliff colonies (though not as large as Guillemot's). Lays single egg under boulders, does not require steep cliff face like Guillemot. Outside breeding season lives far out at sea. *Bill deep* flattened sideways, is held raised as is the fairly long, pointed tail when Razorbill swims. Thicker and shorter neck than Guillemot. Distinguished from southern race of latter at long range by fact that *head and back are jet-black*, not brownish. Underwing-coverts pure white. Razorbill differs from N Atlantic dark-backed Guillemots in having *more white on sides of rump*: white hind area with black central line, actually like Long-tailed Duck (see fig). Also, *holds head and tail higher*, does not look hunch-backed like the guillemots, feet concealed by tail. Display flight startling: suddenly begins to fly in relatively slow motion. Call a grunting, jarring 'urrr', melancholy in tone. RS

Guillemot *Uria aalge* L 40. Nests in large colonies (thousands) on ledges on vertical cliff faces along coast and on offshore islands. Lays single, pear-shaped egg directly on to narrow ledge. Parents recognise their egg by its appearance, their chick by its call. The young jump off more or less all at the same time at late dusk during a few evenings in July, still incapable of flight. The young bird is then guided on the open sea by the male. Heavy body, narrow wings, flies swiftly with propeller-fast wingbeats close over the sea, often several individuals in a line. Has fairly *long and slender bill*, distinguished in other respects from Razorbill when perched by longer and slimmer neck and shorter tail. Southern race (Ireland, southern Scotland southwards) dull blackish-*brown* on back, in intense direct sunlight looks dark grey-brown on back, a major distinction from jet-black Razorbill. Northern race (Scotland and N Europe) is darker, closer to Razorbill. Some individuals, known as 'Bridled' Guillemots, have a white ring around eye and a white line running backwards across top of cheeks. In flight neck is retracted; looks *hunch-backed* in comparison with Razorbill; seems to have larger hind body; feet well visible; *white on sides of rump much more restricted*; underwing-coverts not pure white, have some dark admixed. See also Brünnich's Guillemot. In winter plumage, distinguished from Razorbill and Brünnich's Guillemot by the fact that *white on sides of head extends higher up* and is divided by a dark streak running backwards from eye and also that *sides of body are streaked*. Call a rumbling 'a-orrr', slightly 'happier' in tone than Razorbill's. RS

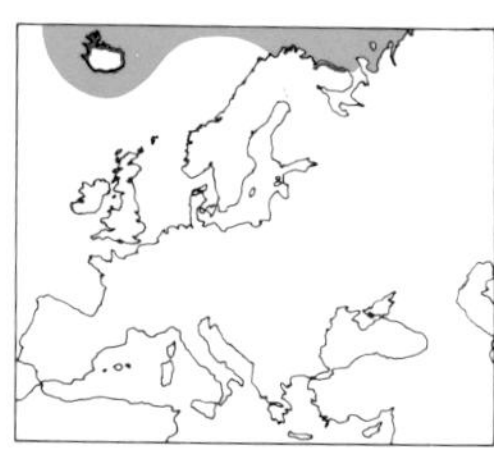

► **Brünnich's Guillemot** *Uria lomvia* L 40. Like Guillemot nests in large colonies on steep sea cliffs but has more northerly distribution. Best distinguished from Guillemot by *shorter and thicker bill* with thin *whitish streak at gape* and also by *unstreaked body sides* (Guillemot always has some amount of dark brown streaking on flanks.) White on foreneck ends pointed (rounded on Guillemot). Underwing-coverts and axillaries appear pale. Also is *darker* brown, almost blackish like Razorbill. In flight quite possible to pick out from preceding two species even at distance by following: *shorter, more compact*, 'pumped up' *body; hunch-backed*, even more so than Guillemot; bill pointing slightly downwards (Razor-bill straight, Guillemot intermediate); *much white at sides of rump*, just like Razorbill; feet visible. In short: head portion like Guillemot, tail portion like Razorbill. In winter plumage white on chin and throat, but black covers a large part of cheek (not the case in Guillemot). Call rumbling, with 'malevolent' tone. V

■□□ **Razorbill** adult summer
□■□ **Razorbill** adult summer in flight
□□■ **Razorbill** adult summer in flight

Razorbill

■□□ **Razorbill** adult summer flock on water with a few Guillemots
□■□ **Razorbill** 1st-winter
□□■ **Guillemot** adult summer southern race in flight

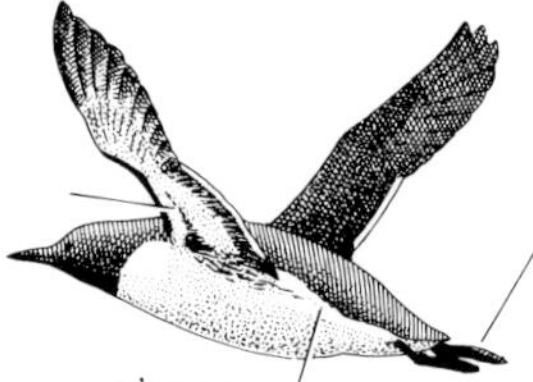

Guillemot

■■□ **Guillemot** adults on breeding ledge, incl. three 'bridled' birds
□■ **Guillemot** adult winter

Brünnich's Guillemot

■□ **Guillemot** adult summer flock on water with six Razorbills
□■ **Brünnich's Guillemot** adult summer

Waders, gulls and auks

Little Auk *Alle alle* L 20. Exceedingly abundant in the Arctic, where it nests in enormous colonies on the mountain slopes, not only on sea cliffs but also inland on nunataks. The egg is laid in a burrow. One of the world's individually most numerous species. Flies around nest mountain in swarms like mosquitoes. Very noisy, high-pitched trilling and nasal laughing calls echo in roaring chorus, 'keerrrr, kehehehehe'. Flies out to sea in flocks at high altitudes, fishes for plankton, returns in undulating bands, low over the water with chock-full throat sac. Outside breeding season lives far out at sea, but occasional individuals can sometimes be seen from land. After severe storms windblown individuals may be found far in over land. Much *smaller* than other auks, only size of a large Starling. Juvenile Puffin is an obvious confusion risk where a single bird is seen flying past at a distance. *Whirring wingbeats, underwings dark.* (Razorbill has white underwings.) Short bill. In flight appears extremely *short-necked.* On water usually swims with head retracted, looks quite neckless. Sometimes, though, stretches up and reveals surprisingly long neck. When resting, floats like a cork high on the water, glistens white, but when fishing, between dives, floats low and carries head even lower than tail, dark wings dragging in the water. W

Black Guillemot *Cepphus grylle* L 33. Nests quite commonly in isolated pairs or small groups under boulders on rocky coasts. Less tied to the sea than other auks, lives all year round nearer shore. In summer dress unmistakable with its *black plumage with large, oval white wing panels.* In flight has certain passing resemblance to male Velvet Scoter, but there should be no confusion even at very long range: Black Guillemot always looks quite different with its short, fusiform body, hunched attitude and *rapidly whirring wingbeats.* Lacquered-red feet glisten. *Always buzzes along low over the water.* In winter plumage sparkling white, though white wing panel still dark-framed. Juvenile is more grey-mottled, including scattering of grey even in wing panel (see fig), on some individuals considerable. One-year-old birds may look all-black (body feathers moulted, wing panels not; see fig). During the mating period Black Guillemots sit in groups and utter Rock Pipit-like 'seep-seep-seep- . . .' calls and drawn-out, thin but far-carrying 'electronic' peeps, at which time they open their bills wide (inside of mouth red). Also raise their wings and show the white wing panel. R

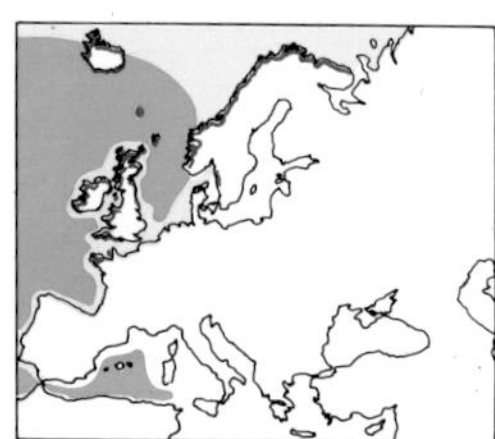

Puffin *Fratercula arctica* L 30. Nests on rocky islands and high rocky coasts in and on the coasts of the Atlantic, in colonies often containing thousands of pairs. Nest is in burrows in the earth or under boulder. In winter goes far out to sea, further out than any other auk except Little Auk. Note 'pot-bellied' body, big head and extraordinarily *deep, sideways-compressed bill,* grooved and gaudily coloured. At the breeding site birds are seen with their bill full of fish, which gives them a 'bearded' appearance. Frequently robbed of their fish by Arctic Skuas. The outer layers of the bill are shed in late summer, producing a narrower bill in winter dress. Immature has an even narrower bill. Greyish-white cheek darkens in winter plumage. When swimming, holds breast higher on the water than other auks, which lends characteristic silhouette. Usually seen in flocks. Flies low over the water in short lines. In flight *big pale head,* small size and short tail are striking. *Underwings fairly dark,* but slightly paler than Little Auk's (see fig.). Call is heard only at breeding site and consists of unmusical 'aaah' notes at the same time creaking and bellowing. R

■□□ **Little Auk** adult summer

□■□ **Little Auk** adult winter (wings held in diving position)

□□■ **Little Auk** summer flock on breeding grounds

Little Auk, winter

Puffin, winter

■□□ **Black Guillemot** adult summer calling

□■□ **Black Guillemot** 1st-winter (note barred wing patch)

□□■ **Black Guillemot** adult summer in flight

Black Guillemot juv.

Black Guillemot, 1st summer

Puffin adult at breeding colony with beakful of sand-eels

Puffin adult summer wing-flapping

Puffin adult summer flock on water

Sandgrouse

Sandgrouse (order Pteroclidiformes, family Pteroclidae) are medium-sized birds, closely related and rather similar to pigeons, but perhaps closer in affinity to waders. Have very short bills and legs, long and pointed wings and tail. Sexes slightly different in plumage. Flight swift and direct, recalls that of pigeons or Golden Plover. Nest on the ground. Clutches of 2–3 eggs. Frequent steppe country and sometimes seen in very large flocks. Noisy. Where fresh water is lacking, breeding sandgrouse fly considerable distances every day, usually at dusk or dawn, between nest sites and waterholes. Several species have capacity to transport drops of water in their belly feathers to young waiting in desert.

Black-bellied Sandgrouse *Pterocles orientalis* L 35. Occurs in SW Europe on steppes and secluded plains. Rarely seen outside its breeding range. Tail shorter than in other sandgrouse. Distinguished in flight from other European sandgrouse by stocky build and *entire belly jet-black*, and by *black wing feathers relieved by pure white underwing-coverts* and brown upperwing-coverts. Tail pointed, but *central tail feathers not elongated.* Female has spotted breast and finely streaked head. Most characteristic call is an explosive snorting 'churrrl-rl-rl', at a distance only 'churrr', a dry rolling snort as from a horse. Sometimes clear 'cheeoo', almost like Little Owl.

Pin-tailed Sandgrouse *Pterocles alchata* L 33. Fairly common in SW Europe on dry steppes and other dry, flat areas. Rarely seen outside its breeding range. Small. On the ground appears extremely short-legged like its relatives but may extend its neck markedly. Flight swift with vigorous wing action, like Golden Plover. Then appears distended and strikingly neckless, the nob of the bill pointing slightly upwards. Paler in plumage than its relatives, has pale brick-brown breast band edged with black. *Central tail feathers elongated.* Best distinguished in flight from Black-bellied and Pallas's Sandgrouse by *white belly*, from Black-bellied Sandgrouse also by *whiter underwings*. Female lacks male's black throat. Usually seen in larger flocks than Black-bellied Sandgrouse. A characteristic, powerful, nasal, guttural 'katar, katar' is given in flight. Variants on this can be heard from flocks, e.g. nasal, persistent 'kow' or 'kraow' calls.

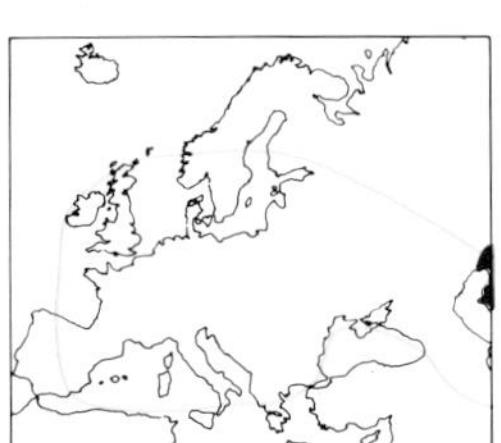

Pallas's Sandgrouse *Syrrhaptes paradoxus* L 38. Common breeding bird on dry steppes in Asia. Mass migration westwards in some years, may then invade W Europe (yellow boundary line on map indicates area concerned), and on such occasions may even breed here. Occasionally appears between invasion years too, but very rarely. Reached Britain and Ireland in 1863 and 1888 (also bred) in association with such invasions. Then often frequents sandy or other dry areas. Characteristic features are *lack of black throat patch, elongated central tail feathers* and black belly patch. *Wings pointed* and pale, *underwings almost pure white.* Male has unstreaked light greyish breast. Female has narrow black throat bar and spotted sides of neck. Often observed in noisy flocks. Call of two or three syllables, 'kirik' or 'kukerik' and also multisyllabic, clucking, rather stifled 'cho-ho-ho-ho'. V

Spotted Sandgrouse *Pterocles senegallus* L 32. Locally common and partly nomadic in deserts of N Africa and Middle East, regularly found in S Israel, in Europe encountered only once (Italy). A medium-sized sandgrouse with *elongated central tail feathers*, pale-winged above, appears fairly uniform *rusty-buff* at distance, at closer range a *smallish black belly patch* in male. Male has dove-grey breast, neck band and eye-stripe; female has these areas rusty-buff with fine dark spotting and also has upper-parts spotted. Usually seen on daily visits to waterholes, and then in flocks, sometimes very large. Call a slightly nasal disyllabic 'quitoo', blurring into a bickering gabble from the flocks performing flight manoeuvres.

■□□ Black-bellied Sandgrouse adult male

□■□ Black-bellied Sandgrouse adult female

□□■ Black-bellied Sandgrouse adult male in flight

■□ Pin-tailed Sandgrouse mixed flock of males and females in flight

□■ Spotted Sandgrouse female

□■ Spotted Sandgrouse male

■□ Pallas's Sandgrouse female

□■ Spotted Sandgrouse mixed flock of males and females in flight

Pigeons and doves

Pigeons and doves (order Columbiformes, family Columbidae) are medium-sized, rather heavy birds with pointed wings and rather long tails. Feed on the ground. Flight swift and enduring. On taking wing a clattering wing noise is often heard, which serves as a warning signal. Can drink with the bill immersed in water (other birds take a billful and lean the head backwards). Clutches of 2 white eggs. Young are fed with a special liquid, 'pigeon's milk', produced in the crop.

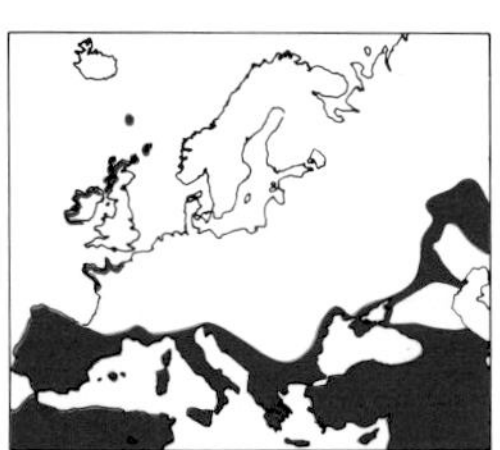

Rock Dove *Columba livia* L 33. Locally common in W and S Europe, in Britain now restricted to W coasts and Ireland and Scotland. Nests in mountain regions and often along coasts and on sea cliffs, where nest is made in caves or on sheltered cliff shelves. City Feral Pigeons (see below) are descended from this species and similar in appearance. Many Feral Pigeons markings almost exactly like the original: light grey upperparts but gleaming *white rump* and *two black bars on the wing. Underwings white* (Stock Dove's grey). Proportions and flight as Feral Pigeon, i.e. smaller more compact in build than Woodpigeon also has faster wingbeats; flight very fast. Usually in small flocks. Cooing consists of series of muffled 'druOO-u' notes, like Feral Pigeon's. R

Feral Pigeon *Columba livia* domest. L 33. Nests in towns and cities throughout almost all Europe, having originally escaped from dovecotes and become wild. Lives in towers, garrets, lofts and in niches on buildings, many broods per year. Fearless, feeds in streets and market places, may become very abundant. Plumage varies enormously, from the ancestral Rock Dove's grey plumage with *white tail base* and *two black wingbars* to *reddish-buff, white, strongly variegated white* or *dark individuals.* Flight and silhouette exactly like Rock Dove's. Resident, but at migration sites carrier pigeons (= Feral Pigeon) can sometimes be seen on 'migration'. Call resembles Rock Dove's. The young beg with drawn-out thin cheeps. R

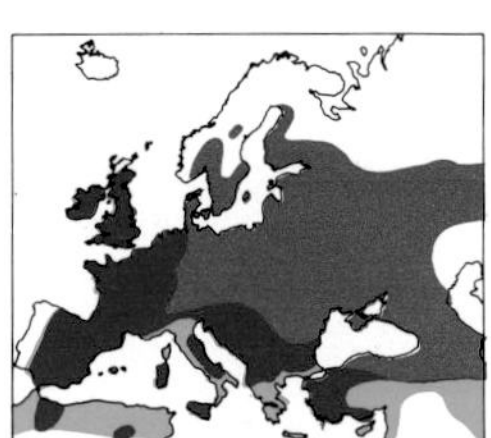

▶ **Stock Dove** *Columba oenas* L 33. Fairly common and widespread in parks, farmland and edges of woodland, sometimes in ruins and on cliffs, nests in holes in trees, buildings, on cliffs. Feeds on fields, often far from nest. Often visits shores. Feeds in small or medium-sized flocks, sometimes with Woodpigeons. Is *smaller and more compact than Woodpigeon*, flies with quicker wingbeats and, apparently, faster. Is richer grey than Woodpigeon, *lacks white markings*, appears rather uniform in colour, but has *lighter ash-grey wing panel and lower back.* Traces of dark wingbars at bases of wings, not very noticeable. Whistling wing noise. Display flight with deep, well-spaced wing strokes and long glides on upraised wings (as Feral Pigeon). Call a monotonous fast croon, 'OO-ooe OO-ooe OO-ooe . . .', more like Feral Pigeon's than Woodpigeon's. RSW

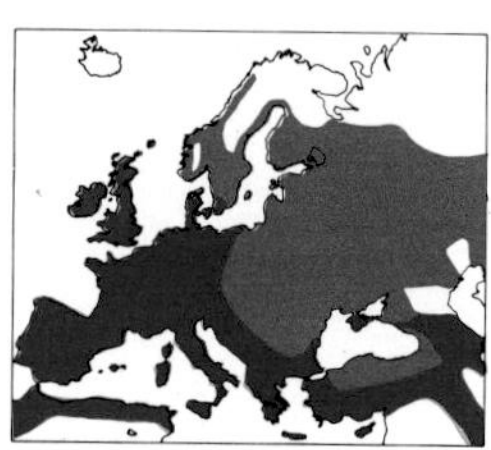

▶ **Woodpigeon** *Columba palumbus* L 40. Most abundant and widespread of Europe's pigeons. Found in farmland, parks, gardens and all kinds of woodland. Breeds in flimsy twig nest. Has entered many larger towns and cities, where it mixes fearlessly with Feral Pigeons. Easily recognised by size, *white patches on sides of neck* (lacking in immatures) together with *broad, white transverse bars on upperwings.* Outside breeding season usually seen in flocks, sometimes of considerable size. Makes loud wing clatter on rising. Flight with looser wingbeats than Stock Dove's and *tail* is proportionately slightly *longer.* Display flight is a short climb with wing clap at the peak, followed by short descending glide on half-closed wings. Muffled, slightly hoarse cooing consists of five syllables, with the emphasis on the first, 'DOOOH-doo doo-doo, du'; final syllable is brief and abruptly cut short; series of notes is repeated three to five times without pause so that final, short syllable seems to belong to and to open next phrase. RW

Rock Dove adult

Feral Pigeons in Trafalgar Square, London

Feral Pigeon

Stock Doves

Stock Dove in flight

Wood Pigeon adult

Wood Pigeons feeding in field

Wood Pigeon adult in flight

15 P PER CUP
PLEASE
RETURN
CONTAINER.

Pigeons and doves

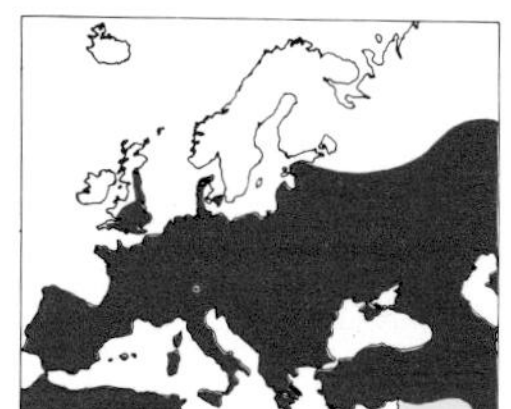

Turtle Dove *Streptopelia turtur* L 27. Common in S and central Europe in agricultural country with hedges and small woods and also in open wooded country. Summer visitor, winters in tropical Africa. Shy and watchful (much hunted). Obviously smaller and darker than Collared Dove, not so strikingly long-tailed. In flight easily recognised by pale belly, fairly dark underwings, *small size* and rapid, flicking wingbeats. Has dark neck patch of crescentic black and white stripes (often with touch of blue-grey – beware misidentification as Rufous Turtle Dove). Juvenile lacks this. Tail dark with broad white terminal band, which stands out well when tail is spread (visible also on closed tail below). Reddish skin around eye obvious. Turtle Dove is considerably smaller than very rare Rufous Turtle Dove, from which it can be distinguished also by *vinous-pink* (not brownish-red) *breast, whiter belly* together with *rusty yellow-brown wing-coverts and scapulars* with small distinct black spots (not dark rusty reddish-brown with larger and more diffuse spots). Also resembles Laughing Dove, though this is an intrepid urban dove, is clearly smaller, has Collared Dove proportions (short-winged, long-tailed) and has large blue wing panels (Turtle Dove's wing panels are smaller and paler grey-blue). Call is a deep rumbling 'toorrrrr, toorrrrr, toorrrrr'. SP

Turtle Dove adult

Turtle Dove juveniles, adult (left)

Turtle Dove adult in flight

Rufous Turtle Dove *Streptopelia orientalis* L 33. Occasional visitor to Europe from breeding places in Asia, mostly in late autumn and winter. Resembles Turtle Dove, but is *considerably larger* (size of Collared Dove or more) and slightly *darker*, has *diffuse white tips to wing-coverts* which produce an almost *scaly effect* and tend to form one or two thin wingbars. Rump and lower back blue-grey (good element of brown in Turtle Dove), nape/hindneck brown (light grey in Turtle Dove). Turtle Dove's whitish neck and tail markings are usually replaced by light blue and grey in Rufous Turtle Dove, but this distinction not always obvious or easy to see; some have greyish-white and black neck patch. (Central Asiatic subspecies *meena* furthermore has white belly and tail markings, exactly like Turtle Dove). Bare skin around eye negligible in most behaviour and habitat as Turtle Dove, but flight almost as heavy as Woodpigeon's, clearly different from the lighter, more nimble Turtle Dove. The call is very particular, almost like Woodpigeon's courtship song, a series composed of two grating notes followed by two clearer, more cooing notes, then two grating ones and so on, 'hroo-hroo oo-oo hroo-hroo oo-oo . . .'. V

▶ **Collared Dove** *Streptopelia decaocto* L 32. Since 1930 has spread considerably northwestwards from the Balkans (first bred in Britain in 1955) and is now found commonly throughout British Isles except on highest mountain areas. Closely associated with towns and villages, where it nests in parks and gardens. Lays several clutches, can be incubating in March and have young in the nest in Nov. Often feeds in company with Feral Pigeons at silos etc. Has nimble flight like Turtle Dove but is clearly stockier and also markedly *long-tailed*. Mainly *sandy-coloured* with darker flight features and *narrow black nape collar* (absent in juvenile). Tail below is white on terminal half, inner half black; on upperside large whitish corner patches, concealed at rest. A loud trisyllabic cooing 'doo-DOOH-do' is given, very frequently from, e.g. TV aerials. Also utters an almost mewing 'krreei' like subdued Black-headed Gull call. R

Collared Dove adult

Collared Dove flock with Starling (far right)

▶ **Laughing Dove** *Streptopelia senegalensis* L 25. Recent immigrant to towns and villages in SE Balkans. Not shy. *Long-tailed* and short-winged like Collared Dove but much *smaller and darker*, more like Turtle Dove at a swift glance. Terminal tail band as latter, but *larger and darker blue wing panel* and characteristic neck markings (*black-spotted 'scarf'*). Has 5-syllable, rapid, subdued cooing in which 3rd and 4th syllables are just a shade higher than the others: 'dododeedeedo'. When several call together, the effect can be like the distant cooing of Black Grouse.

Rufous Turtle Dove adult

Laughing Dove adult

Cuckoos

Cuckoos (order Cuculiformes, family Cuculidae). Medium-sized, long-tailed, with pointed wings. Two toes pointing forwards, two backwards. Some species (e.g. three European ones) are nest parasites.

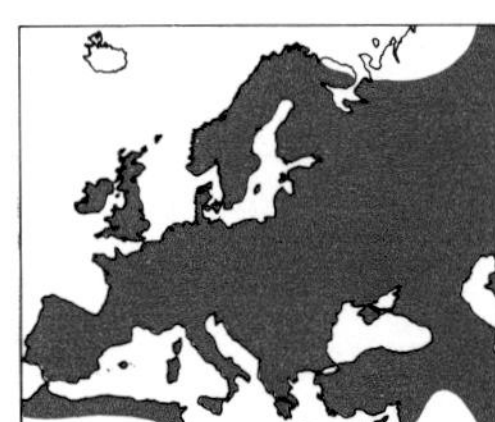

Cuckoo *Cuculus canorus* L 33. Fairly common in all types of terrain, in woodland and in open country right up to mountain slopes. Rarely in the immediate vicinity of densely populated areas, rather shy. Specialises in hairy larvae of bombycid moths. Nest parasite, lays its eggs in other birds' nests, one egg in each nest. Species often exploited include Pied Wagtail, Meadow Pipit, Whitethroat, Reed Warbler and Spotted Flycatcher. Each female Cuckoo specialises in a particular host bird, whose egg colour it imitates. Male Cuckoo is *ash-grey on head, breast and back, with Sparrowhawk-barring on the belly.* Female usually has same pattern apart from *rusty tint and suggestion of barring across upper breast* (grey phase), but a minority of adult females are instead *bright rusty-red* above (rufous phase). Juveniles are quite dark brownish above, some greyer, others more rusty, though not divided into two such different and well-defined categories as the adult females, do not become so bright rusty-red, are always greyer on head/neck. A sure sign of a juvenile is a *white spot on the nape.* Cuckoo's size, its low and unobtrusive flight progression combined with its *long tail* often give a Sparrowhawk impression (females of rufous phase: Kestrel). But quick wingbeats are fairly weak, and *the pointed wings perform without intervals of gliding* and *mostly below the horizontal,* and *small head* with delicate bill *is held pointing clearly upwards.* Often pursued by agitated small birds, e.g. Pied Wagtails. Male's call is the familiar Cuckoo-call, a far-carrying 'COO-koo', repeated in long series. Replaced by an irascible throat-clearing 'gugh-cheh-cheh' when male chases off another Cuckoo. Female has an urgent bubbling call, 'puhuhuhuhuhuhu', like calls of Whimbrel and Little Grebe. Begging call of the young is like that of a small bird, but very penetrating, 'sree, sree . . . . S

Cuckoo adult male

Cuckoo juv., brown phase

Cuckoo adult female in flight

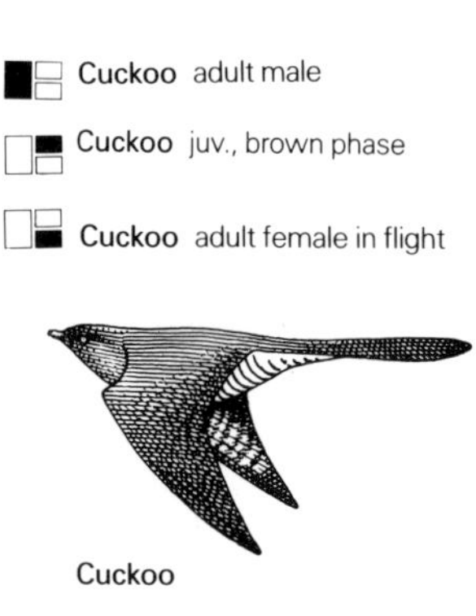

Cuckoo

Oriental Cuckoo *Cuculus saturatus* L 30. Shy bird of the taiga of E Russia and Siberia. Long-distance migrant (winters East Indies), could well overshoot to W Europe (has appeared west as far as Latvia, reported even in Britain). Call disyllabic but obviously different from Cuckoo's: *both syllables at same pitch,* and *equal in stress,* besides being quite Hoopoe-like in tone, 'poo-poo'; repeated in series of 7–8, *at faster tempo* than Cuckoo's. The series is often begun (on alighting) with 5–7 'poo' calls in even, rapid succession. Otherwise depressingly difficult to identify: slightly smaller than Cuckoo, but usually has slightly bigger bill, thicker barring on belly (subtle difference), is a shade darker and colder grey above (crown, back), has rusty-yellow tinge on underparts more often than Cuckoo. The females can also be reddish-brown, sometimes a little more rich than in common Cuckoo. V

Oriental Cuckoo adult male in flight

Great Spotted Cuckoo adult

Great Spotted Cuckoo juv.

▶ **Great Spotted Cuckoo** *Clamator glandarius* L 40. Breeds in SW Europe in open country (scrubland, olive groves etc). Parasities mainly Magpie, may lay several eggs in the same nest. Resembles Cuckoo in shape and flight but is considerably *bigger,* has *crest,* has *broad white feather edges on otherwise quite dark upperparts.* Juvenile has rust-coloured primaries. Male's call, which is uttered frequently, is quite the opposite of Cuckoo's call, a rattling, loud cackle 'cherr-cherr-che-che-che-che-che', reminiscent of Turnstone or well-grown young of woodpeckers. V

Yellow-billed Cuckoo *Coccyzus americanus* L 30. Rare American autumn vagrant. Similar to following species, but in flight shows a rusty-red primary panel and *black tail feathers with broad white tips* (central pair brown). *Yellow lower mandible.* V

Black-billed Cuckoo *Coccyzus erythrophthalmus* L 30. Very rare American autumn vagrant. Resembles the above species, but spread wing uniform brown, *tail feathers brown with only small indistinct white tips.* Red eye-ring. *All-black bill.* V

Black-billed Cuckoo

Yellow-billed Cuckoo

Owls

Owls

(order Strigiformes), families Tytonidae (Barn Owl) and Strigidae (the other owls). Have big heads and short necks, are birds of prey that hunt mostly at night. Broad facial discs conduct sound to the very large ear openings. Head can be turned up to 270°. Noiseless flight. Sexes alike, but females a shade larger. Many species nest in holes. Eggs round, white. *Some species make dangerous attacks in defence of their young.*

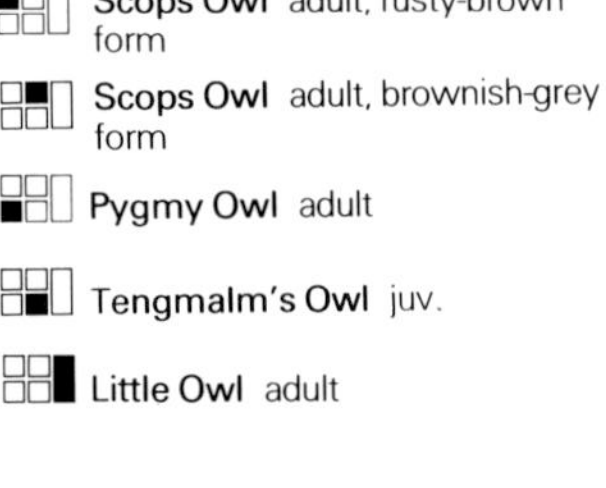

Scops Owl *Otus scops* L 20. Breeds in S Europe in clumps of trees, gardens, also in towns. Nests in hollow in tree or building. Rather uniformly coloured. Some variation: some are brownish-grey, others have more rusty-brown tone. *Small. Broad,* 'thickset' *ear tufts.* Slimmer than Little Owl, perches more upright. Wings proportionately long. Migrant, feeds much on insects. *True nocturnal owl,* noticed mostly by call: a monotonous *deep, monosyllabic whistle, repeated* every 3rd second, 'chook' (resembling midwife toad *Alytes obstetricans*). In duet, female's whistle is heard to be higher than male's. V

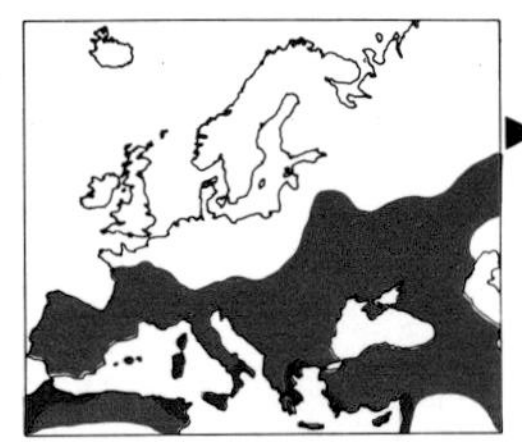

▶ **Pygmy Owl** *Glaucidium passerinum* L 18. Not uncommon in extensive coniferous forest. Nests in woodpecker hole. Hunter of small rodents, but also takes tits and other small birds. More diurnal than most owls. In winter may hunt at birdtables and lay up prey reserves in nestboxes. Europe's *smallest* owl, barely size of Starling, which it resembles when seen overhead; can be called up by imitating its call. Brown with fine white spots and barring. *White supercilia short.* Comparatively small-headed. Flight over long distances undulating like woodpecker. Territorial call, a soft whistle 'hjuuk', rhythmically repeated every other second *at dusk and dawn,* often from very top of a tall spruce. When excited a high stammering hoot is interspersed between the whistles, 'hjuuk . . . huhuhu . . . hjuuk . . . huhuhu . . . hjuuk . . .'. Female may reply with a high 'pseeeee' (this is also begging call of young). Male's 'hjuuk' may also be answered with a thinner, more nasal version, 'hyeelk', probably from female. 'Autumn call' is a short series of shrill fluted notes, rising in pitch, intensity and tempo (recalls sound from bicycle pump, with finger over the hole). Also chattering 'kuee' calls.

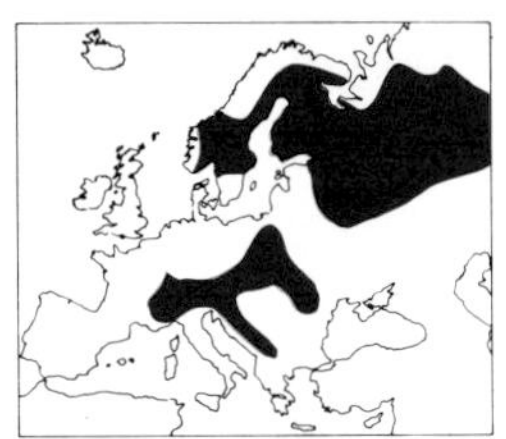

Little Owl *Athene noctua* L 23. Common in S and central Europe in often rocky open terrain, also in towns. Introduced into England in 1880s. Nests in holes in trees, rocks or buildings. Thickset body, *broad head with flat crown, long legs.* Posture usually not so upright as in other owls. Bows and curtseys when agitated. Readily uses fence posts, telegraph wires etc as look-out. Flight undulating like woodpecker. May hover. Wide range of prey: rodents, birds, insects, earthworms etc. *Active by day as well as night.* Territorial call easily told from Scops Owl's, is more *drawn-out and rises at end,* 'gooo(e)k'. Female has a falsetto version. Loud, piercing mew 'kEEoo' is often heard. Alarm shrill, explosive, tern-like 'kyitt, kyitt'. Young beg with drawn-out hiss. R

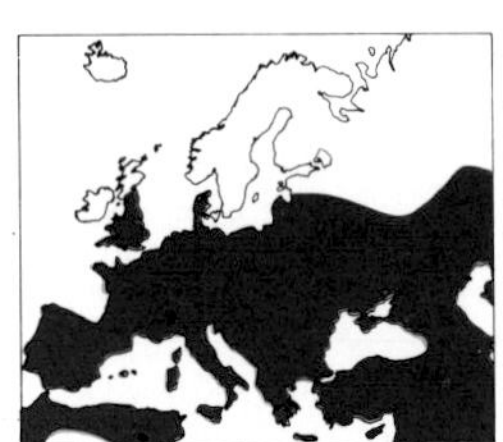

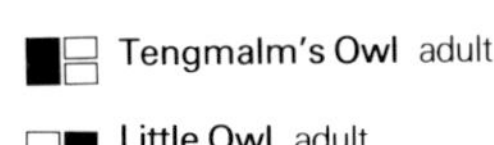

Little Owl adult in flight

Tengmalm's Owl *Aegolius funereus* L 25. Fairly common in extensive coniferous forests. Nests in Black Woodpecker holes and Goldeneye nestboxes. Polygamy occurs. Larger than Pygmy Owl and different in shape (*large-headed,* with look more of open-eyed wonder than frowning) and behaviour (*true nocturnal owl,* avoids showing itself, rarely sits aloft). Face pale, dark-framed. Young are rich dark brown. Territorial call, heard mostly very early in spring, is a *rapid series of deep whistles,* usually 7–8 syllables, slightly rising in tone at the end, 'popopopopopopapa'. Remarkable variations among individuals in pitch, tempo and number of syllables. Can be heard over great distance (over 3km in suitable condition). Calls mostly during late night/midnight, often very persistently. Sometimes an 'interminable' series. Also a nasal and slightly trumpeting 'ku-WEEuk' and, especially on autumn nights, shrill smacking chee-AK' sounds (squirrel-like). Begging calls of young are short, explosive, and hoarse or shrill according to age. V

Owls

Very rare over much of its range

Eagle Owl *Bubo bubo* L 69. Local, mostly rare, in mountainous or rocky terrain, wooded or not. Shyer than other owls but appreciates elements of cultivated country (rubbish dumps). Resident. Nest usually on cliff shelf, at times beside rock on ground. *Largest* and most powerful of Europe's owls. Catches rats, voles, crows, gulls, ducks, even hares. Mainly nocturnal. Mobbed furiously by crows and gulls. Flight fast, with quite shallow wingbeats. Brown (colour of pine bark) above, *rusty-yellow below. Large ear tufts* (not visible in flight). Calls mostly at dawn and dusk a powerful 'HOO-o' (audible up to 5km), repeated at, e.g. 8-sec. intervals (only first note heard at long range). Female replies with higher-pitched, hoarse version, but also has drawn-out hoarse bark 'REEHew'. Alarm a shrill, nasal, fierce 'ke-ke keKAYu', with bill-clicking. Young beg with husky, scraping calls, 'chuEESH' ('planing wood'), into Sep. V

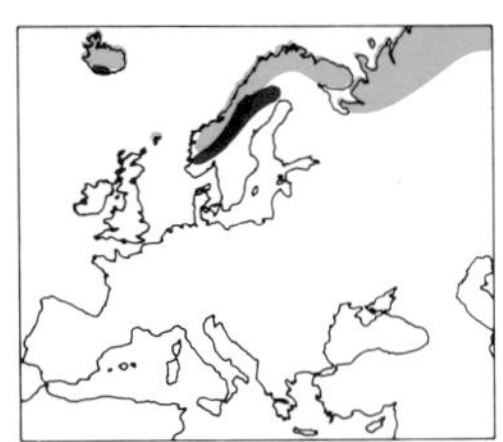

Snowy Owl *Nyctea scandiaca* L 61. Uncommon, arctic owl, has bred Shetland. Nests on high-lying, hummocky upland moor. Known as a diurnal owl but perhaps most active after dusk. Uses mounds and rocks as look-outs. Relatively shy but male may draw blood when defending nest. Breeds in vole and lemming years, is absent in between. May migrate long distances south in winter, then kills larger prey, e.g. medium-sized birds. Stronger flier than most owls. Old males almost all-white, females (much larger) with fine dark spots, young males likewise, while young females are markedly more densely spotted (at a distance look dark grey against snow). Courtship call muffled far-carrying 'gawh', repeated at e.g. 4-sec. intervals. Male has 'krek-krek-krek- . . . ' alarm call, strikingly like agitated female Mallard. Female's alarm is usually 'pyeey, pyeey, pyeey, pyeey', like a falsetto bark, and she also gives a whistled 'seeuuee'. WP

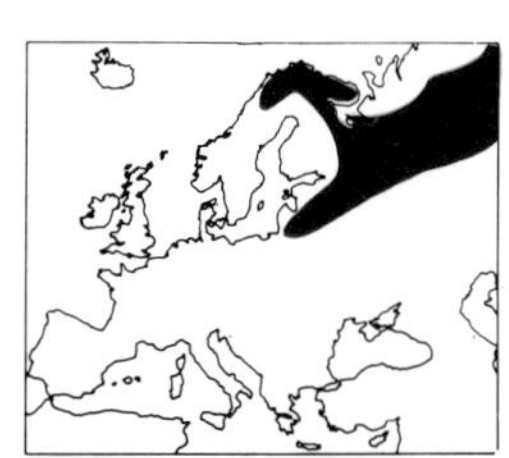

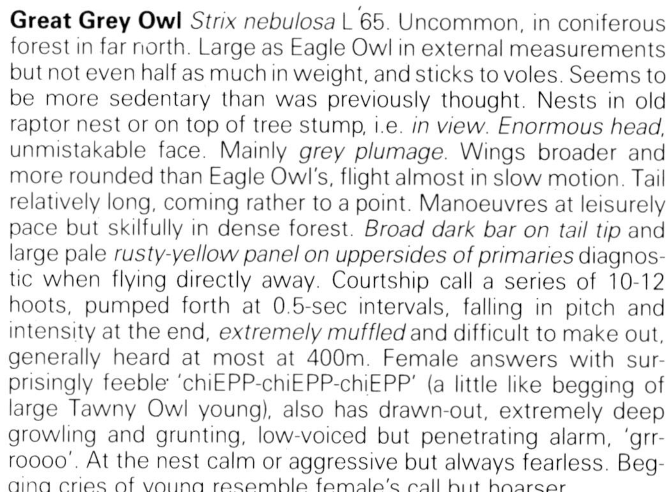

Great Grey Owl *Strix nebulosa* L 65. Uncommon, in coniferous forest in far north. Large as Eagle Owl in external measurements but not even half as much in weight, and sticks to voles. Seems to be more sedentary than was previously thought. Nests in old raptor nest or on top of tree stump, i.e. *in view. Enormous head,* unmistakable face. Mainly *grey plumage.* Wings broader and more rounded than Eagle Owl's, flight almost in slow motion. Tail relatively long, coming rather to a point. Manoeuvres at leisurely pace but skilfully in dense forest. *Broad dark bar on tail tip* and large pale *rusty-yellow panel on uppersides of primaries* diagnostic when flying directly away. Courtship call a series of 10-12 hoots, pumped forth at 0.5-sec intervals, falling in pitch and intensity at the end, *extremely muffled* and difficult to make out, generally heard at most at 400m. Female answers with surprisingly feeble 'chiEPP-chiEPP-chiEPP' (a little like begging of large Tawny Owl young), also has drawn-out, extremely deep growling and grunting, low-voiced but penetrating alarm, 'grr-roooo'. At the nest calm or aggressive but always fearless. Begging cries of young resemble female's call but hoarser.

► **Ural Owl** *Strix uralensis* L 60. Scarce to uncommon in coniferous forests. Waits for voles at clearings, forest marshes etc. Usually nests inside stormbroken dead tree ('chimney stack') but also in old Buzzard nests. Often aggressive at nest. (Do not approach young that have jumped out: they are defended with great determination and the owl aims for the eyes.) Mainly nocturnal. Resident. Much bigger than Tawny Owl but not so huge and imposing as Great Grey, resembles Buzzard when flying away. Tail relatively long, coming to a point, wings rounded. *Faded grey-brown. Face buff-grey,* unmarked. Courtship call deep, far-carrying: 'WHOOhoo . . . (4-sec. pause) . . . whoohoo oWHOOhoo'. Gives muffled series of about 8 syllables 'poopoopoopoo . . . ', gruffer than Short-eared Owl's and with slight rise just before end. Female has hoarse versions of these two calls and begs with scratchy, croaking, heron-like 'kuVEH'. Alarm call like a dog's bark, 'waff'. Begging of young like that of Tawny Owl young.

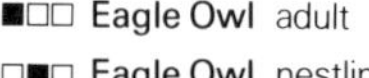

■□□ **Eagle Owl** adult
□■□ **Eagle Owl** nestlings
□□■ **Snowy Owl** adult male

Eagle Owl, young

■□□ **Snowy Owl** young female
□■□ **Snowy Owl** nestling
□□■ **Great Grey Owl** adult in flight

Snowy Owl, young

Great Grey Owl, young

Great Grey Owl adult
Great Grey Owl unfledged juv.
Ural Owl adult
Ural Owl unfledged juv.

Tawny Owl Ural Owl
young

Owls

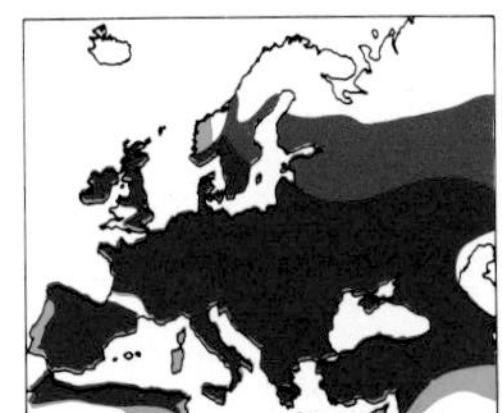

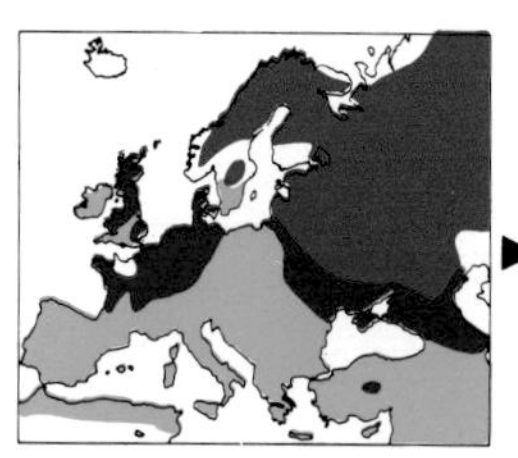

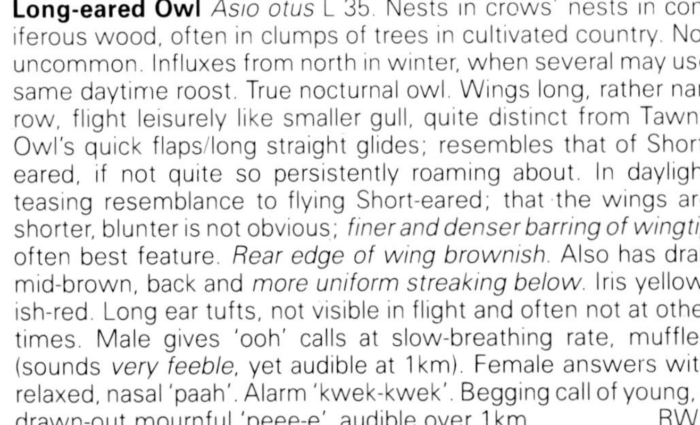

Long-eared Owl *Asio otus* L 35. Nests in crows' nests in coniferous wood, often in clumps of trees in cultivated country. Not uncommon. Influxes from north in winter, when several may use same daytime roost. True nocturnal owl. Wings long, rather narrow, flight leisurely like smaller gull, quite distinct from Tawny Owl's quick flaps/long straight glides; resembles that of Short-eared, if not quite so persistently roaming about. In daylight teasing resemblance to flying Short-eared; that the wings are shorter, blunter is not obvious; *finer and denser barring of wingtip* often best feature. *Rear edge of wing brownish.* Also has drab mid-brown, back and *more uniform streaking below.* Iris yellowish-red. Long ear tufts, not visible in flight and often not at other times. Male gives 'ooh' calls at slow-breathing rate, muffled (sounds *very feeble,* yet audible at 1km). Female answers with relaxed, nasal 'paah'. Alarm 'kwek-kwek'. Begging call of young, a drawn-out mournful 'peee-e', audible over 1km. RWP

▶ **Short-eared Owl** *Asio flammeus* L 38. A subarctic owl, numbers fluctuate with rodent cycles. Breeds locally in Britain. Nests on moorland, bogs. Winter influxes in south, often found on coastal marshes. Longer, narrower wings than other owls, beaten slowly, 'rowing' action with hint of upward jerk. Also active by day. Looks pale in flight. *Breast heavily streaked,* belly *paler, almost unstreaked. Barring of wingtip black, coarse. Trailing edge of wing whitish.* Bends of wing have dark patch above with dull yellow outside, dark comma mark below. Iris yellow. Small ear tufts, revealed when agitated. Male gives muffled courtship call, 'doo-doo-doo-doo-doo-doo- . . . ', in high-level flight, difficult to pinpoint, sounds weak. Also short rattling wing claps. Female replies with husky 'cheeee-oop'. Alarm 'chef-chef'. RSWP

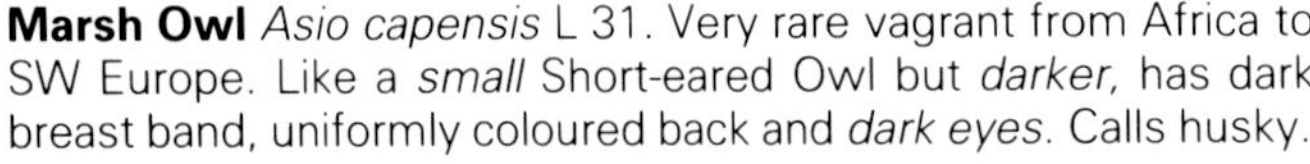

Marsh Owl *Asio capensis* L 31. Very rare vagrant from Africa to SW Europe. Like a *small* Short-eared Owl but *darker,* has dark breast band, uniformly coloured back and *dark eyes.* Calls husky.

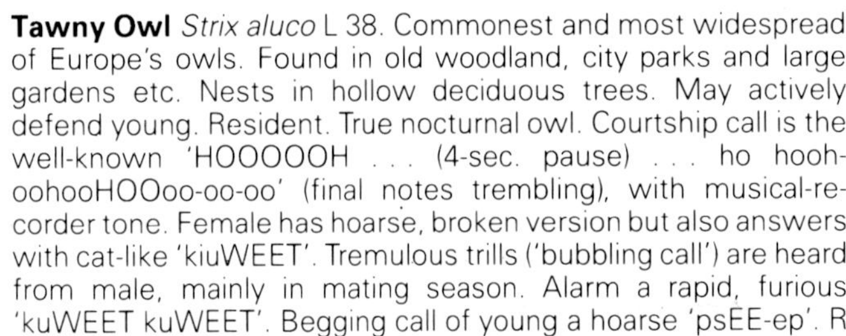

▶ **Tawny Owl** *Strix aluco* L 38. Commonest and most widespread of Europe's owls. Found in old woodland, city parks and large gardens etc. Nests in hollow deciduous trees. May actively defend young. Resident. True nocturnal owl. Courtship call is the well-known 'HOOOOOH . . . (4-sec. pause) . . . ho hooh-oohooHOOoo-oo-oo' (final notes trembling), with musical-recorder tone. Female has hoarse, broken version but also answers with cat-like 'kiuWEET'. Tremulous trills ('bubbling call') are heard from male, mainly in mating season. Alarm a rapid, furious 'kuWEET kuWEET'. Begging call of young a hoarse 'psEE-ep'. R

▶ **Barn Owl** *Tyto alba* L 35. Thrives in open cultivated country, often nests in barns and church towers. Has greatly declined. Resident. Typical heart-shaped face. Flight and wing shape resemble Long-eared Owl's, but plumage is overall *very pale* (even northern-eastern race *guttata*) and often dangles legs. Characteristic pellets: greyish-black, as if varnished. Courtship call a very shrill, hoarse shriek (2 sec. long), given by both sexes, also in flight, varying in intensity and pitch (female's more subdued). Alarm a shrill, fierce shriek. Begs with Nightjar-like hollow snoring. R

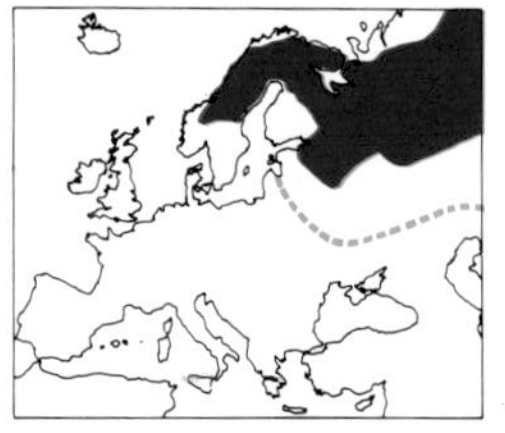

Hawk Owl *Surnia ulula* L 38. Nests in hollow trees, mainly in the subalpine region, especially in upper coniferous forest/lower birch. Almost totally absent between vole years, may then migrate far south. *Longer tail* than other owls, and wings not so rounded. Very like large Sparrowhawk in flight, which is swift and direct with relatively quick wing action. Alights with steep ascent to elevated perch. Noted for being diurnal, but courtship call is heard mainly in black of night: a drawn-out and rapidly shivering trill (e.g. 95 syllables in 7 sec.), resembles Tawny Owl's tremulous trill but more bubbling like female Cuckoo. Audible at about 1km. Female answers, and young begs, with drawn-out hoarse 'kshUUlip'. Alarm a shrill 'quiquiquiqui', recalling Merlin. Exceedingly aggressive at nest. V

■□□ **Long-eared Owl** adult
□■□ **Long-eared Owl** adult
□□■ **Short-eared Owl** adult

■□□ **Long-eared Owl** adult in flight
□■□ **Short-eared Owl** adult in flight
□□■ **Marsh Owl** adult in flight

Marsh Owl

■□□ **Tawny Owl** adult greyish form approaching chick in nest
□■□ **Tawny Owl** adult rufous form
□□■ **Hawk Owl** adult in flight

Hawk Owl, young

■■□ **Barn Owl** adults at nest site, nominate race
□□■ **Hawk Owl**

Nightjars

Nightjars (order Caprimulgiformes, family Caprimulgidae) are noctural insectivores with big, flat heads, small bills and very big mouths. Stiff bristles at the corners of the bill help to catch moths in flight. The big, round eyes are kept virtually closed by day. Plumages brown, vermiculated and well camouflaged. During the day rest on ground or along branches and are difficult to detect. Two eggs are laid directly on to the ground.

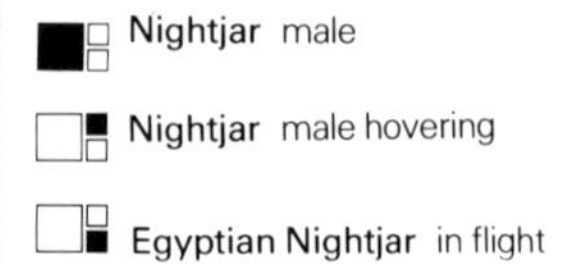

Nightjar male

Nightjar male hovering

Egyptian Nightjar in flight

Nightjar *Caprimulgus europaeus* L 28. Fairly local and scarce, found in light, dry, open woodland and in glades and clearings in denser coniferous wood, also on heaths. By day rests, hard to detect, lying flattened along thick branch, when finely patterned *brown and grey* plumage gives illusion of large flake of bark. In male, note *white spots on wings and tail.* Usually seen at dusk hunting insects. *Silhouette like Kestrel.* Flight silent and buoyant with stiff wingbeats. Often glides on wings held in a shallow V, pitches and turns with great ease and elegance and sometimes stops still for a moment on fluttering wings. Has an advertising flight with occasional wing clap (the wings are struck together above the body). Tiny bill but gigantic mouth – lives on moths, can even swallow cockchafers. Not gregarious except on migration, when flocks may occur. Migrates at night. Most often noticed by far-carrying song, heard without a break at dusk and night during early summer, a characteristic dry, hollow churring roll which runs in two gears, 'errrrrurrrrrrrerrrrrrr . . .'. When singing usually perches in the open, frequently aloft. Male courts female by pitching out and descending with rhythmic wing claps, uttering an intense 'feeOORR-feeOORR-feeOORR- . . .', which changes into a weak, deep and coarse 'ughrrrr . . .' (still producing wing claps), which in turn abruptly becomes silent – the whole gives a strong impression of 'the Nightjar's final sigh'! Call a frog-like, sonorous 'krruit'. S

Red-necked Nightjar *Caprimulgus ruficollis* L 30. Breeds in Iberian peninsula. Found in evergreen woods and on dry, bushy waste. Night bird, closely resembling Nightjar, but bigger, with longer tail, slightly paler colours, *reddish nape band* and often slightly larger white throat patch (often divided by brown along middle of throat). White spots on wings and tail are distinct and are present in both sexes (cf. Nightjar), though fainter in the female. Much larger and darker in plumage than the rare Egyptian Nightjar. Male's song differs altogether from Nightjar's (but has something in common in its hollow ring) and is a protracted, often minutes-long series of repeated disyllabic 'kyoTOK-kyoTOK-kyoTOK- . . .'. female gives a rasping, less far-carrying 'tche-tche-tche- . . .' ('steam engine'). Also wing claps. V

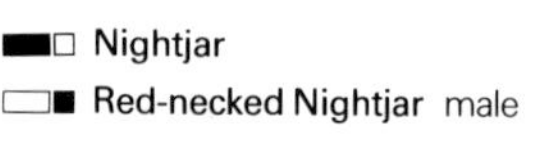

Nightjar

Red-necked Nightjar male

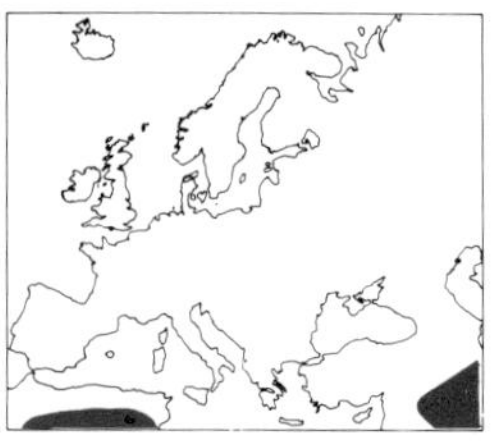

Egyptian Nightjar *Caprimulgus aegyptius* L 25. Very rare visitor to S Europe from breeding areas in Africa and Asia. Found in desert areas, but usually near water. *Much paler* and appears more uniform in colour when perched than Nightjar and Red-necked Nightjar, which it resembles in behaviour and silhouette. In flight, dark primaries contrast with otherwise faded upperparts. White markings of throat at times very indistinct. The song is something between the Nightjar's churring and the Red-necked Nightjar's rhythmic 'spelling out', a hollow-sounding 'kroo-kroo-kroo-kroo- . . .' in long series, in tempo like a slow old-fashioned motor in fishing boat. V

Common Nighthawk, ♂

Common Nighthawk *Chordeiles minor* L 23. Rare vagrant from North America. Small, mottled grey-brown with a *white transverse bar across primaries*, visible in flight. Male has a white throat and a *white band across the tail.* Song a strained, nasal 'pyeet' of the same tone as Goldeneye's display call, repeated every other second. V

Common Nighthawk male

Common Nighthawk female in flight

Swifts

Swifts (order Apodiformes, family Apodidae) resemble swallows and martins but have longer, narrower and more scythe-shaped wings as a result of an extreme adaption to life in the air. Feed exclusively on flying insects. Sexes alike. Nest under roof tiles, on cliffs and in cavities. Clutches of 2–3 white eggs.

Swift adult (background) with two young in nest

Swift juv. clinging to wall

Swift in flight

Swift *Apus apus* L 17. Common. Can be seen in the air almost everywhere but most often near towns and villages. Nests in small colonies, usually under roof tiles and in ventilaton cavities, also in church towers; in wilderness in woodpecker holes. Lives on aerial plankton, gathered at heights of up to 4 km. Bad weather which makes feeding impossible in breeding area can cause mass migration to another part of the country, during which time the young fall into semi-torpor. *Uniform dull brownish-black* with pale chin. Cf. Pallid Swift. Is clearly larger than Swallow and House Martin, has longer, narrower, stiffer, scythe-shaped wings (extremely long hand and short arm) and very streamlined body. Flight outstanding. Standard flight fast with quick wingbeats (may give illusion of wings beaten alternately). Raids (often in screaming parties close above rooftops) exceedingly rapid, and accuracy allows Swift to enter nest almost like an arrowshot. But is often seen floating around quite leisurely high up in the air. Can 'sleep' during flight. Even mates in the air. Has difficulty in taking off from the ground, at least in tall grass. Call a shrill screaming 'srrreeee'. SP

White-rumped Swift

Little Swift

▶ **White-rumped Swift** *Apus caffer* L 14. Has established a few small colonies in S Spain since the 1960s. Nests in old nests of Red-rumped Swallow. Small and uniformly dark with distinct pale chin, *narrow white rump* and *markedly forked tail*. Secondaries tipped white. Call a *jerky series of loud staccato notes*, 'cheet-cheet-cheet- . . .'.

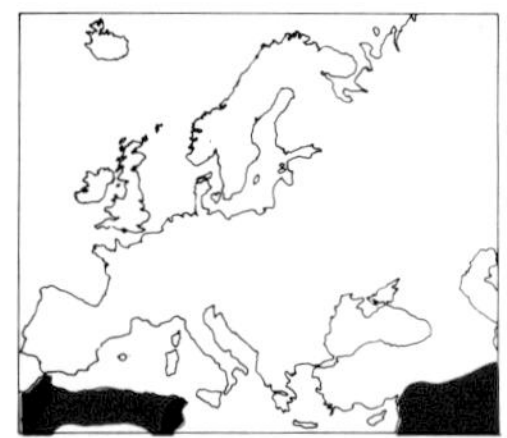

▶ **Little Swift** *Apus affinis* L 12. Very rare vagrant from N Africa and Asia. Distinguished from slightly larger White-rumped Swift by *square-cut tail* and larger *whitc, rectangular rump patch*. Call a *clear*, almost lark-like *twitter*. V

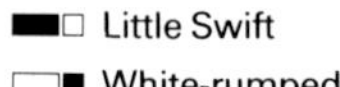

Little Swift

White-rumped Swift in flight

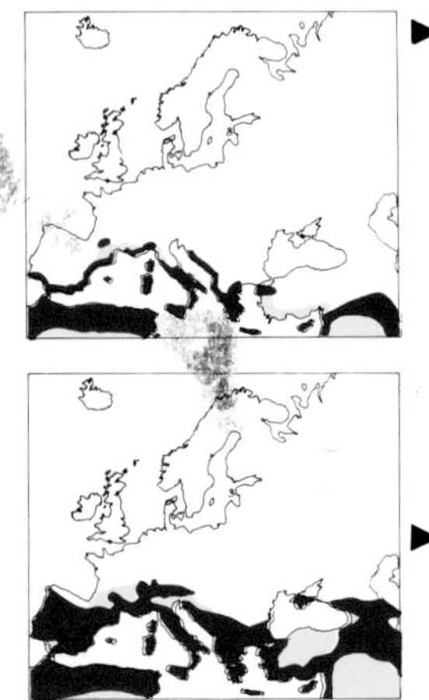

▶ **Pallid Swift** *Apus pallidus* L 17.5. Fairly common in S Europe along rocky coasts, in mountain regions and in towns. Often seen together with Swifts and Alpine Swift. Very like Swift. Overall plumage *slightly paler, more brown* and less sooty, which shows well from above in direct comparison. From below against the sky the colour difference is almost impossible to discern, but with experience one can often see that Pallid Swift's *inner primaries and secondaries are a shade paler* and more translucent; the *outer primaries are darker, creating a contrast*, which is slightly sharper than in Swift. Pallid Swift also has slightly broader wings, and as a result of this and its slightly larger size *beats its wings a trifle more slowly* in normal flight than Swift. It seems also to glide more than its darker relative. *The call is lower* than Swift's and a little *more harsh and strained*, 'vrreeeu', with a slight falling inflection, more so than in Swift. V

▶ **Alpine Swift** *Apus melba* L 23. Breeds in S Europe. Found in mountain districts and cities (incl. at sea level). Nests in colonies. *Much bigger* than the other swifts and has *white underparts* together with *brown breast band*. Has slightly longer tail. Very fast and skilful in flight. Has clearly slower wingbeats than Swift – naturally, in view of its size – but maintains even faster speed. May even recall small, slender falcon. Just like Swift, is seen drifting around in large twittering flocks, especially in mornings and evenings. Call: rapid, *chittering series* 'tititititi . . .', *rising and falling*, accelerating and slowing down again. Sometimes sounds rather hoarse as from small falcon. V

Little Swift in flight

Pallid Swift in flight

Alpine Swift in flight

Kingfishers and their allies

Kingfishers and their allies

(order Coraciiformes) between them make up a group of very different, brightly coloured birds.

KINGFISHERS (family Alcedinidae) have large heads, short tails and long bills together with short legs. Plumages are very colourful. Nearly always seen close to water, either perched on a branch or hovering above the water. Catch fish by plunging. Nest in solitary pairs. Clutch consists of 3–8 white eggs, laid in nests excavated deep in a bank. Nest material usually consists of fish skeletons which serve as 'duckboards'.

BEE-EATERS (family Meropidae) are thrush-sized, slim birds with long, pointed, slightly decurved bills, pointed wings and elongated central tail feathers. They feed on insects which are caught in flight. Rather horizontal posture when perched. Often seen perched on telegraph wires or branches. Nest in colonies. Lay 4–7 eggs in burrows in earth banks.

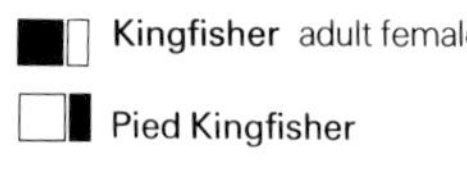

ROLLERS (family Coraciidae) are medium-sized, Jackdaw-like birds with bright blue and brown coloration. Live mainly on insects taken on the ground. Nest in solitary pairs. Hole-nesters that lay 4–5 white eggs in hollow trees.

HOOPOE (family Upupidae) is a bird the size of a Mistle Thrush with long, decurved bill, rounded wings and erectile crest. Nests in solitary pairs in holes. Lays 5–8 greenish-white eggs.

Kingfisher *Alcedo atthis* L 18. Breeds along slow-running rivers and streams with steep, sandy banks, where nest is excavated. Often seen at ponds rich in fish. Manages 2–3 broods. Population often plummets in severe winters. Judicious work with spade on riverbanks will create new nest sites and make it harder for foxes and minks to plunder them. Large head, *long bill*, broad wings, short legs and short tail. *Shimmering blue and green above* – back and tail appear luminous. *Reddish-orange below*. Male's bill is greyish-black while female's has red base to lower mandible (in some females the reddish colour dominates the grey). Perches on branches above the water, under bridges etc, may then sit motionless for long periods, hard to detect, the display of colour then not very prominent. Dives head-first for fish, usually from perch but also after brief hover. Rather shy. Flight swift and direct, close above the water, little is seen of the colours, but back/tail gleam. Even then difficult to catch sight of but announces itself with high, piercing whistles, 'tzeee'. Veritable bursts of whistles, falling in pitch, are heard when two meet. R

■□□ **Kingfisher** male in flight
□■□ **Pied Kingfisher** female
□□■ **Pied Kingfisher** female hovering

Pied Kingfisher *Ceryle rudis* L 25. Very rare vagrant, usually in spring, from breeding areas in Africa and Asia to E and SW Europe. *Black and white* plumage, *large body* and kingfisher-silhouette distinguish this species from other European birds. The male has two more or less complete *breast-bands*, the female has one. Perches on the look-out beside water or hovers above the water surface, sometimes at height of over 30m. Dives are not always so impressive, often descends in stages and may content itself with snatching at the surface. Fishes in salt as well as fresh water. Call short and piercing, 'kwit!', together with sharp, chirping whistles.

Belted Kingfisher, ♂

Belted Kingfisher *Ceryle alcyon* L 33. Very rare vagrant from N America. A real *giant*, as large as a Jackdaw, *blue-grey above* with *white neck and belly*. Male has a blue-grey breast band, the female the same and an additional reddish-brown band below it. Both sexes have a bushy *crest*. Call a hard, rapid rattle. V

■□ **Belted Kingfisher** juv. male
□■ **Smyrna Kingfisher** adult

White-breasted (Smyrna) Kingfisher *Halcyon smyrnensis* L 27. Breeds in S Asia, in west to Turkey. *Big*; has *big red bill*, is brown on head and belly, *white on throat and breast*, shimmering blue on back, tail and wings. Large white wing panels below. Draws attention by its *loud, trilling calls*.

Kingfishers and their allies

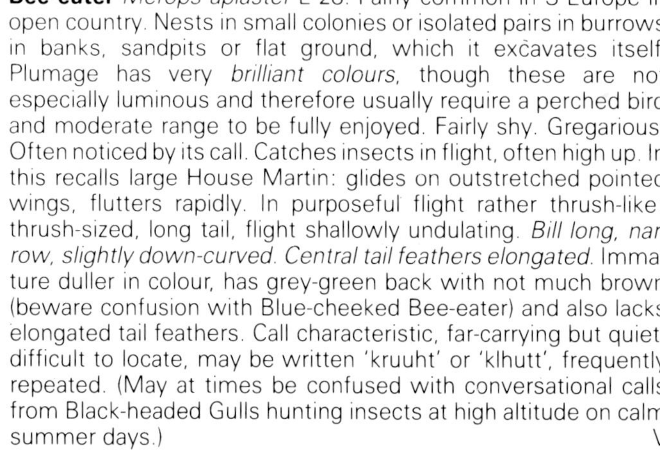

Bee-eater *Merops apiaster* L 28. Fairly common in S Europe in open country. Nests in small colonies or isolated pairs in burrows in banks, sandpits or flat ground, which it excavates itself. Plumage has very *brilliant colours*, though these are not especially luminous and therefore usually require a perched bird and moderate range to be fully enjoyed. Fairly shy. Gregarious. Often noticed by its call. Catches insects in flight, often high up. In this recalls large House Martin: glides on outstretched pointed wings, flutters rapidly. In purposeful flight rather thrush-like: thrush-sized, long tail, flight shallowly undulating. *Bill long, narrow, slightly down-curved. Central tail feathers elongated.* Immature duller in colour, has grey-green back with not much brown (beware confusion with Blue-cheeked Bee-eater) and also lacks elongated tail feathers. Call characteristic, far-carrying but quiet, difficult to locate, may be written 'kruuht' or 'klhutt', frequently repeated. (May at times be confused with conversational calls from Black-headed Gulls hunting insects at high altitude on calm summer days.) V

■□ **Bee-eater** adult male
□■ **Bee-eaters** adults

Blue-cheeked Bee-eater *Merops superciliosus* L 30. Fairly common on steppes in W Asia and Africa. Very rare summer visitor to W Europe. Breeding and behaviour as Bee-eater. *Green colour without any brown on upperparts* and lack of bright yellow throat distinguish it from Bee-eater (juv. Bee-eater looks very green above but has brown crown and lacks tail projections). Blue-cheeked Bee-eater's *tail projections are longer* than adult Bee-eater's. Call resembles Bee-eater's but is lower-pitched and not quite so far carrying, 'cherp'. V

■□ **Bee-eater** adult female winter
□■ **Blue-cheeked Bee-eater** adults

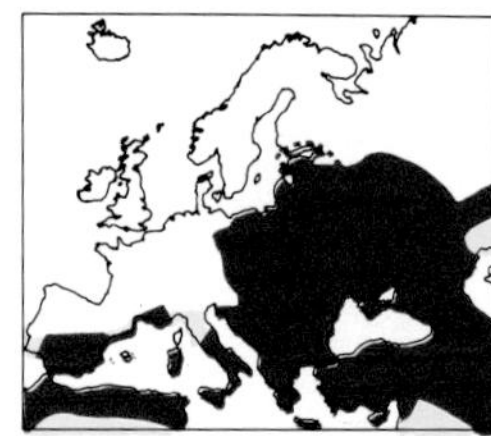

Roller *Coracias garrulus* L 30. Often rather scarce, in S and E Europe in open landscape with large hollow trees. Nests in tree holes, sometimes in ruins etc. The *pale blue on body and wings* has a luminous quality, in strong sunlight appears whitish azure-blue, in evening sun greenish-blue. *Back golden-brown. Carpals and undersides of flight feathers deep violet-blue.* Juvenile is a little duller and browner in colour, and neck and breast are diffusely streaked grey-brown. Perches in the open on dead branch or telegraph wire, flies down on to the ground and takes insect or lizard, in other words behaving like Red-backed Shrike. Flight resembles Jackdaw's but is faster, with more vigorous wingbeats. Display flight is a dive during which the Roller rapidly pitches from side to side (half rolls), like Lapwing. Calls 'CHACK-ack' (like both Magpie and Jackdaw) together with 'rrak-rrak'rrak-rehhh' (like angry Carrion Crow and Jay respectively). V

■□□ **Roller** adult
□■□ **Roller** juv.
□□■ **Roller** adult in flight

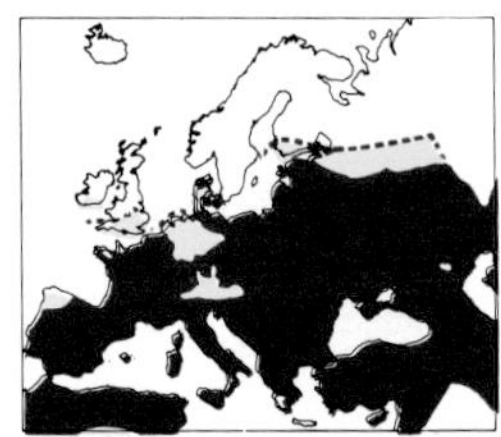

Hoopoe *Upupa epops* L 28. Fairly common in S and central Europe in open country with clumps of trees and cultivations. Nests in tree holes, walls etc. Often seen near buildings but is comparatively shy. In Britain a regular 'overshooting' spring rarity (fewer in autumn), occasionally breeds. Those that turn up in Oct are thought in most cases to be juveniles from distant south-eastern regions that have reached England by reversed migration. Sexes alike: *distinctive pale reddish-buff with striking black and white wing and tail barring*, erectile 'Red Indian chief crest' (raised on landing, otherwise rarely), long decurved bill. Body size as Mistle Thrush. Owing to the broad wings appears larger in *flight*, which *is desultory*, in irregular sweeps, resembles Jay's, often low down. *Broad white bands across the wingtips* are particularly striking. Moves about mostly on the ground, where action very vacillating, continually changes direction (like disturbed compass needle). Sticks its bill in the ground, hauls up insect larvas etc. The male's spring call characteristic: a repeated, three-syllable, hollow 'poo poo poo', sounds weak at close range but carries far. Usually performed out of sight in crown of tree, the Hoopoe perched upright with downward-pointing bill and lowered crest, the neck inflated. Also utters dry, Mistle Thrush-like 'terr' and harsh Jay-like 'schaahr'. P

■□□ **Hoopoe**
□■□ **Hoopoe** at nest site with crest raised
□□■ **Hoopoe** in flight

Woodpeckers

Woodpeckers (order Piciformes, family Picidae) are medium-sized or small birds. Feed mainly on wood-boring insects and their larvae, which are chipped out with their powerful bills. Their stiff tails are used as props when climbing trees. Their tongues are extremely long, and used for seeking food in insect galleries. Most species drum on dead branches, trunks of tree skeletons or telegraph poles when establishing territory in spring. Both sexes drum. The drumming is species-specific. Plumages are often colourful, and most males have red on the crown. Flight undulating (except in Black Woodpecker), and the wings are completely closed after each series of wingbeats. Live mainly in woods and forests, but some species, such as Green Woodpecker, Grey-headed Woodpecker and Wryneck, are often seen in rather open terrain. All are hole nesters, and apart from Wryneck they chip out their own nests in trees, usually a new nest each year; re-use occurs. Clutches consist of 4–8 white eggs. All species except Wryneck are mainly resident.

Green Woodpecker adult female in flight at nest hole

Green Woodpecker adult male

Green Woodpecker *Picus viridis* L 30. Common in deciduous woodland, especially in areas with large glades; also in more open country with isolated trees or clumps. Often seen on the ground searching for ants (green colour considered an adaptation to ground-living habits). In winter digs its way into anthills. *Green upperparts with brightly conspicuous greenish-yellow rump.* Only Grey-headed Woodpecker has same colours, but Green differs by larger size, *more red on crown* (in both sexes) and also *more black on 'face'.* Male has red centre to the moustache (Iberian race *sharpei* almost all-red). Juvenile, in contrast to juvenile Grey-headed, is distinctly spotted on head, neck and underparts, is greener on the back and also has more red on crown. Shy and wary. Flight in *long, marked undulations* with well audible wing noise, silhouette rather thin-necked. Green Woodpecker is voluble and noisy in spring and autumn. Territorial call in spring, which has taken over the role of drumming, is a rich, *full-throated laughing* series, 'kleu-kleu-kleu-kleu-kleu-kleu- . . . , slightly falling in pitch and accelerating at the end; used by both sexes, and duets may be heard. Flight call is a shrill, short, vehement 'kyukyukyuKYUK' or 'kyuKYUK'. Alarm call a more suppressed cackling 'kyakyakya'. Begging call of young is rasping, like sandpaper on wood. Drums rarely; drum bursts almost as fast as Great Spotted Woodpecker's but at least twice as long, and surprisingly weak for such a big woodpecker. R

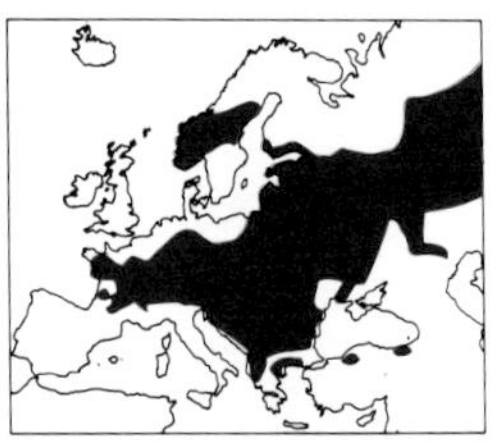

Grey-headed Woodpecker *Picus canus* L 27. Breeds across central Europe but is much less common than Green Woodpecker. Tends to inhabit higher altitudes than latter; also breeds in taiga, habitat avoided by Green; in lowlands accepts smaller woods, e.g. those fringing rivers. Ground-living habits but not so specialised on ants as Green Woodpecker; also feeds up in trees to large extent. Shy and wary. In spring announces itself with frequent calling, in summer is very difficult to find, in autumn/winter finds it way to habitations. Resembles Green Woodpecker but is smaller and has *greyer face*: has black only in form of loral and moustachial streak. This combined with comparatively short bill makes the physiognomy somewhat Wryneck-like. Male has *red only on forecrown*, female has no red at all. Juvenile resembles female, juvenile male has merely a splash of red on the forehead (is not 'freckled' like juvenile Green). Spring call resembles Green Woodpecker's but the *voice is finer, clearer, more musical*, almost flute-like (easily imitated) and lacks full-throated laughing quality of latter, *the notes are better spaced and slow down at the end* instead of accelerating slightly, and the fall in pitch is more marked. Alarm call is an intense, agitated, repeated 'kya'. Unlike Green, drums frequently; rapid bursts a good second long, very like Green Woodpecker's but much louder.

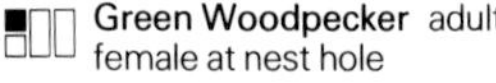

Green Woodpecker adult female at nest hole

Green Woodpecker juv.

Grey-headed Woodpecker adult female

Grey-headed Woodpecker adult male

Woodpeckers

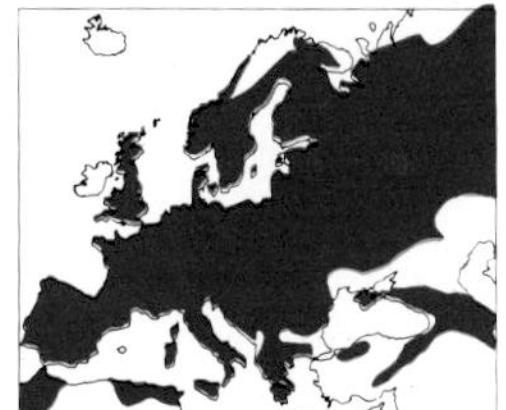

Great Spotted Woodpecker *Dendrocopos major* L 23. Breeds commonly to fairly commonly in both deciduous and coniferous woods, often seen also in gardens and parks (but is the most wary of the pied woodpeckers). Varied diet. More vegetarian than the other woodpeckers. In winter lives to a large extent on seeds from spruce and pine cones, which are pecked out at places known as 'anvils', cavities in stumps or tree trunks where the cones are wedged while being worked on. Undertakes eruptive migrations depending on the seed production. Also eats suet from birdtables. Has *a large white panel on each shoulder, bright red undertail*, unstreaked sides and also very little (male) or no (female) red on head – the male has only a *small red patch where the crown merges into the nape*. Therefore most resembles Syrian Woodpecker, which see. Juvenile, is more like Middle Spotted Woodpecker in having pale red undertail and quite a lot of red on the crown (though not right back to the nape), but *lacks flank streaking* and has *unbroken black band from bill to nape*. Call a high, short and sharp 'kik', may be pounded out in series at 1 sec. intervals. Drums often, bursts being typically *short* (0.4–0.75 sec.), loud and *incredibly rapid*, abruptly cut short. RW

Syrian Woodpecker *Dendrocopos syriacus* L 23. Breeds in SE Europe in comparatively open country: parks, orchards, vineyards, poplar alleys etc. Great expansion northwest in Europe during 1900s. Very similar to Great Spotted, but distinguished by *lack of black line from moustache up to nape, behind cheek*. Also slightly more red on hindcrown (male), whiter forehead, less white on outer tail feathers and Bullfinch-red undertail (instead of scarlet). Flanks may be faintly streaked and barred. Juvenile is distinguished from juvenile Great Spotted by the same characters, from Middle Spotted by moustachial streak extending to bill. The 'kik' call like a scolding Redshank's 'kip, kip'. Drumming rapid, like Great Spotted's, but longer, about 1 sec.

Middle Spotted Woodpecker *Dendrocopos medius* L 20. Breeds in central and S Europe in mature deciduous woods, particularly of oak and hornbeam. Bill comparatively weak, used more as a probe than as a hatchet. Usually moves about in the tree crown. In spring drinks maple sap. Like Great Spotted has white shoulder panels, but also *red crown* (female a little duller red) in all plumages. Note that juveniles of Great Spotted (and Syrian) have red crown, but Middle Spotted differs in having more white on sides of head and neck (moustachial streak does not reach bill), *streaked flanks* and pale *pink undertail* without sharp border with *belly*, which is toned *yellowish-brown*. During breeding season has a nasal, strained, slowly delivered call, 'mjaik, mjaik, mjaik, . . . '. Also common is a whole *series of 'kik' calls at trotting pace*, 'kik, keuk, keuk, keuk, keuk, keuk'. Drumming extremely rare, bursts weak as in Lesser Spotted.

Lesser Spotted Woodpecker *Dendrocopos minor* L 15. Breeds rather scarcely in deciduous and mixed woods, parks and subalpine birch forest. Particularly attracted to waterside areas with profuse tangles of foliage. Sometimes seen in orchards, in winter visits reedbeds where it pecks out pupae from the reeds. *Smallest* of Europe's woodpeckers. In its *deeply undulating flight* resembles an 'ordinary small bird', albeit a quite stocky one (Woodlark if anything). *Back strongly barred white*, can appear predominantly white. *Undertail lacks red*. Commonest call very characteristic: a series of shrill, feeble notes, 'peet peet peet peet peet peet'. Also calls 'kik', though with weaker voice than its relatives. Drums frequently, but more slowly ('rattles') and more weakly than Great Spotted Woodpecker and for longer (c.1.2 sec.). The sound volume of the bursts often varies; they are usually fainter in the middle and louder at beginning and end, may even be split by a fleeting pause. Characteristically, *the drumming is repeated at much shorter intervals* than in the other woodpeckers. R

Great Spotted Woodpecker adult male

Great Spotted Woodpecker adult female

Great Spotted Woodpecker juv.

Great Spotted Woodpecker adult in flight

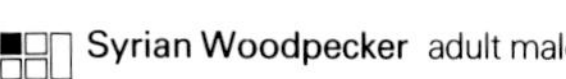
Syrian Woodpecker adult male

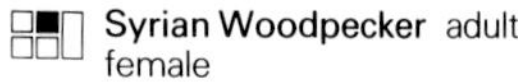
Syrian Woodpecker adult female

Lesser Spotted Woodpecker adult male

Lesser Spotted Woodpecker adult female

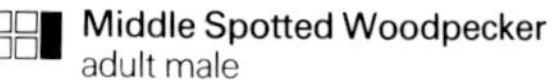
Middle Spotted Woodpecker adult male

Woodpeckers

White-backed Woodpecker *Dendrocopos leucotos* L 25. Rare, and over large parts of range fast retreating, because of its very particular habitat requirements: deciduous and mixed wood with ample supply of old decayed trees (especially aspen, alder, birch, also oak, beech). Often fearless. Often seeks food (larvae of tree insects) at ground level, e.g. on windfallen trees and in old stumps in centre of osier thickets. Bill long and powerful. Makes deep conical holes in rotten wood. Largest of the pied woodpeckers and has distinct white lower back and rump. On perched bird this is not always so obvious (Three-toed is more white-backed); *broad white transverse bar towards wing bend* is then the best mark. *Undertail area pale red,* fading out on belly and *streaked flanks.* Male has red crown, female all-black and juvenile not quite so much red as male. The 'kik' call is quieter and deeper than Great Spotted's, 'kiik' or 'kok', like Blackbird. Drumming powerful and c. 1.7 sec. long, resembling that of Three-toed's but *accelerating and fainter at end* ('shrinking', like diminishing bounces of a table-tennis ball).

Three-toed Woodpecker *Picoides tridactylus* L 22. Not uncommon in the taiga zone, particularly in old spruce forest. Also in subalpine birch forest. Scarce in mountain tracts of central and SE Europe, in coniferous forest. On average the most fearless woodpecker. Often feeds at low level. Habitually makes holes in a ring around trunk of large spruces to obtain sap. Pines, too, may be ringed. Head dark with white chin, *crown brass-yellow* in male, streaked black and white in female. Flanks very grey. Broad white 'blaze' right down back. The 'kik' call is usually soft and like a Redwing call, 'kyuk', but sometimes sharp and shrill like Great Spotted Woodpecker's 'kik'. Drumming powerful, longer (c. 1.3 sec.) than Great Spotted's and distinctly slower ('well articulated'), rather like short Black Woodpecker's.

Black Woodpecker *Dryocopus martius* L 45. Fairly common in older coniferous and deciduous forests. Largest of Europe's woodpeckers. Typically seeks Hercules ants in stumps and on outwardly healthy-looking spruce trunks, makes enormous craters. Size and *uniform black plumage* make it easy to recognise. *Male has entire crown red, female only rear part of crown.* Flight desultory and slightly uneven, but not undulating like other woodpeckers', most like Nutcracker's (i.e. Jay-like). Flight call a far-carrying 'krri-krri-krri . . .', also serves as an alarm call. When perched utters characteristic drawn-out, loud, clear 'klee-ay'. In early spring a loud ringing 'kwee-Kwee-kwee-kwee-kwee-kwee-kwee' is also heard, like Green Woodpecker's but without drop in pitch at end, instead continues at same pitch and with uninterrupted 'wild and crazy' ring. When agitated a sound like a cluck and a nasal squeak run into one is heard. All above calls are given by both sexes. Drums frequently. *Drum bursts long,* from not quite 2 sec. to fully 3 sec. (female's shorter), *open and powerful* ('machine-gun salvo'), accelerating just a shade towards end.

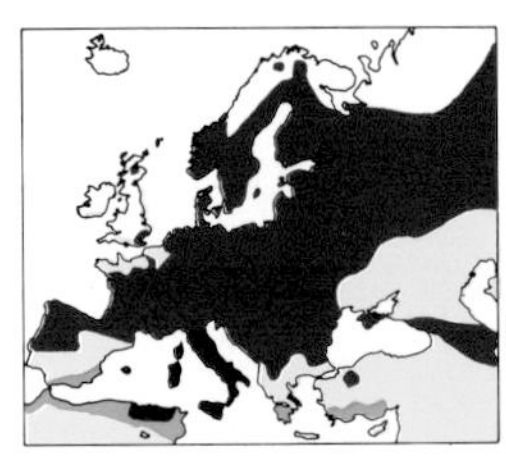

Wryneck *Jynx torquilla* L 17. Fairly common on the Continent in open sunny woodlands (clearings), parks and orchards. Probably now extinct in England, but colonising NE Scotland. Arrives Apr–May, returns to Africa Aug–Sept. Not a 'real' woodpecker – does not climb trunks or chip away at wood, does not drum (in 'real' woodpecker manner). At first glance most resembles an ordinary small bird (large *Sylvia*). In tight situtations, defends itself with snaking, twisting movements of neck (hence the name). *Plumage patterned like lichen in grey-brown with darker bands* along head and back. Tail long, bill relatively short. Specialises on ants. Spends most of time in trees, concealed in foliage, but also visits ground, hopping around. May be seen slipping away in low flight like a small, grey female Red-backed Shrike. Would be anonymous without its call, a series of loud, nasal, slightly croaky or moaning 'TEEe-TEEe-TEEe-TEEe', recalling small falcon. Begging call of young a rapid, high ticking 'tixixixixixix . . .'. SP

White-backed Woodpecker adult male at nest hole

Three-toed Woodpecker adult male

Black Woodpecker adult female

Black Woodpecker adult male with nestling

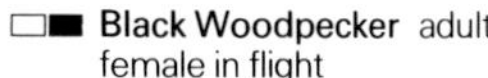
Black Woodpecker adult female in flight

Wryneck

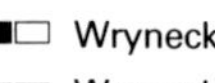
Wryneck

Wryneck

Introduction to passerines

The huge order of Passeriformes – the passerines or perching birds – accounts for some 60 per cent of all the bird species in the world. It embraces 82 families, 24 of which are found in Europe and are represented in the following pages.

All members of this order have feet adapted specially for perching; three of the four unwebbed toes point forwards and the other backwards. The muscles of the syrinx are arranged and developed in such a way that, with very few exceptions, the species are capable of producing real song; indeed, the order includes the best singers and the most remarkable mimics of all birds.

In Europe, the members of this order vary greatly in size, from the Raven (over 60 cm) to the tiny Firecrest and Goldcrest (9 cm). The bill shape also varies, showing adaptations to different food and methods of feeding: insect-eaters generally have thin, rather weak bills, seed-eaters have stout, conical bills, while omnivorous species tend to have deep, powerful bills. While many species are comparatively drab and inconspicuous in colour, an equal number exhibit brilliant plumage coloration.

All the passerines are land birds. Among them they exploit a wide range of habitats and occur in virtually all kinds of environments, from deserts to mountain tops, from swamps and marshes to woodlands, forests and grasslands, and many also live in man-made environments within towns and cities. Dippers have even evolved to inhabit fast-flowing rivers, where they literally walk on the bottom of the river bed.

Their breeding habits may be solitary, as in the case of wagtails and pipits; loosely colonial, as the Reed Warbler; or highly colonial, as the Rook, some of the swallow family and some of the sparrows. While many, such as shrikes and certain thrushes, are highly territorial, others are far less so. Outside the breeding season, most of the finches and buntings, the starlings and some of the thrushes and tits are gregarious and can be seen in flocks occasionally of immense size, while species such as the accentors and the Wren remain solitary. In winter, enormous roosts are formed by Starlings, Pied Wagtails, finches and others.

Nest sites may be on the ground (larks, pipits), in dense shrubbery (warblers), in holes or cavities (nuthatches, flycatchers, tits), on branch forks (many thrushes, some finches) or well up in trees (crows). Some species (e.g. Redstart) regularly use artificial nestboxes. Some nests are of the most intricate design (e.g. Red-rumped Swallow, Penduline Tit), while others are little more than a platform of twigs.

Many passerines are migratory, in particular the insectivores breeding in the northern parts of Europe. Even the smallest warblers cross such dangerous areas as the Mediterranean Sea and the Sahara to reach their wintering grounds in Africa. Others, however, are essentially resident – the House Sparrow, for example – though some make shorter movements to escape the rigours of the northern winter – such as the Greenfinch.

As with the non-passerines, the sequence of families within this order follows one of the more familiar arrangements.

Mistle Thrush at nest with young

Passerines

Larks (family Alaudidae) are small and medium-sized birds, rather uniform in colour, mainly brown. In Britain only two breeding species and one scarce winter visitor; most are found in S Europe. Inhabit open country. Rather like pipits, but stockier and with broader wings and shorter tails. Sexes usually alike (exception is Black Lark). Good singers, usually during prolonged song flight at high altitude. Eat insects and seeds. Nest on the ground. Clutches of 3–5 eggs.

■□ Dupont's Lark
□■ Dupont's Lark

Dupont's Lark *Chersophilus duponti* L 18. In recent years a tiny population has nested in central Spain (only a few pairs), otherwise breeds in N Africa. Lives on dry steppes with isolated bushes. Fairly *long, narrow and slightly decurved bill.* Head has no suggestion of a crest. Has pale supercilium and white outer tail feathers. *Lacks white on wings.* Unobtrusive, often hides in the vegetation. Runs quickly. *Long-legged* and *stands* more *upright* than other larks. The song, which is performed in flight, is delivered at a slowish tempo and contains both clear, fluty whistles and rasping, strained notes.

■□ Short-toed Lark
□■ Short-toed Lark

Short-toed Lark *Calandrella brachydactyla* L 15. Breeds in S Europe in open, dry country, often on dry mudflats. Like a small *pale* Skylark with 'swollen' bill. Distinct *pale supercilium.* Usually a dark eye-stripe. Rusty crown. Unmarked sandy lesser wing-coverts, dark median coverts. Underparts *unstreaked* except for a few, diffuse spots on the breast in the juvenile (adult plumage from Aug–Sept). Dark patch on side of neck in adult as a rule difficult to see in the field and may be absent. Very like Lesser Short-toed Lark, but adult distinguished from that species by lack of clear streaking on breast, generally paler and rustier-toned colours and often also, at close range, by dark patch on side of neck and longer tertials (covering tips of primaries). Call resembles Skylark's though more of a *dry chirrup,* 'drreet-it-it' or 'drri-e' etc. The song is composed of short, simple phrases, *little variation,* less often mimicking calls, mostly a dry chirruping similar to the call. *Second-long phrases, a good second between each,* the song is delivered in synchrony with the wingbeats in the *undulating song flight* – Skylark-like *rapid fluttering wingbeats* succeeded by descending glide with tightly closed wings. Song flight wandering and erratic at high altitude. V

■□ Short-toed Lark
□■ Lesser Short-toed Lark

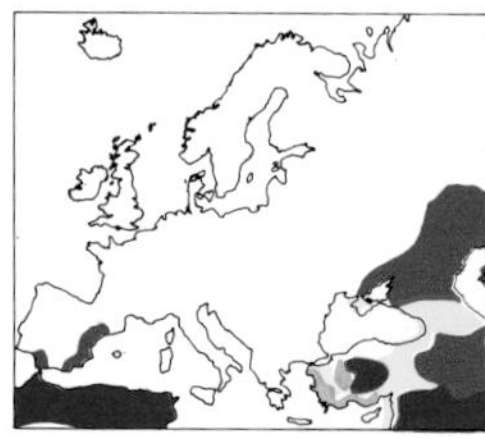

Lesser Short-toed Lark *Calandrella rufescens* L 14. Breeds locally in SW and SE Europe in dry, open country, though also on rather damper meadows than Short-toed Lark. Very like latter, but adult is *distinctly streaked on the breast* and (more faintly) on the sides and is also usually slightly darker and *more greyish-brown,* has shorter tertials. Call a dry buzzing 'drrrr-drr' or simply 'prrrrt', like House Martin with dry ring of Sand Martin or like a scolding sparrow. Song *long, varied,* pleasing, *full of good mimicry.* Often it sounds like a Crested Lark, cleverly mimicked, changes over to trills like Calandra Lark's, strikes up Green Sandpiper, Common Sandpiper, Linnet and others, now and then relieved by the call. Song flight drifting around at random fairly high up, *wingbeats at times slow and deliberate* as in Greenfinch display – thus like Calandra Lark. V

Calandra Lark, song flight

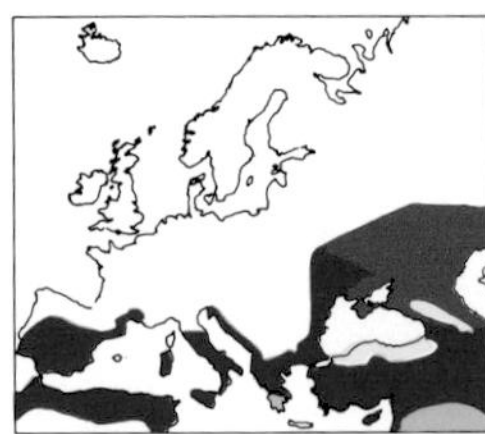

Calandra Lark *Melanocorypha calandra* L 20. Breeds in S Europe in dry, open country. Very *big* with proportionately short tail and *broad, long wings with white trailing edge* and typically *dark underwings* in flight. *Bill thick.* The large, black neck patches can sometimes be difficult to see and are less conspicuous in the female. Flight usually low and undulating, wingbeats comparatively slow (may recall wader). Call powerful and *raucous, dry roll,* 'tshrreet' (like quarrelling Starling). The song, melodic and like Skylark's though more powerful and even richer in mimicry, is delivered during circling flight from high altitude, *wingbeats* for long periods *slow,* deliberate. V

■□ Calandra Lark
□■ Calandra Lark adult at nest with chicks

Passerines

White-winged Lark *Melanocorypha leucoptera* L 19. Breeds on steppes in Kazakhstan west to Black Sea. Slightly bigger than Skylark. Has *characteristic wing pattern* of three colours: brown fore edge, black central band and broad white rear edge. White rear edge makes it look extremely *narrow-winged* in flight. Crown, wing bend and uppertail-coverts red-brown in male, weaker in colour and streaked in female. Legs pale brown. Song like Skylark's but slightly dryer and harder and also lacks clear notes. V

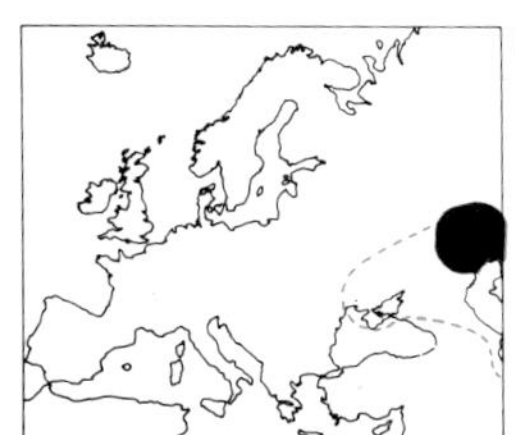

Black Lark *Melanocorypha yeltoniensis* L ♂ 21, ♀ 19. Breeds on steppes in Kazakhstan, by wetlands. Resident. Big and stocky. Male *all-black* in summer, at distance can be taken for a Starling (perched). In winter most of the black is hidden by *broad buff fringes*. Female so *much smaller* that appears to be of different species, is very like Calandra Lark, incl. similar blackish-brown neck mark and dark underwings; *but lacks white trailing edge to wing*, and legs are dark. The big male courts like a House Sparrow, hops close around female, ruffles up head/neck, holds out carpals, cocks tail; flies in pursuit close above ground, a little unsure, when broad, rounded wings beat only above level of back, high and improbably sparsely; slow butterfly-like display flight higher up, usually without song. Has primitive lark song, delivered mostly from ground.

Crested Lark *Galerida cristata* L 17. Fairly common in dry, open country with sparse vegetation, along roadsides and in open places in towns. Often seen close to grain silos, along embankments and, in coastal regions, in dock areas. *Striking, pointed crest* (Skylark may sometimes raise crown feathers to a blunted crest), which distinguishes it from all other larks except Thekla Lark (which see). Fairly pale, long and heavy bill. Rather pale brown (with slight ochre tone) with diffuse back markings. Often very fearless. Runs fast. Looks *big-winged and short-tailed* in flight. *No white on trailing edge of wing*, and tail sides ochre. Juvenile has shorter crest and pale scaly pattern on back. Call clear, melancholy and a little languorous, e.g. 'dee dee düh'. Also utters hoarse mewing 'dwuee" and creaky, rolling 'drrUee'. Song partly primitive, with pauses, combinations of clear call notes which are mostly delivered from perch, partly flowing, rich in mimicry, *Calandrella*-like, delivered in flight. V

Thekla Lark *Galerida theklae* L 16. Breeds in SW Europe in dry, open country with sparse vegetation. Usually prefers rockier areas and higher altitudes than Crested Lark but also occurs in similar kinds of habitats. Very difficult to distinguish from Crested. A shade smaller, has *shorter and slightly darker bill with convex lower mandible* (Crested: straight), is usually greyer above and paler below, with *better-defined breast streaking* and grey-brown underwings (light brownish-pink in Crested). Uppertail-coverts usually rusty-toned, contrasting with greyer rump and tail feathers (only slight rusty tone and contrast in Crested), but this hard to see in the field. Often flies up in to trees, which Crested seldom does. Call often of five syllables, 'tee-ti-tiuee'; can be shorter but always slightly softer (tone recalls Rustic Bunting song) and weaker than Crested's. Song resembles Crested's but has *softer, more melodious tone*, greater variation and complexity.

Bimaculated Lark *Melanocorypha bimaculata* L 17. Breeds on dry plateaux in SW Asia incl. Caucasus, Turkey and NE Israel. Similar to Calandra Lark in build and markings (e.g. has *marked black neck patch*) but has even heavier bill, *shorter tail* and slightly *more pointed wings* (Starling impression in flight). *White terminal tail band* but no white on tail sides. Brown underwing and only negligible white on trailing edge. Call like Skylark but gruffer. Song very like Calandra's. In song flight wingbeats often fast like Skylark but sometimes fairly slow, which gives bat impression, emphasised by short tail (spread, unlike in Calandra Lark). V

■□□ White-winged Lark adult male singing
□■□ White-winged Lark flying away
□□■ Black Lark adult male

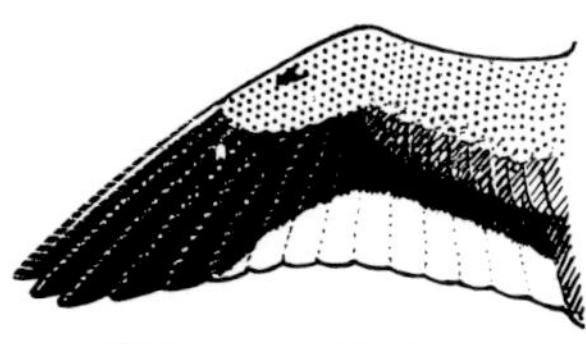

White-winged Lark, upperwing

■□□ Crested Lark
□■□ Crested Lark
□□■ Crested Lark

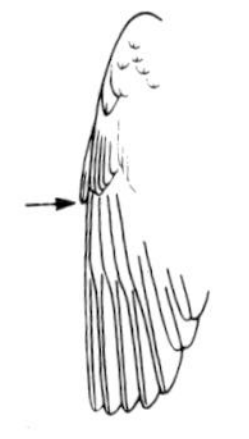

Thekla

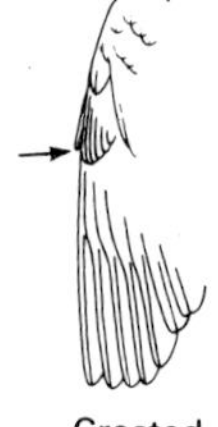

Crested

■□□ Thekla Lark
□■□ Thekla Lark
□□■ Thekla Lark

Bimaculated Lark, song flight

■□ Bimaculated Lark
□■ Bimaculated Lark

Passerines

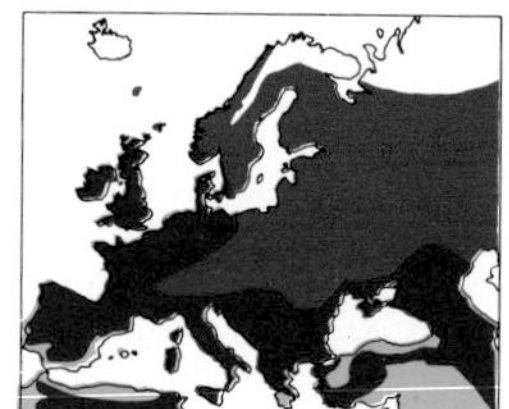

Skylark *Alauda arvensis* L 18. Very common breeding bird in open country, cultivated as well as natural (arable land, coastal meadows etc). Terrestrial. Rather pale *brown-spotted with whitish trailing edge to wing* and medium-length white-edged tail. Has small crest (Crested Lark has much longer and more pointed crest. Other rather similar species are Woodlark, Calandra Lark and Corn Bunting, which see). Juveniles wear a scaly patterned plumage until late summer, and lack pale trailing edge to wing. Usual call is a dry, full chirrup, 'prriee' and 'prreet' etc. The song is an *endless outpouring* based on high rolling notes repeated in long series, often containing notes of mimicry. It starts up as early as the first hours of dawn (mass starting up, strikingly simultaneous) and can then be heard all day. It generally begins on the ground or from a fence post but is usually performed for the most part high in the sky, for 10–15 minutes without stopping. The lark at this time hangs still on fluttering wings difficult to detect. Towards late summer the larks become silent. During the autumn loose flocks can be flushed on the stubble fields. In winter larger flocks are present, and in severe weather sometimes huge flocks and massive migratory movements may occur. RSWP

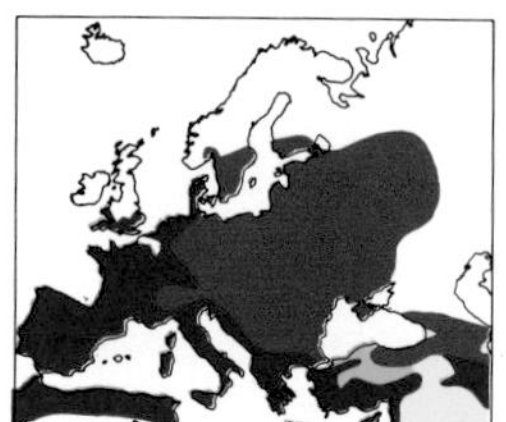

Woodlark *Lullula arborea* L 15. Scarce breeding bird on heaths and brecks with scattered trees, also felled woodland, burnt ground, occasionally nurseries. Resembles Skylark but has much *shorter tail*. Prominent pale supercilia which practically meet on the nape. Short crest which is usually not raised. Totally characteristic of the species is a *dark spot, enclosed by brownish-white, on the fore edge of the wing* (upperside). Has a more distinctly undulating flight than Skylark (may actually recall Lesser Spotted Woodpecker), and seen from below it appears rather bat-like with its broad, rounded wings and obviously short tail. The tail lacks white outer feathers, instead has pale band at tip. The Woodlark often perches in trees and bushes (in exposed position on ends of branches, in the tops etc) but feeds on ground. The song consists of runs of mellow notes with a delightful ring, which begin tentatively but accelerate and increase in intensity at the same time as they fall in pitch 'lee lee lee lililililiiluluhululooloo, EElu, EElu EElu-EElu . . .'. It is heard mainly on early mornings and evenings, in June (2nd brood) sometimes at midnight – completely solo then! Most often delivered in song flight, which is high up and often drifts away out of earshot, but also from perch (tree, telegraph wire, even on ground). Call a mellow, quiet, melodic 'deedlooEE' or with a ring more like the song, 'TLOee-TLOee'. Small single-species flocks in autumn. R

Shore Lark *Eremophila alpestris* L 17. In Europe an alpine species. The northern race (*flava*) has recently declined markedly in Fenno-Scandia, with a consequent reduction in numbers in W. European wintering areas. Nests on dry mountain heath, often highest parts such as the top of low mountains. Rarely seen on migration. In winter found along sea coasts and on fields, on roughly the same ground as Snow Buntings. Under reasonable conditions easily recognised by *head markings of black and yellow*. Juveniles, however, have a completely different plumage: back, crown and cheeks dark brown with cream-coloured spots, supercilium and throat cream, broad brown-blotched breast band; feet black. The Shore Larks in Greece and Turkey (*penicillata*) have more black on the head (see fig.) and more evenly grey upperparts. Distinguished in flight from Skylark by greater contrast between pale belly and blackish undertail. Flight like Skylark's. Usually, however, slips away low in Rock Pipit fashion. Call is a thin 'EEH tutu' (a squeaky note and two soft ones in rapid succession). Song short, jingling and irregular, resembles Lapland Bunting's and Snow Bunting's but more 'jolty', opens up almost like Corn Bunting, lacks drawn-out clinking notes of Lapland and mellow voice of Snow. Is usually delivered from a rock on the heath but also in circling flight, high up, with wings extended; tail then looks surprisingly long. WP

■□□ **Skylark**
□■□ **Skylark**
□□■ **Skylark** hovering in song flight

Woodlark adult at nest with chicks
Woodlark adult
Shore Lark adult male, race *penicillata*

Shore Lark, adult ♂
SE Europe, Turkey

■□ **Shore Lark** adult male at nest with chicks
□■ **Shore Lark** female or 1st-winter

Passerines

Swallows

Swallows (family Hirundinidae) have long pointed wings and often clearly forked tails. Their flight is swift and elegant with more fluent wing action than in the rather similar swifts. Legs and bills are short, mouths wide. Catch insects in flight. Often seen perched on telegraph wires, seldom on the ground. Long-distance migrants, the great majority leave Europe to winter in Africa. Often appear in large mixed flocks. Most species are colonial breeders; several build characteristic sealed nests of mud, blades of grass and saliva. Clutches of 4–7 white or spotted eggs.

Sand Martin *Riparia riparia* L 13. Fairly common, colonial breeder in steep riverbanks, gravel-pits, sandpits etc, the nests excavated in the steep sides. Arrives in Britain mid Mar, a little earlier than the other swallows. Often seen near water. On migration, roosts in reeds in immense flocks. The smallest swallow. *Upperparts brown* with no white. Characteristic of species is the *brown breast band*. See also Crag Martin. Call a low noteless rasp. S

Crag Martin *Ptyonoprogne rupestris* L 15. Nests in colonies locally in S Europe in mountain regions and on rocky coasts. The Crag Martins of the Alps migrate south in winter, while Spanish breeders may stay behind. The nest is placed on cliffs. Larger and stouter than Sand Martin and *lacks breast band*. *Underwing-coverts markedly dark*, forming distinct contrast with rest of underparts. *Wings broader* than Sand Martin's, and tail only slightly forked. Flight more restlessly agile and acrobatic than the other swallows'. When turning, the tail is spread, showing the *characteristic white spots*. Call a fairly weak 'tshree'.

Swallow *Hirundo rustica* L 19. Breeds commonly in cultivated, open country. Nests in single pairs or small, loose colonies. The open nest is made of mud and straw, usually inside buildings (on rafters, in recesses etc in barns and stables) or under bridges (similar siting). Roosts in large flocks in reeds on migration. *Outer tail feathers greatly elongated and narrow*. Red forehead and chin good specific characters but difficult to see at some distance – look instead for *all-dark chin/throat. No white on rump*. Flight jerky and flicking (glides on extended wings are relatively short and fast, not as House Martin's). Call a short 'wit', 'wit-wit'. A fuller 'glit-glit' announces, e.g. a Sparrowhawk. Sharp 'si-VLIT' when mobbing. Song a rapidly delivered chatter with abruptly interposed croaking sounds. S

▶ **Red-rumped Swallow** *Hirundo daurica* L 18. Fairly common in S Europe in open, preferably rocky country. The nest, with its tube-shaped entrace, is built entirely of mud and placed under projecting rocks, in the roof of a cave, under a bridge or on a building. Nests in single pairs or in small, loose colonies. Resembles Swallow, but note *pale, rusty-coloured rump and narrow nape band, pale chin* and not such long tail projections. *Undertail-coverts jet-black* (white in Swallow). (Note: hybrids between Swallow and House Martin can resemble this species.) Flight like House Martin's with glides on outstretched wings. Flight call a nasal 'tweit', rather like Tree Sparrow. Alarm a sharp 'keer'. The song recalls Swallow's but is slower, more grating and is often delivered in shorter phrases. V

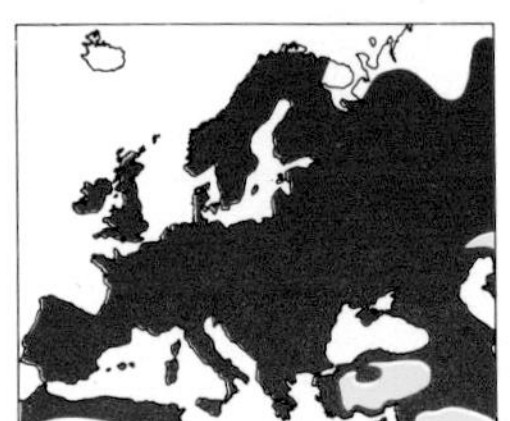

▶ **House Martin** *Delichon urbica* L 14. Nests commonly in colonies, mainly in villages and cities but also in mountain regions. The nest, in the shape of a bowl and sealed with mud, is fixed under the eaves of buildings or on to cliff faces. Roosts in nests or treetops (not reeds). The House Martin is recognised by *blue-glossed black upperparts with white rump* together with white underparts. The tail is short and moderately forked. Flight more fluttering than Swallow's, with rather long, relaxed glides on extended wings (not flicking jerkily). Call a dry twitter, 'prreet' (not rasping like Sand Martin's). Alarm call a repeated high 'seerr' (may mean Sparrowhawk, small falcon or – usually – internal quarrel). Song chirruping, on same pitch as the call. S

■□ **Sand Martin** in flight
□■ **Sand Martin** colony

■□□ **Crag Martin** in flight
□■□ **Crag Martin** in flight
□□■ **Crag Martins**

■□□ **Swallow** adult
□■□ **Swallow** in flight by nest site
□□■ **Red-rumped Swallow** collecting mud for nest

■□□ **Red-rumped Swallow** in flight
□■□ **House Martins** at nest
□□■ **House Martins** collecting mud for nest

Passerines

Pipits and wagtails (family Motacillidae) are birds barely the size of sparrows, slender in build, with long tails with white outer edges and with slender, pointed bills. Lively and always on the go, very much terrestrial, able to walk and run well. Insectivorous. The wagtails have a habit of wagging their long tail up and down. The long tail serves as a balance in dashing runs. The pipits are brown and streaked and are best distinguished from the larks by more slender shape and longer tails. Clutches of 4–7.

song-flight

Tree Pipit *Anthus trivialis* L 15. Fairly common (in places abundant) in open woods, in glades and in more open country with bushes and trees. Resembles Meadow Pipit, but can be distinguished by slightly *more yellowish-brown colour*, not so grey-green, *belly whiter*, not yellowish tinged *more distinct dark malar stripe*, flanks more finely streaked, almost completely unstreaked rump and comparatively short, curved hindclaw, but *best by voice*. Call a characteristic, hoarse 'speez'. Alarm a quiet but distinct, slowly repeated 'sit'. The song is sometimes delivered from a treetop but usually during a short song flight, in which the bird descends on stiff wings – like a little paper plane. The song is loud and is a repetition of short series of notes at varying tempo, 'cha-cha-cha-cha weeweeweewee trrrrrr uee uee uee uee, ooee SEEa-SEEa-SEEa'. SP

Olive-backed Pipit *Anthus hodgsoni* L 14.5. Breeds in the taiga in NE Russia and Siberia. Rare autumn vagrant to NW Europe. Very like Tree Pipit, but is a shade smaller, more *olive-green above* with *fainter streaking on back*; underparts on the other hand are more heavily streaked. Supercilium broad and distinct, buff in front of eye. *Also a small pale and a small dark spot behind the ear-coverts* in most individuals (see fig.). Rump is unstreaked. Call a fine 'tseet', very like Tree Pipit's but clearer, recalling Red-throated Pipit, though more powerful and slightly harsher and briefer, not drawn-out and dying away. From perch sings a Tree Pipit-like song but with less variation. Does not slow down with drawn-out 'SEEa' like Tree Pipit, changes phrases more quickly, includes dry trills reminiscent of Red-throated Pipit. V

Olive-backed Pipit

Pechora Pipit *Anthus gustavi* L 14.5. Breeds on the tundra in NE Russia (from the Pechora) and Siberia. Extremely rare autumn vagrant in NW Europe. Often skulks like a *Locustella*, hard to flush. Resembles Tree Pipit but is slighlty *darker*, has long hindclaw, *two pale stripes on back, strong rather pale bill, indistinct supercilium, faint malar stripe*, and *streaked rump*. Outer tail feathers edged buffish-white and not pure white (rarely discern ible in the field). Rather silent on migration; call when heard a characteristic, hard, often repeated 'tsip', quite different from other pipits. Song a throaty buzzing on a few themes. V

Richard's Pipit *Anthus novaeseelandiae* L 18. A rare but annual visitor to W Europe, mainly at end of Sept and Oct, from breeding grounds in Asia. Usually stops off on coastal meadows and dry long-grass fields. *Big and long-legged*, stands in *upright posture*, has *very long hindclaw*, streaked upperparts and a band of short streaks across breast. *Bill long* and stout, but can appear less striking on some. Most easily confused with immature Tawny Pipit, which also has streaked breast in summer and early autumn but differs in *call*, hindclaw, comparatively pale lores and often also in leg length and posture. Sometimes hovers immediately above ground before landing (which Tawny does very rarely indeed). Call an explosive and loud, harsh 'schreep' on rising or in flight; at a distance sounds like a spluttery 'hissing' 'psch'. V

Blyth's Pipit *Anthus godlewskii* L 17. A very rare vagrant from Asia. Size between Tawny and Richard's Pipits, in the field almost indistinguishable from latter. Can be identified in the hand by leg and hindclaw length and tail pattern. Call more like a harsh Yellow Wagtail call than Richard's Pipit's, 'pscheeoo', distinctly louder and harsher than any Tawny Pipit call. V

Tree Pipit at nest with food
Tree Pipit with food
Tree Pipit adult spring
Olive-backed Pipit
Olive-backed Pipit

Pechora Pipit
Richard's Pipit 1st-winter

hind claws
Tree Pipit
Meadow Pipit
Tawny Pipit
Richard's Pipit
(Life size)

Blyth's Pipit spring
Blyth's Pipit 1st-winter
Richard's Pipit adult

Passerines

Meadow Pipit *Anthus pratensis* L 14.5. Breeds commonly on heaths, moors, pastures, coastal meadows, dunes; in winter often found on fields, lowland marshes, coasts. Resembles Tree Pipit but a shade smaller, is rather *more grey-green*, has *less clearly defined malar stripe* and straighter, longer hindclaw. Rump very lightly streaked, clearly less so than back. Rises with bounding flight and utters a thin 'ist-ist', 2 or 3 syllables, very unlike Tree and Red-throated Pipits but very like Rock Pipit call (which see). Alarm a disyllabic trembling 'tirrEE'. Has brief song flight. Song simple: a few rapid and sharp series of notes, e.g. 'zi zi zi-zi-zi-zi-zi-zu-zu zurrrrr seea seea seea seea seea seea seea'. RSWP

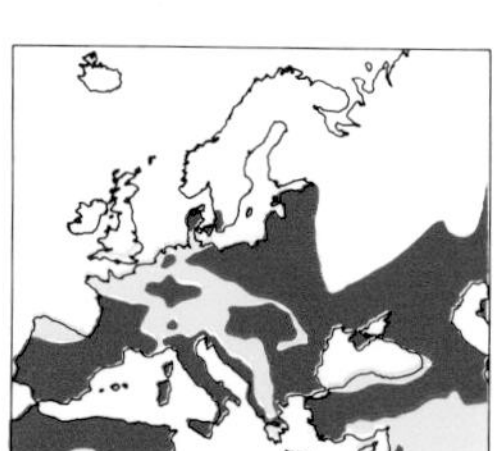

Tawny Pipit *Anthus campestris* L 16.5. Locally common breeder in open, dry and sandy country with sparse vegetation, in S Europe sometimes on bare mountain heath. Annual spring and autumn in Britain. *Sandy-coloured, rather faintly streaked*, above as well as below, and *big*, which distinguishes it from other European pipits. Pale supercilium generally well marked, *median wing-coverts dark*, tipped light in fresh plumage. Juvenile in summer/early autumn is streaked above and spotted on breast like Richard's Pipit, but differs in weaker bill, darker lores, shorter legs and hindclaw and – above all – in *call*. Call very like House Sparrow's 'chilp'; some variation in articulation. Song a slowly repeated 'tseerLEE', delivered in flight or from ground. Variations occur, e.g. a vibrant tremble descending in pitch: 'sr-r-ree-u'. P

Red-throated Pipit *Anthus cervinus* L 14.5. Breeds sparsely in *Salix* scrub on subarctic bogs, mainly above tree line. Migrates south across E and central Europe, rare vagrant in west. In summer easily told from other pipits by *rusty-red throat, cheeks and upper breast*. Adult retain throat colour in autumn. Juvenile resembles Meadow Pipit but has *heavily streaked rump*, is *rustier brown*, has two conspicuous *pale streaks on back* and prominent dark malar stripe. *Call* a thin, drawn-out 'pseeh' (or 'pssss'), distinctly different from Meadow and Tree Pipits. Alarm 'chup', like Ortolan Bunting. Song, often delivered in flight, most resembles Tree Pipit's but finer, has typical Redpoll-like dry trills and thin, drawn-out 'pseeeu-pseeeu-pseeeu- . . . '. V

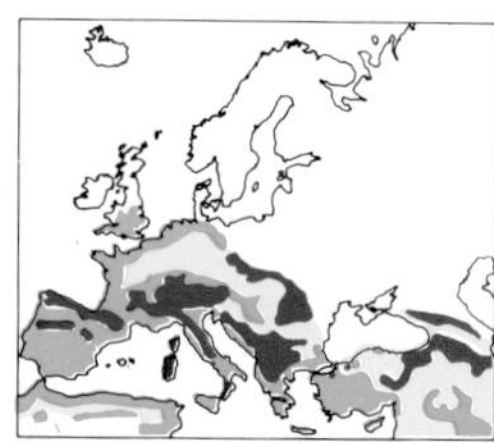

Water Pipit *Anthus spinoletta* L16 (Recently split from the Rock Pipit (below) to form a separate species). Breeds central and S Europe above tree line, usually beside torrential watercourses. In winter found in open country at lower altitude, occurs S Britain by watercress beds, lakes. In summer plumage *crown and nape grey, back and wings warm brown*, back very faintly streaked; *prominent white supercilium; unstreaked below* (or almost so), with more or less *pink tinge*; pale wingbar rather prominent; *pure white on outer tail feathers* (exceptions recorded). *Dark brown legs*. Occasionally Rock Pipits in summer have underparts almost unstreaked pale pinkish-buff, but are separated by more uniform and olive-tinged upperparts and dusky outer tail feathers. In winter Water Pipits are brownish above, *whitish below*, sparsely but *distinctly streaked*. Voice as Rock Pipit (which see). WP

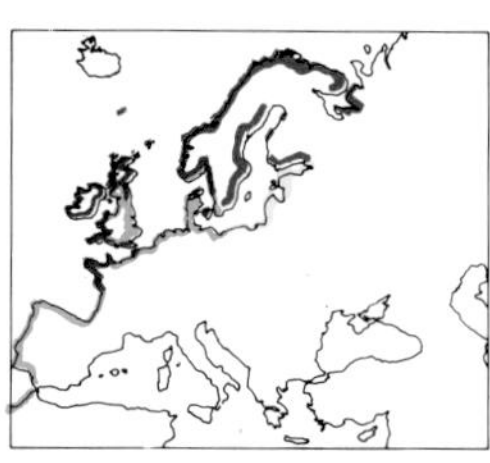

Rock Pipit *Anthus petrosus* L 16. Fairly common along rocky coasts of Britain and NW France; Scandinavian race *littoralis* occurs in Britain Oct–Apr. In summer plumage *upperparts rather uniform greyish-olive*, only slightly tinged brown (become greyer with wear), back faintly streaked; supercilium and wingbar *ill-defined*; breast and flanks usually well streaked, *streaks prominent but diffuse on yellowish-dusky ground; outer tail feathers marked dusky or greyish-white* (a little paler in *littoralis*). Variant summer plumage described under Water Pipit. Distinguished from Meadow and Tree Pipits by *dark brown legs* (but juveniles in summer reddish-brown), heavier bill and more diffuse streaking below on duskier ground. Song plain like Meadow's. Call like Meadow's though not so short and excitedly jumpy but more emphatic and usually only single or double note: 'weest-weest'. Alarm a Tree Pipit-like 'sit, sit'. RWP

■□□ **Meadow Pipit**
□■□ **Meadow Pipit**
□□■ **Meadow Pipit** juv.

■□□ **Tawny Pipit** adult summer
□■□ **Tawny Pipit** juv.
□□■ **Red-throated Pipit** adult female at nest

■□□ **Red-throated Pipit** adult summer
□■□ **Red-throated Pipit** adult
□□■ **Red-throated Pipit** adult female winter

■□□ **Water Pipit** adult summer
□■□ **Rock Pipit** adult summer, race *littoralis*
□□■ **Rock Pipit** 1st-winter

Passerines

Yellow Wagtail *Motacilla flava* L 16.5. Fairly common breeder on damp meadows; race *thunbergi* on delta-land, and bogs, damp openings in birch forest on mountain slopes, vast clearings in coniferous forest. On migration often seeks company of grazing cattle, gets in close to hooves in search of insects. Flight undulating. Before migration often roosts in large flocks in reedbeds. Departs Aug–Oct, returns Mar–May. Long tail, *yellow underparts* and *greenish back* typical. Colour of head and neck in summer plumage male varies depending on race (see table). Females in all regions are fairly alike. Some 1st-winter females are confusingly pale below, but generally have some yellow on vent. Juvenile plumage (moulted before southward migration) grey-brown above, dirty-white below, throat bordered by brownish-black upper breast band and malar stripe, pale supercilium with dark edges. Call a high 'pseet' or a fuller 'TSLEEe'; race *feldegg* calls 'psrreet'. Song a mediocre 'srree-SRRIT' (or trisyllabic) with sharp scratchy tone, often delivered from bush top or barbed wire. SP

■□□ **Yellow Wagtail** adult male summer, race *flava*

□■□ **Yellow Wagtail** adult male summer, race *flavissima*, at nest

□□■ **Yellow Wagtail** adult female winter, race *flavissima*

Races of Yellow Wagtail *Motacilla flava*

Race	Male in summer plumage	Distribution
Motacilla f. flava	Blue-grey head, yellow throat, white supercilium	Southern Fennoscandia, W Europe except Britain and Iberian peninsula
M. f. thunbergi	Dark grey head, blackish ear-coverts, yellow throat, no supercilium	N Fenno-Scandia and Russia
M. f. flavissima	Greenish-yellow head, yellow throat, yellow supercilium	Britain and locally on adjacent Continental coast
M. f. iberiae	Grey head, white throat, narrow white supercilium	Iberian peninsula, S and SW France, Balearics
M. f. cinereocapilla	Grey head, white throat, generally no supercilium	Italy, central Mediterranean islands, Albania
M. f. feldegg	Black head, yellow throat, no supercilium	Balkans and Black Sea coast
M. f. beema	Grey (often pale) head, white supercilium and cheek-stripe	SE Russia
M. f. lutea (not illustrated)	Yellow head, yellow throat, pale yellow-green ear-coverts	Extreme SE Russia (lower Volga region)

■□□ **Yellow Wagtail** adult male summer, race *beema*, dark-headed bird

□■□ **Yellow Wagtail** adult male summer, race *cinereocapilla*

□□■ **Yellow Wagtail** adult male summer, race *feldegg*

■□□ **Yellow Wagtail** adult male summer, race *iberiae*

□■□ **Yellow Wagtail** adult male summer, race *thunbergi*

□□■ **Yellow Wagtail** adult female, race *thunbergi*

The Yellow Wagtail complex of races is one of the avian systematist's hardest nuts to crack. Some prefer, e.g. to place *flavissima* and *lutea* in a separate species, *M. lutea*. Within one race's range individual males are often seen which resemble males of other races. These may be stray individuals of these races, but also simply colour variants of the race breeding locally. At times birds are seen whose appearance does not tally with any known race. In the field one should therefore be temperate in racial identification, especially as, furthermore, intermediate forms that are difficult to identify appear in border areas between the ranges of different races.

Citrine Wagtail *Motacilla citreola* L 18. Nearest breeding areas in W Russia. Rare vagrant in W Europe. Male unmistakable with *yellow head* and black hindneck, grey back and *two broad, pure white wingbars*, visible also in flight. Female has grey-brown on crown and cheeks; at most a suggestion of black nape. The juvenile, most often encountered in W Europe, is grey above (faintly tinged brown, not green), has bold white wingbars, blackish uppertail-coverts, and sometimes slightly paler, brown-tinged forehead; below whitish, with buff tinge on breast (occasionally spotted), *undertail-coverts and vent white* (Yellow Wagtail: almost invariably pale yellow), flanks often grey like Pied Wagtail. Tail longer than Yellow Wagtail's, about same as Pied. *Call on passage more piercing* than Yellow Wagtail's, which it resembles, more straight and *harsher* (hint of an 'r' sound), 'tsreep', can recall Richard's Pipit, but most resembles Yellow Wagtail song. One population (race?), however, can call exactly like Yellow Wagtail. V

■□ **Citrine Wagtail** adult male summer

□■ **Citrine Wagtail** adult female

Passerines

Grey Wagtail *Motacilla cinerea* L 18. Breeds beside upland streams and along swift-flowing brooks, sometimes beside lakes and slow rivers. Widespread and fairly common in S and W Europe, incl. Britain. The nest is placed on a rock ledge, under a bridge (often of stone) or in a similar site. Less particular outside breeding season; then also on coast, beside lakes, on sewage farms, watercress beds, cultivated land etc. Has *very long tail*, even longer than Pied Wagtail's. *Yellow on underparts*, especially *intense on vent, grey on upperparts* (white edging on tertials). Male's throat black in summer, female's faintly or profusely marked with black. When flying away *yellowish rump* and a *white wingbar* formed by white bases to flight feathers are visible. *Wingbar even more prominent from below, translucent* against the light. Immature *is yellow only on rump and vent*, the breast is buff. Distinguished from immature Yellow Wagtail by yellowish rump, extremely long tail, brownish-pink legs (blackish in other wagtails). White wingbar is also present in the immature. The long tail makes its mark on all the Grey Wagtail's movements; *the flight is even more markedly undulating* than Pied Wagtail's, the action on the ground *even more rocking and see-sawing*. Runs and skips deftly among the rocks of the rushing waters, often hovers above water in search of insects, is very much inclined (more than Pied Wagtail) to perch in tops of overhanging trees. Usual call resembles Pied Wagtail's but is markedly more metallic and higher-pitched, 'tsiziss'; this, together with wingbar, extreme tail length and extremely undulating flight, is what gives it away in overhead flight. Alarm 'SEE-eat', mixed with excited version of call. Song consists of short series of sharp notes. R

Grey Wagtail adult male summer at nest

Grey Wagtail adult female winter

Grey Wagtail adult flying up to nest

Grey Wagtail

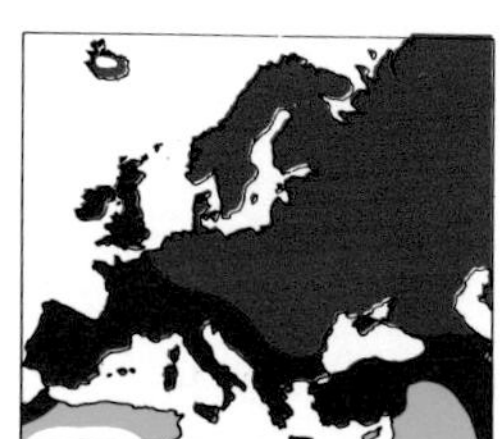

White and Pied Wagtails

Pied Wagtail *Motacilla alba yarrellii* L 18.5. British Isles race of White Wagtail, also breeds sporadically on adjacent Continental coasts: locally in Norway, Germany, Holland, Belgium and NW France. Breeds commonly in open country, around farmyards, in towns, usually near water. Nests in recesses or holes, often under roof tiles and in stone walls, under stones, even on moored boats. *Black, dark grey and white plumage* together with *constantly wagging tail* distiniguish it from all other birds. Male can often be told from female by back being pure black; female usually has dark grey back. Juvenile is grey on face and has a grey patch across breast. At end of summer moults into 1st-winter plumage with dull yellowish face and *prominent black crescent on upper breast*. Adult in winter similar but is white on face and throat. Juvenile resembles juvenile Grey Wagtail, but has white (not yellow) undertail-coverts and the dark patch across breast. Birds in 1st-winter plumage and females in 1st-summer plumage resemble White Wagtail (see below), but *rump is almost black*, not grey, and *flanks are dark grey* (with green tone), not pale ash-grey. Outside breeding season usually seen in small parties, but sometimes gathers in large flocks to roost communally in reeds, orchards etc (at times even inside factories and glasshouses). Feeds on insects taken on the ground as well as captured in the air in flycatcher fashion. Runs very quickly. Wags tail up and down and nods head as it moves. Flight deeply undulating. Call a disyllabic, kind of 'rebounding', 'tsee-LITT' and variants. Juveniles often sound higher-pitched, more metallic, the call is more rapid and often of three or even four syllables, 'tseeziLITT', 'tseeziziLITT'. Song twittering, composed, to large extent of the call, always sounds very excited and lively. Also heard when chasing off Cuckoos and smaller birds of prey. RSWP

Pied Wagtail adult male winter

Pied Wagtail adult female winter

See map above

White Wagtail *Motacilla alba alba* L 18. Nominate race of Pied, breeds throughout Europe except within Pied's range. Male easily told from Pied Wagtail by *medium grey back* contrasting sharply with pure black nape. Female similar but grey back colour usually merges imperceptibly into black of crown. Occasional females may lack all trace of black on crown. Juvenile impossible to distinguish in field from juvenile Pied (but 1st-winter birds often separable – see above under Pied). Calls as Pied. P

White Wagtail adult male summer

White Wagtail winter

White Wagtail juv.

Passerines

Shrikes

Shrikes (family Laniidae) are medium-sized passerines with proportionately large heads, strong, hooked bills, long tails and often striking colour patterns. Feed on insects, small birds and small rodents, which are sometimes speared on thorns or barbed wire. Often seen perched alone on bush tops or on telegraph wires in open country. Flight is low and undulating. Clutches of 4–6 eggs.

Declining as breeding species in northwest; almost extinct in Britain

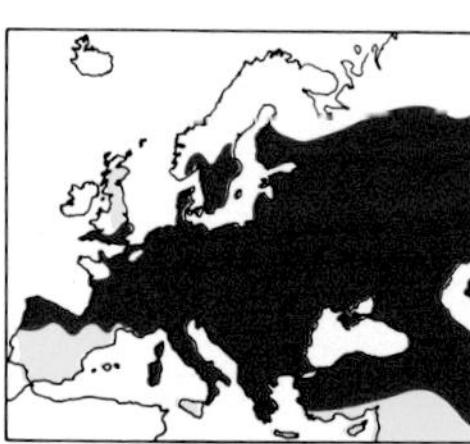

Red-backed Shrike *Lanius collurio* L 18. Breeds in open bushy country and in clearings. Now very rare in Britain, but colonising E Scotland. Male has warm *brown back, ash-grey crown/nape,* black and white tail and unbarred white underparts with rosy tone. Female and juvenile are brown with *close crescentic markings on breast.* Occasional females may be more contrastingly marked and can even be very like male; the underparts, however, always show crescentic barring and the tail is dark brown with just a little white basally on the outer edges. Call a short 'cheve'. Alarm a series of hoarse smacking noises. The song is pleasant, quiet and full of mimicry. SP

Isabelline Shrike *Lanius isabellinus* L 18. Very closely related to the Red-backed Shrike. Rare vagrant from Asia. Is *considerably paler* and slightly longer-tailed than Red-backed Shrike. Sexes much alike: red-toned sandy colour or light brownish-grey above, buffish-white below with *reddish-brown tail* and *dark eye mask* – blackish in male, brown in female. Female also has fine crescentic barring on the sides of neck and sides of breast, which male lacks. (Similar species: Brown Shrike *L. cristatus,* in Siberia. This, however, has tail not so vividly reddish-brown, and the tail feathers are distinctly narrower and finely barred.) V

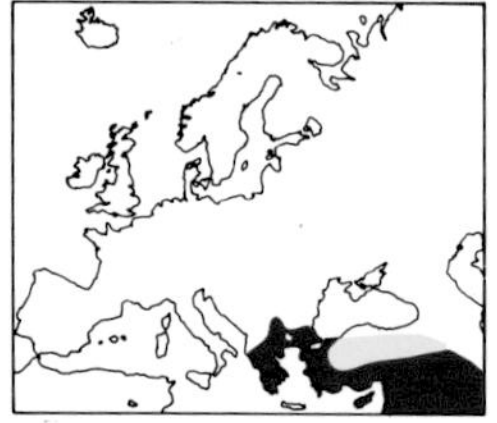

▶ **Masked Shrike** *Lanius nubicus* L 18. Breeds in SE Europe in semi-open country. Note black (male) or grey (female) upperparts and *long, narrow tail. Large white wing panels,* conspicuous in flight. Juvenile is barred and lacks yellowish-brown tone below, is *entirely black, white and grey,* best identified by narrow tail and the large white wing panels in flight. Song is uneven and grating, rather monotonous, at slow tempo.

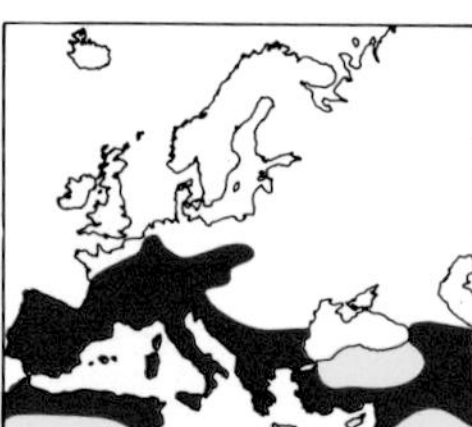

Woodchat Shrike *Lanius senator* L 19. Breeds in central and S Europe in open, dry country with trees and bushes, sometimes in more wooded terrain. Note dark upperparts with *white shoulder patches and rump* and striking *reddish-brown crown and nape.* Race *badius* (e.g. Mallorca) lacks white wingbar. Juvenile resembles juvenile Red-backed, but has paler upperparts with hint of white shoulder patches and pale rump. Head slightly bigger than in Red-backed. Song attractive, full of mimicry, for the most part scratchy; repeats each phrase 2–5 times. V

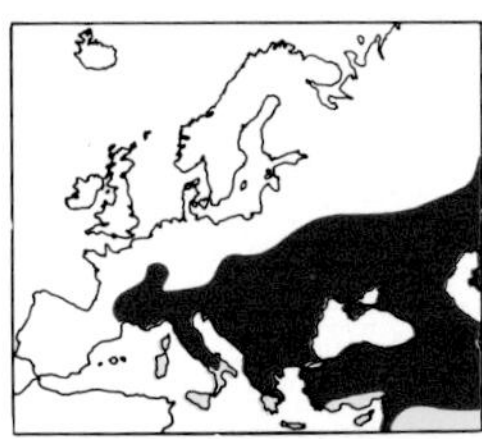

Lesser Grey Shrike *Lanius minor* L 20. Breeds in central and SE Europe in open country with isolated trees and bushes. Told from Great Grey Shrike by smaller size, slightly shorter tail, more upright posture and *black forehead*; white wingbar short but broad. Juvenile lacks black on forehead (thus has a mask like Great Grey's) and has upperparts barred. Song very like Woodchat Shrike's but is perhaps a little harder in intonation and slower in tempo. V

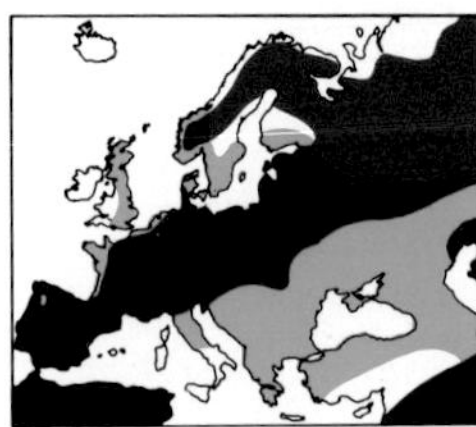

Great Grey Shrike *Lanius excubitor* L 24. In S Europe breeds in dry, semi-open country, in Fenno-Scandia by bogs and clearings in coniferous or birch forest. Scarce winter visitor to Britain, in open areas. Easy to spot, *perches exposed* on top of tree/bush. Fieldfare size, *gleaming whitish. Flight strongly undulating, white wingbar conspicuous.* Often hovers, takes voles. Pursues small birds in flight. Scolds angrily with an emphatic, grating 'vaaech'. A hard, rolling, ringing 'dirrrrp' is often heard. Song is subdued, delivered at slow pace, containing both harsh and melodic calls repeated several times. WP

■□□ **Red-backed Shrike** adult male
□■□ **Red-backed Shrike** adult female
□□■ **Red-backed Shrike** juv.

■□□ **Isabelline Shrike** adult male
□■□ **Isabelline Shrike** adult female/imm.
□□■ **Masked Shrike** adult male

■□□ **Masked Shrike** adult female
□■□ **Woodchat Shrike** adult male
□□■ **Woodchat Shrike** juv.

■□□ **Lesser Grey Shrike** adult male
□■□ **Great Grey Shrike** adult
□□■ **Great Grey Shrike** juv.

Passerines

Golden Oriole (family Oriolidae) is a thrush-sized, brightly coloured bird that frequents woods and parklands. 3–5 eggs are laid in a nest suspended in a fork high in a tree.

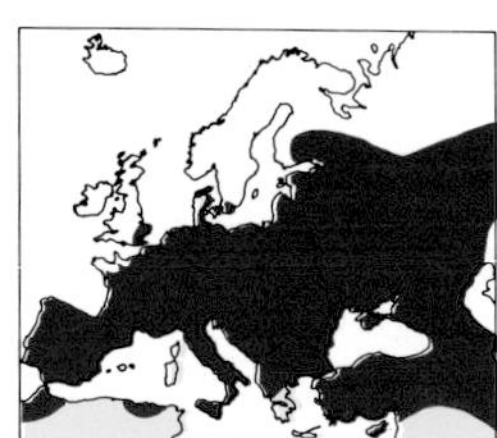

Golden Oriole *Oriolus oriolus* L 24. Breeds in central and S Europe in groves in cultivated country, prefers deciduous woods with mature trees. Rare breeder in S Britain. Very shy and difficult to get good views of, persistently spends its time in the upper parts of the tree canopy. Appears restless, often on the move. Adult male *bright yellow and black*, female and one-year-old male greenish above, yellowish-white and streaked below. Flight rather like Fieldfare if anything. Song is a yodelling, mellow as a Blackbird, 'oh-weeloh-WEE weeOO' with many variants – the same bird habitually varies the details of the calls. 'Contemplating' males may restrict themselves to quieter 'weeOO' notes. A hoarse and nasal, Jay-like 'kwa-kwaaEK' is often heard. SP

Starlings (family Sturnidae) are medium-sized, short-tailed and sociable birds. The 4–6 eggs are laid in holes.

Rose-coloured Starling *Sturnus roseus* L 21. Breeds irregularly in SE Europe in open country. Follows the big swarms of locusts, may nest en masse in an area for a year or two, then be gone for many years. Rare visitor to NW Europe, mostly in summer. Adult typical, but beware partially albinistic Starling. Juveniles resembles juvenile Starling, but is *considerably paler, especially on rump and lores*. The *bill* is quite *pale* and not so long and pointed as Starling's. Gregarious, readily associates with Starlings. Resembles Starling in behaviour and calls. V

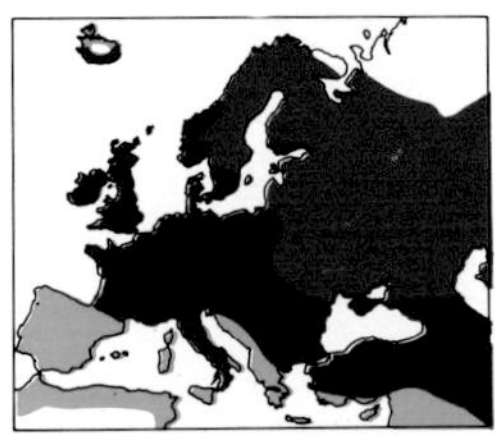

Starling *Sturnus vulgaris* L 21. Breeds very commonly in or close to cultivated country, especially near human habitations. Makes its home in nestboxes and holes in trees and walls, under roof tiles etc. Note *short tail, speckled plumage* and long, pointed bill. Wanders quickly and without pausing over lawns searching for insects (cf. Blackbird). Flight swift, silhouette characteristic with short tail and *pointed wings*. Gregarious. Noisy packs of drab brown juveniles emerge in early summer. Flies in tight flocks, sometimes thousands of birds together in association with roosting in reeds (also city centres) after the breeding season. Call in flight is a short weak buzzing 'tcheerrr'. Alarm a hard 'kyett' (bird of prey) or a grating croak 'stah' (at the nest). The song is varied with whistles, clicking noises and much expert mimicry, recognised by its whining, strained tone and by recurring descending whistles 'seeeooo'. RW

▶ **Spotless Starling** *Sturnus unicolor* L 21. Replaces the Starling in Iberian peninsula. Resembles Starling, but *lacks pale spots completely in summer plumage*. In winter the pale spots in the plumage are much smaller than the corresponding ones in Starling. The metallic sheen is also slightly weaker in the Spotless Starling. Nests colonially. Song resembles Starling's.

Waxwing (family Bombycillidae) is a starling-sized bird with a crest on the crown. Sexes alike. Builds open nest in tree. 3–5 eggs.

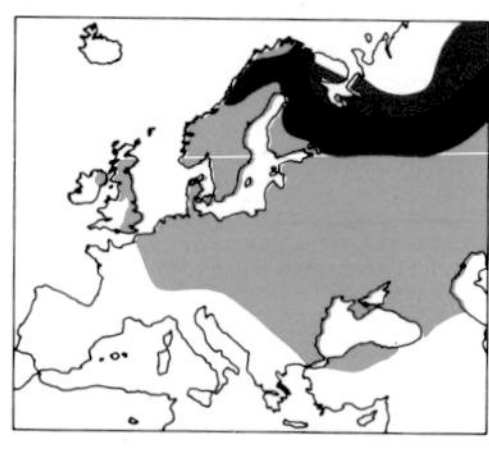

Waxwing *Bombycilla garrulus* L 18. Breeds sparsely in the coniferous woods of Lapland and eastwards. In some years undertakes long-distance movements of invasion proportions. In winter often seen in flocks in gardens and in city avenues, eats rowan berries. Easy to recognise by the *long crest* and exquisite *cocoa-brown colour* (with tinges of hazel-nut brown and grey). Adult has yellowish-white 'V' marks on the primary tips while juvenile has only a pale-coloured straight line (see fig.). Flight is very like Starling's but more regular undulations and slightly slimmer silhouette (no 'shoulders'). Call a clear and high trilling 'sirrr', silvery clear. Song is simple, slow and quiet, consists of the trill call together with harsher notes. W

■□ **Golden Oriole** adult male at nest with young

□■ **Golden Oriole** adult female

■□□ **Rose-coloured Starling** adult

□■□ **Rose-coloured Starling** juv.

□□■ **Starling** juvs.

■□□ **Starling** moulting into 1st-winter plumage

□■□ **Starling** adult male moulting into winter plumage

□□■ **Starling** adult male summer

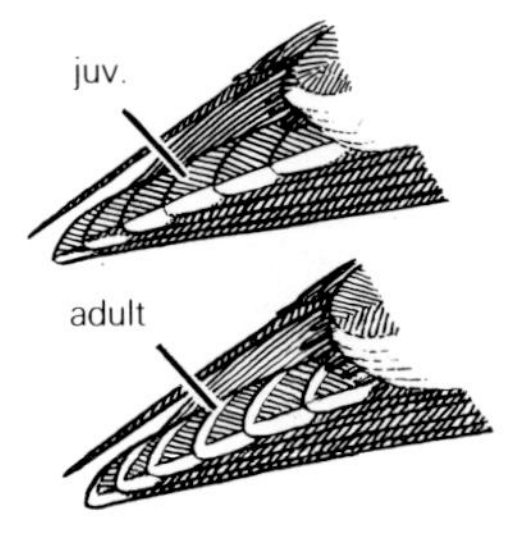

Waxwing

■□□ **Spotless Starling** adult male summer

□■□ **Waxwing** 1st-winter female

□□■ **Waxwing** adult female winter

Passerines

Crows

Crows (family Corvidae) are a successful, fairly highly developed group of birds with almost worldwide distribution. The crows and their allies are medium-sized or large, sociable, omnivorous passerines with powerful bills and legs. Raid nests of other birds when chance is offered. Colours most often black, grey and white. Wings rounded. Sexes alike. Have harsh calls for the most part. The 3–7 eggs are usually blue-green and spotted.

Siberian Jay *Perisoreus infaustus* L 28. Fairly common to scarce breeding bird in northern coniferous forest. Sedentary, hardly ever found outside its breeding area. *Fluffy grey-brown with elements of rusty-red,* mainly on the tail. Fearless and inquisitive but also alert. Comes flying noiselessly along and alights right beside camp fire or hops around silently inside dry spruces, will cling upside down like a gigantic tit. Flies with series of relatively quick wingbeats alternating with glides. The rusty-red colours on rump, tail and wings are clearly visible in flight. Quite silent, but sometimes produces loud outbursts. Rich repertoire of calls. Usual calls are a mewing 'geeah', a harsh 'tchair' and a shrill 'kij, kij'.

Jay *Garrulus glandarius* L 35. Common in coniferous and mixed woodland. By no means avoids human habitation, but is wary and therefore difficult to see properly. Usually seen on feeding excursions moving from wood to wood and is then recognised by the broad, rounded wings and the laboured flight with rather irregular wingbeats. When glimpsed at closer range in woodland, the *white on rump and wings* is conspicuous (blue wing panel will not be noticed then). Announces itself mainly by calls: most often the typical sudden hoarse shout, 'kshehr', but also the very Buzzard-like mewing, 'peeay'. Also often mimics Goshawk's 'kyek-kyek-kyek- . . .'. Clucking and intense bubbling sounds given as well. RWP

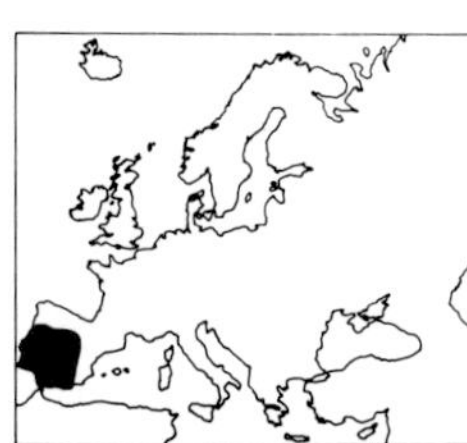

Azure-winged Magpie *Cyanopica cyana* L 35. Breeds only on the Iberian Peninsula. Found mainly in stone-pine woods. Builds open nest in small colonies. Easy to recognise by *black hood, blue wings* and *long, blue tail.* Back, breast and belly are grey-buff, the *throat white.* Usually seen in small parties. Flight and general behaviour like Siberian Jay's. Quite shy and restless, roaming around a lot, hops about in the crowns of the stone-pines, darts off among the trunks in undulating gliding flight, gleaming azure-blue. Calls include a jay-like, harsh but high-pitched 'zhruEE', with faintly rising diphthong, and a clear 'kwee'.

Magpie *Pica pica* L 45 (half of which is the tail). Breeds commonly in vicinity of human habitation; in farmland, by settlements, in towns. The domed twig nest is built in the centre of the crown of a deciduous tree, looks like a huge dark ball. Builds a new nest each year. Very alert. The Magpie's reputation as a 'silver thief' is partly undeserved; true it sometimes takes glittering objects to the nest, but authentic cases of such kleptomania appear to be exceedingly few. The *black and white colour pattern* and *extremely long tail* with green metallic sheen make the Magpie unmistakable. Flight characteristic, with quick, fluttering wing-beats interspersed with short glides. Lives in pairs, but quite large flocks are often seen, e.g. in winter and in association with roosting or good food supply. Apart from the well-known harsh, laughing call, the Magpie makes diverse smacking and plaintive noises and has a quiet song with chirping and twittering sounds. R

Siberian Jay

Jay adult

Jay in flight

Azure-winged Magpie adult at nest

Azure-winged Magpie in flight

Magpie adult

Magpie juv. just out of nest

Magpie adult flying to nest with twig

Passerines

Nutcracker *Nucifraga caryocatactes* L 33. Sparse breeder in central Eruopean mountains, and in Fenno-Scandia and Russia in lowlands, in coniferous forests with arolla pine or hazel in the vicinity. Arolla pine seeds and hazelnuts are favourite foods – cached. Shy at breeding site. In autumns with poor harvest of cones/nuts, Nutcrackers may invade W Europe, thick-billed European race as well as the more numerous Siberian slender-billed race *macrorhynchos*. Invasion birds, sometimes in small flocks, are often quite fearless, may be seen in gardens etc. *Dark brown white-spotted plumage* and characteristic flight silhouette with somewhat upslanted body, short tail and rounded wings. Dark tail base contrasts with *white tail tip and undertail area*. Flight desultory and unsteady, reminiscent of Jay's. Call a hard 'rrraah', more rolling than Carrion Crow's, and has a hard, typically hollow and dry, almost buzzing ring. V

Chough *Pyrrhocorax pyrrhocorax* L 40. Breeds in mountain districts and along steep rocky coasts in S and W Europe, respectively. *Glossy black* with *long and curved red bill*. Juvenile's bill brownish-yellow. The wings have short 'arm' and long 'hand', are broad and have *6 clearly spread, flexible 'fingers'* (much more obvious than Alpine Chough's). Tail rather short, square. Black underwing-coverts, darker than flight feathers. Often plays in groups in the air in front of rock faces. Superb aerial acrobat, dives headlong at breakneck speed with closed wings. Call a characteristic 'keeach', basically like Jackdaw but considerably more 'caustic' and hoarser and 'thicker'. Other high-pitched unmusical calls are given, e.g. 'krree-aw'. R

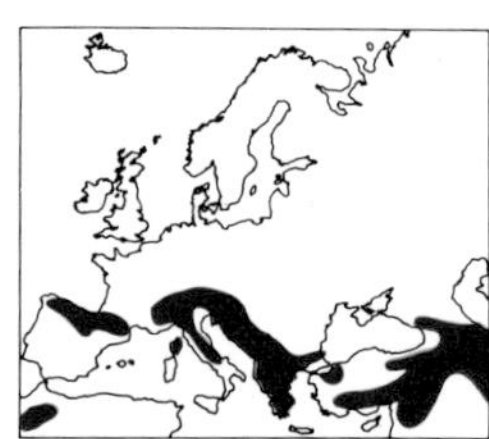

Alpine Chough *Pyrrhocorax graculus* L 38. Breeds in S Europe in high mountains up to the snow line. Visits the valleys in winter and is then often seen in villages, but even then usually met with at the top stations of ski resorts. Nests in colonies in rock crevices and caves. Much resembles Chough, but has shorter, *yellow bill*, not such glossy plumage, decidedly *less prominent 'fingers' at the wingtips, longer tail*. Juvenile has darker legs than adult and sulphur-yellow bill (in juvenile Chough brown-toned). Distinguished from Jackdaw even at a distance by more obviously fingered wingtips, slightly longer tail with narrower base, and also in the right lighting conditions by black underwing-coverts, distinctly darker than grey flight feathers (Jackdaw an even-grey below). Commonest calls are very peculiar and characteristic. Typical is a clear, piercing 'tsi-eh' (sharp beginning, whining). Also a rolling 'krrrree' (something like a noisy young Starling in nest hole). Both calls have a particular 'electric' quality, reminiscent of sound produced by throwing a stone on to fresh ice. Other minor calls are more akin to Chough calls.

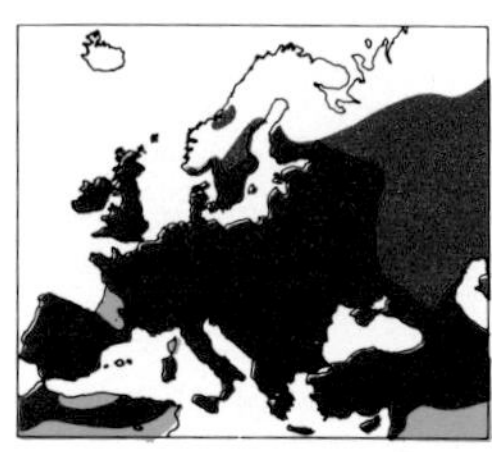

▶ **Jackdaw** *Corvus monedula* L 33. Breeds commonly in cultivated country, in older deciduous wood, in towns and in rocky mountains and coastal cliffs. Nests in hollow trees, chimney stacks etc, cliffs, with tendency towards colonial breeding. Black with *grey nape. Iris greyish-white*. Flight powerful and fast, always quicker and with deeper wingbeats than Carrion Crow's, may somewhat recall that of the pigeons. Is very sociable, almost always seen in pairs or in flocks; division into pairs obvious even in the flocks, which otherwise are much more closely packed together than, e.g. those of Carrion Crow. Feed on fields, often together with other crow species and Starlings. Are often up circling in flocks at quite high altitude, playing tag and performing acrobatic tricks. Gather in autumn to roost in certain selected towns; remarkable mass flight display in the gathering dusk and loud, noisy cackling in the twilight. The Jackdaw is distinguished from the Chough and Alpine Chough even at long range by *broader head/neck, only slightly fingered wingtips* and *broader tail base*, and also by *even-grey underparts*. The Jackdaw's usual calls are a loud, jarring, nasal 'kye' and a more drawn-out 'kyaar'. When giving alarm against birds of prey, a hoarse 'cheehr'. RSW

Nutcracker

■□ **Nutcracker** slender-billed race *macrorhynchos*

□■ **Chough** adult

Chough

■□□ **Chough** juv.

□■□ **Chough** in flight

□□■ **Alpine Chough** adult

Alpine Chough

Jackdaw

■□□ **Jackdaw**

□■□ **Jackdaw** in flight

□□■ **Daurian Jackdaw** adult
Very rare vagrant from East Asia

Passerines

Rook *Corvus frugilegus* L 46. Typical bird of cultivated lowlands, where it nests in colonies (rookeries) in groups of trees and small woods. Common over whole of Britain and Ireland except N Scotland. Nests are placed close together high in the tops of the trees. Gregarious all year. Feeds in flocks in fields, performs aerial games in flocks above the nest trees. *Black plumage with violet sheen,* comparatively long and evenly tapering bill and, in adult, a *pale bare area where bill joins feathering* are characteristic. Peaked crown and bushy 'trousers' are normally apparent, but not invariably. Wings slightly longer and narrower than Carrion Crow's, flight more elagent with slightly deeper, more elastic wingbeats; also glides more. Immature is duller and does not have bare skin at bill-join (may retain feathering there until one year of age), is therefore extremely like Carrion Crow. Distinguished, however, by *bill shape* (see fig), by *pale mouth flanges* and also by call (differences in flight certainly exist but difficult to judge in case of single individual; odd birds may give wrong impression). Call more nasal and hoarser than Carrion Crow's, not so open, coarse and rolling, 'kah'. RW

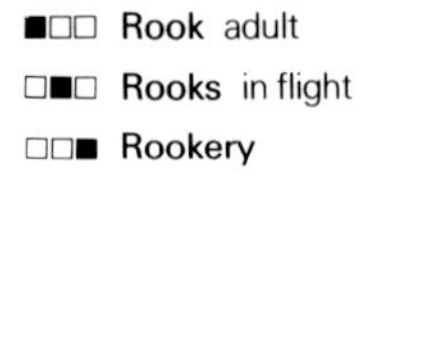

■□□ **Rook** adult
□■□ **Rooks** in flight
□□■ **Rookery**

Rook, young

Carrion Crow *Corvus corone corone* L 46, W 85. Common in W Europe in all types of fairly open country, but also in towns and cities. Builds open twig nest in treetop in clump of trees, well concealed, not exposed as Magpie. Never breeds in colonies, is a territorial bird. Black with *moderate, blue sheen.* Best told from Rook by black feathering at bill base (though immature Rooks also have this), *stouter bill more downcurved at tip* and by much coarser, less nasal croaking call. *Mouth flanges always dark.* Does not have 'trousers'. *Tail slightly shorter and not so rounded at the tip.* Outer wing on average slightly shorter than Rook (Rook can look like Raven in silhouette, which Carrion Crow hardly does). Also has slightly slower, more listless wingbeats than Rook. Distinguished from Raven by smaller size, smaller bill and square-cut tail. Gathers in flocks, especially for roosting, but does not nest in colonies. Omnivorous, nest-raider in summer, often eats refuse and carrion. Call a harsh croaking 'kraa' often repeated several times. In internal quarrels and also when warning of 'harmless' birds of prey give persistent, grating 'krrrr' calls. (Superior birds of prey are showered with furious 'kraa' calls.) RW

■□□ **Carrion Crow** adult
□■□ **Carrion Crow** juv., newly fledged
□□■ **Hooded Crow** in flight

Carrion Crow

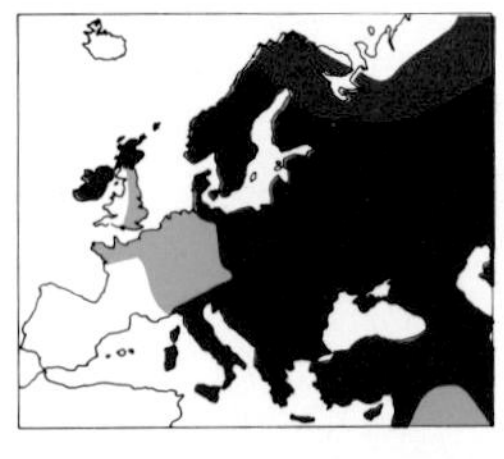

▶ Hooded Crow *Corvus corone cornix* L 46. The grey and black crow of NW Scotland, Ireland, the Isle of Man and the eastern half of Europe is the same species as the Carrion Crow, but a different race. Breeds in cultivated country, commonly but in single pairs. Wary, well used to man. Easily recognised by grey and black plumage. In habits resembles Carrion Crow, with which it often associates and also interbreeds where the two races meet. *Flight fairly listless and lazy, wingbeats steady and quite shallow.* Flies singly or in loose formation. Hooded Crows from NE Europe visit east coast of Britain in winter, mainly Oct–Apr. Habits, as well as voice, like Carrion Crow. RW

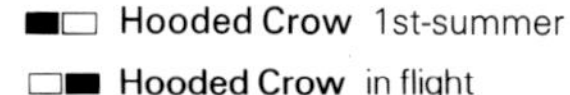

■□ **Hooded Crow** 1st-summer
□■ **Hooded Crow** in flight

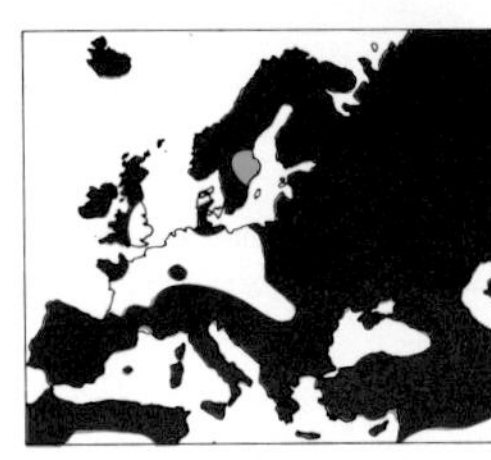

▶ **Raven** *Corvus corax* L 65, W 125. Breeds fairly commonly on rocky coasts and mountains and in extensive woodland. Maintains lifelong pair bonds. Also outside the breeding season is very often seen in pairs; two dots moving along a ridge are often Ravens. But may sometimes gather in quite large parties. The nest is placed on cliff shelf or in tree. An early breeder, often incubating in Feb-Mar. Feeds on small animals, carrion and refuse. Roams widely, visits refuse tips, slaughter houses and similar. *Largest* of the passerines, clearly bigger than Buzzard. *All-black* plumage, powerful bill and *long, wedge-shaped tail* distinguish it from the smaller crow species. Flight with quite measured but very driving wingbeats. Soars more often than other crows. Confusion with birds of prey often a real problem, but Raven never holds its wings raised in soaring flight. Often performs half-rolls in play. Shy and wary. Call 'prruk', deep, resonant; alarm 'krra-krra-krra'. In spring various clucking noises. R

Raven

■□□ **Raven** adult
□■□ **Raven** adult
□□■ **Raven** adult in flight

Passerines

Dipper (family Cinclidae) is, because of its powerful feet, solid skeleton and special oil gland, well adapted to a life in water. Sexes alike. 4–6 eggs, laid in large, domed nests in association with running water.

Dipper *Cinclus cinclus* L 18. Nests along rapid-flowing water-courses, mostly in more hilly areas. In winter thinly distributed along rivers, streams and forest brooks, but a hardy species, will remain in areas where rivers are half-frozen. Perches on boulders etc, bobbing and curtseying, short tail slightly cocked. *White breast* conspicuous. Hops in the water, swims (sits low), dives for worms etc, swims underwater with powerful wingstrokes. Can even run along on the bottom. Also in mid winter sings its quiet, squeaky, scratchy song. Flight is low and quite straight and fast. Then utters short, harsh 'zrets' which penetrates through the roar of the torrent. Birds from Fenno-Scandia blacker below, lacking chestnut band, occasionally visit E coast of Britain in winter. RW

Wren (family Troglodytidae) is a small, very active, brown bird. The delicately barred tail is usually held cocked. Sexes alike. The 5–7 eggs are laid in a large, domed nest.

Wren *Troglodytes troglodytes* L 10. Breeds commonly in wide variety of habitats, in woodland, gardens, reeds, upland moors, cliffs etc – anywhere with good low cover, incl. on barren islands far offshore. *Diminutive, cocked tail* and *rusty-brown plumage* distinguish it. (Several island races off N and W Scotland are larger, vary in strength of plumage colour.) Lives near the ground, often well hidden. Call a dry rolling 'zerr'. Alarm a loud metallic 'zek, zek . . .'. Song melodious and unexpectedly loud, consists of rapid series of high, clear notes and trills, e.g. 'tee lu ti-ti-ti-ti-ti turrr-yu-tee-lee zel-zel-zel-zel-zel yu terrrrrrrrrr-zil'. In Britain (and elsewhere) sings loudly in mid-winter. RW

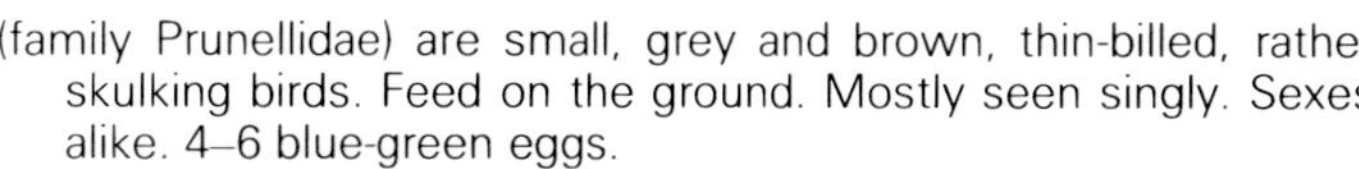

Accentors (family Prunellidae) are small, grey and brown, thin-billed, rather skulking birds. Feed on the ground. Mostly seen singly. Sexes alike. 4–6 blue-green eggs.

Alpine Accentor *Prunella collaris* L 18. Breeds in central and S Europe on high mountains above the tree line. Lark-sized. At a distance looks dull brownish-grey, almost like a Rock Pipit. The character visible at greatest range is the *dark bar across the wing* (greater coverts), and next the *heavy rusty-brown markings on the flanks*. The throat markings are apparent only at close range. Yellow gape patch. Sexes alike. Gives quite loud, rolling, lark-like 'drrreup-drrreup- . . .' and thrush-like 'chep-chep-chep- . . .' calls. Song something between Dunnock and Shore Lark, tuneful and irresolute chirruping. Also delivered in song flight. V

Siberian Accentor *Prunella montanella* L 16. A rare visitor from the Urals to W Europe. Note the distinct, ochre-yellow streak above the eye. Sexes similar.

Black-throated Accentor *Prunella atrogularis* L 15. Breeds in the Urals in birch and coniferous forest. Like Siberian Accentor but has black bib. Flanks streaked. Sexes alike.

Radde's Accentor *Prunella ocularis* L 16. Breeds in E Turkey, the Caucasus and N Iran. Crown dark, back grey-brown, breast yellow-ochre, throat pale, flanks with ill-defined streaking.

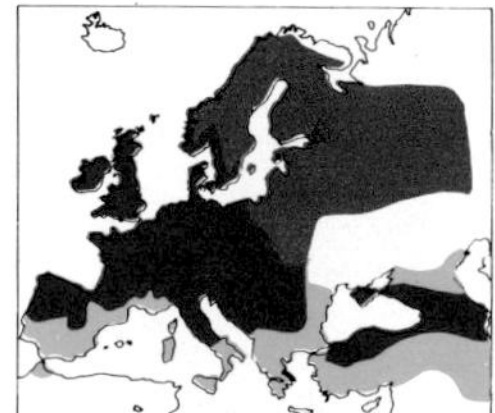

Dunnock *Prunella modularis* L 15. Common breeder in denser gardens and parks, also in scrubland, preferably half-grown spruce forest and subalpine birch forest. Note *slate-grey head and breast* together with streaked warm brown upperparts. Feeds much on ground. Skulking, but song is delivered from exposed perch such as top of bush or very top of spruce. Song characteristic, a high-pitched, clear jingle, somewhat irresolute and markedly cyclic, 'tutelliTEEtelleTEEtutelliTUtelliTEE'. Common call (excitement, alarm) is a loud piping with a cracked tone, 'teeh'. Flight call (migration) a thin and frail ringing, 'sissississ'. RW

Dipper N. European race *cinclus*
Dipper at nest site
Dipper British race *hibernicus*
Wren in flight
Wren

Alpine Accentor
Dunnock juv.
Dunnock adult

Black-throated Accentor

Black-throated Accentor
Siberian Accentor
Radde's Accentor

Passerines

Cetti's Warbler *Cettia cetti* L 14. Breeds in S and W Europe in dense and low vegetation by ditches, watercourses and marshes. Has in recent years expanded northwest and now has an established breeding stock in England. Keeps well concealed and is always difficult to see. Note *unstreaked, dark reddish-brown upperparts,* greyish-white underparts and *white streak above the eye* (a bit Wren-like). *Tail broad and rounded,* appears 'dishevelled'. Often jerks tail downwards or sideways. Wings short and rounded. Bill slender and pointed. Sexes alike. Heard more often than seen. Has an explosive lip-smacking/cracking 'pex'. Alarm a furious 'tett-ett-ett- . . .', rather similar to Wren. *Song* begins suddenly and ends abruptly, *is very loud and explosive,* often sounds 'tsi-tsi-chuut! CHUti-CHUti-CHUti!'. Sings from well-concealed perch. R

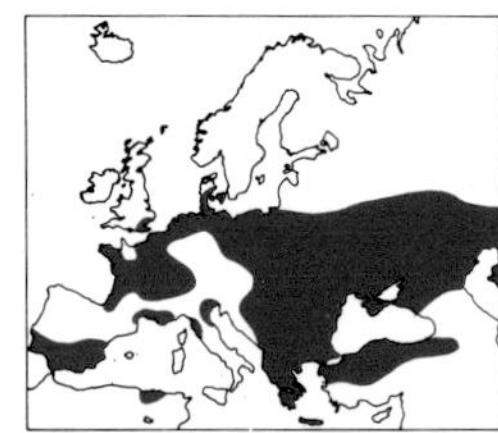

Savi's Warbler *Locustella luscinioides* L 14. Breeds in S and central Europe, incl. SE Britain (rare), in thick reedbeds. *Unstreaked, reddish grey-brown above,* pale below with pale *reddish-brown breast, flanks and vent.* Undertail-coverts pale rufous-brown, in some with indistinct light tips. *Weak supercilium.* Tail long, broad and rounded. Legs dark, reddish-brown. Utters a surprisingly Great Tit-like 'ching-ching'. Song resembles Grasshopper Warbler's, but is delivered at a deeper pitch and is faster, lacks Grasshopper Warbler's reeling, ringing quality, sounds more of a *hard buzzing,* 'surrrrr . . .'. Can be confused with reeling of mole-cricket. Song often begins quite gently. Often sings from exposed sites in reeds or bushes, mainly at dusk and dawn but also quite often during the day. S

River Warbler *Locustella fluviatilis* L 13.5. Breeds in E Europe, rare visitor to W Europe. Lives among shrubbery and sparse alder growth on damp ground with rich undergrowth. *Unstreaked olive-brown upperparts,* pale underparts with sparse *diffuse streaking on throat and breast.* Poorly marked pale supercilium. Tail broad and rounded. Undertail-coverts are pale brown with white tips. Keeps well hidden in dense vegetation. Call harsh. Sings from bush or smallish tree. Typical *Locustella* song with quality of machine or insect, but very distinct from Grasshopper Warbler's in having *fast shuttling rhythm of sewing machine* with well separated syllables, an energetic 'zezezezeze . . .'. Most closely resembles a low-frequency but very loud wart-biter bush-cricket *Decticus verrucivorus.* At close range a metallic background noise can be heard. Sings mostly at dusk and dawn. V

Gray's Grasshopper Warbler *Locustella fasciolata* L 18. Very rare vagrant to W Europe from Asia. Lives in luxuriant vegetation of plants and bushes, often on marshy ground or close to rivers. *Large* as a Great Reed Warbler, coloration as a River Warbler, but *undertail-coverts* not white-tipped but *uniformly rusty-yellow.* Does not arrive at its breeding sites until end May/early June. Song startlingly *loud* and *explosive* like a bulbul's, accelerates, 'TEUkoo, TIkoo CHIKoo-tuk-CHIKoo-teuKEE'. Sings at night.

▶ **Paddyfield Warbler** *Acrocephalus agricola* L 12. Breeds in SE Europe in dense vegetation beside marshes and lakeshores. Often lives in reeds but said to adopt songposts in trees. Always stays near water, incl. on migration. Very rare vagrant to W Europe. Resembles Reed Warbler, but is *smaller* and has a *more distinct supercilium. The bill* is also *smaller* (comparatively short). Colour of upperparts varies somewhat but is usually paler than in Reed Warbler. Can also be confused with Booted Warbler but has more rounded tail without white, and rump always has a rusty-brown tone. Wings strongly rounded. The call is described as 'tschik'. Song resembles Marsh Warbler's, rich in mimicry and delivered at the same quick tempo, but *is somewhat softer,* lacks the harsh notes incl. the typical 'zi-cheeh zi-cheeh'. May recall ecstatically singing *Sylvia* warbler. V

Cetti's Warbler showing tail

Cetti's Warbler at nest with young

Savi's Warbler

River Warbler

River Warbler

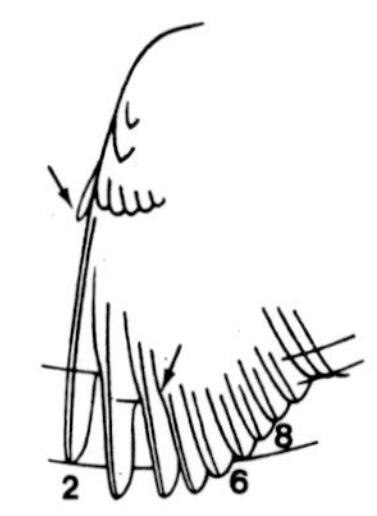

Paddyfield Warbler

Gray's Grasshopper Warbler

Paddyfield Warbler

Passerines

Pallas's Grasshopper Warbler *Locustella certhiola* L 13.5. A very rare autumn vagrant to NW Europe from Asia. Found in swamps, marshes and in meadows with dense vegetation. Resembles both Sedge and Grasshopper Warblers, e.g. in general coloration and pale, buff-white supercilium, but has *rusty-brown and unstreaked rump* contrasting with heavily streaked back and uppertail-coverts. *Tail feathers are cross-barred and darker towards the tips*, and all except the central pair have *white tips* (sometimes abraded or difficult to see). Juvenile usually has a yellowish-brown tone on throat and rest of underparts, and the breast is streaked. Habits resemble Grasshopper Warbler's, keeps well hidden in dense vegetation, often close to the ground. Call sharp and disyllabic. Song is short, begins tentatively, then picks up speed and ends with some rapid sharp notes: 'tik, chuk, tet-tet sree-sree-sree- chuk-chuk-chuk sree-sree swee-swee-swee' (The terminating series, 'swee-swee-swee', can be heard at long distances.) One would rather think that it came from an *Acrocephalus* than from a *Locustella*. V

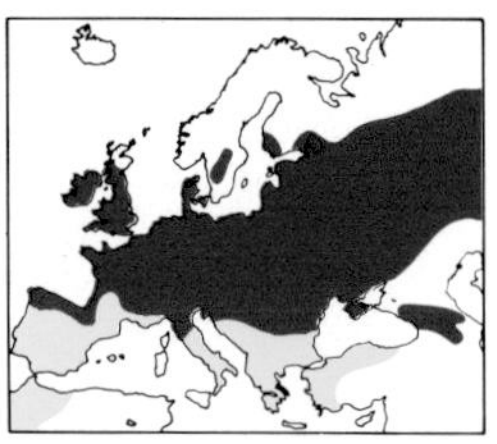

Grasshopper Warbler *Locustella naevia* L 13. Fairly common but local in damp, open country with dense ground vegetation, prefers tussocky meadows with isolated bushes. Also occurs on dryer ground such as young conifer nurseries and cornfields. Numbers vary annually. A migrant from Africa: arrives mid Apr/May, departs Aug/Sep. Plumage colours vary somewhat, but typical are heavily *streaked olive-brown upperparts, diffuse supercilium* and pale underparts, often with a few, indistinct spots on the breast. Indistinct supercilium togther with heavily streaked back are best field characters. Identification, however, is best made from the song. Lives well out of sight and keeps well hidden in the dense ground vegetation. Takes wing only reluctantly when disturbed, and then flies away as short a distance as possible and very close above the grass. Call a short 'chik'. Sings from low songpost, mostly at dusk and dawn. The song is a fast, *dry 'interminable' reeling*, like a small alarm clock with muffled clapper. Goes on for long periods without a break. The song seems to change volume as the bird turns its head. Savi's Warbler has similar song, but Savi's is shorter, deeper in tone and harder. River Warbler 'chuffs'. Cf. Lanceolated Warbler's song. S

Lanceolated Warbler *Locustella lanceolata* L 12. Breeds in easternmost Europe in dense vegetation beside swamps, marshy ground and along lakeshores. On migration may stop off in ordinary woodland. Very rare autumn and spring vagrant to NW Europe. Resembles Grasshopper Warbler, but is *smaller* and more *distinctly streaked on upperparts* and also has *heavy streaking on the breast*, often some well-marked streaks on the flanks and sometimes also on the throat; the most heavily streaked birds are probably first-year. Supercilium poorly marked. As in Grasshopper Warbler the colours may vary. Habits and call resemble Grasshopper Warbler's, and the bird keeps itself permanently well concealed in the vegetation. Sometimes flies up if disturbed at close range. Song is extremely like Grasshopper Warbler's 'svirrrrr . . .', but sounds slightly sharper, higher-pitched and more metallic, has faint suggestion of River Warbler's 'chuffing'. V

Pallas's Grasshopper Warbler

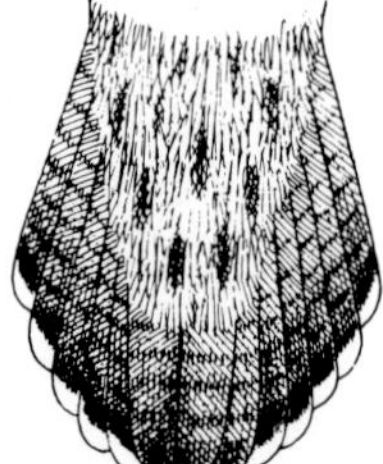

tail from above

Grasshopper Warbler adult at nest

Pallas's Grasshopper Warbler adult

Pallas's Grasshopper Warbler 1st-winter male

Grasshopper Warbler adult in full song

Pallas's Grasshopper Warbler 1st-winter male

Lanceolated Warbler

Lanceolated Warbler

Passerines

Moustached Warbler *Acrocephalus melanopogon* L 12.5. Breeds in S Europe in reedbeds and swamps with dense vegetation, often stands off bulrushes. Resembles Sedge Warbler, but has more *reddish-brown back, darker crown and ear-coverts* which contrast with *purer white supercilium* and white throat. Flanks and sides of breast tinged rufous. Supercilium is *broad and abruptly square-ended*. Sometimes gently cocks its tail. Often sings from well visible song post. Song resembles Reed Warbler's, but it is slightly softer and livelier and is recognised sooner or later by *a series of drawn-out, rising, Nightingale-like whistling notes*, 'we we wee wih'. Alarm 'trrrt'. V

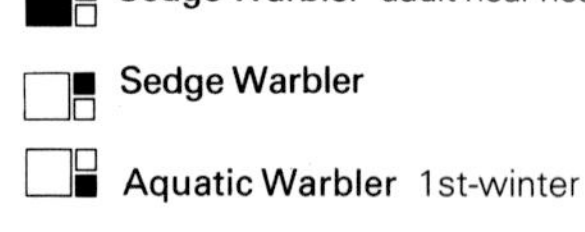

Sedge Warbler adult near nest

Sedge Warbler

Aquatic Warbler 1st-winter

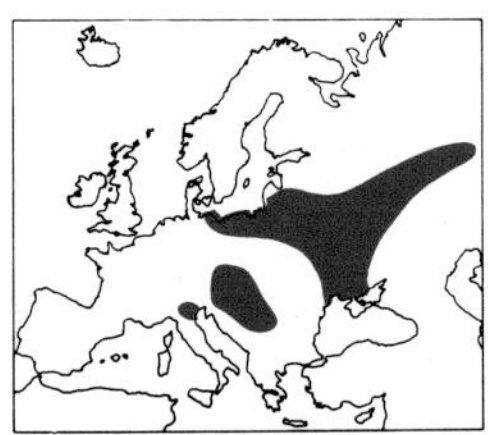

Aquatic Warbler *Acrocephalus paludicola* L 12.5. Rare and local breeder in central and S Europe in wet meadows with tall growth of *Carex* species. Like Sedge Warbler, but has *paler yellow-brown plumage* and a *pale longitudinal stripe on the crown*. (Note that juvenile Sedge can have rather a pale central line.) Distinct yellowish-white supercilium. *Heavily streaked back* with *pale, buff longitudinal stripes on the mantle*, moderately streaked rump. Has sparse indistinct streaks on breast and flanks. Tail is more rounded than in Sedge Warbler. Keeps well concealed in the vegetation. Song resembles a 'sleepy' Sedge Warbler's – the stanzas are short and delivered without 'spirit' – and is sometimes executed in short song flights. The major differences from Sedge Warbler seems to be the absence of changes in tempo: dry, flat trills are overtaken by series of whistled sounds, separated by short pauses, e.g. 'trrrrr . . . pee-pee-pee-pee-pee-pee . . . cherrrr . . . kyee-kyee-kyee-kyee . . . trrrrr . . .' and so on. V

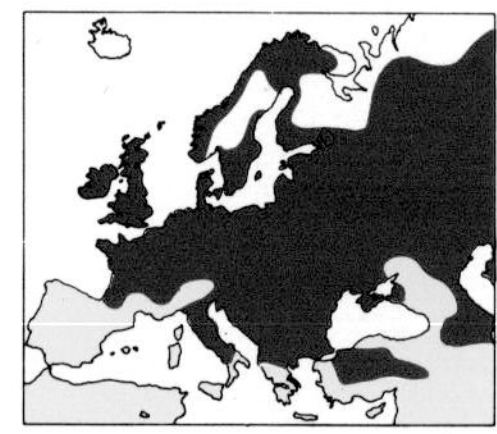

Sedge Warbler *Acrocephalus schoenobaenus* L 12.5. Breeds commonly (though recently declining) in reedbeds in swamps and in other dense vegetation along lakeshores and riverbanks, sparingly in the far north in osier beds. Upperparts are streaked, albeit quite lightly (in worn plumage the back is fairly uniform grey-brown). *Supercilium distinct* and long, *buff-white or dirty-white*. Resembles Moustached and Aquatic Warblers (cf. these). Rump unstreaked yellowish-brown. Juvenile can have faintly streaked breast and a faint crown-stripe, though never so obvious as in the considerably paler and yellower Aquatic Warbler. Call 'tsek'. Alarm 'trrr'. Often sings in pitch-dark night (Reed Warbler prefers dawn and dusk). In daytime often performs a short vertical song flight. Song *varied, full of mimicry and harsh, jittery calls*. Song resembles Reed Warbler's but *the tempo is more hurried* and more varied, giving a feverish and hectic quality. (Remember the basic rule: Sedge Warbler Spirited singer, Reed Warbler Relaxed.) Often recognised by rapid accelerating crescendo of excited notes that turns into tuneful whistles, e.g. 'zreezree trett zreezreezreė trett, zreezreezree PSEET trutrutru-peerrrrrrrrrrrr-urrrrrr wee-wee-wee LULULU zitri zitri . . .' etc. S

Fan-tailed Warbler

Fan-tailed Warbler

Aquatic Warbler adult male

▶ **Fan-tailed Warbler** *Cisticola juncidis* L 10. Breeds in S Europe in open country, on plains with tall grass, in cornfields etc. Recognised by *small size*, clear streaking on crown and upperparts together with *very short, rounded tail* with black and white tip. Very unobtrusive, keeps well hidden except for extensive, bounding song flights at c. 10m height. These take place even in middle of day at height of summer. Song consists of series of slowly repeated, penetrating 'zreep' notes, one 'zreep' with each bounce. V

Thick-billed Warbler *Acrocephalus aedon* L 18. Very rare vagrant to W Europe from Asia. Not tied to water like its relatives, but does not avoid proximity of water either; found in open terrain with scattered trees and bushes, sometimes in swamps. Active by day. *Large* as Great Reed Warbler, but has *short, thick bill, pale lores* and *lacks supercilium*. Wings and tail strongly rounded, *tail long*. Song something between Marsh Warbler's and Moustached Warbler's. Anxiety call a loud 'tshok-tshok'. V

Thick-billed Warbler

Thick-billed Warbler

Moustached Warbler

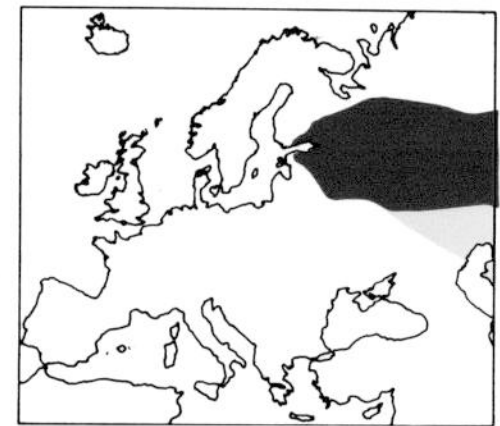

Blyth's Reed Warbler *Acrocephalus dumetorum* L 12.5. Breeds in NE Europe (incl. SE Finland) in bushy swamps, damp wood edges and glades with dense thickets. Very rare summer visitor to NW Europe. Resembles Marsh Warbler, but rump slightly more rusty in tone and wings more rounded (2nd primary shorter than 5th, confirmable only when bird is captured), primary projection thus being shorter. Bill slightly longer than Marsh's. Supercilium normally short and indistinct, but exceptions recorded. Alula and tertials pale brown, make wing even more lacking in contrast than in other *Acrocephalus* species. Also on average darker, greyer feet than its relatives. The song, heard mainly at night, is often given from rather a high perch. Brilliant mimic. Song, however, very distinct from Marsh's in its *calm tempo* and fact that *every phrase is repeated* five or six, sometimes even ten times. Many individuals have a characteristic phrase ('the stairs'), a clear, rising, 'lo leu LEEa', with long note breaks. Nearly always *interposed between the phrases is a typical tongue-clicking* 'chek chek'. V

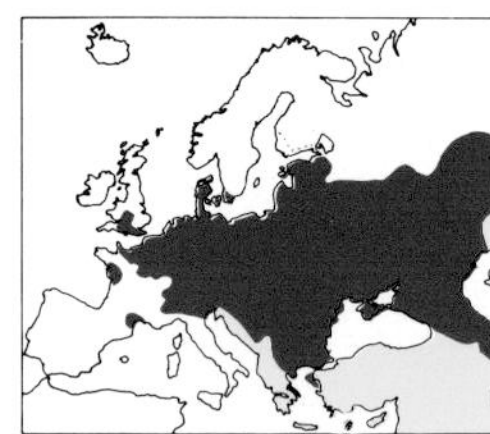

Marsh Warbler *Acrocephalus palustris* L 13. Breeds in rank, often damp areas of weeds along marshy banks and river margins, preferably among nettles and meadowsweet, also in drier growth of reeds with interspersed weeds. Extremely local in Britain. Very like Reed Warbler but has slightly shorter bill and is more *greenish-brown above* in adult. Juvenile very similar to juvenile Reed but has pale pink legs compared with juvenile Reed's browner legs, but difference slight and difficult to use in the field. As a rule different habitat (is rarely seen in dense reedbeds growing in water), and more outstanding song is a better guide. Sings mainly at night. Tempo of song is *varied*, sometimes it slows right down, sticks on several mimicking calls which are repeated (cf. Blyth's Reed Warbler); but then identifies itself by an *acceleration* and an *explosion of masterful mimicry* (often Blue Tit, Magpie, Swallow, Chaffinch and Blackbirds calls) interwoven among series of quite unmelodic, dry trilling calls (even these are imitations, but of tropical species). Characteristic, harsh 'zi-CHEH zi-CHEH' is often heard. S

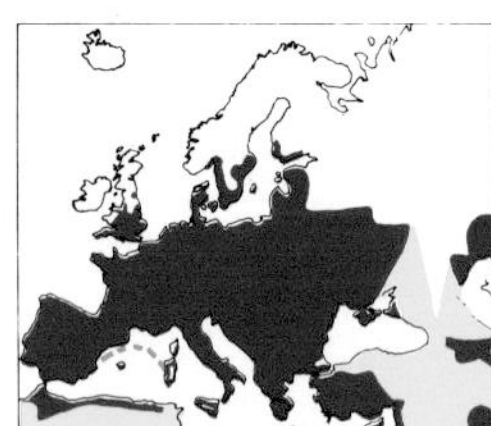

Reed Warbler *Acrocephalus scirpaceus* L 12.5. Breeds commonly in reeds. May also visit dense shrubbery, bushy gardens etc. Skilfully weaves a well-formed nest basket which is suspended around three or four reed stems out in the reedbed. Often exploited as foster host for young Cuckoo. *Unstreaked, brown upperparts* with *only faint suggestion of supercilium* separate it from Sedge Warbler, which occurs in similar habitats. Warmer brown above than adult Marsh Warbler; rump always rust-coloured. Note: juvenile Marsh is almost as warm brown above as Reed, can be practically inseparable even in the hand. Song, heard mostly at dawn and dusk, is not so fast and varied as Sedge Warbler's, which it otherwise resembles. The *predominantly harsh notes, repeated two or three times*, are delivered at *fussily chattering tempo*, 'trett trett trett tirri tirri trü trü . . .' etc. Like other *Acrocephalus* species, readily imitates other bird calls. S

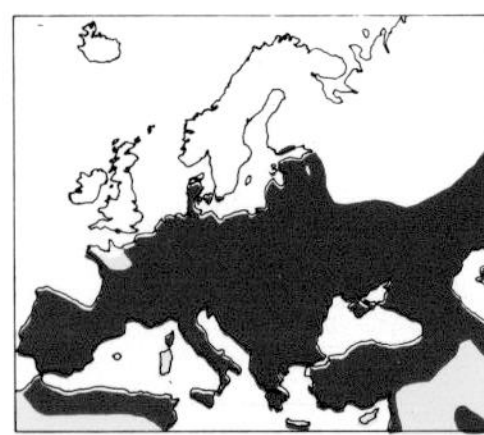

Great Reed Warbler *Acrocephalus arundinaceus* L 19. Breeds both in extensive reedbeds and in smaller curtains of reeds along canals etc. Sometimes 'overshoots' to S Britain where may establish territory. *Very big* with *long powerful bill*. Resembles a giant-sized Reed Warbler but with more distinct supercilium; faintly streaked crop visible at closest ranges only. Less retiring in behaviour than other *Acrocephalus* species; often perches right out in the open, particularly when it sings at sunrise. Song, heard at dusk and dawn but also frequently in daytime, is Reed Warbler-like in its chattering repetitive character but is *considerably louder and more powerful* (as powerful as Thrush Nightingale), has Fieldfare-like creaky elements. A common verse runs 'trr trr trr KARRa-KARRa-KARRa KREEe-KREEe-KREEe trr-trr-KEEe-KEEe'. V

Reed Warbler adult at nest with cuckoo chick

Blyth's Reed Warbler adult spring

Marsh Warbler adult at nest

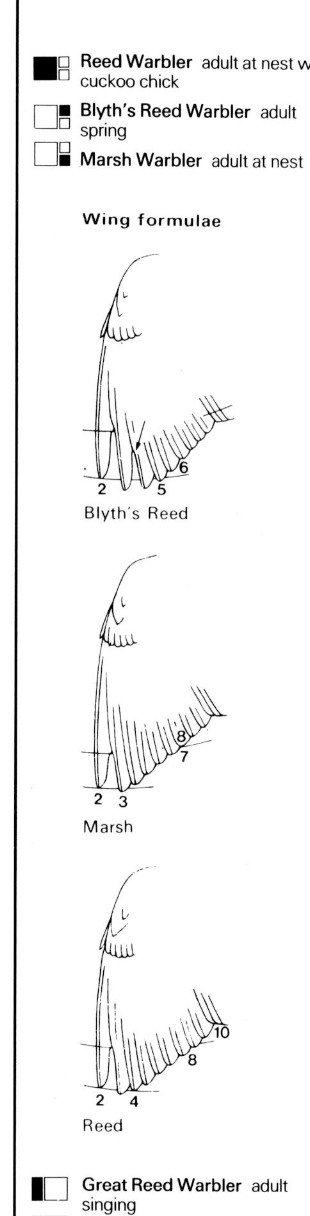

Great Reed Warbler adult singing

Great Reed Warbler adult at nest

Passerines

Icterine Warbler *Hippolais icterina* L 13. Breeds rather commonly in eastern half of Europe in deciduous woods with undergrowth, dense parks and larger gardens. Greenish-grey upperparts and usually *clear pale yellow underparts, including belly,* distinguish it from other warblers except very similar Melodious, which replaces it in SW Europe. Pale edges to secondaries form *pale panel on folded wing* in fresh plumage. Face fairly plain, lacks dark lores and eye-stripe. Longer winged than Melodious Warbler. *Legs blue-grey.* Perches more upright than *Phylloscopus* species and is not so active. Often raises crown feathers when excited. In alarm gives series of hoarse and tongue-clicking notes, 'tettettet-tett . . .', heated and with rather uneven rhythm. The hoarse clicking note is included in call, a short, musical 'tete-LUeet'. Song very varied and pleasing, full of masterful mimicry. It also contains churring notes, and a *nasal and creaky* 'GEEa' is peculiar to the species. Some individuals repeat the verses more pedantically than most, and may even throw in a 'tett' (risk then of confusion with Blyth's Reed Warbler). Sings from elevated perch. Usually does not sing at night. P

■□□ **Icterine Warbler** at nest
□■□ **Icterine Warbler** juv.
□□■ **Melodious Warbler** at nest

Hippolais

Phylloscopus

► **Melodious Warbler** *Hippolais polyglotta* L 13. Breeds in SW Europe in open deciduous wood with rich undergrowth, parks and gardens and also riparian scrub. Much resembles Icterine Warbler, but is a shade *yellower below,* has shorter wings, often *brown legs* and *less prominent pale edges to secondaries.* (Yellow underparts not always striking in the field; can in fact be taken for Marsh Warbler.) *Call a House Sparrow-like chatter,* 'krrrrrr'. Song *faster* and more chattering, does not contain so many imitative notes as Icterine's. The rattling call is interwoven into the song, but Icterine's 'GEEa' is always lacking. The only major confusion risk is a Subalpine Warbler in ecstatic song. P

■□ **Melodious Warbler** autumn
□■ **Melodious Warbler** juv.

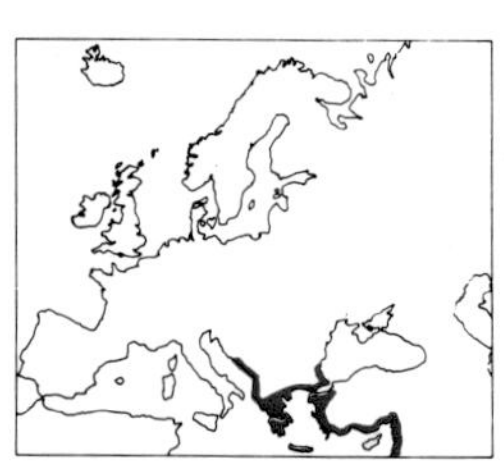

► **Olive-tree Warbler** *Hippolais olivetorum* L 15.5. Breeds in SE Europe in olive and almond groves and open oakwoods. *Large size,* brownish-grey upperparts, pale underparts, *white-edged secondaries* (except autumn adult) and *markedly long bill* distinguish it from all other warblers. Wings are longer than in other *Hippolais* species. Resembles Icterine in behaviour but keeps more concealed. Song loud, hard and raucous, the stanzas relatively short, most reminiscent of Great Reed Warbler. Call a hard tongue-clicking 'tack'.

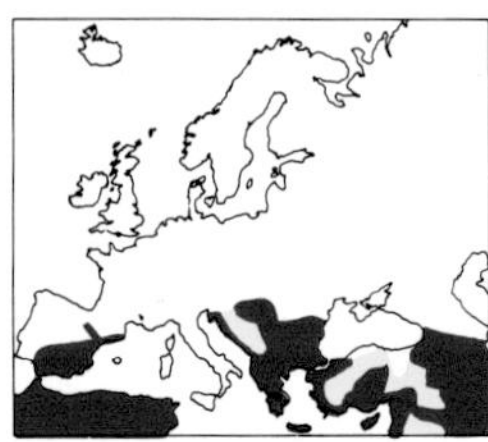

Olivaceous Warbler *Hippolais pallida* L 13. Breeds in S Europe in open, damp woodland, parks and gardens. Note *faintly green-toned brownish-grey upperparts* with slightly darker wings and tail, and *pale underparts.* Best told from similarly coloured Garden Warbler by typical *Hippolais* appearance, with *long, pointed bill* with broad base and peaked head profile. Often flicks tail downwards in nervous manner. Song rather reminiscent of Reed Warbler's (same *slow* tempo) but *more monotonous, harsher and more chattering.* Often contains *high, almost choking notes.* Alarm call is series of quiet hard tongue-clicking notes, distinguished from Lesser Whitethroat's and Subalpine Warbler's by 'thicker', less pure and slightly more nasal ring (recalling Garden Warbler). Also a chattering 'krrrt'. V

■□ **Olive-tree Warbler** adult
□■ **Olivaceous Warbler**

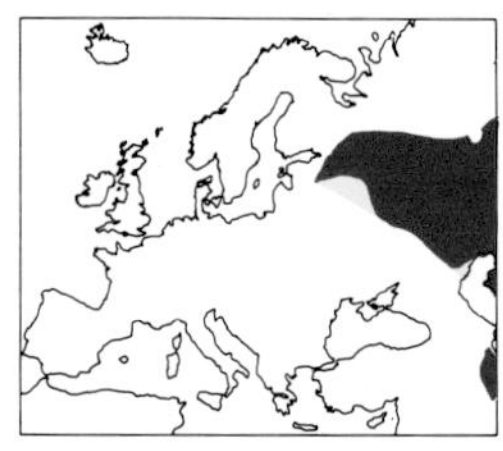

► **Booted Warbler** *Hippolais caligata* L 11.5. Breeds in E Europe in bushes and scrub. Often frequents the ground vegetation, yet difficult to see. Very rare autumn vagrant to W Europe. Very like Olivaceous Warbler, but *smaller* and has *shorter, finer bill* and slightly more discernible supercilium and more darkish lores. Legs greyish-brown. At close range narrow whitish edges to tail (square-cut) sometimes discernible. Rump *not* contrastingly reddish-brown (cf. Paddyfield Warbler). Song *fast and chattering,* trills and churrs at random, rather monotonous, and not very loud, most like 'heated' *Sylvia* song. Tongue-clicking call like Lesser Whitethroat. Alarm either a Bluethroat-like 'trak' or a churring 'zerrr'. V

■□ **Booted Warbler** adult summer
□■ **Booted Warbler** adult summer

Passerines

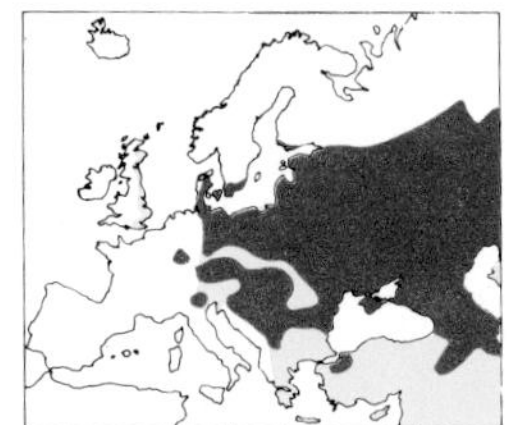

Barred Warbler *Sylvia nisoria* L 15.5. Breeds sparsely in eastern half of Europe in open country with bushy thickets with scattered trees or glades with bushes; often same terrain as Red-backed Shrike. Adult has *delicate crescentic barring below* and *pale yellow eye*, but the barring at least is not always so easy to see in the field. White tips to tertials, wing-coverts, uppertail-coverts, together with *white outer corners on fairly long tail.* Young birds in Aug have dark brown or grey eye, are unmarked below, resemble Garden Warbler, but are larger and have a longer tail and also *pale edges to tertials and greater coverts.* Often keeps well hidden. A Barred Warbler flying away can be confused with Red-backed Shrike owing to similar kind of habitat, body size and manner of flight, but the back is greyer and the tail differently marked (see above). Call a rattling 'trrrrr-tt-t-', slowing down towards end, rather like upset House Sparrow. Song like Garden Warbler's but harder and more scratchy in voice, and the verses are often shorter; moreover, the rattling call is often added. Can be confused with ecstatic song variant of Whitethroat. Song flight, similar to that of Whitethroat, is often seen. P

▶ **Orphean Warbler** *Sylvia hortensis* L 15. Breeds in S Europe in open woodland, groves and parks. *Large* with *dark hood*, narrow *pale iris* (exceptions occur), white outer tail feathers and whitish underparts. Similarly coloured Sardinian Warbler is considerably smaller and has red orbital ring (adult). Juvenile resembles a large Lesser Whitethroat. Call a sharp 'tak'. Song is loud, composed of series of repeated phrases. It sounds quite different in Spain from in Greece: the SE European race *crassirostris* sounds almost as rich as a Blackbird, the verses are fairly long and varied, e.g. 'tru tru tru sheevu sheevu, yoo-yoo-yoo-bru-treeh . . .' and so on – and the major confusion risk is rather surprisingly Nightingale; the nominate SW European race *hortensis* sings more monotonously, the song composed of alternating high and low notes with tone like Ring Ouzel; a common theme runs 'TEEroo TEEroo TEEroo'. V

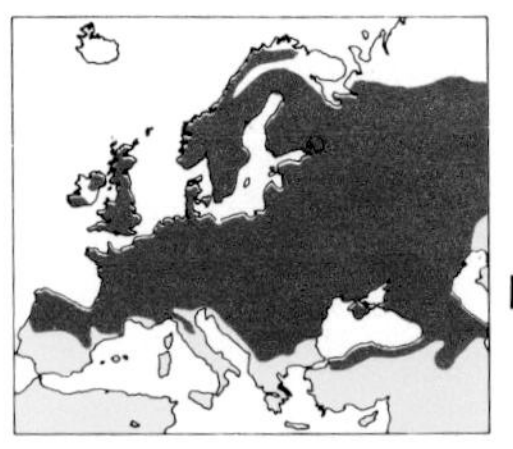

▶ **Garden Warbler** *Sylvia borin* L 14. Breeds commonly in open woodland with rich undergrowth and also in larger thickly wooded gardens and parks. *Olive-tinged brownish-grey upperparts* and *greyish-white underparts*, legs grey-brown. Lacks particular distinguishing features. Most easily confused with Olivaceous, Booted Marsh and juvenile Barred Warblers. Note rounded head profile, the *short and rather heavy grey bill* and also almost total lack of supercilium. Often slightly grey-toned on sides of nape/hindneck. Keeps well hidden in the foliage even when singing. Song has no clear tune, it ripples forth in a charming babble, like Blackcap's, but the verses are longer and lack latter's clear final notes. Alarm a hoarse note with a slightly nasal clucking quality, 'interminably' repeated, 'chek-chek-chek- . . .'. SP

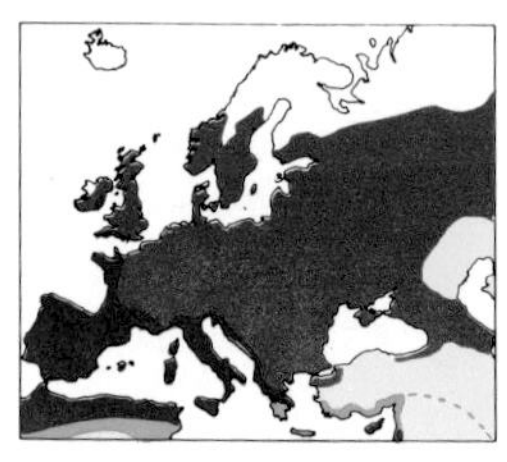

▶ **Blackcap** *Sylvia atricapilla* L 14. Breeds commonly in woods with rich undergrowth and in parks and gardens. Medium-sized grey warbler. *Black cap distinguishes the male* and *reddish-brown cap the female.* Juvenile resembles female. Easier to catch sight of than Garden Warbler, but nonetheless usually keeps well concealed. Hardy, capable of enduring quite severe cold. Often eats berries. Sings from well-concealed songpost. Song resembles Garden Warbler's, but verses are shorter, and the rippling babble turns towards the end into a few characteristic, *clear and powerful fluted notes* with a melancholy ring. Alarm is a series of hard, loud, hurried tongue-clicking notes, 'tett-ett-ett-ett- . . .'. SWP

■□□ **Barred Warbler** adult male

□■□ **Barred Warbler** adult female at nest with chicks

□□■ **Barred Warbler** 1st-winter

Barred Warbler

■□ **Garden Warbler** 1st-winter

□■ **Garden Warbler** adult at nest

Garden Warbler juv. at bathing pool

Orphean Warbler adult male at nest

Orphean Warbler female at nest (dark iris, probably 1st-summer)

Blackcap adult male at bathing pool

Blackcap adult female at nest with chicks

Passerines

Whitethroat *Sylvia communis* L 14. Breeds commonly in scrub and bushy areas (common, e.g. on heaths with blackberry and low juniper), in cultivated country wherever hedges and shrubbery are present. Fond of rank plant vegetation, thrives in more open habitats than Lesser Whitethroat. *White throat*, buff-toned breast (pink tinge in adult male), brown-grey head (greyest in adult male), *pale reddish-brown wings* and quite long tail with pale outer feathers are characteristic. Best distinguished from Lesser Whitethroat by *paler legs* and reddish-brown wings. Very active, constantly on the move in bushes and scrub. Call a harsh 'whett whett whett'. Alarm a harsh, drawn-out 'chairr'. Song is delivered from a bush top or telegraph wire and is a rapid and quite short, jerky verse, harsh in tone; a common rhythm runs 'CHUCK-a-ro-CHE, CHUCK-a-ro'. Now and again the Whitethroat flies up a few metres and performs a protracted, ecstatically chattering flight song of rather general *Sylvia* character. SP

■□□ **Whitethroat** adult male at nest
□■□ **Whitethroat** adult female
□□■ **Whitethroat** adult female in flight

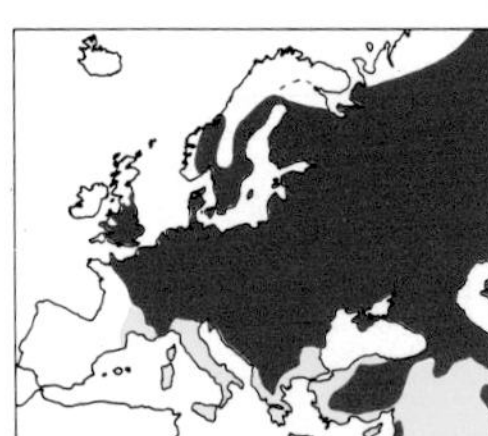

Lesser Whitethroat *Sylvia curruca* L 13.5. Breeds quite commonly in dense bushy thickets, in hedges in gardens and in young pine groves. Resembles Whitethroat, but is a shade smaller with shorter tail, grey-brown upperparts with *greyish-brown wings* and *dark grey ear-coverts*. Entire *underparts very pale*, almost pure white, breast without buff tone as in, e.g. female Subalpine Warbler, which can be a confusion risk in the Mediterranean countries. *Iris grey, legs dark grey.* Keeps well concealed. Call a short tongue-clicking 'tett'. Numerous in SE Europe (Asia Minor), on migration, where has a further call, a Blue Tit-like hoarse scolding 'chay-de-de-de'. Song, delivered usually from concealed songpost, consists of two parts: first a brief, muffled chatter, then a fast, loud, rattling trill, 'tellellellellellellell'. SP

■□□ **Lesser Whitethroat** worn adult
□■□ **Lesser Whitethroat** 1st-winter
□□■ **Lesser Whitethroat** adult at nest with chicks

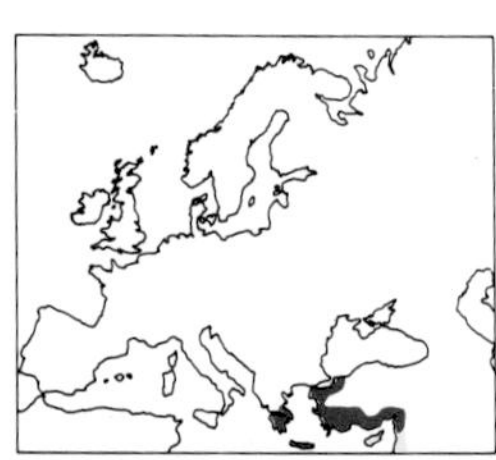

Rüppell's Warbler *Sylvia rueppellii* L 14. Breeds locally in SE Europe in thorny scrub in mainly rocky areas. Male easily recognised by *black hood and throat* separated by *narrow, white moustachial stripe*, and grey upperparts. Female has more of a dark grey hood, and she often has *diffusely dark-spotted chin* separated from dark head by thin white line; looks all-grey above with light edges to tertials and a few greater coverts. Orbital ring and *legs reddish-brown* in both sexes. Call a sparrow-like rattle, like Barred Warbler's but weaker and not slowing down as in that species, and also a series of hard tongue-clicking notes, harder than corresponding call of Subalpine Warbler, not so much like a 'mechanical rattle' as in Sardinian Warbler. Song very like Sardinian's but not quite so loud; more 'chugging' or like a pulsating rattle, e.g. 'prr-trr-trr prr-trr-trr see-tree-wee-prr' and similar. Song flight with slow-motion flight like Greenfinch and occasional glides on upwards-angled wings. V

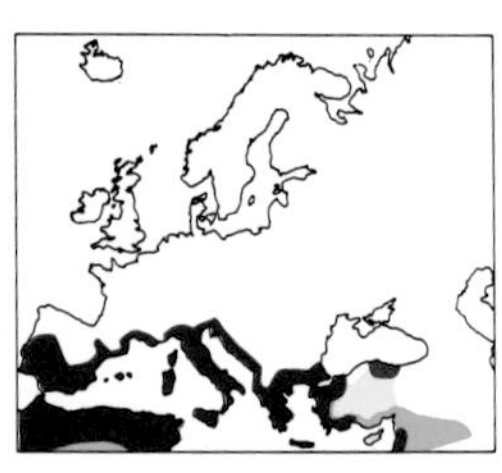

Sardinian Warbler *Sylvia melanocephala* L 13. Breeds commonly in S Europe in scrub and bushes in open or rocky country, but also in woods with undergrowth. Characteristic of the male are *jet-black hood* with well visible *reddish-brown orbital ring*. Female and juvenile more difficult to identify, but note fairly *dark upperparts* and *grey-brown flanks* together with *long* rounded *tail*; underparts look sullied, contrasting with white throat. Female also has rather prominent reddish-brown orbital ring, juvenile a more indistinct brown one. Main confusion risk is Ménétries's Warbler (which see). Orphean Warbler is much bigger and lacks red orbital ring. Calls are an explosive chattering mechanical rattle, 'churrrr, trit-trit-trit-trit-trit' or slower 'terit terit terit terit', and also, when agitated, series of more grinding tongue-clicking notes or occasional loud, hard 'tsek'. Song a typical *Sylvia* chatter, should be learnt thoroughly for easier comparisons and identification of other *Sylvia* warblers in S Europe. Tempo speedy, length of verses varying but normally 2–5 sec. Composed of hard 'trr-trr' call-like notes intermingled with exceedingly short whistles. Song flight like Whitethroat's. V

Rüppell's Warbler adult male
Sardinian Warbler adult male
Sardinian Warbler adult female at nest with chicks

Passerines

Ménétries's Warbler *Sylvia mystacea* L 13.5. Breeds in easternmost Europe in tamarisk scrub, often in rocky areas, but also along river valleys. Extremely rare vagrant to W Europe. Very like and closely related to Sardinian Warbler. Male has *black hood which blends into brown-tinged dark grey upperparts*. Reddish-brown orbital ring. Has *rosy tone on underparts, sometimes almost brick-red on throat, breast and flanks*. Tail not so strongly rounded and long as on Sardinian Warbler. Female is paler and browner on upperparts and has *buff tone on underparts* (not dull brown tone as in Sardinain). Very active, keeps well hidden in shrubbery. Call a sharp, repeated 'tak' and also a sparrow-like chattering series of notes like Rüppell's Warbler. Song similar to Sardinian's, not surprisingly, but more musical and varied, appears to be delivered slightly more jerkily and at slower tempo; phrases longer.

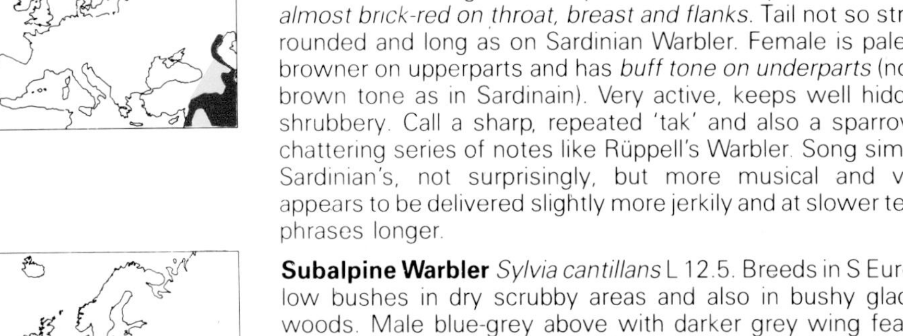

Subalpine Warbler *Sylvia cantillans* L 12.5. Breeds in S Europe in low bushes in dry scrubby areas and also in bushy glades in woods. Male blue-grey above with darker grey wing feathers, below *rusty-orange on chin, throat, breast and flanks*; distinct *white moustachial stripe* and red orbital ring. Female duller in colour, less blue-grey and rusty-orange, but pale moustachial stripe is usually visible; has indistinct reddish-brown orbital ring and outside this a clear *whitish eye-ring*. Female and juvenile best distinguished from Spectacled Warbler by *grey-brown upperwing*, not reddish-brown, from juvenile Sardinian Warbler by paler and browner colours, and from Lesser Whitethroat by *pale brown legs*, pale eye-ring, *buff tone on underparts* together with lack of darker ear-coverts. Skulking in behaviour, keeps well concealed in shrubbery. Calls comprise individual 'tett' notes, very like Lesser Whitethroat (but not quite so loud), and also series of tongue-clicking notes that are more subdued than Sardinian Warbler's and sound more dry, 'tett-tett-tett-tett-tett-tett'. Often one or two 'tett' notes tacked on to the end. When highly agitated a more bubbly rattle, 'prrrrt', is uttered, vaguely reminiscent of Crested Tit. The song is most likely to be confused with Sardinian Warbler's and Rüppell's Warbler's, but the voice is clearer and the verses more varied, 'bouncing' and chattering like Linnet, the verses also usually longer. Sings from top of bush or in short song flight. V

▶ **Desert Warbler** *Sylvia nana* L 11.5. Breeds in easternmost Europe on bushy steppes and in desert. A very rare autumn vagrant to W Europe. Asiatic race looks like a pale small Whitethroat. Sexes alike. Upperparts pale grey-brown with ochre tone, most obvious on edges of tertials, which can be reminiscent of Whitethroat. *Tail rusty-brown in tone*. Underparts pale. *Iris pale yellow*. In the North African race the plumage strikingly pale and lacking in contrast. Keeps well concealed in shrubbery and flies low above the ground from one bit of scrub to another. Also hops on the ground. Call a short trill. Song short like Whitethroat (1–2 sec.) but clearer and faster. Some notes are often clear like Blackcap's. V

▶ **Spectacled Warbler** *Sylvia conspicillata* L 12.5. Breeds in SW Europe in open, dry localities with scrub. Looks like a Whitethroat but is *smaller*, has *finer bill* (dark, with yellowish-white base) and proportionately *shorter tail*; adult male has darker grey forecrown shading to *blackish on lores and around eye*, a *more obvious white eye-ring* and darker pink breast (greyish on upper breast). Female very similar. Distinguished from Subalpine Warbler female by *reddish-brown wings*, but a few are tricky, being less vividly rufous. Call a very dry, clear, rattlesnake-rattle, 'zerrrrr'. Song a typical *Sylvia* chatter; fast tempo, quite short phrases, *high-pitched voice*; the phrases usually open with one or a few notes of Crested Lark clarity. Sings from perch in full view or during song flight. V

■□□ **Ménétries's Warbler** adult male summer

□■□ **Ménétries's Warbler** female

□□■ **Ménétries's Warbler** 1st-winter female

■□ **Subalpine Warbler** adult male summer

□■ **Subalpine Warbler** 1st-winter

■□□ **Subalpine Warbler** female at nest

□■□ **Desert Warbler** Asiatic race *nana*

□□■ **Desert Warbler** Asiatic race *nana*

■□□ **Spectacled Warbler** adult male summer

□■□ **Spectacled Warbler** 1st-winter male

□□■ **Spectacled Warbler** juv.

Passerines

Dartford Warbler *Sylvia undata* L 13. Breeds in SW Europe (incl. S England) in dry, bushy localities, on heath with scrubland, often among gorse, broom and thornbushes. Mainly resident. In northern part of the range the birds are very hard pressed during severe winters and in consequence numbers there fluctuate considerably. *Long-tailed*, very dark grey-brown above, *dark red-toned below* (not so red as in the plate). Female's brown colour considerably duller, can appear entirely grey at swift glance. Darker than any other warbler except Marmora's, which has grey, not red-brown, breast. Often clearly demarcated white belly. *Bill base yellowish. Throat with pale spots.* Usually a small white spot at the edge of the wing next to the alula. Often holds tail cocked and frequently flicks it. Flight low and weak with characteristic jerky tail movements. Usually keeps well concealed in the vegetation. In winter sometimes seen in small flocks which rove about like tits. Calls are a harsh, drawn-out and slightly inflected 'chaihrr-er', repeated at a grinding tempo when agitated, and also a 'tak', which may be repeated in a rattling, fast series. The song is rather rugged and hard-voiced (actually somewhat recalling short, fast pieces from Barred Warbler song). Normal phrase length 2-3 sec. Can be heard singing throughout the year. Song flight often performed. RS

Marmora's Warbler *Sylvia sarda* L 13. Breeds locally in W Mediterranean region in dry, scrubby localities, often in rocky country. Resembles Dartford Warbler, but has *grey*, not red-brown *underparts*. Differs from Dartford also in *reddish* or *orange bill base*, lack of clearly defined white belly, pale spotting on throat and also white spot on wing edge next to alula (cf. Dartford). *Long tail* and *dark colours* distinguish it from all other warblers. Habits as Dartford Warbler. Commonest call is a subdued, short, gently simmering, disyllabic 'churu' (actually resembles a weak call of rising Snipe). Alarm a soft 'trrt'. Song very distinct from Dartford's, somewhat lower in pitch, consists of fairly simple series repeated in cycles, at distance reminiscent of Sardinian Warbler's rattling call but is slightly more irregular and varied in details, and often the phrase begins with a clear note, 'heet, chUree-chUree-chUree-chUriree'. The phrases are short, but during song flight the song is protracted as in other *Sylvia* species. V

Thrushes

(family Turdidae) are described on pages 236–251, apart from Rufous Bush Robin which is dealt with below.

Rufous Bush Robin *Cercotrichas galactotes* L 15.5. Now included in the thrushes, and rather reminiscent of a nightingale. Breeds sparsely in Southern Europe in open, dry and bushy localities, in vineyards, hedgerows and gardens, preferably in prickly pear hedges. Arrives late in spring, not until May. Two clearly separated races occur in Europe: *C. g. galactotes* in SW Europe has reddish-brown toned crown and back; *C. g. syriacus* in SE Europe is paler and more grey-brown. Characteristic of both races is the *long tail with striking black and white markings at the tip.* Often behaves quite boldly, often seen perched right out in the open with tail raised and fanned, showing the prominent pattern. Often seen on the ground. Call a sharp 'tak'. Song like both Song Thrush and Nightingale, consists of clear, flute-like notes at an even rhythm. Phrases short, the song 'recited'. Sings from perch or in pipit-like, parachuting song flight. Sings frequently. V

Dartford Warbler adult female at nest

Dartford Warbler adult male

Marmora's Warbler adult female

Rufous Bush Robin at nest race *galactotes*

Rufous Bush Robin race *syriacus*

Passerines

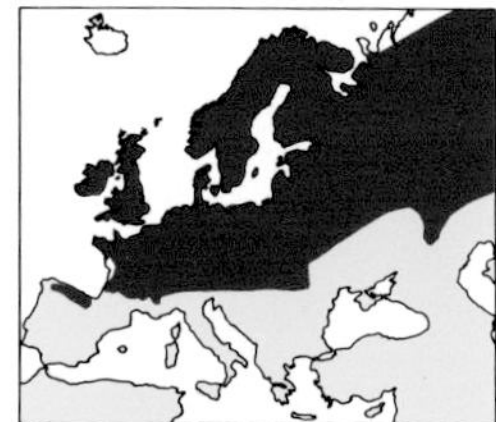

Willow Warbler *Phylloscopus trochilus* L 11.5. Very common summer visitor, in deciduous and mixed wood from lowland copse to highest subalpine birch, requires simply a group of trees with undergrowth. Even brown-grey, green-toned upperparts without wingbars (in high boreal and subarctic tends to be more grey-brown above). *Breast has touch of yellow.* Juvenile quite strong yellow below. Similar to Chiffchaff but on average less brown and has more distinct supercilium. Usually *paler leg colour* (but legs *can* be mid brown). Like other *Phylloscopus* warblers is very active and restless in foliage of trees. Call a weak, soft 'HOOeet'. Song very melodic, flowing and melancholy; starts with high, fast notes, drops slightly down scale, slows down momentarily, speeds up to end in a cadence with tender and languorous, soft notes which die away. SP

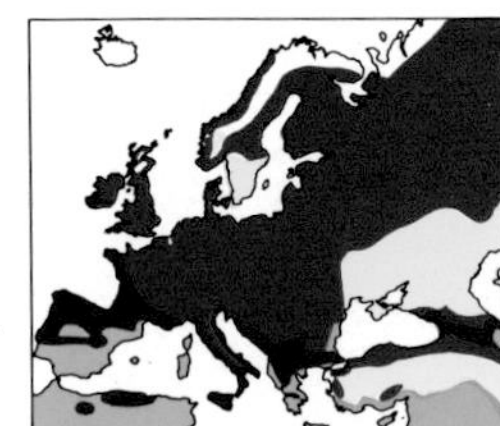

Chiffchaff *Phylloscopus collybita* L 11. Common summer visitor, in parks and open wood (incl. coniferous on Continent and in far north) with undergrowth. Small numbers winter in Britain. Very like Willow Warbler, but *more grey-brown*, has less distinct supercilium, usually *dark legs* (*can* be mid brown). Rarely may show hint of pale wingbar. E Siberian race *tristis* (straggles to W Europe) has buff supercilium and breast, lacks yellow and green on head, mantle and underparts; feet black. Call not so clearly disyllabic as Willow Warbler's, a little stronger, slightly harsher with stress more on second syllable, 'huEET'. More easterly populations give plainer, more urgent, Coal Tit-like 'peet' ('chicken in distress' call). Song chatting: 'chiff chiff chaff chiff chaffa chiff . . .', may be interrupted by occasional muffled 'terr, terr'. RSP

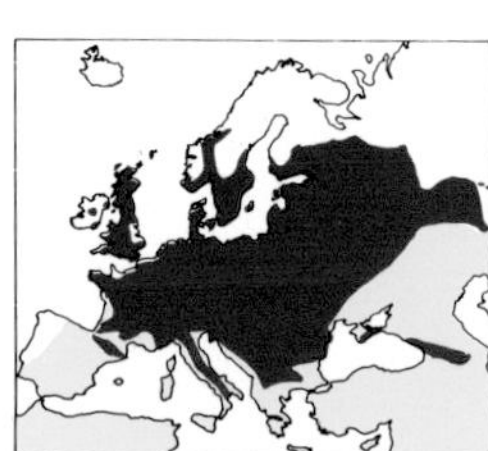

Wood Warbler *Phylloscopus sibilatrix* L 12. Fairly common in woods with tall trees ('pillared hall'), typical bird of old beech wood. Clear *yellow throat and yellow breast with pure white belly* and *vivid yellowish-green upperparts.* Distinct, yellow supercilium. Song an accelerating series of 'zip' notes ending in metallic trill, 'zip, zip zip-zip-zip-zwirrrrrrrrrr' ('coin spinning on marble slab'). Also often gives intensified, melancholy 'deeu-deeu-deeu-deeu- . . .'. Frequent short horizontal song flights in canopy, often low down, in which flies while making 'zip' sounds and lands while trilling. Call sharp 'zip'. Alarm a single 'deeu'. S

Green Warbler *Phylloscopus nitidus* L 11.5. Breeds in deciduous mountain forests, incl. birch forest, in Caucasus. Merely a race of ► Greenish Warbler? *Yellowish-white wingbar* (sometimes a hint of a second one). *Supercilium, cheeks and entire underparts weakly tinted yellow.* Calls and song similar to Greenish. V

Dusky Warbler *Phylloscopus fuscatus* L 11. Very rare autumn vagrant from Asia. Very like Radde's Warbler, but *narrower bill and legs* (medium brown), somewhat darker upperparts (rufous-brown), and supercilium always narrow above lores, often rustier at rear (can be entirely whitish). *No yellow on underparts,* breast and flanks buffish-brown. Told from E Siberian Chiffchaff (*tristis*) by leg colour, longer, more prominent supercilium, darker upperparts, pale base to bill (not all-black). Often seen near ground (much of a bush dweller). *Call a hard tongue-clicking* 'chak', like Blackcap.

Radde's Warbler *Phylloscopus schwarzi* L 12. Very rare vagrant from Asia. Olive-brown above, white below with yellowish-brown tone on breast and flanks. Vent tinged rufous. *Bill and legs stout,* legs pale yellowish-pink. Distinct, *broad, buff supercilium,* whitest at very rear, often widest and slightly diffuse in front of eye. Dark eye-stripe. Often seen near ground. *Call a nasal tongue-clicking* 'chap' or 'chrep' (a trifle slurred, not so dry as Dusky's), can be rather quiet. V

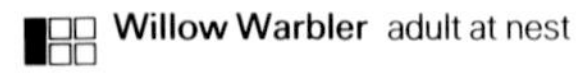

Willow Warbler adult at nest

Willow Warbler adult

Willow Warbler juv.

Chiffchaff adult at nest

Chiffchaff 1st-winter

Willow Warbler

Chiffchaff

Chiffchaff Siberian race *tristis*

Wood Warbler

Wood Warbler

Green Warbler adult

Dusky Warbler adult singing

Radde's Warbler 1st-winter

Passerines

Bonelli's Warbler *Phylloscopus bonelli* L 11. Breeds in central and S Europe in wooded mountain regions, preferably in forests of cork oak and pine, but found also at lower level. Rare visitor to NW Europe. Pale olive-brown upperparts (greyer in SE European race *orientalis*) with *greenish-yellow edges to flight and tail feathers, greenish-yellow tone on rump* (in adult) together with *white underparts* and *pale ear-coverts* are typical characters. Juvenile usually has only indistinct contrast between back and rump. Active, usually keeps well concealed in the foliage. Call when agitated a loud but 'silky', slightly strained 'huu-eef', distinctly disyllabic with equal stress on both syllables. A variant sounds quite like Greenfinch, 'dyooee'. Often has two song variants, one slightly the faster. In SE Europe the call is different, a characteristic 'chiff', very like young House Sparrow.Song a second-long, single-note trill, tender and clear, as if laughing, resembles end of Wood Warbler's song but runs at slower tempo, 'swee-wee-wee-wee-wee-wee'. V

Yellow-browed Warbler *Phylloscopus inornatus* L 10. Breeds in northeasternmost Europe and in Asia. Rare but regular autumn visitor to NW Europe, mainly in late Sept–Oct. *Very small* with *greenish upperparts*, off-white underparts, pale yellow supercilium, *two distinct wingbars* and *broad pale edges to tertials*. Sometimes has a faint suggestion of a paler longitudinal stripe on the crown (especially on rear part). Resembles Willow Warbler in habits and often mixes with other *Phylloscopus* species or tits on passage. *Often calls*, call a high 'tsWEEST', rather like Coal Tit but higher-pitched and with distinct upwards inflection, sometimes given twice. Song is very high-pitched and thin, may be described as a mixture of Hazel Grouse and Goldcrest. Geographical variations within the wide range are documented, and these seem to apply to the calls too. The form *P. inornatus(?) humei* in the mountain regions of central Asia thus calls 'tseelü', with downward inflection, often uttered twice; its song, too, differs markedly and resembles Redwing's call, 'steeep'; this form has been recorded as a very rare straggler to Europe. P

▶ **Arctic Warbler** *Phylloscopus borealis* L 12.5. Rare and local breeder in far north in birchwood on mountain slopes, usually near watercourses. Arrives extremely late, up to midsummer, this as a result of record migration route distance: winters in SE Asia, and therefore covers, despite its body weight of 10 g, 25,000 km annually. A very rare visitor to W Europe. A quite large and slim *Phylloscopus* with a *distinct wingbar* (a second, faint, bar sometimes visible, *clearly marked and long, narrow supercilium ending before base of forehead*, distinct dark *eye-stripe* which *reaches bill base*, olive-grey toned breast sides and flanks and pale brown legs. Bill heavy. Can be confused with Greenish, but has different call, is bigger, has different supercilium (on Greenish reaches forehead, eye-stripe usually does not reach bill base), olive-grey flanks and usually paler legs. Usually keeps hidden in the treetops. Call a short, penetrating 'drzE', rather like Dipper. Song is a fast reeling trill, 'sresresresresresre . . . ., reminiscent of a series of notes from Tree Pipit's song or, perhaps more, like Cirl Bunting's song. V

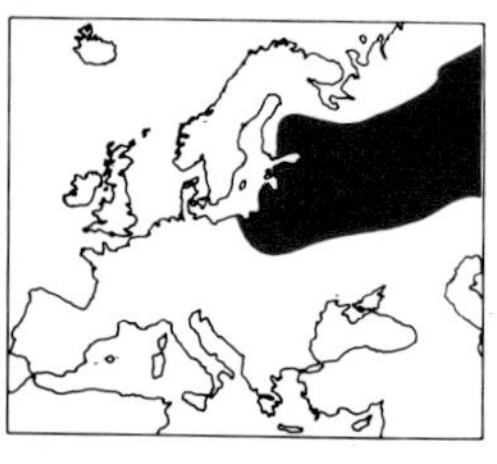

▶ **Greenish Warbler** *Phylloscopus trochiloides* L 11. An eastern species, rare visitor to W Europe (spring and early autumn). Usually found in mixed forests with rich undergrowth, often in spruce forest with some deciduous trees. On migration often in deciduous copses. Resembles Willow Warbler and Chiffchaff, but has *more distinct and long supercilium* and a narrow *wingbar*. (Beware of confusion with odd autumn Chiffchaffs with hint of wing bar – note dark legs of that species). For differences from Arctic Warbler, see that species. Call a loud 'seeLEE', slightly like Pied Wagtail. Song loud and 'frothy', a short, reeling verse, high-pitched and rapid, a little jerky, slightly reminiscent of excited Pied Wagtail song. Some individuals occasionally relieve this with, or stick almost exclusively to, a slightly longer and more trilling verse, confusingly like Wren's. V

■□ **Bonelli's Warbler** adult
□■ **Bonelli's Warbler**

■□ **Yellow-browed Warbler** autumn
□■ **Yellow-browed Warbler** autumn

■□ **Yellow-browed Warbler** summer race *humei*
□■ **Arctic Warbler**

■□ **Arctic Warbler** autumn
□■ **Greenish Warbler**

Passerines

Pallas's Warbler *Phylloscopus proregulus* L 9.5. Very rare (but recently regular) vagrant in late autumn to NW Europe from Asia. Usually breeds in coniferous and mixed forest, but on migration normally found in deciduous wood and shrubbery and thickets. *Very small* and resembles Goldcrest, but has conspicuous, *bright yellow rump* (rarely, white; quite exceptionally, obscure). This is especially striking in flight. Green above with pale yellow *double wingbar* and broad *pale edges to tertials*. Very *dark crown* with *pale yellow central stripe* and long supercilium. Dark eye-stripe very strongly marked, terminates in slight downward curve. Appears big-headed. Best distinguished from similar Yellow-browed Warbler by yellow rump and *distinct* central crown-stripe (a *faint* stripe is sometimes also visible on Yellow-browed). Sometimes associates with feeding flocks of Goldcrests or tits. Habits as Goldcrest's, incl. manner of fluttering in the foliage after insects. May also be seen hanging upside down like a tit, which Yellow-browed does not do. Rather silent on migration. Call a high, drawn-out 'tweep' or disyllabic 'twooeep', quite unlike Yellow-browed's call, more like a Chiffchaff or a subdued Greenfinch. Song is faintly like Wren's, pleasing and clear, surprisingly *loud and varied*, 'tsee yu-yu-yu-tsree, weecha weecha seewoo seewoo seewoo sitt, choot choot choot tsee', and similar. In a way, it resembles Olive-backed Pipit's song. V

Pallas's Warbler autumn
Pallas's Warbler autumn

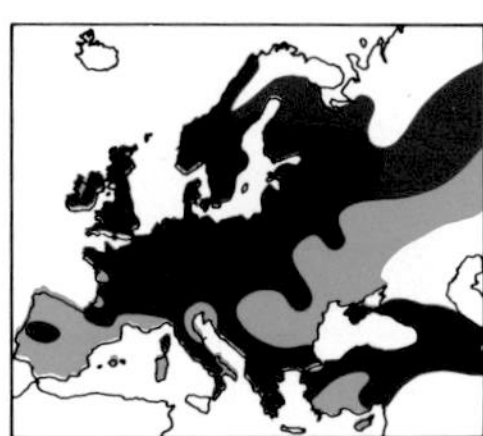

Goldcrest *Regulus regulus* L 9. Breeds commonly in spruce wood, also in other coniferous and even mixed wood, incl. gardens. In most old spruce forests, one can hear the Goldcrests' high, thin calls from high up in the trees. To see them is harder; they usually dodge about high up, skip and climb quickly along the branches, flutter momentarily on the outside of the tip of a branch etc. The Goldcrest is *Europe's smallest bird*. It has a plain grey-green plumage but is adorned with a *broad yellow crown-stripe., edged with black*. The male has in addition a touch of orange in the yellow. The juvenile lacks the crown markings in its first plumage, but this is very seldom seen since juvenile Goldcrests rarely have cause in summer to descend to the level where man lives, and in the autumn they moult and acquire the crown pattern. Outside the breeding period Goldcrests roam around in loose groups, often with tits, and when they find themselves outside coniferous woods they often show themselves very well, e.g. in bushes and tall herbs and are very fearless. In very hard weather they can suffer severe losses, but these are compensated for by the fact that the Goldcrest lays two clutches per year with up to 10 eggs in each. The call is a very thin and high-pitched 'sree-sree-sree'. Alarm call is high but plain and emphatic 'tseet'. The song is likewise very high and treble; a theme repeated *in cycles* and with a short flourish as an ending. RWP

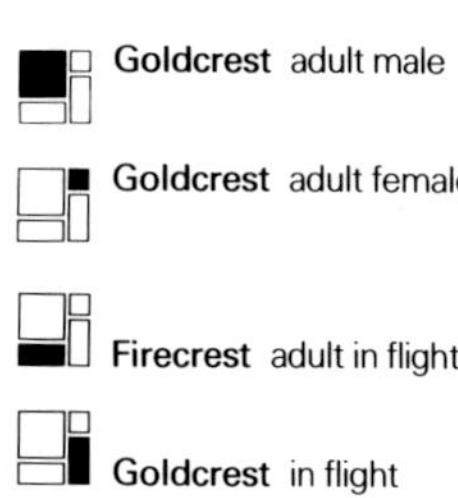

Goldcrest adult male
Goldcrest adult female
Firecrest adult in flight
Goldcrest in flight

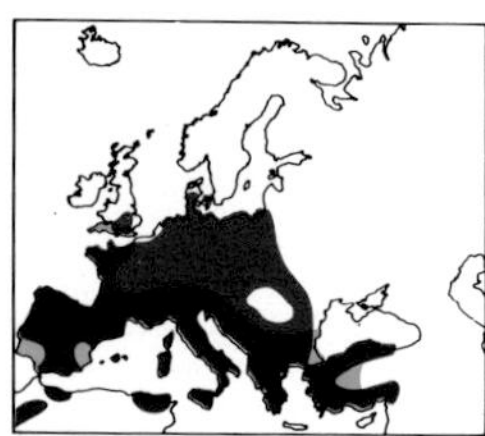

Firecrest *Regulus ignicapillus* L 9. Breeds in central and S Europe in deciduous, coniferous and mixed woodland and also in parks. Resembles Goldcrest but distinguished from that species in all plumages by *distinct white stripe above the eye* and *black stripe through it. The shoulders are rather bright bronzy-green* (in Goldcrest dull grey-green like the back), which is characteristic. Easily told from Pallas's Warbler by lack of sharply demarcated, bright pale yellow rump. Habits as Goldcrest's. Call as sharp as Goldcrest's and very difficult to tell from latter's, but last note in a series of a few *rises in pitch*; also has a more Coal Tit-like call. The song is a monotone series of high notes that accelerate and rise slightly; it is not so well articulated as Goldcrest's, and the tempo is a shade faster. RWP

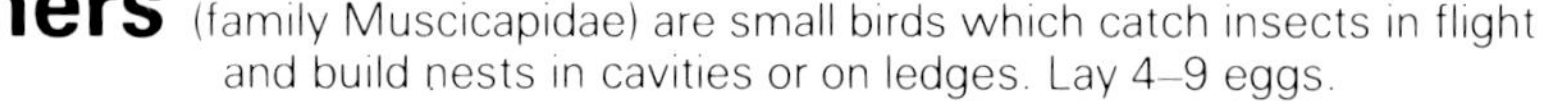

Flycatchers

Flycatchers (family Muscicapidae) are small birds which catch insects in flight and build nests in cavities or on ledges. Lay 4–9 eggs.

Pied Flycatcher *Ficedula hypoleuca* L 13. Breeds commonly in woods with at least some deciduous element, in parks and gardens but also in remote forests. Readily uses nestboxes. Not quite such a specialist at taking flying insects as Spotted Flycatcher. Flicks wings (often one higher than other) and cocks tail when perched on look-out. Some males (especially in E Europe, occasionally further west) are browner, though always have *white forehead patch* (female never has). ▶ Male is easy but female very difficult to distinguish in the field from corresponding sexes of Collared Flycatcher (see that species). Song quite powerful, sprightly and rhythmic, e.g. 'see tseevree tseevree tseevree yu lee tseeplee tseeplee tseeplee tseeplee'. Alarm a persistent, short metallic 'pik, pik, pik, . . .'. Also gives quiet tongue-clicking 'tett'. SP

■□□ **Pied Flycatcher** male at nest hole
□■□ **Pied Flycatcher** female
□□■ **Pied Flycatcher** 1st-winter in flight

Semi-collared Flycatcher *Ficedula semitorquata* L 13. Breeds sparsely in the Balkans, Crimea and also in the Caucasus. Very closely related to Collared Flycatcher (normal calls similar), and females indistinguishable in the field. Male on the other hand resembles Pied Flycatcher but has *more white on wings* incl. *white-tipped median coverts* and often *more white on sides of neck* (semi-collared). Song like Pied's but higher and weaker.

Collared and Semi-collared Flycatchers combined range

Collared Flycatcher *Ficedula albicollis* L 13. Breeds fairly commonly in deciduous wood and gardens in central and SE Europe (also SE Sweden). Male told from male Pied by broad *white neck collar, large white forehead patch,* noticeably more white on wings and *greyish-white rump.* Is never brownish. Many females separable in the field from female Pied under favourable circumstances by greyer upperparts, pale grey nape and more obvious white on folded wing (*pure white also on bases of primaries*; none or only a little buffish-white on inner primaries on female Pied). Song surprisingly unlike Pied's, consists of drawn-out squeaky notes, as if pumped and squeezed out. Alarm persistently repeated, loud 'eehlp' notes. Also gives quiet tongue-clicking call. V

■□□ **Collared Flycatcher** adult male
□■□ **Collared Flycatcher** adult female
□□■ **Semi-collared Flycatcher** male

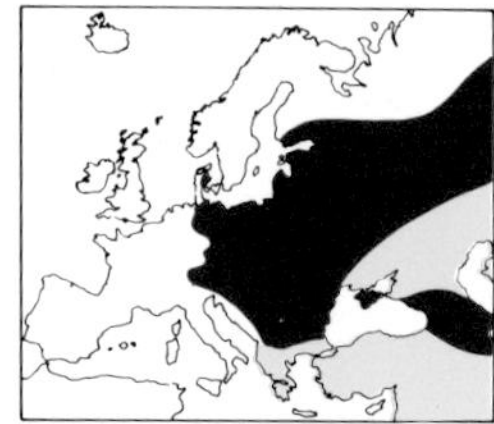

Red-breasted Flycatcher *Ficedula parva* L 11.5. Fairly common but local in luxuriant, shady, often slightly damp parts of wood, deciduous or mixed. In Britain scarce migrant. Nests in tree crevices. Behaves like a Willow Warbler. Cocks tail (characteristic). *White patches on tail base.* Adult male has *rusty-orange throat.* Female nondescript buffish-white on chin/breast. First-year males (both sing and breed) have female-like plumage. Song begins rhythmically like Pied's, ends with characteristic series of descending (not dying away) notes, 'sree . . . sree, sree, seewut seewut seewut seewut wut wut wiu wiu wiu wew'. Call a dry rolling 'serrrt', weaker than Wren. A clear 'TEElu' (alarm, agitation) is often heard, as is a Lesser Whitethroat-like 'tek'. P

■□□ **Red-breasted Flycatcher** male
□■□ **Red-breasted Flycatcher** sub-adult male
□□■ **Red-breasted Flycatcher** 1st-winter

Spotted Flycatcher *Muscicapa striata* L 14. Common in open woods, woodland edges, parks and gardens. Nests in recesses, often in inconventional sites. Perches on look-out on jutting branch, launches out in short sally and snatches some small flying insect. Upright posture when perched, flicks wings. Plumage *plain brownish-grey* with streaking on breast and (diagnostically) *on forehead.* Sexes alike. Call a sharp 'zreet', alarm 'isst-tec'. Song extremely simple, consists of 3 or 4 call-like notes. SP

Brown Flycatcher *Muscicapa latirostris* L 12. Breeds in Asia. Brown-grey above (tertials narrowly edged pale; thin pale wing-bar in fresh plumage), unstreaked brownish-grey forehead, pale below. *Narrow pale ring around eye* and *broad pale lores.* Bill flat, *broad-based and* proportionately *long*; dark, but *base of lower mandible pale yellowish or pinkish.* Sexes alike. Song squeaky like over-excited Robin. Call a thin 'see'.

■□□ **Spotted Flycatcher** adult
□■□ **Spotted Flycatcher** juv.
□□■ **Brown Flycatcher**

Passerines

Wheatears

Wheatears are small, ground-dwelling birds which live in open country. Tail dark with white pattern. Males are more brightly coloured than females. Often perch on stones or tops of bushes. Bob and flick tail. Catch insects, mostly on the ground. Clutches of 4–6 bluish eggs are laid in nests in hollows in the ground or among stones.

European wheatears can be difficult to distinguish, especially the females. The approximate distribution of black and white on the tail (the ratio lengthwise between the black terminal band and total length of tail) is given below together with general characteristics of males and females and also where they occur in Europe in summer.

Species	Male	Female	Ratio of terminal tail-band: tail length (cf. above)	Range
Wheatear *Oe. oenanthe*	Black ear-coverts, grey back	Brown-grey ear-coverts and back	1:2	All Europe
Isabelline Wheatear *Oe. isabellina*	Pale, large, long-billed	Very like male; lores less dark	1:1.5	NE Greece, Bulgaria
Pied Wheatear *Oe. pleschanka*	Black throat and breast, black back	As Black-eared Wheatear	1:4	East coast of Black Sea
Black-eared Wheatear *Oe. hispanica*	Black ear-coverts, black throat in some, greyish-white to rusty-buff back	Dark wings, dirty-brown back	1:4	Mediterranean countries
Desert Wheatear *Oe. deserti*	Black throat, sandy-coloured back	As Black-eared Wheatear	1:1	Vagrant
Black Wheatear *Oe. leucura*	Black	Brownish-black	1:2	Spain, Portugal, S France

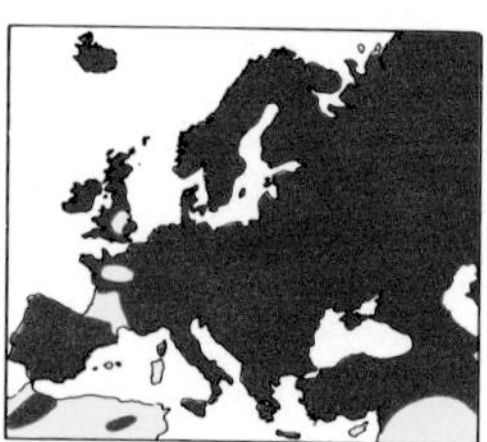

Wheatear *Oenanthe oenanthe* L 14.5. Breeds commonly in open, stony country and prefers areas with sparse vegetation. In all plumages *tail has* characteristic *black and white pattern.* Male is recognised by *ash-grey back and crown,* black eye-stripe together with pure white supercilium in summer plumage. Faint rosy buff tone on underparts fades to white in summer. Female is brownish-grey above and has distinct creamy-white stripe above the eye inclining to buff in front of eye. Juvenile resembles female but has light wavy barring. Greenland race *Oe. oe. leucorhoa* is slightly larger and heavier-billed, browner above and tinged rufous below; passes through Britain, especially W coast, in good numbers in both spring and autumn. Utters a sharp whistle, 'heet', and a hard 'chak'. Sings from stone or in short song flight, frequently at night. Song consists of a short, crackly and rippling phrase at fast tempo, always with whistled 'heet' interwoven. SP

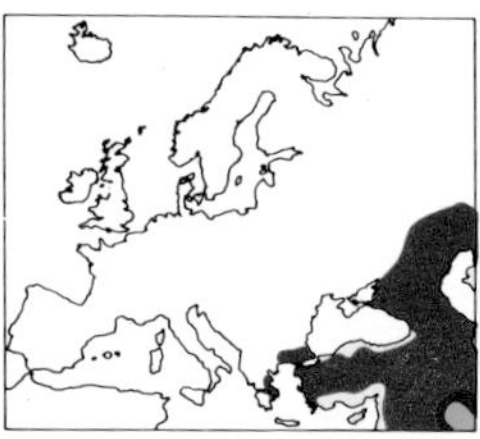

Isabelline Wheatear *Oenanthe isabellina* L 16. Breeds in SE Europe on steppes and in semi-desert. *Large,* uniformly sandy-coloured with *paler wings* than other wheatears (visible especially in flight). In particular, lesser and median *secondary coverts and also primary coverts are pale buff, so that brownish-black alula feather stands out* against these. (Wheatear, which can be confusingly similar in autumn, has dark feather centres in wing-coverts, and alula does not contrast.) Tail as a rule has more black than in Wheatear. Has long bill. Sexes usually alike, males on average slightly more contrasty with black lores. Supercilium whitish, especially in front of eye (cf. Wheatear). Often observed to *stand a little more upright* than is usual for Wheatear. Call a high and metallic pipe, 'cheep'. Song completely different from other wheatears' in its length – can continue for 15 sec. – its 'chattering' character and its mimicry. Series of clear 'wee-wee-wee-wee' often included. V

Wheatear 1st-summer male

Wheatear adult-female

Wheatear juv.

Wheatear autumn (female or non-adult male)

Wheatear autumn (female or non-adult male)

Isabelline Wheatear adult male

Isabelline Wheatear adult male

Passerines

Pied Wheatear *Oenanthe pleschanka* L 14.5. Breeds in SE Europe on stony, arid slopes and erosion gullies. Often perches high above ground (trees, telegraph wires), from where flies down on to ground like a shrike to catch insects. Male has *black back which meets on sides of neck with the large black bib.* Tail pattern roughly as in Wheatear, but the *black terminal band generally narrower* and can be broken up. Female extremely like female Black-eared Wheatear of eastern race, but is more *dull grey-brown* (not so warm buff-brown) *on the back*; also, the majority has a *more obvious dark throat bib* (only rarely so in black-eared), and below the dark throat there is a tawny-coloured pectoral band (more orange-buff in Black-eared). Calls include hard 'tack'. Song very like Black-eared Wheatear's, short twittering phrases, sometimes with interwoven mimicry. V

Black-eared Wheatear *Oenanthe hispanica* L 14.5. Breeds commonly in open, stony or rocky country, including maquis and vineyards, at lower level than Wheatear. Tail pattern as Pied Wheatear's. Male occurs in two colour morphs, one with black throat and one with white throat. Black-throated morph distinguished from Pied Wheatear by *buff,* not black *back,* from male Desert Wheatear by tail pattern. Female distinguished from female Wheatear by ill-defined supercilium, on average *browner,* less grey *back,* often *paler lores,* more of an orange-buff pectoral band, some more white in tail, on a few, grey-mottled throat. Female of eastern race (*melanoleuca*) is grey-brown on the back (not so buff-brown as western race *hispanica*) and close to impossible to distinguish from female Pied Wheatear (which see). Calls include hard 'tack', usually followed by whistling notes. Sings in flight (considerably more often than Wheatear) or from perch. Song like Wheatear's, though individually quite variable, sometimes mostly dry and twittering, at other times quite clear and thrush-like. V

Finsch's Wheatear *Oenanthe finschii* L 15. Breeds in E Turkey, the Caucasus and eastwards. Can be confused with black-throated form of Black-eared Wheatear, but male has more *black on throat – meets black of the wing* (only rarely the case on Black-eared when head hunched down), pale back is more restricted, breast less buff and head appears somewhat larger and feet stronger; wing feathers rather paler below, contrasting markedly with jet-black underwing-coverts. Female is pale grey above with brown tone to cheeks and greater coverts; chin and throat grey-shaded to varying degree, breast lacks brown traces.

Red-tailed Wheatear *Oenanthe xanthoprymna* L 15. Breeds in rocky terrain in Iran and eastwards. Nominate race migrates through Sinai to African winter quarters, recognised by *brown crown and back* and *rusty-red rump, narrow white supercilium* and white base to tail feathers.

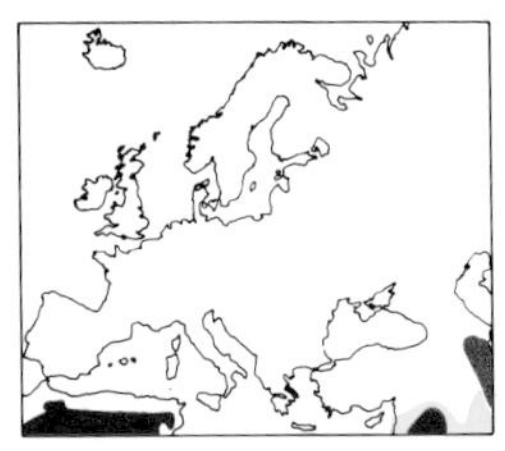

▶ **Desert Wheatear** *Oenanthe deserti* L 15. Very rare visitor in autumn from breeding sites in Africa and Asia. Frequents dry, open country. Resembles black-throated form of Black-eared Wheatear, but only the rump is white – the *tail feathers are almost wholly black.* Furthermore, the *wings are more pale-edged,* not so sooty-black. There are often a few dark feathers on the nape. Female resembles females of Black-eared and Pied Wheatears, but pattern of tail is characteristic. Call a shrill whistle. Song *short* and very *plaintive* in tone, a *descending* trill. V

▶ **Black Wheatear** *Oenanthe leucura* L 18. Breeds in SW Europe in arid, rocky mountains. Always easy to recognise: in all plumages is *uniformly black* (females and juvenile males brownish-black and dull black, respectively) except for the white rump and outer parts of tail. Also *obviously bigger* and heavier than the other wheatears. Utters a 'tshek tshek' and also shrill whistles, 'peee-e' (downwards inflected). Song a varied, short trill, resembling Rock Thrush's. V

■□□ **Pied Wheatear** adult male summer

□■□ **Pied Wheatear** adult female summer

□□■ **Pied Wheatear** 1st-winter male

■□□ **Black-eared Wheatear** adult male summer (black-throated morph) eastern race *melanoleuca*

□■□ **Black-eared Wheatear** adult male winter (white-throated morph) eastern race *melanoleuca*

□□■ **Black-eared Wheatear** adult female summer

Finsch's Wheatear ♂

■□□ **Finsch's Wheatear** female autumn

□■□ **Red-tailed Wheatear** adult male autumn race *xanthoprymna*

□□■ **Desert Wheatear** adult male summer

■□□ **Desert Wheatear** 1st-winter male autumn

□■□ **Desert Wheatear** female

□□■ **Black Wheatear** adult male

Passerines

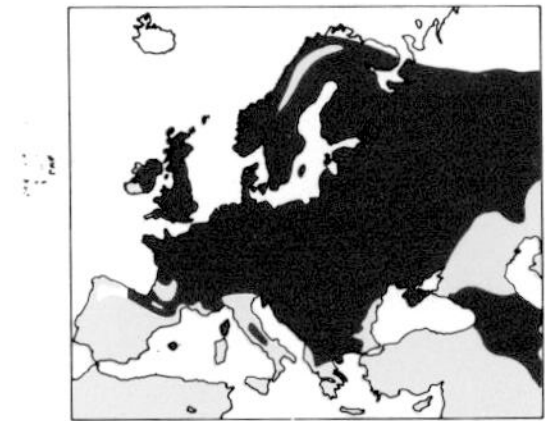

Whinchat *Saxicola rubetra* L 12.5. Breeds fairly commonly on open commons, damp tussocky meadows with scattered bushes, mosses and heaths, in low vegetation along ditches. Male has prominent, *white supercilium*, and the *rusty-orange coloured throat is distinctly white-edged*; cheeks and lores very dark. White marks on wing. Female duller in colour. Distinguished in all plumages from European Stonechats by *white base to outer tail feathers* (noticeable in flight but hardly conspicuous); *upper-tail-coverts always streaked* brown. Perches upright, usually on top of a low bush, thistle or fence wire. Often flicks tail. Alarm call 'yu tek, yu tek-tek'. Song short and fast, beginning and ending abruptly; a few clear notes mixed with occasional creaking sounds. Phrase variable, often contains mimicry; one variant is like Corn Bunting song. Sings mostly at night. SP

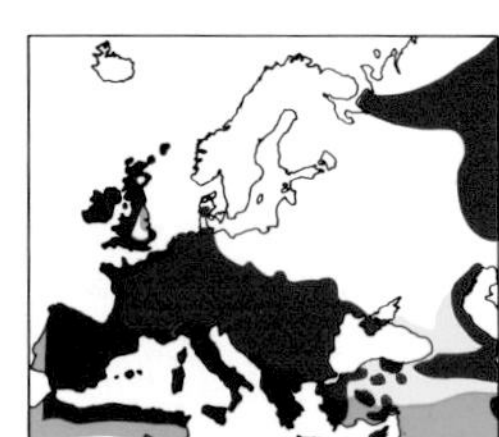

Stonechat *Saxicola torquata* L 12. Breeds in central and S Europe, incl. Britain and Ireland, on heaths and grassy plains with bushes, often gorse. Usually prefers more broken country than Whinchat. Male's *all-black head* including throat is characteristic. Female has duller, brown head. Both sexes have some *white on mid-wing*, male also *white on rump*. *No white on tail* (exception: Stonechats from Caspian region and Iran). Siberian race (*maura*) – rare late autumn vagrant to W Europe – has *unmarked buff-white rump*, is in fresh autumn plumage almost as pale as female Whinchat; pale supercilium, although not so prominent as in Whinchat, and pale sandy throat contrast with darker buff breast; lacks dark moustachial stripe of Whinchat. The Stonechat perches upright, and its head appears big and very round. Alarm 'weest trak trak'. Song short, has features of both Dunnock's (squeaky voice) and Whitethroat's (phrasing). RS

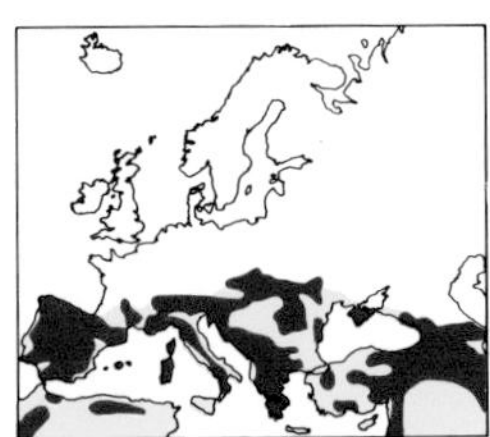

Rock Thrush *Monticola saxatilis* L 19. Breeds in S Europe in rocky and mountainous areas with or without scattered trees, usually at fairly high altitude but sometimes also at lower levels. Migratory, winters in Africa. Male in summer easily recognised by its attractive, variegated plumage. Female brownish with crescentic barring. In winter plumage male is more like female, but is recognised at close range by intimation of blue-grey and white feathers on head and back, respectively. In all plumages short *orange-red tail* is characteristic. Can quiver tail like Redstart. Unobtrusive, often hides among rocks. Call a short 'chak'. Songs from perch or, less often, in song flight (ends with glide), a tuneful, fluting phrase which is very variable. At a distance can recall Blackbird song, but at shorter range is totally different, is faster and more varied and embellished, lacks deep fluted notes. Not such a melancholy ring as Blue Rock Thrush's but otherwise quite like latter's. V

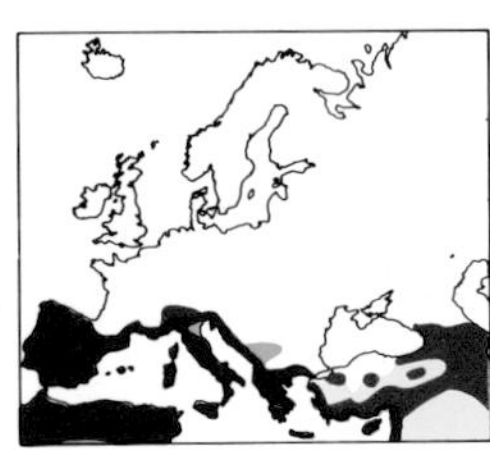

Blue Rock Thrush *Monticola solitarius* L 20.5. Breeds in S Europe, in particular on sheer precipices exposed to the sun and in ruins, usually at lower level than Rock Thrush. Male easily recognised by *blue plumage*. *Bill strikingly long.* In winter the blue becomes slightly more greyish-black. Female has crescentic barring and resembles female Rock Thrush, but has *dark grey-brown*, not rusty-brown *tail*. Readily perches out in the open on a rock but usually seen only at long range, for is very shy and retiring in habits. Like Rock Thrush, disappears quickly among the rocks when disturbed. Call a hard 'tik' and a deeper 'chuk'. Song recalls Rock Thrush's, is loud and clear like latter's but more melancholy, resembles Crested Lark's song with thrush voice. It is given from perch as well as, more rarely, in song flight. V

■□□ **Whinchat** adult male summer
□■□ **Whinchat** female summer
□□■ **Whinchat** autumn (1st-winter or adult female)

Stonechat, Siberian race *maura* ('Eastern'), autumn female

Stonechat male summer
Stonechat female summer
Stonechat 1st-winter female
Stonechat adult male summer, race *maura*
Rock Thrush adult male summer

■□□ **Rock Thrush** adult female summer at nest site
□■□ **Blue Rock Thrush** adult male summer with lizard
□□■ **Blue Rock Thrush** adult female summer at nest

Passerines

Redstart *Phoenicurus phoenicurus* L 14. Breeds fairly commonly in parks and open forest, in suburbs as well as in remote taiga. Nests in tree holes and nestboxes. Male in summer attractive in black, white, ash-grey and rust-red. In September, before departing, the colours are much subdued by pale brown feather edges. Female is brownish apart from tail. In all plumages has *rust-red tail* which is constantly quivering – by this it is readily distinguished from all other W European birds apart from Black Redstart. Female Redstart is similar to female Black Redstart, but is paler below (buffish grey-white) and generally warmer in tone. Agile, often catches insects in flycatcher fashion. Alarm call very similar to Willow Warbler's but usually with ticking notes at end: 'hueet tick-tick'. Song short, with melancholy ring, is heard as early as very first light. The verses start characteristically 'SEEH TRUee-TRUee-TRUee see see seewuh . . . . SP

Güldenstädt's Redstart *Phoenicurus erythrogaster* L 18. Breeding resident in the Caucasus, in winter moves only down to lower altitude. Nest is in rock crevice. Resembles Redstart, but is *considerably bigger,* and male has *black back, greyish yellow-white crown* and *white wing flash.* Female resembles female Redstart apart from size.

Black Redstart *Phoenicurus ochruros* L 15. In Britain breeds locally and uncommonly in old ruins and power stations in towns, in S Europe also very common in mountain districts. Adult male *blackish with rust-red tail* and *white wing panel.* Female similar to female Redstart but a shade darker and drabber, especially below. One-year-old male as female, but often shows some black on throat or white on wing. Alarm 'weet, tick-tick-tick- . . .', dry, treble voice. Sings, mainly at night and dawn, from elevated perch on building; a short, fast and loud phrase with a pause and *an interposed quiet crackling noise,* 'tee tee srrui CHILL-CHILL-CHILL-CHILL . . . (krshkrsh) . . .SREE-wee-wee-wee'. RSWP

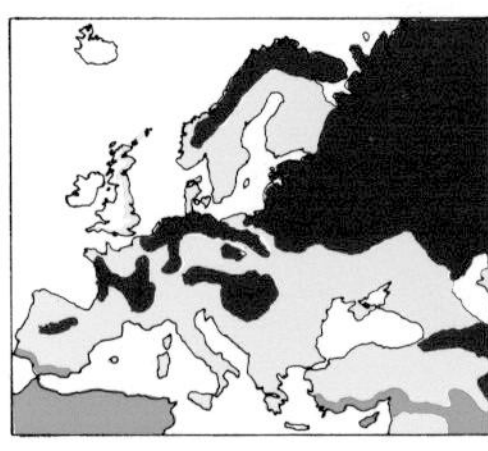

Bluethroat *Luscinia svecica* L 14. Scandinavian race *L. s. svecica* (red-spotted Bluethroat) is common in damp willow thickets and luxuriant subalpine birch forest. Frequently hops on ground. Long legs. Flicks tail. In all plumages has characteristic *rust-red patches at tail base. Prominent supercilium.* Male's *cornflower-blue gorget* has an enamel lustre. Adult female has creamy throat framed by a varying amount of blue and black, often also some rust-red. Juvenile, as in Robin and many other Turdidae, is earth-brown with rusty-yellow spots, moulted to 1st-winter plumage before departing. Song masterful, is composed of mimicry and species-specific bell-like sounds which increase in tempo and intensity (like balalaika). Call 'trak' (like minature Fieldfare). Alarm exactly like Wheatear's, 'heet'. Southern race *L. s. cyanecula* (White-spotted Bluethroat) breeds in reedy swamplands, turns up sporadically farther north (singing at night). In breeding plumage may virtually lack white breast spot. Racial determination impossible in autumn. P

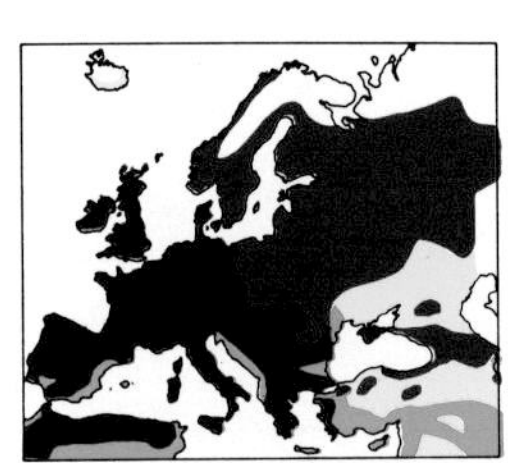

▶ **Robin** *Erithacus rubecula* L 14. Breeds commonly in gardens, woods, parks and hedgerows, in boreal region typical of luxuriant coniferous forests. Fairly unobtrusive habits but not shy. Hops along on ground in long bounds, gazes in upright posture, bobs. Adults characteristically *rusty-orange on whole breast* and also up across forehead. Juveniles brown with dense yellowish-brown spotting and dark scaly pattern, moult to adult plumage by end of summer. Sings from low perch, often in cover, but also from top of trees, bushes etc. Song crystal clear, begins with very high notes, then tumbles into a lightning fast series of wildly rippling notes, checks, goes bounding off again. Autumn and winter song quieter, much more melancholy. Typical call is a series of hard, emphatic clicks, 'tic-ic-ic- . . .', sounding like old grandfather clock being wound up. Also extremely high, thin 'tseeh' (cf. Blackbird and Penduline Tit). Nocturnal migrants from N and E Europe give a thin, weak, slightly harsh 'tsEE-e'. RSWP

■□ **Redstart** adult male summer
□■ **Redstart** adult female summer

■□□ **Black Redstart** adult male summer
□■□ **Black Redstart** adult female or imm. male
□□■ **Güldenstädt's Redstart** adult male

■□□ **Bluethroat** adult male summer, race *svecica*
□■□ **Bluethroat** adult female
□□■ **Bluethroat** 1st-winter female

■□□ **Bluethroat** adult male summer, race *cyanecula*
□■□ **Robin** adult
□□■ **Robin** juv.

Passerines

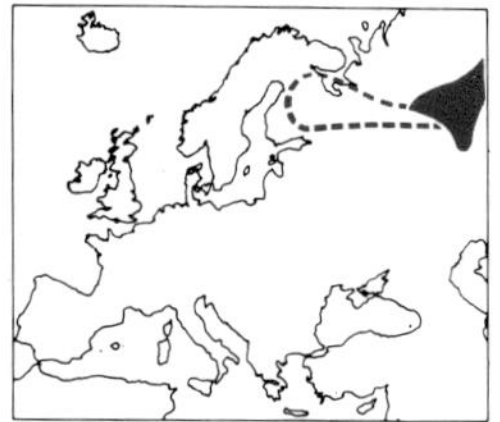

Red-flanked Bluetail *Tarsiger cyanurus* L 14. Breeds in NE Europe in luxuriant coniferous forests, often in broken ground. Has clear blue (adult male) or grey-blue uppertail-coverts and sides of tail feathers and also in all plumages *orange tone on flanks*. Females, juveniles and first-year males (the latter hold territories) are plain like female flycatchers, especially as blue of tail is difficult to see in the field – the tail simply looks dark. *Throat strikingly white, framed with grey.* Upperparts are olive-brown. Adult male's upperparts are dark grey-blue with clear cobalt-blue carpal areas. Most resembles Redstart in habits, but is often seen on the ground and does not quiver tail but jerks it. Shy, as a rule keeps well hidden, but most often sings from top of a spruce, often high up on steep slopes. Song is a loud, clear twitter, most closely resembling Redstart's in its thin, melancholy tone, with four or five syllables, sometimes ending in a trill. When agitated, a short 'weet', and also a hard 'trak'. V

■□ Red-flanked Bluetail adult male

□■ Red-flanked Bluetail adult female or 1st-year male

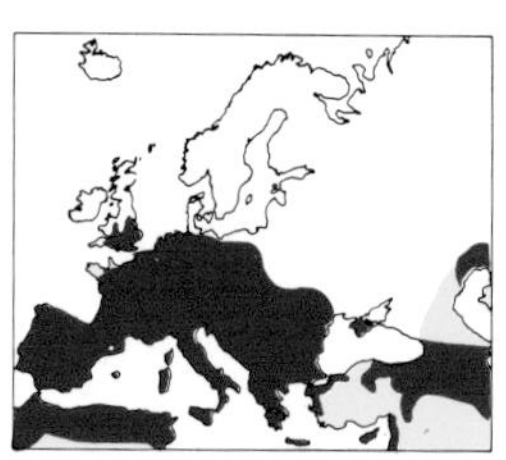

Nightingale *Luscinia megarhynchos* L 16.5. Breeds in thickets, in damp undergrowth in woodland and parks. Rather big and long-tailed. Uniform brown with *reddish-brown tail* in all plumages. Juvenile is spotted all over the body as juvenile Robin. Almost impossible to distinguish in the field from Thrush Nightingale, but has warmer brown (not grey-toned) back, redder tail and also *lacks obvious mottling on breast*. Wary, keeps well concealed in bushes. More often heard than seen. Alarm call is a shrill, drawn-out whistle with a faint tendency towards upward inflection, '(u)EEhp'. Sings from dense thickets, often at night but also by day, a loud, beautifully warbling song. In comparison with Thrush Nightingale's it is more languorous and weak, not quite so powerful; contains *typical crescendo* of soft whistled notes, 'lu lu lü lü lee leee'. The song phrases are in addition shorter, and the Thrush Nightingale's harsher, more rattling series of notes, 'zr-zr-zr-zr-. . .' and the like, are missing. S

■□ Nightingale

□■ Thrush Nightingale

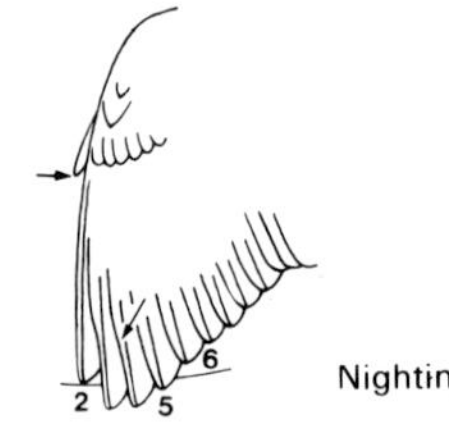

Nightingale

Thrush Nightingale *Luscinia luscinia* L 16.5. Breeds fairly commonly in E Europe and the Baltic areas in leafy groves and along lakeshores in large shady copses. Very like Nightingale, but can sometimes be separated by greyer back and less vivid red tail together with *diffuse grey spotting on breast*. Juvenile looks like juvenile Nightingale (see above). Sings from concealed songpost almost throughout the day, but mostly at night. Song resembles Nightingale's in structure with series of rapidly repeated notes, but is much *more powerful and less melodic*, contains more rattling themes and characteristic very far-carrying, fast series of deep 'chok' notes. Alarm is hard, shrill, drawn-out 'eehp' notes, persistently repeated (rather like call of Collared Flycatcher). Another call is a hard rolling 'errrr'. V

Thrush Nightingale

■□□ White-throated Robin female

□■□ White-throated Robin female

□□■ White-throated Robin adult male

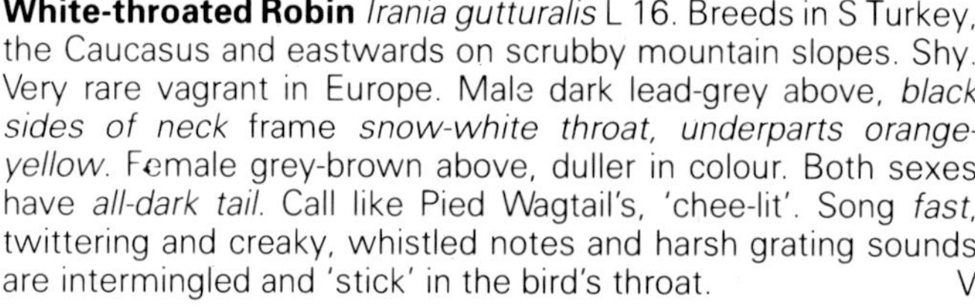

White-throated Robin *Irania gutturalis* L 16. Breeds in S Turkey, the Caucasus and eastwards on scrubby mountain slopes. Shy. Very rare vagrant in Europe. Male dark lead-grey above, *black sides of neck* frame *snow-white throat, underparts orange-yellow*. Female grey-brown above, duller in colour. Both sexes have *all-dark tail*. Call like Pied Wagtail's, 'chee-lit'. Song *fast*, twittering and creaky, whistled notes and harsh grating sounds are intermingled and 'stick' in the bird's throat. V

White-throated Robin, ♂

Siberian Rubythroat *Luscinia calliope* L 15. Breeds in coniferous forest with rich undergrowth, in thickly wooded parks and similar places. Very rare vagrant in W Europe. Male easily recognised by *ruby-red throat, white supercilium, white moustachial stripe* and *all-dark tail*. Female distinguished from female and juvenile Bluethroat by all-dark tail and lack of black breast band. Occasional females have a little rosy-pink on throat. Resembles Thrush Nightingale in behaviour (shy, skulking). Song powerful and melodic, *calm* and 'chatty', contains both clear and hard notes and superb mimicry. Calls: loud whistling 'EE-lu' and 'chak' (miniature Fieldfare). V

■□ Siberian Rubythroat adult male

□■ Siberian Rubythroat 1st-winter female

Passerines

Thrushes

Thrushes form a fairly homogeneous group within the family Turdidae. The group consists of three genera: *Turdus*, the largest genus and to which all native European species belong; *Zoothera*, to which two Asiatic accidental visitors belong; and also *Catharus*, in which four vagrants from N America are classed.

The thrushes are medium-sized birds with fairly slender though not weak bills, and rather long to medium-length tails. All are spotted in juvenile plumage, several species also when older. Seen mostly on the ground. Feed on worms, insects and berries. Mainly nocturnal migrants. Gregarious outside the breeding season. Build open cup-shaped nests in trees or bushes. Clutches of 3–6 eggs.

Grey-cheeked Thrush *Catharus minimus* L 19. A very rare autumn vagrant from N America. Similar to Swainson's Thrush. Small, brownish-grey above, greyish-white below with heavily spotted breast. *Ear-coverts have mixed shades of grey. Lacks clear pale eye-ring.* Broad white wingbar below. Call a shrill whistling, drawn-out 'keeep', slightly descending. V

Swainson's Thrush *Catharus ustulatus* L 18. A very rare autumn vagrant from N America. Similar to Grey-cheeked Thrush. Small, grey-brown above with warm olive-brown tinge, dirty-white below with heavily spotted breast on yellowish-buff ground. *Ear-coverts finely patterned in grey and yellowish-buff.* Usually has *distinct buffish-white eye-ring and supercilium* from the eye forward to side of forehead. Broad white wingbar below. Call a soft, slightly rising 'weeyt', also a high 'peee' on nocturnal migration. V

Hermit Thrush *Catharus guttatus* L 17.5. A very rare vagrant from N America. Similar to Swainson's Thrush but has distinctly *rusty-brown tail and uppertail-coverts. Breast* is even *more heavily spotted* than in Grey-cheeked and Swainson's Thrushes, and wing is more rounded. Broad white wingbar below. The tail is raised jerkily and lowered slowly when bird is perched. Call a tongue-clicking 'chak', also a mewing sound. V

Veery *Catharus fuscescens* L 19. A very rare autumn vagrant from N America. Similar to Swainson's Thrush but has *whole of upperparts distinctly rusty in tone* (not just the tail as in Hermit Thrush) and also *lacks clear white eye-ring* and has *only diffuse spotting on breast.* Broad white wingbar below. May raise and lower tail. Call an easily imitated whistle, 'wheew' (downward inflected). V

Eye-browed Thrush *Turdus obscurus* L 19. A very rare autumn vagrant from Asia. Male is *grey on head, neck and breast* with distinct *white supercilium*, olive-brown back and rusty *yellow-brown flanks.* Female and younger males are browner and have *white, spotted throat.* Call a thin, drawn-out 'zeee'. V

Dusky Thrush *Turdus naumanni eunomus* L 24. A rare autumn vagrant from Asia. Despite quite different appearances, Dusky Thrush and Naumann's Thrush (below) are regarded as subspecies of the same species. Dark and with variegated markings with distinct *white supercilium, dark breast-band, rusty-brown wing panel* (also on underwing) and dark rusty-brown, spotted rump. Breast and flanks heavily spotted. Sexes alike. Calls resemble Fieldfare's: shrill 'geeh', often repeated twice, and 'chak-chak'. V

Naumann's Thrush *Turdus naumanni naumanni* L 24. A rare autumn vagrant from Asia. Male is grey-brown above, has buff supercilium; *breast and tail reddish-brown.* Female is browner with more spotted breast.

■□ Grey-cheeked Thrush

□■ Eye-browed Thrush adult female

■□ Veery 1st-winter

□■ Swainson's Thrush adult autumn

Hermit Thrush

■□ Naumann's Thrush race *naumanni*

□■ Dusky Thrush adult at nest race *eunomus*

Passerines

Ring Ouzel *Turdus torquatus* L 24. In Britain breeds fairly commonly on hilly moorland with rocky outcrops and scrubby areas, on the Continent in alpine spruce forest. *White, crescent-shaped breast band* distinguishes adult. Male not so jet-black as Blackbird, and in particular *the wings are paler.* Female is browner in tone, and the whitish crescent has brown wavy barring (but occasional individuals are confusingly like male). Juvenile is less uniform than juvenile Blackbird, e.g. has whitish-buff throat and distinctly spotted breast; is moulted by end of summer. Some 1st-winter birds confusingly all-dark, though still showing tendency to pale wings. Shy and wary. On migration associates with other thrushes. Utters a hard tongue-clicking, 'tek-tek-tek-tek' but also soft, shrill, more Fieldfare-like chatter. Song has dialectal variants but is always simple and melancholy, e.g. 'treenk-treenk-treenk' or 'teeLIU-teeLIU-teeLIU', followed by a quiet twitter; resembles certain dialects of Redwing song, but pace is calm as Song Thrush's. SP

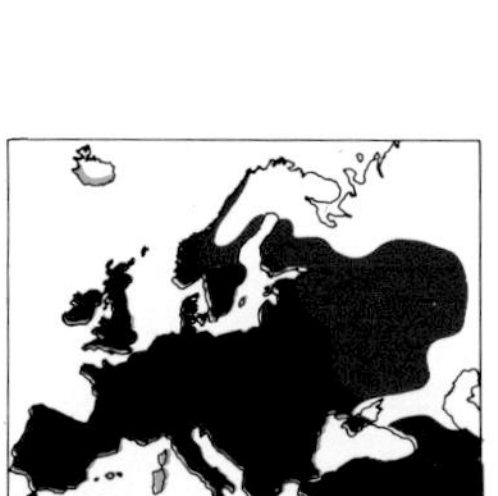

Blackbird *Turdus merula* L 24. Breeds commonly in gardens, parks and woods (incl. deep forests). Male easily recognised by *jet-black plumage* and bright *yellow bill.* Female is recognised by almost uniformly brown plumage. Juvenile has paler and warmer colours and has pale, narrow flecks above. Feeds right out in the open on the ground. Distinguished from Starling by lack of pale spots in the plumage, by *long tail* and two-legged hops or nimble steps succeeded by dead still gaze (not waddling restless gait). Calls include: a startled series of tongue-clicking 'chak-ak-ak-ak' notes which may be heightened to an intense, shrill 'pli-pli-pli-pli-. . .' (before going to roost and confronted by, e.g. Tawny Owl); an enticing, slowly repeated 'kok'; an extremely thin, high, 'tseeh' (similar to Robin); a slightly rolling, ringing 'srree' (also heard from night migrants). Sings from well-visible songpost, mostly at dusk and dawn. The song is very tuneful and pleasing, consists of clear fluting, slowly sliding, alternating high and low notes, almost always followed by a quieter, short twitter. RSWP

▶ **Black-throated Thrush** *Turdus ruficollis* L 23. Breeds in easternmost Europe and in Asia in clearings and at edges of coniferous forests; in winter seen in more open country. Rare visitor to W Europe, mainly during late autumn and winter. Two races, males of which easily distinguishable: *T. r. ruficollis* (Red-throated Thrush), with Asiatic distribution, in which male has *reddish-brown throat and breast* and *rusty-brown toned tail,* and also *T. r. atrogularis* (Black-throated Thrush), with distribution in easternmost Europe and W Siberia, in which male has *black throat and breast* together with *brownish-black tail.* Female and juvenile brownish-grey with densely spotted breast. Both races (even male Black-throated) have rusty-red undersides to wings. Only the Black-throated race has been found (a few times) in Britain, and mostly males – presumably females are easily overlooked. Resembles Fieldfare in behaviour. Song similar to Song Thrush's. V

Siberian Thrush *Zoothera sibirica* L 23. Rare autumn visitor to Europe from Asia. Male *very dark with white supercilium,* female looks like a scaly Song Thrush with prominent supercilium. Both sexes have conspicuous *black and white bands on underwing* like White's Thrush and white spots on tail. Juvenile resembles female but is more heavily spotted. Shy and retiring in behaviour. Call 'zit', like Song Thrush's. V

American Robin *Turdus migratorius* L 25. Rare visitor during autumn and winter to W Europe from N America. Easily recognised by *rust-red breast, dark grey upperparts* and *distinct white eye-ring.* Juvenile has spotted, not bright reddish-brown breast. Behaviour and calls resemble Blackbird's. (In spite of the name, it is not related to the Robin.) V

■□□ **Ring Ouzel** adult male
□■□ **Ring Ouzel** adult female
□□■ **Ring Ouzel** female at nest with young

■□ **Blackbird** adult male
□■ **Blackbird** adult female

■□□ **Blackbird** juv.
□■□ **Black-throated Thrush** adult male race *atrogularis* in autumn showing underside of wing
□□■ **Black-throated Thrush** 1st-winter

Siberian Thrush, ♂

■□ **Black-throated Thrush** male race *ruficollis*
□■ **American Robin** adult

Passerines

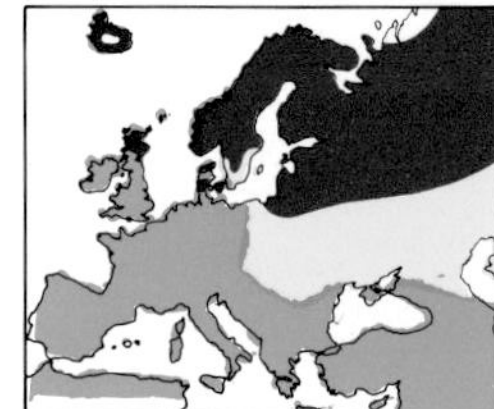

Redwing *Turdus iliacus* L 20. Breeds commonly in open mountain birch forest in far north, less commonly at lower levels (incl. in small numbers in Scotland). In winter in fields, often loose flocks mixed with other thrushes, and in open woods. *Prominent supercilium,* streaked underparts and *rusty-red flanks together with underwings.* Call 'gak', alarm a persistent 'trett-trett-trett- . . .'; on migration (often at night) an inhaled, thin, slightly harsh 'steeef', often heard on October nights, not least over towns and cities. The song has many local variations. Consists of a short series of melancholy notes, usually on descending scale, followed by a low, squeaking chatter. Common variants are 'tree triu tru tro', 'CHIRRe-CHURRe-CHUHee', very fast 'til-lil-lil-lil-lil', 'teeDJI-tee-DIUe' and more simple 'truee-trae'. A buzzing chorus is heard from flocks resting on spring migration. RW

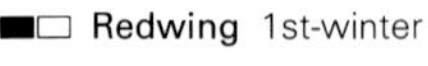

Redwing 1st-winter
Redwing juv.

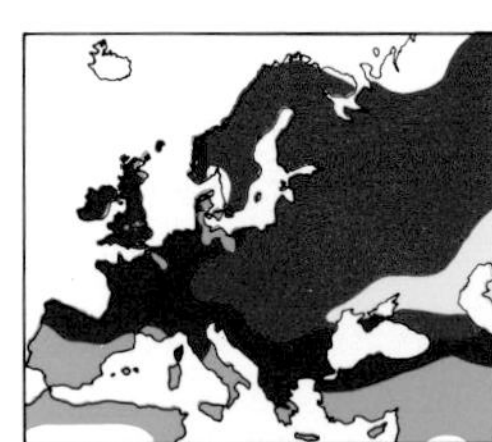

Song Thrush *Turdus philomelos* L 22. Breeds commonly in woodland, parks, gardens, hedges and in rough terrain with good cover, also in deep forest in Fenno-Scandia. Less gregarious than Redwing. *Even-brown upperparts,* spotted underparts together with *pale yellowish-brown underwing* distinguish it from all other thrushes. Call a short, sharp, 'zit'. Alarm a persistent, sharp 'xell-xellxell . . .'. Powerful song, with fluted notes alternating with shrill, sharp notes. Many elements are repeated two to four times at calm tempo, which is very typical, e.g. 'kukleeWEE kukleeWEE kukleeWEE . . . kru-kru-kru . . . kwee-kwee . . . peeoo peeoo peeoo . . . chuwu-ee chuwu-ee . . .' and so on. Often mimics. RSWP

Song Thrush adult

Mistle Thrush adult at nest with chicks

Song Thrush juv. at pool

Mistle Thrush *Turdus viscivorus* L 28. Breeds fairly commonly in woods, parks, scattered conifers. Shy and wary. In winter often on fields, usually in small numbers, associates with other thrushes. *Big,* heavily spotted below with *white underwings* and uniformly *grey-brown upperparts* together with *white tips to outer tail feathers.* Stands more upright on ground than other thrushes. Call a characteristic *dry and churring* 'zerrrrr'. Song similar to Blackbird's but has more desolate ring, the phrases are shorter and delivered at faster tempo and with shorter pauses than in Blackbird; also lacks latter's slow and considerable shifts in pitch as well as the final twittering notes. Song may run, e.g. 'truEEtrüwu . . . chuREEchuRU . . . chüWÜtru . . . churuwüTRÜ' and so on. Does not join in the general thrush chorus at dawn and dusk, prefers to sing on sunny mornings and afternoons, and then dominates the neighbourhood. Alarm a hard rattle, like Fieldfare's corresponding call but drier. RW

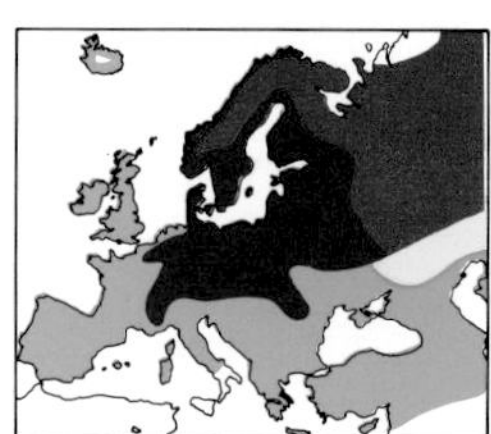

Fieldfare *Turdus pilaris* L 25. Rare and local breeder in Britain but common in N and E Europe, in parks and most types of forests bordering open ground. Typical of subalpine birch forest. Nests solitarily or in colonies in treetops (Merlin often nests in Fieldfare colonies in far north). Hardier than other thrushes. Common winter bird in Britain; large flocks haunt fields and plunder rowan trees. Better flier than most other thrushes, migrates by day in large loose flocks. Flight slightly undulating. Big. *Head and rump grey, long tail dark* and *back chestnut-brown. Spotted yellowish-brown breast,* pale belly. *White underwings.* Call a loud frothy 'shak-shak' and a thin, slightly nasal and strained 'geeh'. Song an unmusical squeaky chatter, delivered without pauses for breath as bird flies among the trees. Gives hard rattle when dive-bombing crows. WP

White's Thrush *Zoothera dauma* L 28. Breeds in easternmost Europe in woods with rich undergrowth. Rare winter visitor to W Europe. Very shy and wary, takes cover in vegetation at slightest danger. Therefore rarely seen flying in the open. May also fly into treetop and 'freeze', when plumage pattern makes it very difficult to detect. *Big* and entirely *covered with* striking *black, crescent-shaped marks* on yellowish ground. Heavy *black and white bands on underwing.* Flight undulating. V

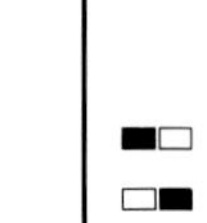

White's Thrush
Fieldfare

Passerines

Tits (family Paridae) are small, short-billed and agile birds. Often quite fearless. The sexes are alike, and the juveniles rather like the adults. Normally sedentary, but several species move south or west in some years. Outside breeding season often seen in mixed flocks, known as roving tit flocks, which may also contain Nuthatches, Treecreepers and Goldcrests. They often find their way to birdtables, particularly in winter. Most species are hole nesters and readily use nestboxes. The clutches vary between 5 and 16 eggs. Eggs are white with red speckles.

Marsh Tit *Parus palustris* L 12. Breeds commonly in deciduous and mixed woods and seems particularly fond of dense leafy thickets and neglected gardens. Nests in natural hole in tree or nestbox. Tends not to accompany roving flocks; very sedentary; most often seen in pairs. Zealous hoarder of seeds, often seen low down in the undergrowth. Resembles Willow Tit, but black crown is glossy and *wings uniformly coloured without white panel.* Cheeks not pure white. Juvenile cannot be safely distinguished from juvenile Willow Tit by appearance. Best distinguished from Willow Tit by calls. Typical are a short, explosive 'piCHAY' and a clear and full 'cheeü', and also a hoarse, slightly Blue-Tit-like, excited series, 'ziche dededededede'. The song has several patterns but is always a rapid series of full and loud notes. Common variants are 'chiup-chiup-chiup- . . .' (recalling Greenfinch) and 'TEEta-TEEta-TEEta- . . .' ('saw-sharpening', like Coal and Great Tits). R

Willow Tit *Parus montanus* L 12. Breeds commonly in coniferous and mixed forest, also mountainous areas and subalpine birch forest, in Britain also in damp birch and alder woods without conifers. Usually excavates own nest hole in rotten tree stumps. In winter joins roving tit flocks. Distinguished most easily from Marsh Tit by calls (see below), and by *whitish panel along wing* formed by pale edges to secondaries, also by matt-black crown. British race *P. m. kleinschmidti* has buffish flanks, especially noticeable outside breeding season. Fenno-Scandian and N Russian race *P. m. borealis* is larger, paler, with pure white cheeks. Juveniles cannot be reliably distinguished from juvenile Marsh by appearance. Willow Tit's most characteristic call is 'tee-tee CHAY CHAY', the two final sounds strongly stressed, drawn-out and harsh. The song is a series of pensive and well-articulated 'tiU tiU tiU. . .' (recalling Wood Warbler), less commonly a straight 'teeh teeh teeh . . .' (the same individual may alternate between the two). Sometimes an odd, short phrase, rapid, cheerful and chuckling. R

► **Sombre Tit** *Parus lugubris* L 13.5. Breeds in SE Europe in deciduous wood (often oak), also in mountainous areas. Big, has heavy bill, gives Great Tit-like impression. Plumage appears shabby. *Large bib* and *large cap* are *dull brownish-black* (browner in female). Not gregarious, and more shy than other tits. One call is like Long-tailed Tit's, 'zreeh-zreeh-zreeh' with sharp, grating tone; another a very House Sparrow-like chattering series, 'cher-r-r-r-r'. The song recalls Marsh Tit song, but the voice is gruffer and more grating, the tempo slower: 'cheeEW-cheeEW-cheeEW- . . .'.

► **Siberian Tit** *Parus cinctus* L 13. Breeds sparsely in the northernmost coniferous forests, reaches right up to the subalpine birch forest. Recognised by *rusty-yellow flanks* (less obvious in summer), dull brown cap and *large black bib.* Plumage more 'bushy' than in other tits (save Azure Tit). Commonest call a fast 'tee-tee TAYee TAYee', in which the hoarse final syllables are not so straight and drawn-out as in corresponding call of Willow Tit. The song is a thin and fast purring 'chee-ÜRRR chee-ÜRRR chee-ÜRRR chee-ÜRRR chee-ÜRRR'. Besides this, a Marsh Tit-like 'che che che che che . . .' and a cheerful, short, chuckling phrase 'see see diTWUY' occur.

■ Marsh Tit

■□ Willow Tit race *borealis*

□■ Willow Tit adult, race *kleinschmidti*, at nest hole

■□□ Siberian Tit

□■□ Siberian Tit

□□■ Sombre Tit adult at nest site

Passerines

Crested Tit *Parus cristatus* L 12. Breeds in coniferous forest, mainly pine, in Britain confined to Caledonian forest of Scotland. Extremely sedentary. Nests in hole in decayed trunk, capable of excavating own nest hole. Easily recognised by well-visible *crest. Black and white head markings*, in all plumages ages and sexes alike. Sometimes associates with Coal Tit, but spends more of its time near the ground. Call a characteristic purring or 'bubbling' trill, 'burrurrlT' (somewhat recalling Snow Bunting call), and a thin 'SEEH-lili'. Song: 'SEEH-burrurrlT-SEEH-burrurrlT- . . . ', at a fast rate. R

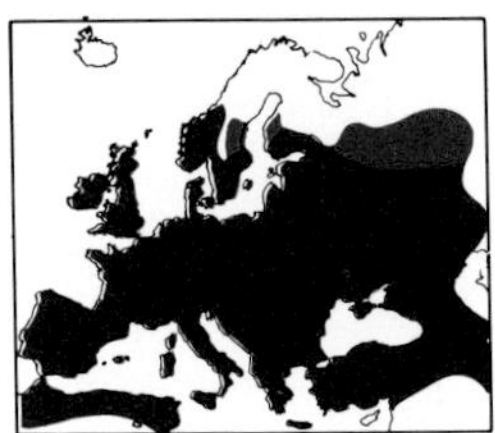

Blue Tit *Parus caeruleus* L 12. Breeds commonly in deciduous wood (also mixed wood), parks and gardens. Outside breeding season often visits reedbeds. *Yellow underparts* as in Great Tit but has *bright blue cap* enclosed with white and is also distinctly *smaller*. Wings and tail blue. Juveniles in summer have yellow cheeks and greyish-green cap. Searches branches and trunks in typically clambering fashion, seldom seen on ground. Behaviour in winter at birdtable self-assured, often drives away the large Great Tit. Has many calls, but most often heard is a clear 'seeseedu' and a quarrelsome churr 'cherrrrrr-errr-errr-ett'. The song consists of two thin, drawn-out notes followed by a crystal-clear trill, 'zeeh zeeh sirrrrr'. A song variant with two short phrases in rapid succession, 'zizi-serr zizi-serr', is sometimes heard. RW

Azure Tit *Parus cyanus* L 13. Breeds in E Europe in deciduous and mixed wood, especially around lakes and rivers. Very rare visitor to central and W Europe. In winter often frequents reedbeds. Conspicuously white, plumage 'fluffy'. Tail rather long. Distinguished from atypically pale Blue Tits by *all-white throat, white on tail* and by the two *broad white wingbars* which are particularly prominent in flight. Calls 'tsirr' and 'tsee-tsee-dze-dze'.

Coal Tit *Parus ater* L 11. Basically a bird of coniferous forest, but in Britain also fairly common in gardens and in deciduous wood. Mass eruptions in N Europe when spruce crop fails. Outside breeding season associates with other tits. Black head with white cheeks and *white nape patch* together with faint buff tone on underparts are characteristic. Rather short-tailed. Common calls are thin, clear, very melancholy 'TEEH-e, tü'. Also less characteristic, Goldcrest-thin squeaks. The song is a fast and nimble 'sipiTEE-sipiTEE-sipiTEE- . . . ' (totally characteristic) or a 'saw-sharpening' 'sitchoo-sitchoo-sitchoo- . . . ' (like variants of Great Tit song, although faster and more feeble, and also resembles Marsh Tit song). RW

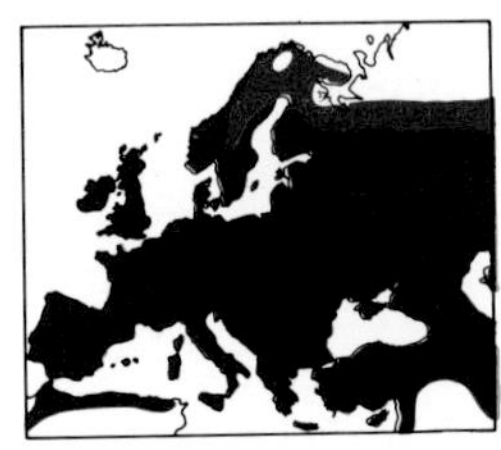

Great Tit *Parus major* L 14. Breeds commonly in all kinds of wood, in parks and gardens. In some autumns sets off southwards from northern areas, when many may reach Britain (especially east coasts). Size, *glossy black crown*, white cheeks and *black band down centre of yellow underparts* make it easy to identify. Band wider and blacker in male than in female, particularly obvious on the belly (see fig.). Young in summer have yellowish cheeks without black lower border. Often seen in mixed flocks with other tits, size then separates out the Great Tit at first glance. Often feeds in low bushes and also on ground. Calls innumerable and usually more powerful than other tits', e.g. rather Chaffinch-like 'ping-ping', a slightly 'wondering' and melancholy 'tee tü tüh' (autumn call) and also confident and rapid 'see-YUtti-YUtti'. Song very characteristic, a penetrating 'saw-sharpening' series, e.g. 'TEE-ta TEE-ta TEE-ta . . .' or trisyllabic 'tee-tee-TÜ tee-tee-TÜ tee-tee-TÜ . . .', the last variant like Mozart's (from The Marriage of Figaro) 'Say goodbye butterfly to merriment' without the final note. RW

■□□ Crested Tit
□■ Blue Tit adult
□■ Blue Tit juv.

■□□ Coal Tit
□■□ Coal Tit
□□■ Azure Tit

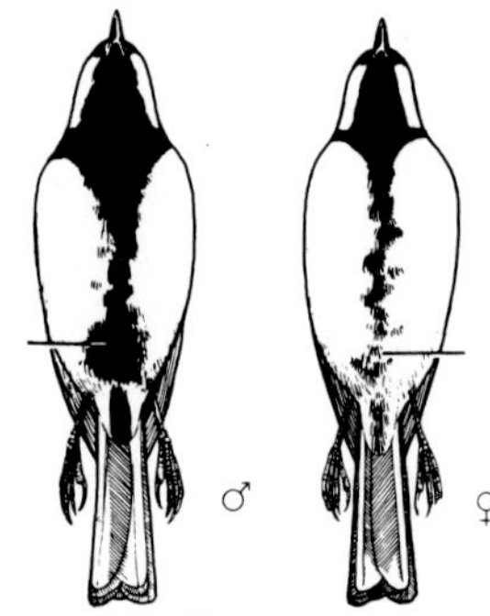

Great Tit

■□□ Great Tit adult male
□■□ Great Tit juv.
□□■ Great Tit in flight

Passerines

Long-tailed Tit

Long-tailed Tit (family Aegithalidae) is closely related to the true tits. Apart from long tail is distinguished by the architecture of its nest. Clutches of 8–12 red-spotted white eggs.

Long-tailed Tit *Aegithalos caudatus* L 16. Breeds fairly commonly in deciduous and mixed wood, often with hazel or thick bushes. Nest skilfully built, with dome covered with lichens and sited in bushes or tree forks. In winter may be seen in company with other tits but always keeps together in small flocks, even within a roving tit flock. *Very long tail* (in most of range) characteristic. British and Irish race *A. c. rosaceus* has *white head with broad black stripe above eye,* strong pinkish-buff tone on scapulars, rump and vent, and whitish wing panels. Juvenile has dark cheeks, little pink and shorter tail. Adults of northern/eastern race *A. c. caudatus* have all-white head, whiter wings, look much whiter. Intermediate forms occur in N central Europe. Spanish Long-tailed Tits are very swarthy, have stripy sides of head, wine-red tone on flanks and almost all-black back; tail is comparatively short. Resembles other tits in habits, but rarely comes to bird-tables. Calls are a dry churring 'tserr' (recalling Wren), clicking 'tett' and also a high 3-syllable 'sreeh-sreeh-sreeh'. The song is a thin metallic trill on the same note, 'seeh wiwiwiwiwiwi', recalling Blue Tit's song. R

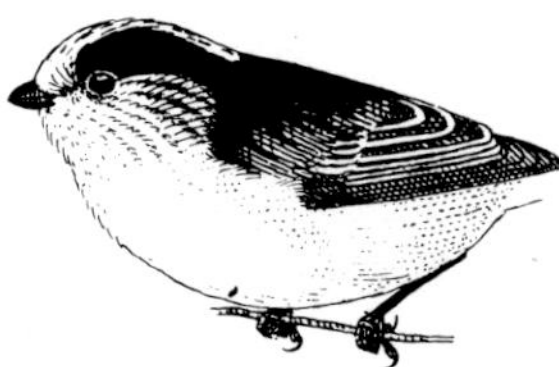

Long-tailed Tit, Spain

Long-tailed Tit adult at nest, continental/British race

Long-tailed Tit adult, race *caudatus*

Long-tailed Tit adult, continental/British race

Bearded Tit

Bearded Tit (family Timaliidae) resembles the tits in most respects, but is nevertheless placed by the taxonomists in the babbler and laughing thrush etc family. Clutches of 5–7 eggs are laid in open nests low down in reeds.

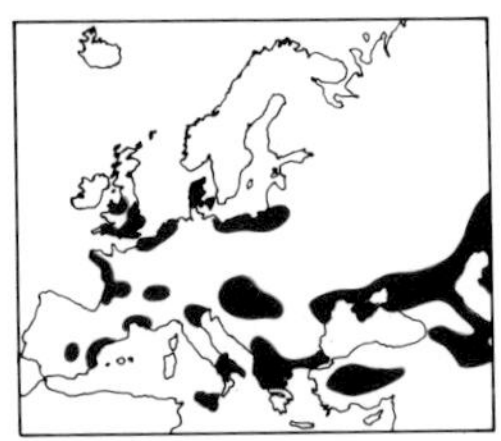

Bearded Tit *Panurus biarmicus* L 16.5 Scattered distribution in central and S Europe in larger reedbeds. Increasing and spreading in NW Europe. In summer feeds on insects, in winter on reed seeds. Easily recognised by *buff and cinnamon-brown colours* and *very long tail.* Male has distinct *black drooping moustache* and black undertail-coverts, which are absent in female and juvenile. Juvenile told from female by black lores (lacking in female), middle of back and sides of tail. Very active, clambers around in reeds with hopping movements, often at lowermost levels. Flight weak with very rapid wingbeats, usually low over reeds. In autumn, however, seen working its way high up into the sky in dense flocks, usually only to dive headlong back (still in closed formation) but sometimes to migrate. Outside breeding season seen almost exclusively in flocks. Main call a twanging, lively 'pching' (may also be written 'pchew'), very characteristic (but can be imitated expertly by Reed Warbler!). Song twittering. RW

Penduline Tit

Penduline Tit (family Remizidae) is a small bird resembling a tit, with a thin, pointed bill. Sexes similar. Nests in finely woven, domed nest with entrance provided by tunnel, suspended from thin branches and often built over water. Clutch of 6–8 eggs.

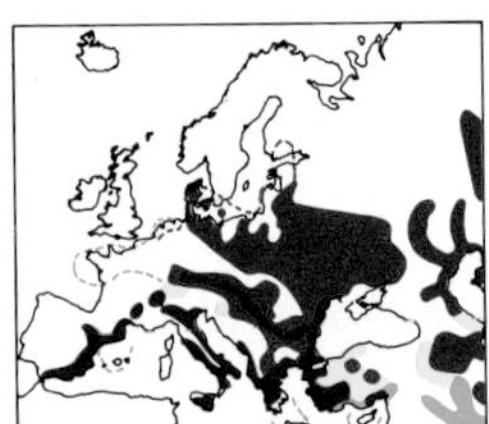

Penduline Tit *Remiz pendulinus* L 11. Breeds mainly in S and E Europe. Locally common in shoreline thickets and shrubbery in or near reeds. Currently expanding northwestwards (several recent British records). Builds a curious pouch-shaped nest suspended from the very end of a twig of a tree, close to water. A quite small bird, smaller than Blue Tit. *Black band on 'face'* distinguishes adult. Juvenile lacks the black band, has evenly sandy head. Behaviour much like that of tits. Call a very thin, drawn-out 'zeeeeu', as fine as Red-throated Pipit's call but dropping slightly at the end like Robin's thin peep. (If Robin can be said to sound sharply 'alert', Penduline Tit sounds if anything 'good-natured' and 'dreamy'.) Song quiet and heard only for brief moments, rather Coal Tit-like, 'zeeu-seewut zeeu-seewut zeeu-seewut' and other variants. V

Bearded Tit adult male

Bearded Tit juv. male

Penduline Tit adult female at nest

Penduline Tit adult male in song

Passerines

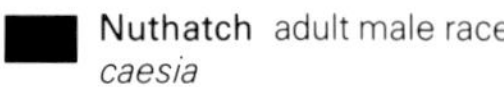
Nuthatch adult male race *caesia*

Nuthatches

Nuthatches (family Sittidae) have strong feet, large heads, short tails. Climb trees or cliffs. Pick insects out of crevices with the long, straight bill. Very agile and even move downwards head first, which treecreepers and woodpeckers cannot do. This feat is accomplished by one foot being held higher up on the trunk so that the bird is almost suspended from this foot. Outside breeding season often associate with the tits. Calls loud and characteristic. Flight jerky and undulating. Sexes similar. Hole nesters. Clutches of 5–7 white eggs with red spots.

Nuthatch *Sitta europaea* L 14. Breeds fairly commonly in older deciduous wood, in parks and gardens. Regular visitor at bird-tables during winter months. Nests in hollow trees and often reduces size of entrance hole by plastering it with mud. Has a profile all of its own, with long, pointed bill, short tail and crouched posture. *Climbs head first down trunks. Back blue-grey, long black streak through eye.* Colour of underparts in adult varies from white in *S. e. europaea* (Fenno Scandia, N Russia) to pale reddish-brown in *S. e. caesia* (W. Europe). Intermediate forms occur. Male's flanks vivid chestnut-red, female's duller rusty-brown. Does not drum like the woodpeckers, but often hammers at nuts and seeds of various kinds to get at the contents. Has several characteristic, *very loud calls.* Common call a sharp, emphatic 'seet, seet', alarm/scolding call an excited 'twett-twett-twett, . . .'. Song loud, has tone like a musical whistle, may be drawling, 'uEEH uEEH uEEH . . .' (alternatively 'WEEu WEEu WEEu . . .') or fast, wiwiwiwiwi . . .'. A further variant is often heard, a rapid 'jujuJU jujuJU . . .'. R

Corsican Nuthatch *Sitta whiteheadi* L 12. Breeds on Corsica in montane pinewoods. Looks like a small Nuthatch, but note the distinctive markings on the head with *black crown/nape* and clear, *white line above eye.* Female and juvenile darker in colours, but markings the same. Habits as Nuthatch's, but rather shyer. Excavates own nest hole in tree. Has hoarse scolding call, 'chay-chay-chay- . . .'. Song consists of clear notes in fast, accelerating series: 'dewdewdewdewdew-di-di-di-di-di'.

Corsican Nuthatch, ♂

Rock Nuthatch *Sitta neumayer* L 15. Breeds in SE Europe on rocky slopes and mountains with scattered bushes. Looks like a *big, pale* Nuthatch, but lacks latter's white spots on tail and has proportionately *longer bill.* Resembles Nuthatch in movements and posture. Climbs cliffs instead of trees. Nests on cliff faces, on which voluminous nests are plastered with mud. Very 'talkative' with loud and high-pitched calls. Song sounds sometimes very like Marsh Tit's, 'tew tew tew . . .', sometimes more complex: trilling and loud, begins like Wood Warbler song, drops in pitch and tempo, ends almost like Chaffinch trill without final flourish.

Krüper's Nuthatch *Sitta krueperi* L 12. Breeds in Europe locally in SE Greece (Mytilene) in montane pinewood. Closely related to Corsican Nuthatch and accordingly small. Glossy black crown patch (does not extend to nape), black eye-stripe and blue-grey back like Corsican Nuthatch, but overall impression of face paler, and is easily recognised by *reddish-brown patch on breast.* Calls in essence very like Corsican Nuthatch's. Include Greenfinch-like 'dyuee' and hoarse scolding 'chay-chay . . .' and (in flight) a Brambling-like 'jek'. Song consists of a shrill, yodelling, rather Blue Tit-like trill.

Krüper's Nuthatch, ♂

Nuthatch adult male race *europaea*

Rock Nuthatch

Passerines

Wallcreeper

Wallcreeper (family Tichodromadidae) is a close relative of the nuthatches, but has a long, curved bill and behaves like the treecreepers. Builds bulky nest in cleft in a cliff. The 4–5 white eggs have red spots.

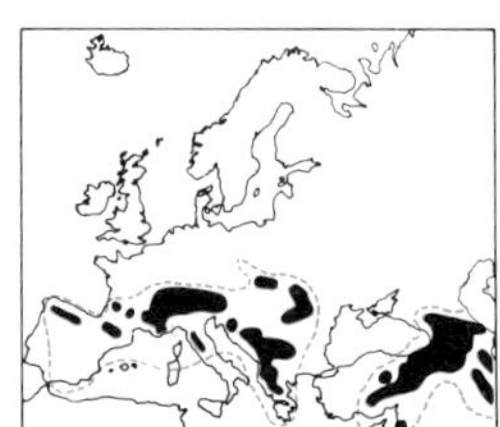

Wallcreeper *Tichodroma muraria* L 16. Uncommon and local in occurrence in high mountains up to the snow line. Seems to be easier to find in its eastern range of distribution. Nests in the Alps usually at between 1000m and 2500m altitude, but nests have been found down to 350m above sea level. In winter moves further down, and can then be seen on church towers, walls of castles and in quarries. Longer movements are very rare (though several have even reached Britain). Appearance odd, unmistakable. *Bill long, curved,* upperparts grey, underparts black in summer and pale grey in winter. Female, however, has merely a black patch on throat in summer. Shape and pattern of *wings* very striking: *broad and round with large, red panels and white spots.* Flight characteristically fluttering. Climbs cliffs in search of insects, when all the time it flicks its wings so that the red flashes. On the other hand it does not use its tail as a support like a treecreeper. Call thin and piping. Song consists partly of vaguely twittering series, and partly of – and totally diagnostic – peculiarly strained, drawn-out notes with glissando 'tu, ruuee zeeeeeu' repeated in the same way several times in succession. V

Wallcreeper adult male winter

Wallcreeper adult male summer

Treecreeper roosting on tree trunk

Wallcreeper, ♂

Treecreepers

Treecreepers (family Certhiidae) are small, short-legged, brown-speckled birds with thin, curved bills. Seek food on outside of tree trunks, when climb in spirals which start at the foot of the trees. Usually seen singly. Very active. Build nest in clefts or hollows (often behind loose bark). The 5–7 eggs are white with red spots.

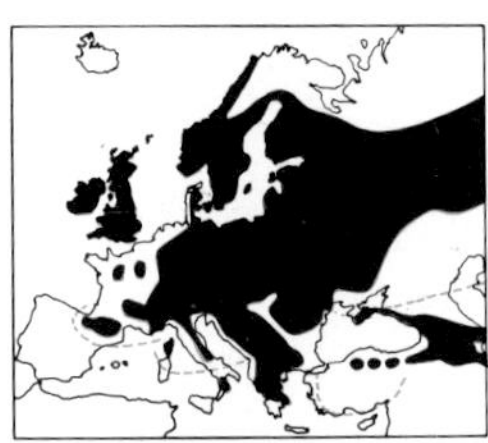

Treecreeper *Certhia familiaris* L 13. Breeds fairly commonly in older woodland, parks and gardens, both coniferous and deciduous wood. In S Europe where it occurs within the same area as Short-toed Treecreeper, it prefers coniferous woods at higher altitudes. Easily distinguished from other birds except Short-toed Treecreeper. Often has more distinct pale supercilia than latter, especially in front of eye above lores; can even meet narrowly over base of bill. Usually lacks the pale brown colour on the flanks and has *slightly paler, more contrasty plumage* and more of a red tone on rump. Bill is on average a shade shorter than Short-toed's. Call a repeated, very high, thin and sharp but yet rollng 'srrree, srrree, . . .'. Also gives pure, plain 'teeeh' (quite pronounced, rather Coal Tit-like, may be repeated in a series, though not rapidly as in Short-toed Treecreeper). Song is a sharp and thin, quite low-voiced, clear ditty which accelerates, falls in pitch and ends with a short, melodic flourish, rather like Willow Warbler. R

► **Short-toed Treecreeper** *Certhia brachydactyla* L 13. Breeds in central and S Europe in older deciduous wood, parks and gardens, usually at lower altitudes than Treecreeper and this particularly so in the southern part of the range. Very similar to Treecreeper, but is *a shade darker* and less rusty-toned above and also has *pale brown tone on flanks.* In the hand can usually be separated by shorter hindclaw. Bill averages slightly longer than Treecreeper's. Call a powerful, clear and Coal Tit-like 'teeut', repeated at well-spaced intervals or in very typical 'dripping' series (crystal clear) which accelerate to fast trotting rhythm and fall in pitch. In addition a very Treecreeper-like (but somewhat looser) 'srree' may be heard, and a short 'tit' from flying birds. The song has a more plaintive tone (Coal Tit-like) than Treecreeper's, is a short clear phrase with a slightly jolting rhythm, 'TÜte toh etitITT', final notes slightly rising in pitch. V

Short-toed Treecreeper

Treecreeper

Passerines

Sparrows

Sparrows (family Passeridae) are small, thick-billed, rather short-legged birds, more dumpy than most other passerines. In some species the sexes are alike. Sociable, most breed colonially. Feed on the ground. Hole nesters or build domed nests. Lack well-developed singing ability. The Snow Finch belongs to this family, but is illustrated with Snow Bunting for easier comparison.

House Sparrow *Passer domesticus* L 14.5. Closely associated with human habitation, breeds very commonly around farmyards, in towns and villages. Sociable. Nests under roof tiles, in holes, cavities or sometimes builds own domed nest in bush or tree. Looks drab grey-brown at a distance, but if a male is studied at close range it will be found to be quite an attractive bird with *grey crown area* broadly bordered chestnut-brown, with pale grey cheeks and *black bib*. Female and juvenile more uniformly shabby grey-brown with unstreaked breast and pale supercilium. Both sexes have rusty-brown, black-streaked back. In southern race, 'Italian Sparrow' *P. d. italiae*, of the Italian peninsula, Corsica and Crete, male has chestnut-brown crown and whitish cheeks. Call and song consist of a number of monotonous 'chirp' sounds varying in pitch. When mobbing and in excitement, a rattling series of scolding calls, 'cherrr-r-r-r-r', is heard. RWP

■□□ **House Sparrow** female
□■□ **House Sparrow** male summer
□□■ **House Sparrow** male winter

Spanish Sparrow *Passer hispaniolensis* L 14.5. Despite its name this species seems now to be very difficult to find on the Iberian peninsula. Breeds in southeasternmost Europe, Asia Minor and in parts of N Africa, mainly in open country without any association with villages etc, often in windbreak trees, in large colonies, many nests in the same tree. May also bred in stork nests. Appears to be a migrant, at least in northern parts of range; large flocks can be seen moving during migration periods. Male is easily distinguished from male House Sparrow by *larger black bib, black streaking on flanks and back* and *greyish-white cheeks* together with *chestnut-brown crown*. Extent of black varies but is generally much greater than in House Sparrow; some are very close to 'Italian Sparrow' (see above). Female and juvenile usually indistinguishable, but have on average slightly heavier bill, whiter belly and, in some, a trifle more well-marked streaks on breast than House Sparrow. Call and song resemble House Sparrow's, but are slightly more powerful and deeper. V

■□□ **Spanish Sparrow** males winter
□■□ **Spanish Sparrow** male summer
□□■ **Spanish Sparrow** female

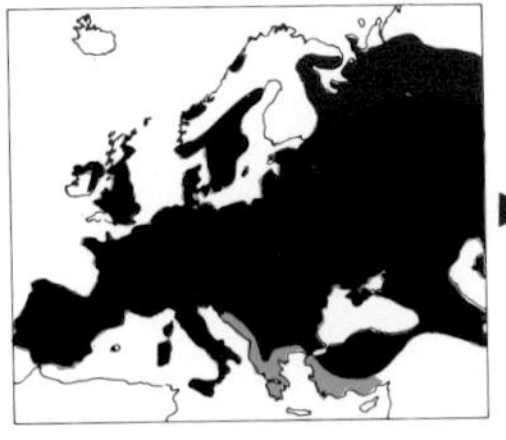

▶ **Tree Sparrow** *Passer montanus* L 14. Breeds commonly in parks, gardens and cultivated country with trees. Less tied to human habitations than House Sparrow and can be found breeding in pure woodland. Nests in holes, mainly in trees. Also uses nestboxes. Smaller and slimmer than House Sparrow. Note *chestnut-brown crown*, small bib and a *small black spot on pale grey cheek*. Sexes alike. Calls resemble House Sparrow's, but are both harder and clearer in voice. Typical is a slightly nasal 'tsooWIT' and a nasal but dry 'tett' or a rapid series, 'tett-ett-ett-ett', in flight. Song consists of repeated 'tsveet' notes. RWP

▶ **Rock Sparrow** *Petronia petronia* L 15. Breeds locally in S Europe in rocky country, cultivated as well as wild. Sometimes nests in ruins, within towns or in hollow trees in plantations. Resembles female House Sparrow with *broad pale supercilium*, but has a *moderately pale crown-stripe* and *whitish tail band* (noticeable mostly in flight). Small yellow spot on breast not very conspicuous, shows mostly when bird puffs up its feathers. Much more active than House Sparrow, with which it may associate. Usually in small loose flocks. A variety of short calls like 'wed' and 'dliu', also a characteristic very sweet 'peeUH-ee'. V

▶ **Pale Rock Sparrow** *Petronia brachydactyla* L 14. Breeds in the Caucasus and Asia Minor in desert-like terrain. Resembles a pale female House Sparrow with *white spots at tip of tail*. Supercilium less prominent than in Rock Sparrow, *head more uniform*.

Tree Sparrow
Rock Sparrow
Pale Rock Sparrow

Passerines

Finches

Finches (family Fringillidae) are small or medium-sized with short, heavy bills. Seed-eaters. Usually brightly coloured. Nest in trees, shrubs and other dense vegetation. Build cup-shaped nests. Clutches of 3–6 eggs.

Chaffinch *Fringilla coelebs* L 15. One of Europe's commonest birds. Nests in both deciduous and coniferous woods, gardens and parks. The nest is most often in a tree fork, skilfully constructed and well camouflaged with moss and lichen. Migrant in north and northeast, large movements in early October. In winter common in flocks in fields, usually rather close to woods. Much drawn to beech woods. Male brightly coloured, female and juvenile dull grey-brown with greenish tinge; they all have prominent, *white wingbars*, white on outer tail feathers and green rump. One of the most zealous singers in the wood, song loud. From well-visible songpost gives a tuneful, short but forceful rattle which drops down the scale and ends with a flourish, e.g. 'zit-zit-zit-zit-sett-sett-sett-chitterEEEdia'; sometimes a woodpecker-like 'kik' is added to the final flourish. Flight call (close contact) is a short, low 'jup jup'. Loud call and alarm a metallic 'fink'. The so-called rain-song is variable, often a loud whistle, 'huitt, huitt . . .' (in SE Europe this call sounds like 'heep', uninflected and in fact confusingly like Thrush Nightingale), in other areas a short, rolling 'wrrret'. RWP

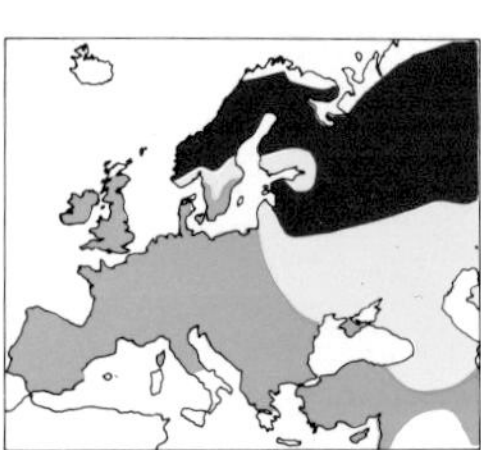

Brambling *Fringilla montifringilla* L 15. Breeds commonly in taiga and subalpine birch forest. On migration and in winter frequents woods, parks, gardens and fields, usually in flocks. Passage flocks tighter than migrating Chaffinch flocks. Note *white rump, dark back* and *white wingbars*. Flocks are often mixed with Chaffinches. In some 'invasion years' flocks of thousands and even millions can occur in areas of beech woods; eats beechnuts. Song is a dreary, monotonously repeated, rolling and wheezing 'rrrrhee' (at a distance slightly reminiscent of a cross-cut saw). Sings from well-exposed songpost. Flight call (close contact) 'jek jek', like Chaffinch but more nasal and a little harder. Loud call a characteristic wheezing, nasal 'teh-ehp'. Alarm call at breeding site a hard ringing 'slitt, slitt'. WP

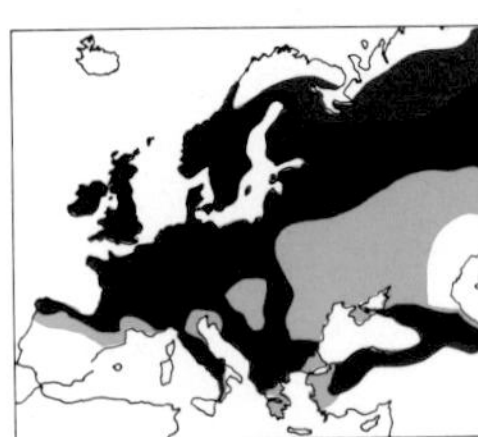

Bullfinch *Pyrrhula pyrrhula* L 16. Breeds fairly commonly in deciduous as well as coniferous wood (taiga), also in gardens and orchards. Note *white rump*, black and grey upperparts, *red underparts* in male, more dull brown colours in female, and also *short and heavy bill* in both sexes. First juvenile plumage is predominantly pale brown with no black on face other than peppercorn eye. Quiet. In winter sometimes in small flocks, incl. in gardens, in summer very shy and withdrawn. Eats berries, buds and seeds. Call a soft, sad, melodic 'pew'; when perched a more downwards inflected 'pee-u'. Song weak, unmusical: calls mixed with wheezing notes. RWP

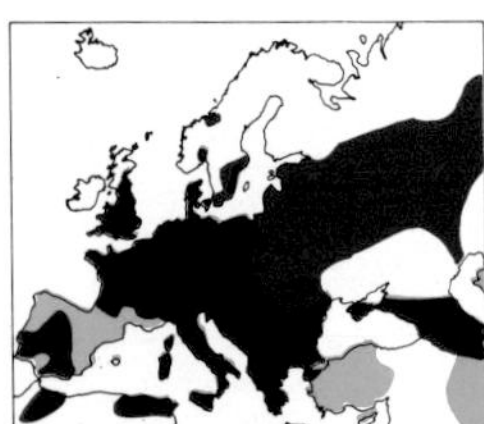

Hawfinch *Coccothraustes coccothraustes* L 18. Breeds sparsely in deciduous and mixed wood with dense undergrowth. Attracted to cherry orchards, easily splits kernels with its colossal bill. Hornbeam seeds also form a popular food. Easy to overlook as it is shy, rather silent and spends most of time in foliage of treetops. Note *very large and powerful bill* (blue-grey in breeding season, yellowish-white rest of year), short tail and *broad white wingbar*, characters which are well visible in flight. Female is basically like male but has pale grey secondary panel on folded wing, is less warm and rich in colours, tending towards grey-green. Apart from the white bars on the wing and tail, juvenile is a rather nondescript yellowish-brown bird (lacks among other things black markings on face). Can be sexed by the secondaries character. Call a metallic, very hard 'pix' like a powerful, single Robin 'tic', a Blackbird-like 'srree', and 'chi' with harsh quality of Spotted Flycatcher. Song consists of low, strained 'tee-eeh' notes mingled with the calls. R

■□□ **Chaffinch** adult male
□■□ **Chaffinch** adult female
□□■ **Brambling** male in late winter plumage

■■□ **Brambling** mixed flock of winter males and females

□■ **Brambling** female

Bullfinch, juv.

■□□ **Bullfinch** adult male
□■□ **Bullfinch** adult female
□□■ **Bullfinch** juv.

■□□ **Hawfinch** adult male summer
□■□ **Hawfinch** adult female summer
□□■ **Hawfinch** juv. male

Passerines

Citril Finch *Serinus citrinella* L 11.5. Breeds in central and SW Europe in mountain districts with coniferous wood. In Corsica and Sardinia (race *corsicana*) not so confined to woods – found among broom and heather. Its presence depends on spruce seeds, but it also eats such items as dandelion seeds from the alpine meadows. In winter descends to lower level. *Unstreaked, greenish-yellow underparts and rump,* yellow wingbars *and ash-grey nape* distinguish adult. Juvenile is browner and heavily streaked. The race *corsicana* has warm brown back. Usually seen in flocks. Call a melancholy, characteristic 'pjee-u', with a more cracked tone than Siskin's. A metallic 'chik' and other short calls are also given. Has a twittering, fast song, often given in song flight, reminiscent of Siskin and Goldfinch. V

■□ **Citril Finch** adult male
□■ **Citril Finch** juv.

Serin *Serinus serinus* L 11. Common over most of the Continent, in Britain rare and very local in summer (irregular breeder). Found in parks, coniferous belts, gardens, often in villages. Streaked plumage, largely *yellow underparts and rump* are characteristic. In summer, when greyish-green feather fringes are worn away, head can look almost all-yellow. Juvenile lacks yellow and is streaked. Most easily recognised by *small size* and *very short bill.* Often feeds on the ground. Common call a high-pitched, metallic twittering, 'zr-r-litt', not unlike call of juvenile Pied Wagtail in tone. Sings frequently from high and exposed songpost or in Greenfinch-like song flight with slow wingbeats, a jingling, chirping and harsh twitter at fast tempo (somewhat reminiscent of glass being ground). SP

■□□ **Serin** adult male
□■□ **Serin** adult female at nest
□□■ **Serin** juv.

Red-fronted Serin *Serinus pusillus* L 11. Breeding resident in the higher regions of the Caucasus; also found in mountains of Turkey and central Asia. Resembles Serin, but male easily recognised by *black head with red forehead.* Female similar but a little less contrasting in pattern, has smaller red patch. Juveniles are surprisingly different, with rusty *yellow-brown face* and lack of black and red. Call like Serin's but weaker and more soft, a singing, slightly nasal, drawn-out 'drrrrt'.

Red-fronted Serin ♂

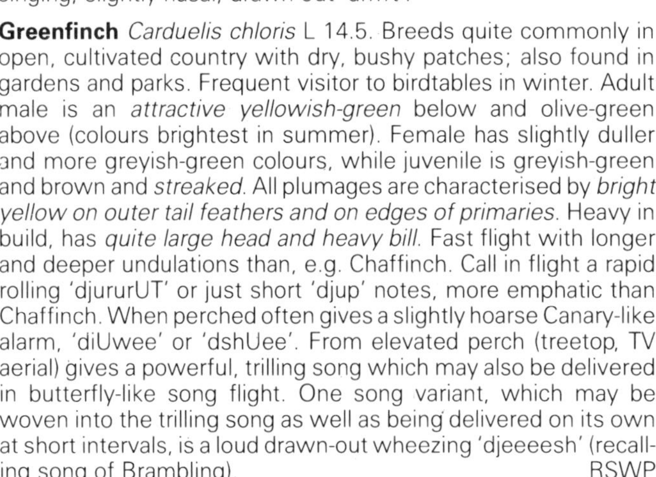

▶ **Greenfinch** *Carduelis chloris* L 14.5. Breeds quite commonly in open, cultivated country with dry, bushy patches; also found in gardens and parks. Frequent visitor to birdtables in winter. Adult male is an *attractive yellowish-green* below and olive-green above (colours brightest in summer). Female has slightly duller and more greyish-green colours, while juvenile is greyish-green and brown and *streaked.* All plumages are characterised by *bright yellow on outer tail feathers and on edges of primaries.* Heavy in build, has *quite large head and heavy bill.* Fast flight with longer and deeper undulations than, e.g. Chaffinch. Call in flight a rapid rolling 'djururUT' or just short 'djup' notes, more emphatic than Chaffinch. When perched often gives a slightly hoarse Canary-like alarm, 'diUwee' or 'dshUee'. From elevated perch (treetop, TV aerial) gives a powerful, trilling song which may also be delivered in butterfly-like song flight. One song variant, which may be woven into the trilling song as well as being delivered on its own at short intervals, is a loud drawn-out wheezing 'djeeeesh' (recalling song of Brambling). RSWP

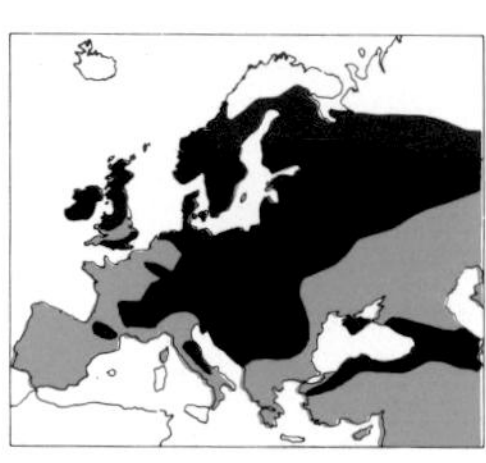

Siskin

Siskin *Carduelis spinus* L 12. Breeds fairly commonly but locally in coniferous forest, especially tall spruce. Numbers vary with seed production. Smallest finch of N Europe. *Greenish and streaked,* has yellow tail sides and wingbars. Male has *black forehead and chin patch.* Outside breeding season gathers in dense flocks (often mixed with Redpolls), feeds silently, hanging upside-down in birches and alders, suddenly launches out in dense swarm in short circular trip uttering buzzing twitter. In Britain often visits garden nutbag feeders in winter. Flight light, in long, deep undulations. Call a drawn-out, clear, sad 'DLU-ee' or 'DLEE-u', as well as a dry 'ketteKETT'. Song fast, twittering chatter, ends with a feeble wheeze. Performs song flight. RWP

Greenfinch adult male
Greenfinch adult female
Siskin adult male
Siskin adult female
Siskins on garden nutbag feeder

Passerines

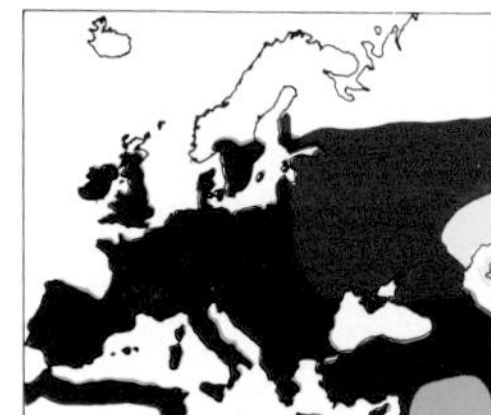

Goldfinch *Carduelis carduelis* L 14. Breeds fairly commonly in open country at woodland edge, also often seen in parks and gardens. Easily overlooked during breeding season. Many move south for the winter. Adult easily recognised by *red face* with rest of head black and white. Wing black with a broad *bright yellow bar*, particularly striking in flight. *Rump white.* Sexes are impossible to separate in the field. Juvenile has wing and tail feathers as adult's (broad bright yellow wingbars), but is otherwise insipid grey-brown with dark streaking. Last to be moulted is the head, and so in early autumn immature Goldfinches are seen which look like adults except for the pale grey head. Sociable outside breeding season and often occurs in small flocks. Specialises on seeds of thistles; in autumn and winter is usually found on open 'untidy' meadows with many thistles. Call a characteristically sharp and high-pitched 'tickeLIT'; rasping Sand Martin-like calls are also heard from larger flocks. Song resembles both Greenfinch's and Siskin's, recognised by the call being mixed in, as well as attractive mewing sounds and Sand Martin-like rasps. RS

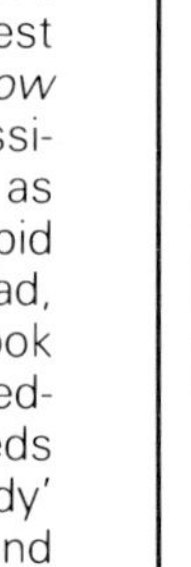

Goldfinch adult male

Goldfinch juv. drinking

Linnet adult male at nest

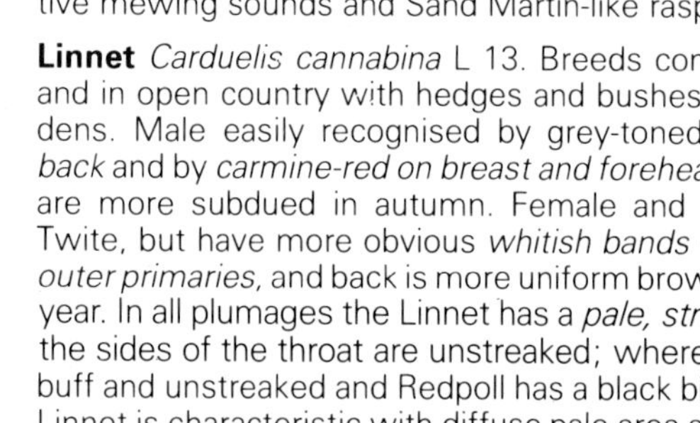

Linnet *Carduelis cannabina* L 13. Breeds commonly on heaths and in open country with hedges and bushes, in parks and gardens. Male easily recognised by grey-toned head, *nut-brown back* and by *carmine-red on breast and forehead.* The red colours are more subdued in autumn. Female and juvenile resemble Twite, but have more obvious *whitish bands* (broad, diffuse) *on outer primaries,* and back is more uniform brown. Bill dark grey all year. In all plumages the Linnet has a *pale, streaked throat* (only the sides of the throat are unstreaked; where the Twite is pale buff and unstreaked and Redpoll has a black bib. Side of head on Linnet is characteristic with diffuse pale area around the eye and on the cheek, framed in grey. Nearly always seen in pairs or in family groups, on migration in small or medium-sized flocks (single-species) that are closely knit. Feeds on ground, in autumn and winter on stubble and other fields among other finches and buntings, when often in giant flocks. Has many calls, is voluble. On migration usually a slightly nasal 'tett' or 'terretett', sometimes combined with short trills or thin, soft whistles, e.g. 'peeuu', 'trrreu' and 'tukeeYEU'. Gives a very varied and pleasing, twittering song from well-visible songpost. RSW

Linnet adult female

Linnet juv.

Twite *Carduelis flavirostris* L 13. Breeds on upland moors, also near coast. In winter on cultivated lowlands, rubbish tips, along flat coasts and similar places, where seeks food in flocks among tall weeds. Fearless but restless and therefore difficult to see properly, often flies a long way off. In general most resembles Redpoll and Linnet. Often associates with both. Compared with Redpoll, longer-tailed, more *yellowish-brown in tone* and *lacks dark areas on forehead and throat*; resembles female Linnet, but *bill is bright yellow* (though in summer grey-brown, as in female House Sparrow), cheeks and breast yellower brown, *throat unmarked dull yellow* (not whitish and streaked), the wing has a Redpoll-like pale bar (tips of greater coverts), does not have such obvious white on outer primaries as Linnet. Legs black. Male has pink on rump, though this is very difficult to discern in the field, especially in autumn/winter (when brown fringes conceal). Most typical call is a nasal, hoarse, fine 'TWEit' (hence the name), which is totally characteristic and is heard in particular from large flocks. Also has a more conventional chattering call 'jek, jek', which is related mainly to calls of Redpoll and Brambling but also to those of Linnet and Greenfinch. Song chattering, with calls intermingled. RSW

Twite winter

Twite summer

Twite juv.

Passerines

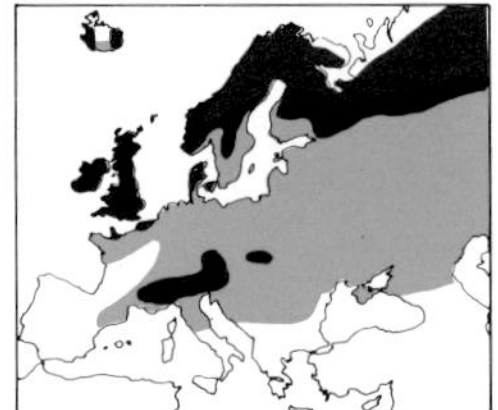

Redpoll *Carduelis flammea* L 12.5. In Britain breeds in birch and alder scrub, conifer plantations, gardens and parks, in Fenno-Scandia mainly in subalpine birch forest but also in coniferous. Northern populations move south in winter, in widely varying numbers, occasionally in invasion proportions. *Red forehead* (though not until Aug in first-years) and *small black chin patch* distinguish it from all other species (except very closely related Arctic Redpoll, which see). Adult male rose-red on breast and rump, the latter sometimes almost unmarked. Race *flammea* (Fenno-Scandia, Russia) is medium-sized, rather pale and grey. Race *cabaret* (Britain and Ireland, Alps) is smaller and darker, more brown. Race *rostrata* (Greenland) is largest, is dark, heavily streaked and has stout, heavy bill. Sociable, often nests in loose colonies. In winter in dense flocks (often with Siskins) in birches and alders, though also feeds in tall weeds like Twite. Call 'chut, chut-chut', cracked, with metallic echo. A hoarse Greenfinch-like 'djuee' is often popped in. Flight song consists of the call, alternating with a dry rattle: 'chut chut chut serrrrrr . . .'. RSWP

Arctic Redpoll *Carduelis hornemanni* L 12.5. Breeds sparsely in the subarctic region, in the willow zone (exceptionally in upper birch forest). In winter seen rarely among Redpolls. Very like Redpoll. Distinguishing marks are *unstreaked, white rump* (particularly characteristic of adult male; first-years at least may have faint streaking on rump), fewer and narrower streaks on flanks and *paler head and back*. On average shorter bill and looser plumage than Redpoll, but these differences subtle. In practice many 'pale redpolls' must be left unidentified (even trapped ones can be intermediates, difficult to identify). Calls similar to Redpoll's. V

Trumpeter Finch *Bucanetes githagineus* L 14. N African and W Asiatic species, also in SE Spain (Almeria). Male in summer plumage buff with *rose-red elements*, e.g. the bill and outer tail. In winter plumage duller, resembles female and juvenile. Very *short, stout, bill.* Spends most of time on the ground. Song a peculiarly nasal, monotonous, very loud buzzing ('toy trumpet'). V

Scarlet Rosefinch *Carpodacus erythrinus* L 14. Has recently colonised N Europe. Inhabits luxuriant scrub with tall herbs and scattered trees. Arrives very late in spring. Male in full summer plumage *strawberry-jam red on head, breast and rump.* Female and juvenile insipid grey-brown with hint of streaking and faint wingbars (cf. females of House Sparrow and Linnet). *Stout, heavy bill.* One-year-old males breed in female plumage. Attracts attention mostly by its song, a short, sharply whistled phrase, 'WEEje-wü WEEja' or 'pleased to see you' etc (the theme varies), typically pure and soft in voice. Call a fresh, pure 'ueet', with same voice as in song. Alarm an almost Greenfinch-like 'JAY-ee'. P

Pallas's Rosefinch *Carpodacus roseus* L 15. Very rare visitor to E Europe from Asia. Male *paler red* than Scarlet Rosefinch, with *whitish glossy streaking on throat and forehead.*

▶ **Great Rosefinch** *Carpodacus rubicilla* L 20. Breeding resident in the Caucasus and in Asia. *Whole of underparts dark pink* in male, *bestrewn with pale blotches. Big.* (Not illustrated.)

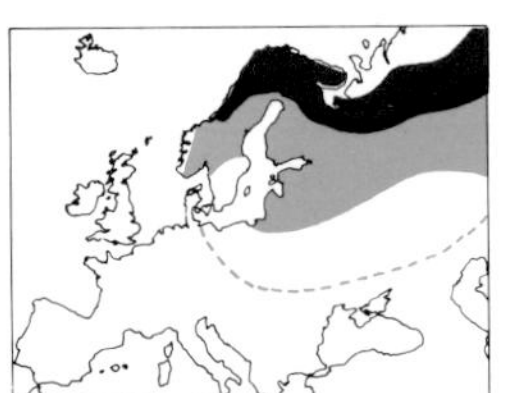

Pine Grosbeak *Pinicola enucleator* L 20. Breeds sparsely in northern taiga, may go up into subalpine birch forest. Feeds on buds up in the spruces, searches for berries while hopping on ground. Quiet, easy to overlook. Male *raspberry-red*, female and juvenile both grey-green and dull orange, all with *two distinct white wingbars.* In some winters moves south and west in large numbers, plundering the rowans, amazingly fearless. Big and sturdy, obviously long-tailed. In flight resembles small Fieldfare, but flight more undulating. Call a clear, strongly fluting 'peelee-JEEH, peeleeJÜ'. Conversational call a subdued 'büt, büt'. Song a fast, crystal-clear series, rather like Wood Sandpiper display. V

■□□ **Redpoll** female or 1st-winter male
□■□ **Redpoll** female or 1st-winter male
□□■ **Redpoll** adult male winter

■□□ **Arctic Redpoll** female or 1st-winter male
□■□ **Arctic Redpoll** female or 1st-winter male
□□■ **Arctic Redpoll**

■□□ **Trumpeter Finch** male
□■□ **Trumpeter Finch** winter
□□■ **Scarlet Rosefinch** adult male

Pallas's Rosefinch, ♂

■□□ **Scarlet Rosefinch** 1st-winter
□■□ **Pine Grosbeak** adult male
□□■ **Pine Grosbeak** female or 1st-winter male

Passerines

Crossbills

Crossbills (family Fringillidae, genus *Loxia*). Live on conifer seeds. Specialists in cutting off and prising open cones (each species its particular sort) with their powerful, crossed bills. Breeding usually takes place in late winter (severe cold!), since the seeds of the cones (the food of the young) ripen at that time. Breeding may, however, occur also in summer or early autumn. Crossbill populations lead a roving existence, descend on those regions which have a rich cone production just in that actual year. In years of cone failure mass long-distance movements take place.

Crossbill *Loxia curvirostra* L 16. Spruce-cone specialist; a characteristic bird of the coniferous zone. Numbers vary greatly, however: in some years Crossbills fill the wood with their calls, in others shortage of spruce seeds has made them emigrate in full force. May then appear in invasion proportions well outside normal range, must then make do with emergency foods, e.g. rowanberries. Sometimes very fearless. Usually nests in Feb–Mar, in severest cold. Mass movements can therefore begin as early as summer. Outside breeding season they roam about in flocks (5–30 individuals), calling eagerly with typical, metallic ringing 'glipp-glipp- . . .' (Parrot Crossbill sounds similar, see that species.) When eating, they are noticed less: hang nimbly in the spruces (exceptionally pines), flutter with large cones hanging from bill, then work out the seeds industriously and in silence; only muffled 'chük-chük' calls and clatter of dropped emptied cones are heard. Song (sometimes soaring song flight) loud but hesitant, with call interwoven: 'cheeree-cheeree cheuf glipp-glipp-glipp cheeree . . .' Males red, females grey-green (more yellow-green on rump), juveniles greyish and markedly streaked. An element of yellow in male's red plumage is not a certain sign of immaturity. *Bill not so heavy* as Parrot Crossbill's. R

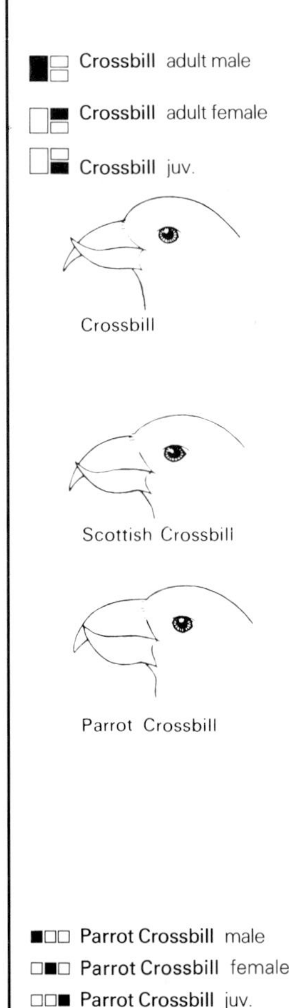

Scottish Crossbill *Loxia scotica* L 16.5. Sedentary breeding bird in Scotland, in pine forest. Between Parrot Crossbill and Crossbill, has intermediate dimensions and calls. R

Parrot Crossbill *Loxia pytyopsittacus* L 17. Pine-cone specialist; distributed across the coniferous belt but less numerous than Crossbill and not known for mass eruptions (though one in 1982/83 led to breeding in Britain). Colour pattern identical to Crossbill's, but *bill markedly heavier and deeper* (*contour of lower mandible has stronger S-curve*); this can often be judged. Sometimes fearless. Calls problematically like Crossbill's. In both species the repertoire is basically monotonous but different moods are expressed by variations in pitch, strength and timbre, so that a wide spectrum of calls exist. Parrot Crossbill's are consistently slightly stronger and deeper than Crossbill's, but the two species' spectra of calls overlap to large extent. The extremes are species-specific, e.g. the 'chok' as deep as a Blackbird's heard from Parrot Crossbills calmly eating. With great practice even crossbills flying over can be identified on call. The alarm calls (in N Europe easily elicited by imitation of Pygmy Owl) are also clearly different: Crossbill alarm is 'chük-chük' (deep enough), Parrot Crossbill's is 'cherk-cherk' (deeper, very hard). Song contains 'cheeLER-cheeLER' (may be species-specific). V

Two-barred Crossbill *Loxia leucoptera* L 15. Larch-cone specialist. Rare vagrant to W Europe from east, in some years in greater numbers, from summer to late winter. Apart from larches, often seen in rowans. Fearless. *Broad white wingbars* in all plumages. Has slightly weaker bill than Crossbill and is *smaller*, and male has more *rosy-red hue*. Call weaker and thinner than Crossbill's, with less of a metallic ring: 'kip-kip' rather than 'glipp-glipp'. Also Redpoll-like 'chut-chut' occurs. Canary-like cheeps, 'tweeht', are heard from feeding flocks, which seem to have no equivalent in other crossbills (also act as alarm). Song comparatively long, rich and varied, rather Siskin-like. V

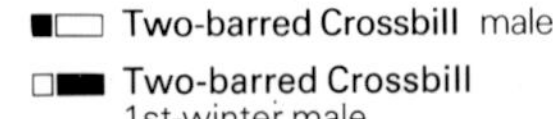

Passerines

Buntings

Buntings (family Emberizidae) are quite small birds, with short, thick bills with S-shaped cutting edges. Live in open country with bushes, often in cultivated districts with hedges and windbreak trees but also in upland tracts on bare moorland and in willow or in reeds and damp thickets. Only Rustic Bunting and perhaps Little Bunting thrive in more enclosed woodland. In spring and summer often noticed by species-specific song. Males usually have brighter plumages than females. Juveniles are for the most part like females. In some species sexes are alike. Outside breeding season often seen in flocks. Feed mainly on seeds on ground, but nestlings are often fed on insect larvae and the like. Nest on ground or in low bushes. The 3–6 eggs are blotched and scribbled.

Corn Bunting *Miliaria calandra* L 18. Breeds fairly commonly in open, cultivated country and in downland. Some males are polygamous. Outside breeding season seen in flocks. *Grey-toned brown*, heavily streaked without particular identification features. Sexes alike. Looks *bulky*. Flight heavy and even at a distance easily distinguished from larks' flight, also by *lack of pale trailing edge to wing*. Often flies with *legs dangling*. Call a hard, sharp, almost clicking 'tik'. Usually sings from well-visible perch, often from telegraph wire. Song metallic, a monotonously repeated accelerating jarring sound, 'tük tük zik-zee-zrrississ'. RW

Little Bunting *Emberiza pusilla* L 13. Breeds uncommonly in far NE Europe, probably annually in NE Finland but irregular farther west. Prefers damp, fairly open wood. Very rare migrant southwards. In summer plumage recongised by *reddish-brown head* (adult male also chin) with black stripes on sides of crown (*pale, reddish-brown stripe down centre of crown* characteristic) together with narrow black lines partially framing rusty-brown cheek. Despite smaller size can be confused with juvenile Reed Bunting in autumn, but recognised by *evenly rusty-yellow-brown cheek patch* (not dark and variegated black-brown-white) on which the bordering black streak below does *not* reach bill, proportionately *slightly longer bill* with *straight* (not convex) *culmen, dull brown* (not reddish-brown) *lesser wing-coverts above* (not always seen on perched bird), paler feet and usually narrower, shorter and blacker streaks on underparts. Usually distinct *pale eye-ring* and *pale buffish-white covert bar*. Call a hard, sharply clicking 'zik', like Hawfinch call in miniature. Song fairly quiet, varying, contains several motifs recalling Ortolan and Reed Buntings among others. V

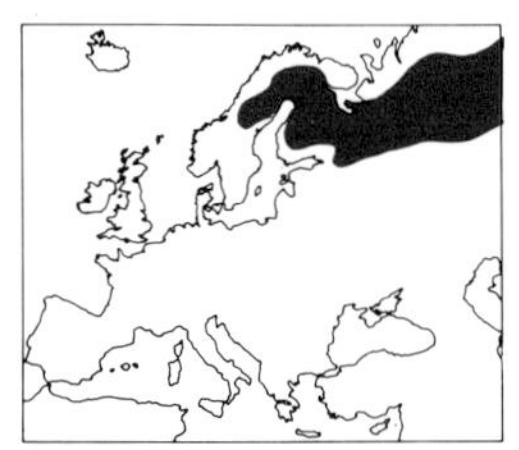

Rustic Bunting *Emberiza rustica* L 14.5. Fairly common in far NE Europe in swampy spruce forest, sometimes in damp birch forest, bounded by small bogs and streams. Migrates southeast, but annual vagrant (most autumn) to Britain. Male in summer plumage has characteristic black and white markings on head. Also characteristic are *reddish-brown breast band, reddish-brown* flanks together with white belly. Female and autumn birds most easily confused with Reed Buntings, but latter is dark-streaked on breast and flanks, lacks red-brown colour; Rustic Bunting's *rump is reddish-brown*, Reed Bunting's brownish-grey; bill has straight culmen in Rustic, convex in Reed; more prominent light wingbars in Rustic, and legs paler (pink). Call very like Song Thrush's but slightly higher and more distinct, 'zit'. Song clear and melodic, fairly short, has mournful ring like Lapland Bunting and is irresolute like Dunnock's in character, e.g. 'DUdeleu deLUU-delee', very mellow in tone. V

Yellow-browed Bunting *Emberiza chrysophrys* L 14. Very rare vagrant from Asia. A trifle smaller than Rustic Bunting. Male has *black hood* with *white crown-stripe, yellow supercilium* becoming white at rear, white submoustachial stripe and black malar stripe; whole of underparts white, streaked dark on breast and flanks. Female duller in colour. Call similar to that of Rustic Bunting, a short, distinct 'zit'. Song rather like Chestnut Bunting's. V

Corn Bunting adult singing
Corn Bunting juv.

Little Bunting

Little Bunting adult male singing
Little Bunting adult summer
Little Bunting autumn

Yellow-browed Bunting ♂

Rustic Bunting adult male with load of insects
Rustic Bunting female autumn

Passerines

Rock Bunting *Emberiza cia* L 16. Breeds in central and S Europe on rocky mountain slopes, both heather-clad and thickly wooded ones. In winter descends to lower levels. Male is recognised by *ash-grey and black markings on head*, female is more diffusely patterned. In both sexes note unstreaked throat and also vivid *chestnut-brown rump* (seen well when bird flies up). Median secondary coverts are white-tipped, form narrow wingbar. Juvenile is streaked below, rather resembles juvenile Yellowhammer in having chestnut-brown rump and white on outer tail feathers, but distinguished by *reddish underparts*. Distinguished from juvenile Cretzschmar's Bunting and Ortolan Bunting by chestnut-brown rump and *grey bill*. Often seen on ground, but also readily alights in trees. Call a thin, weak 'zeet' or a very high drawn-in whistle, 'seeee', just a shade down-slurred or totally straight. Sings from elevated and open perch. Song pleasing, *fast* and varied as Wren but with *squeaky* voice, 'seut wit tell-tell wit drr weeay sit seeay'. V

■□ **Rock Bunting** adult male

□■ **Rock Bunting** adult female

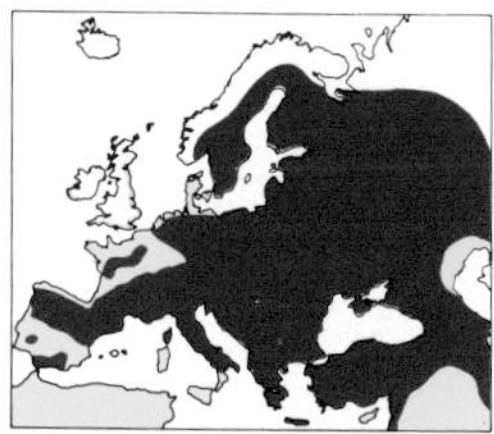

Ortolan Bunting *Emberiza hortulana* L 16.5. Breeds rather sparingly in open, cultivated country (lowland) with clumps of trees (N Europe) or in open mountainous terrain with scattered trees (S Europe). Adult male distinguished from other buntings by *greenish-grey, unmarked head* and *pale yellow throat*. At close range *narrow yellowish-white eye-ring can be seen*. Legs and *bill pinkish*. Outer tail feathers edged white. Distinguished from Cretzschmar's Bunting by yellow (not orange) throat and greenish-grey (not blue-grey) head and also greenish-grey breast band. Female similar to male but has brown-toned greenish-grey head with dark streaking and distinctly streaked greyish breast band. Juvenile is brown and streaked as a pipit, has grey-toned brown, streaked rump (not reddish-brown as in Yellowhammer and Rock Bunting); bill grey. Call a clear, metallic 'SLEEe'; also heard from night migrants in Aug, repeated loosely (3–5 times per flight over). A contact call, heard, e.g. from diurnal migrants, is a muffled, dry 'plett'. When agitated a short 'chu' (or 'SLEEe' and 'chu' alternating at 2-sec. intervals). Song varies individually, but ringing tone is specific, and typically the second part has lower notes than first: 'swee swee swee swee drü drü' or 'drü drü drü seea seea'. In S Europe the second part usually is only one cracked, falling note (cf. Cretzschmar's). P

■□ **Ortolan Bunting** adult male at nest

□■ **Ortolan Bunting** adult male

Cretzschmar's Bunting *Emberiza caesia* L 16.5. Breeds in SE Europe in dry, rocky country with isolated bushes. Resembles Ortolan, but has *blue-grey* (not greenish-grey) *head* and rather *orange* (not yellow) *throat*. Female distinguished from male by distinctly streaked crown and faintly streaked breast band. Juvenile is very like that of Ortolan Bunting and in the field they are indistinguishable. Distinguished from juvenile Rock Bunting by more *grey-toned brown* (not reddish-brown) *rump*. Usually seen on the ground. Call a metallic 'spit', sharper than in Ortolan Bunting. Song is similar in structure to a defective or primitive Ortolan song, is thin and lacks the pleasantly ringing tone, invariably has only *one* final note, not two or three. The final note is moreover straight and drawn-out, not ringing or with a diphthong. Two song types are used alternately, one a little stronger and deeper, 'jee jee jee jü', the other higher and almost wheezing, 'wee wee wee wüh'. V

Cretzschmar's Bunting adult male

Cretzschmar's Bunting adult female

Grey-necked Bunting adult male

Grey-necked Bunting *Emberiza buchanani* L 16.5. Breeds in the southernmost Caucasus and eastwards in barren terrain on mountain slopes, often at over 2000m, but occasionally at only 400m. Like Cretzschmar's Bunting, has blue-grey head and dull *brick-red underparts* (many feathers tipped white; 'untidy' effect), but *without dark breast band*, has paler, whitish chin and throat with reddish-brown tinge, paler also under tail. *Upperpart streaking fainter* than in Ortolan and Cretzschmar's Buntings. Sexes similar, female just slightly duller in colour. Song recalls Ortolan's.

Passerines

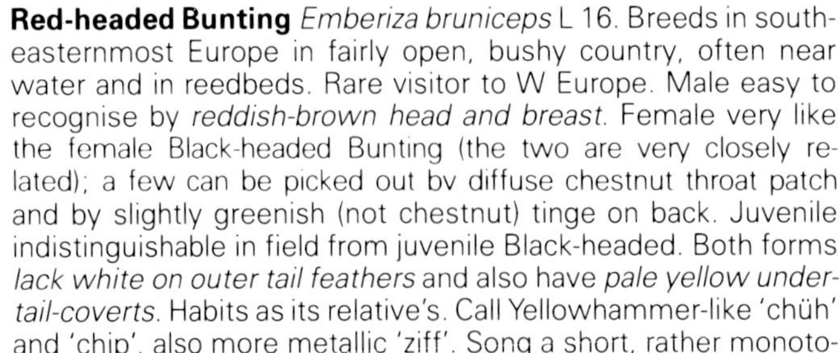

Red-headed Bunting *Emberiza bruniceps* L 16. Breeds in south-easternmost Europe in fairly open, bushy country, often near water and in reedbeds. Rare visitor to W Europe. Male easy to recognise by *reddish-brown head and breast.* Female very like the female Black-headed Bunting (the two are very closely related); a few can be picked out bv diffuse chestnut throat patch and by slightly greenish (not chestnut) tinge on back. Juvenile indistinguishable in field from juvenile Black-headed. Both forms *lack white on outer tail feathers* and also have *pale yellow under-tail-coverts.* Habits as its relative's. Call Yellowhammer-like 'chüh' and 'chip', also more metallic 'ziff'. Song a short, rather monotonous verse, very like Black-headed. V

Chestnut Bunting *Emberiza rutila* L 14.5. Very rare vagrant from Asia. Smaller than Reed Bunting, male *unmarked deep red-brown on head, throat, upper breast and whole of upperparts; belly yellow.* Female and juvenile have merely red-brown rump, distinctions from Yellowhammer include much smaller size and *lack of white on tail.* Call 'zic', like Little Bunting. Song pleasing, brief, opening like Tree Pipit, ending like Redstart.

Pine Bunting *Emberiza leucocephalos* L 16.5. Very rare vagrant from Siberia (breeds from European side of Urals to Sea of Okhotsk). Has roughly same habitat requirements as Yellowhammer, of which may be said to be eastern counterpart. (In W Siberia, where both species breed side by side within a vast area, limited interbreeding occurs; some taxonomists consider them to be races of the same species.) Pronounced migrant. Male easily recognised by *striking white and red-brown head markings.* Female and juvenile like Yellowhammer (rust-coloured rump), but have *white ground colour to underparts* instead of more or less yellow. Some females have in addition a little white on the crown. Calls and song like Yellowhammer's ('little bit of bread' etc). V

Cinereous Bunting *Emberiza cineracea* L 16.5. Very rare and local in Europe, breeds on Mytilene in Aegean Sea. Visits the island from Mar to Aug. Prefers barren and rocky country. ▶ Plumage brownish-grey, male with *unmarked, pale greyish-yellow head*; female has yellowish tone only on throat, while the head is otherwise grey-brown and diffusely streaked. Juvenile lacks all yellow, is browner and more clearly streaked. Calls 'kleup' and 'chiff'. Song a simple, ringing series, 'deur deur deur-deur drEE-do'.

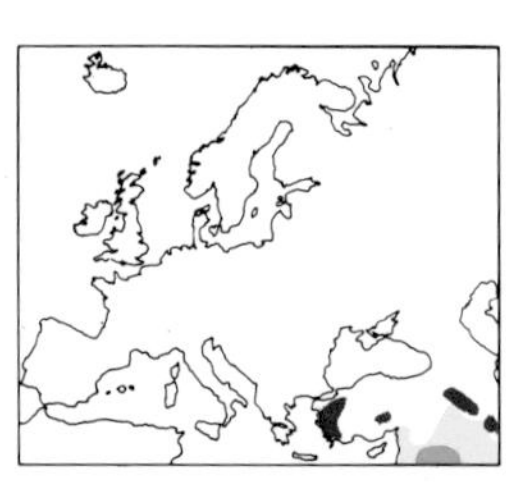

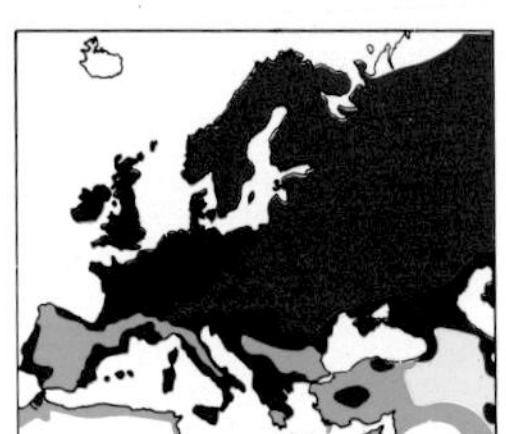

Reed Bunting *Emberiza schoeniclus* L 15.5. Breeds commonly in and near reedbeds, also in dryer areas, e.g. young conifers, in winter also visits cultivated fields, sometimes in company of other buntings and finches, often in small flocks. Male in summer plumage easy to recognise by *white neck ring, black hood and bib.* Neck ring is actually mainly a nape band which ends in a wedge up to the bill (submoustachial stripes). Female has boldly marked head, and pale throat is bordered by *dark malar stripes.* White outer tail feathers are visible when bird jerks tail. Can be confused with female and juvenile Rustic Bunting, but told by black streaks over breast and on flanks, not rusty-coloured. Slightly bigger than Little Bunting (though this not always easy to see) and also lacks evenly rusty-brown cheeks (see Little Bunting for more distinguishing details). Call a finely drawn-in 'tseeU' and a hoarse 'bzü'. Song rather monotonous, slow and jumpy but varies greatly, often 'tsee tsee, tseeA, tsisisirrr'. RWP

Pallas's Reed Bunting *Emberiza pallasi* L 13. Very rare vagrant from E Siberia. Differs from European brown-backed Reed Bunting (apart from size) in that back is *paler, yellowish-grey* and rump is greyish-white. *Lesser coverts grey or grey-brown, culmen straight, base of lower mandible pink.* (Siberian Reed have similar plumage but always red-brown lesser coverts and heavy, stubby bill.) Male in fresh plumage has *yellow-toned nape collar.* Female has *fine markings on neck sides,* which often meet in narrow line across breast, is otherwise very *lightly* streaked below. V

Red-headed Bunting male
Red-headed Bunting female

Chestnut Bunting

♀ ♂

Pine Bunting female
Cinereous Bunting male

Reed Bunting female
Reed Bunting male winter moulting into summer plumage
Reed Bunting male summer
Pallas's Reed Bunting male
Pallas's Reed Bunting female

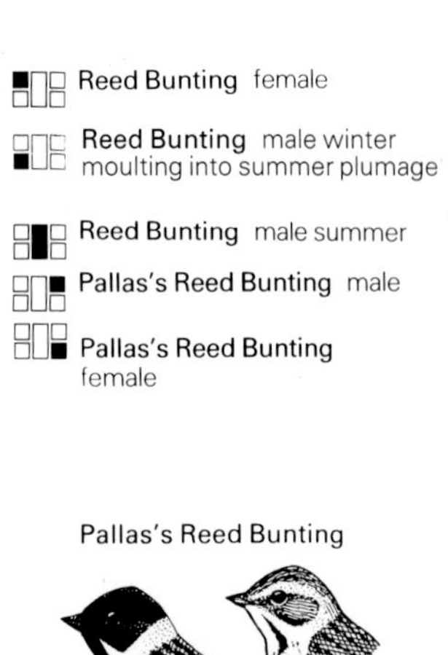

Pallas's Reed Bunting

♀ ♂

Passerines

Yellowhammer *Emberiza citrinella* L 16.5. Breeds commonly in open country with some bushes, also young conifers, in arable farmland, in juniper country, birch meadows, in clearings in woodland etc. In winter in flocks, feeds in stubble fields, rests in blackthorn scrub, slumps of conifers and the like. Big and long-tailed. In all plumages *reddish-brown rump* and *white on outer tail feathers* together with some yellow in the plumage, even though some juveniles have little of this. Adult male in spring and summer has *unmarked bright yellow crown patch and throat.* (In winter much of the yellow is concealed by grey-brown and green feather edges.) Female and juvenile less strongly coloured and usually more streaked. Distinguished from female and juvenile Cirl Bunting by reddish-brown, not grey-toned brown, rump. Call an impure 'steuf' and quiet clicking 'steeLIT' or 'pittiLIT' in flight. Song characteristic and well known, varies individually but most often runs 'see-see-see-see-see-see-suuuu'. Sometimes the penultimate note higher than the others ('little-bit-of-bread-and-NO-cheese'). Some individuals have a more buzzing, River Warbler-like tone, 'dze-dze-dze-dze-. . .'. RW

Yellow-breasted Bunting *Emberiza aureola* L 15. Breeds in NE Europe in damp scrubland and birch forest. Male easily recognised by *black 'face', chestnut-brown crown and breast band* contrasting with *yellow underparts* and also distinct, *white wingbars* (almost as Chaffinch), which are also visible in otherwise more subdued winter plumage. Female rather resembles female Yellowhammer, but has duller brown (not reddish-brown), streaked rump, *prominent pale supercilium* and a faint suggestion of paler crown-stripe; median secondary coverts tipped white, forming distinct wingbar; *underparts almost uniformly buffish yellow-white,* streaked only on flanks and sometimes narrowly across the breast. Juvenile like female, but has less obvious markings. Call a short 'tik'. Song most like Ortolan Bunting's owing to its tone, but is slightly weaker, is quietly jingling a little like Lapland Bunting, also has jumpy elements like Reed Bunting. E.g. 'treeU-treeU-treeU-huhuhu TREEa-TREEa trip-TREEEH'. Typically it rises in pitch towards the end (the last note in the example is the highest). V

Cirl Bunting *Emberiza cirlus* L 16.5. Breeds in W and S Europe in open country with bushes, trees and hedges. Now rare in Britain. In winter seen on open fields, often in flocks together with other buntings and finches. Male is recognised by head pattern. Distinguished from Yellowhammer by *brown-grey,* not reddish-brown, *rump,* from Yellow-breasted Bunting by completely or almost completely *unstreaked rump* and uppertail-coverts, from adult Ortolan Bunting by more distinct head markings and *grey,* not pink, *bill.* Call a Song Thrush-like 'zit'. Also gives thin, down-slurred 'siu', and a very fast series of clicks, 'zir'r'r'r'r' (like crackling electricity). Song does not resemble other buntings' songs but more Arctic Warbler's, a rapid, slightly harsh, rolling trill, 'zezezeeze . . .'. R

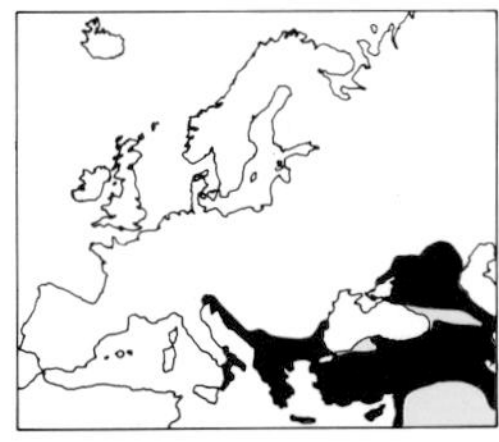

Black-headed Bunting *Emberiza melanocephala* L 16.5. Breeds in SE Europe in rather open country with scattered bushes and trees. Male easy to recognise by *black head* and *yellow* or yellowish-white *underparts* together with *lack of white tail markings.* Female very like female Red-headed Bunting, but has if anything *reddish-brown tone on back,* not greyish-green. Juvenile cannot be distinguished in the field from juvenile Red-headed Bunting. Red-headed is incidentally considered by some authorities to be a race of Black-headed. Call a Yellowhammer-like 'cheuh' or 'styu' and also Ortolan-like clicking 'plüt'. Song is quite short, has something of Lapland Bunting's desolate ring, 'sitt, süt süt süterEE-süt-süte-ray', but is not so jingling. It bears strong resemblance to Red-headed Bunting's song, and some appear inseparable. V

■□□ **Yellowhammer** adult male summer

□■□ **Yellowhammer** adult female at nest

□□■ **Yellowhammer** juv.

■□□ **Yellowhammer** male winter

□■□ **Yellow-breasted Bunting** adult male

□□■ **Yellow-breasted Bunting** adult female

■□□ **Yellow-breasted Bunting** female

□■□ **Cirl Bunting** adult male

□□■ **Cirl Bunting** adult female at nest

■□ **Black-headed Bunting** adult male

□■ **Black-headed Bunting** adult female

Passerines

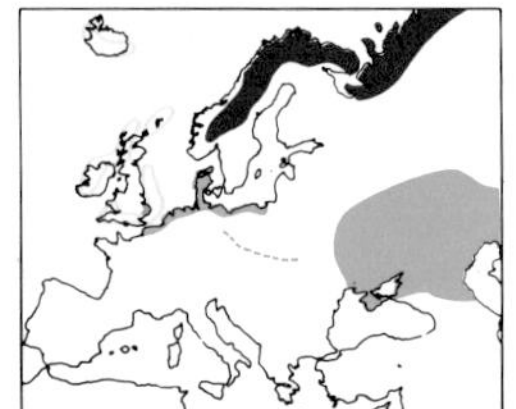

Lapland Bunting *Calcarius lapponicus* L 15.5. Breeds fairly commonly in open tundra landscape, preferably next to low willow in damp recesses. Also on cloudberry bogs in upper birch zone. A few breed in Scotland on hummocky moors. On migration and in winter seen on stubble fields and dry short meadows, mostly singly or in small groups. Spends most of time on ground, where it runs freely. Male in summer plumage unmistakable with black face, throat and breast, *pale yellow streak from the eye backwards,* white neck markings and *reddish-brown nape.* Female more diffusely marked but likewise has fox-red nape, also *pale central crown-stripe.* In winter plumage the face pattern of both is broken up by pale edges, but red nape discernible. Juvenile has insignificant markings on face/nape, instead has *rusty-red on greater wing-coverts,* also broad pale central crown-stripe (which Reed Bunting lacks). More robust build and shorter-tailed than most buntings. Has *long, fairly straight hindclaw.* Call on migration a hard, dry 'prrrt', sometimes followed by an almost clicking short 'chu' (may at times be extremely like Snow Bunting's 'piU'), alternatively harsh 'jeeb' (also heard from night migrants). At breeding site metallic 'TEElu' also heard. Song short and jingling, like Shore Lark in tone, but the phrases are not so varied but are repeated fairly constantly. A common phrase runs 'kretle-krlEEE-trr kritle-kretle-tru'. Has song flight, descends on outspread wings. WP

■□□ **Lapland Bunting** adult male at nest
□■□ **Lapland Bunting** adult female at nest
□□■ **Lapland Bunting** 1st-winter male

■□□ **Lapland Bunting** juv.
□■□ **Snow Bunting** adult male summer
□□■ **Snow Bunting** adult female summer

Snow Bunting *Plectrophenax nivalis* L 16. Breeds fairly commonly at high altitude in mountains among rocks and patches of snow. In winter often visits open coastal areas or extensive arable plains. Male in summer is shining white, has *all-white head* and underparts together with large *white panels on wings and tail*; the rest is black. Female is dirty grey-brown on head and has elements of brown in the dark back. In autumn and winter both sexes are considerably more brownish-buff in tone, but in flight still flash very white. Juveniles in their first plumage (Jul-Aug) have grey head and brown-spotted breast. By autumn they have moulted into a plumage resembling that of the adults. On average, though, they have less white in the wing; the immature female has only bases of secondaries white, forming a broad, white, translucent wing bar (see fig.). Flies in long undulations, the flocks glistening white. Call a short but full whistle, 'piU' (usually from single birds) and a softly twittering 'dirrirrlT', recalling Crested Tit, softer than similar call of Lapland Bunting. Sand Martin-like rasping calls are heard from large flocks. The song is short and clear, with resemblances to both Rustic and Lapland Buntings (though lacks latter's jingling tone), e.g. 'swEEto-süweeweetüta-süWEE'. It is given from boulder or in descending gliding flight. RWP

Snow Bunting, 1st winter, ♀

■□ **Snow Bunting** adult male winter
□■ **Snow Bunting** winter

Sparrows

(family Passeridae) are described earlier apart from the Snow Finch, which is dealt with here for easier comparison with Snow Bunting.

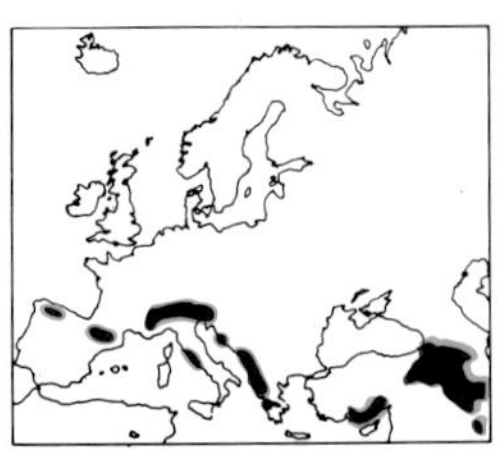

Snow Finch *Montifringilla nivalis* L 18. Breeds in the Alps and S Europe on high mountains above the tree line and below the snow. Nests in crevices and under boulders. Outside breeding season often seen in small flocks. In winter moves to lower level, but can certainly be seen in Feb at the top stations of ski resorts. Often encountered near human habitations. In all plumages easily distinguished from Snow Bunting by *grey head* (exception: juvenile Snow Bunting in Jul–Aug has grey head). Male in summer has a *small blackish bib,* female some grey visible on chin. Note white markings on wings and tail, less extensive in female and juvenile. Juvenile resembles female. *Bill colour* changes in male from *yellow in winter* to *black in spring.* Often jerks tail. Calls include a somewhat hoarse 'tseeh' and a purring 'prrt'. The song, uttered from perch on a boulder, is very jerky and jolting, somewhat recalling Twite's.

■□□ **Snow Bunting** juv.
□■□ **Snow Finch** adult male summer
□□■ **Snow Finch** winter

Vagrant North American passerines

An increased interest and a greater knowledge of field identification has led to an increasing number of North American species being identified in W Europe, and particularly in Britain and Ireland. Most records have been in autumn. A selection of the species most often encountered is described here.

Red-eyed Vireo *Vireo olivaceus* L 15. Recalls a warbler but has heavier bill with a hooked tip and more ponderous movements. The bolder white supercilium is bordered above with black. Crown grey. Iris reddish. Immatures have brown iris.

Northern Parula *Parula americana* L 11. Double wingbar, white eye-ring, yellow breast, and yellow-green back patch on otherwise bluish upperparts.

American Redstart *Setophaga ruticilla* L 13. Has habit of fanning tail and dropping wings. Catches insects in flycatcher fashion. Male black with orange markings on wings and tail, female and imm. greyish green-brown above, white below, with yellow tail markings.

Blackpoll Warbler *Dendroica striata* L 13. Note streaked back, double white wingbar and pure white undertail-coverts. Tail feathers have a large white patch on outer part. Feet usually brownish. Adult male in summer has white cheeks and black cap together with dark malar stripe and streaking on breast. In autumn very like female and first-winter, less contrasting. (Not illust.)

Yellow-rumped Warbler *Dendroica coronata* L 14. Pale eye-ring and yellow rump and a little yellow on flanks in all plumages. Adult has yellow patch on crown and obvious yellow on sides. White (northern race) or yellow (western race) throat, distinctly set off against very dark ear-coverts.

Northern Waterthrush *Seiurus noveboracensis* L 15. On migration, will occur in damp areas, e.g. reedbeds. Superficially like a pipit. Movements much like a Common Sandpiper. Note fine bill, yellowish-white supercilium and streaked throat. Call 'explosive', sharp and somewhat metallic.

Bobolink *Dolichonyx oryzivorus* L 19. Male's autumn plumage similar to female plumage, dull buffish-yellow with predominantly streaked back and faintly streaked underparts. Pale band along dark bordered crown. Bill heavy. Tips of tail feathers are narrow and very pointed. Lives in reeds. Call a characteristic, metallic 'pink'.

Northern Oriole *Icterus galbula* L 19. Females and immatures of the eastern race (vagrant to Europe) have dull orange-buff underparts and rump, and have grey-brown head and olive-brown back. Call a rich, fluty whistle, 'pew-li'. (Not illustrated)

White-throated Sparrow *Zonotrichia albicollis* L 16. Adult has well-defined white throat and also an orange-yellowish loral spot. Note also the distinctly striped crown. Juvenile duller in colours, dirty yellowish-white below with heavy, diffuse streaks except on throat and belly. A common call is a thin, drawn-out 'fseet'.

Fox Sparrow *Zonotrichia iliaca* L 18. Note coarse reddish-brown spotting on underparts (spots triangular) merging together into a large patch in middle of breast, reddish-brown on wings and tail together with grey nape and sides of crown.

Song Sparrow *Zonotrichia melodia* L 15. Best recognised by narrow, distinct light crown stripe, heavily streaked underparts (including throat), generally with a prominent malar streak. Supercilium prominent, greyish-buff. In flight it bumps its long, rounded tail which has no white visible. Call a characteristic 'chimp'.

Dark-eyed Junco *Junco hyemalis* L 15. Note slate-grey colour with pale pink bill and much white on outer tail feathers. Several races exist, differing in coloration.

Rose-breasted Grosbeak *Pheucticus ludovicianus* L 20. Female and juvenile look like large female House Sparrow, but have striped crown, *prominent white supercilium, very powerful bill,* double white wingbars and orange-yellow underwing.

■□□ Red-eyed Vireo autumn
□■□ Northern Parula 1st-winter male
□□■ American Redstart female/1st-winter male

■□□ Yellow-rumped Warbler autumn
□■□ Bobolink autumn
□□■ White-throated Sparrow adult

■□□ Song Sparrow
□■□ Dark-eyed Junco
□□■ Northern Waterthrush

■□ Fox Sparrow
□■ Rose-breasted Grosbeak female

Index

This index contains the common and scientific names of species. The page reference is to the text page, and the illustration appears on the opposite page. A number of commonly used alternative names have been indexed and cross-referenced to the names used in this book.